AF352690

Blood Ritual in the Hebrew Bible

Blood Ritual in the Hebrew Bible

Meaning and Power

William K. Gilders

The Johns Hopkins University Press
Baltimore and London

The Johns Hopkins University Press
2715 North Charles Street
Baltimore, Maryland 21218-4363
www.press.jhu.edu

Library of Congress Cataloging-in-Publication Data

Gilders, William K., 1967–
   Blood ritual in the Hebrew Bible : meaning and power / William K.
Gilders.
       p.   cm.
   Includes bibliographical references and index.
   ISBN 0-8018-7993-0 (hardcover : alk. paper)
   1. Sacrifice—Judaism. 2. Blood in the Bible. 3. Blood—Religious
aspects—Judaism. I. Title.
BM715.G54 2004
221.6—dc22   2004001112

A catalog record for this book is available from the British Library.

Contents

Preface

This study of Hebrew Bible blood ritual—the manipulation of blood of sacrificial animals by such means as tossing, sprinkling, pouring, and daubing it—is an outgrowth and expression of my broader interest in ancient Israelite sacrificial cult, and still more general interests in theoretical and comparative study of ritual and of sacrifice as a mode of religious practice. Thus, it is my hope that this study will be of interest not only to scholars of the Hebrew Bible and ancient Israelite religion but also to those who share my general interest in ritual practice, particularly sacrifice.

Work on this study has convinced me that no worthwhile intellectual endeavor is ever truly "finished." This book, as a cultural artifact, is completed, but my interest in the questions it addresses is far from exhausted. In the study itself I have dealt only tentatively with a number of significant questions and problems, and with others I have had to emphasize that lack of data prevents a firm answer or solution. The resulting "agnosticism" that runs through this work may be disappointing to some readers. However, I am convinced that it is valuable not only to establish knowledge but also to clarify what we *do not* (yet) know. By shining a light into our knowledge gaps, and at times by removing fragile camouflage laid across those gaps, I have sought to establish a basis for further explorations into this fascinating aspect of ancient Israelite religious practice.

Throughout this work, all translations from Hebrew and Greek are my own unless otherwise indicated.

My study of cultic blood manipulation in the Hebrew Bible began with my doctoral work in the Judaism in Antiquity program in the Religion Department at Brown University. Thus, my first acknowledgments must go to my teachers there: Saul M. Olyan, Shaye J. D. Cohen, and Stanley K. Stowers. I am particularly appreciative of Saul Olyan's steady guidance and mentoring, as well as his warm and generous friendship. His advice has made this a better book. At Emory University, I have had the good fortune of being a member of the Religion Department and the Rabbi Donald A. Tam Institute for Jewish Studies, and an active participant in the Hebrew Bible doctoral program of the Graduate Division of Religion. Each of these affiliations has had a positive impact on the completion of this work. In particular, I must recognize the support and guidance provided by Laurie L. Patton, Chair of the Religion Department. I also acknowledge the following colleagues, who have variously assisted my work on this project: David R. Blumenthal, Vernon K. Robbins, Mark D. Jordan, Eric Reinders, Carol A. Newsom, and Brent A. Strawn. Special words of thanks must be directed to the office staffs of the Religion Department, the Institute for Jewish Studies, and the Graduate Division of Religion for their indispensable assistance with technical matters related to the preparation of the manuscript: Tony Avery, Joy Wasson, Anny Varghese, Pescha Penso, and Arlene Robie. It is a pleasure also to acknowledge the work of three graduate student assistants. Julie S. Pfau and Beatrice J. Wallins Lawrence both proofread the complete manuscript and checked references; Jordan D. Rosenblum checked references during the final stages of work on the manuscript and also functioned ably as a teaching assistant, freeing up time for me to spend with this study. Finally, I wish to thank Henry Tom of the Johns Hopkins University Press for his advice and assistance from the initial submission of the manuscript for consideration through to its acceptance and preparation for publication. I also acknowledge the help and guidance of his assistant, Claire McCabe.

My mother, Donna Gilpin, my stepfather, George Gilpin, my grandparents, Esther Clarke and the late Roy and Letitia Gilders, have all been unfailingly supportive of my scholarly pursuits, as have my brother, Clinton Gilders, and my sister-in-law, Andrea Gilders. Their children, Charlotte Anabelle and Silas Bennett, have been constant sources of pleasure and useful reminders that there is much more to life than writing books. I dedicate this book to my niece and nephew, with many thanks for smiles, laughter, and play.

Abbreviations

The following abbreviations appear in the text and notes. The list does not include abbreviations for journal and series titles, which appear in full in the Bibliography.

AHw	W. von Soden. *Akkadisches Handwörterbuch.* 3 vols. Wiesbaden: Harrassowitz, 1965–81.
AV	Authorized (King James) Version of the Bible
*ANET*³	James B. Pritchard, ed. *Ancient Near Eastern Texts Relating to the Old Testament.* 3d ed. Princeton, N.J.: Princeton University Press, 1969.
BDB	F. Brown, S. R. Driver, and C. A. Briggs. *A Hebrew and English Lexicon of the Old Testament.* 1907. Reprint, Peabody, Mass.: Hendrickson, 1979.
BHS	*Biblia Hebraica Stuttgartensia.* Edited by K. Elliger and W. Rudolf. Stuttgart, 1983.
CAD	*The Assyrian Dictionary of the Oriental Institute of the University Of Chicago.* Edited by Ignace J. Gelb et al. Chicago: Oriental Institute, 1956–.
EBT	Johannes B. Bauer, ed. *Encyclopedia of Biblical Theology.* 3 vols. Translated by Joseph Blenkinsopp, David J. Bourke, N. D. Smith, and Walter P. van Sigt. London: Sheed and Ward, 1976.
EM	U. Cassuto et al., eds. *ʾenṣîqlopedyâ miqrāʾît.* 9 volumes. Jerusalem: Mosad Bialik, 1950–88.
ET	English translation
EV	English version (chapter and verse division of the Bible)
GKC	*Gesenius' Hebrew Grammar.* Edited by E. Kautzsch. Translated by A. E. Cowley. 2d ed. Oxford: Clarendon Press, 1910.

Joüon, *GHB*	Paul Joüon. *Grammaire de l'hébreu biblique.* 2d ed. Rome: Institut biblique pontifical, 1947.
KBL3	L. Koehler, W. Baumgartner, and J. J. Stamm, eds. *Hebräisches und aramäisches Lexicon zum Alten Testament.* 3d ed. Fascicles 1–5. Leiden: E. J. Brill, 1967–95.
LXX	Septuagint Greek translation of the Pentateuch
MT	Massoretic Text of the Hebrew Bible
NEB	New English Bible
NIV	New International Version of the Bible
NJPS	New Jewish Publication Society Version of the Bible
NRSV	New Revised Standard Version of the Bible
RSV	Revised Standard Version of the Bible
SCTT	Jacob Milgrom. *Studies in Cultic Theology and Terminology.* Studies in Judaism in Late Antiquity 36. Leiden: E. J. Brill, 1983.
TDOT	G. J. Botterweck and H. Ringgren, eds. *Theological Dictionary of the Old Testament.* Translated by J. T. Willis, G. W. Bromiley, and D. E. Green. Grand Rapids, Mich.: Eerdmans, 1974–.
THAT	E. Jenni and C. Westermann, eds. *Theologisches Handwörterbuch zum Alten Testament.* 2 vols. Munich: C. Kaiser, 1971–76.
TLOT	E. Jenni and C. Westermann, eds. *Theological Lexicon of The Old Testament.* Translated by M. E. Biddle. 3 vols. Peabody, Mass.: Hendrickson, 1997.
TWAT	G. J. Botterweck and H. Ringgren, eds. *Theologisches Wörterbuch zum Alten Testament.* Stuttgart: W. Kohlhammer, 1970–.
Williams, *Hebrew Syntax*	Ronald J. Williams. *Hebrew Syntax: An Outline.* 2d ed. Toronto: University of Toronto Press, 1976.

Blood Ritual in the Hebrew Bible

Introduction

There is power, power,
Wonder working power
In the blood of the Lamb;
There is power, power,
Wonder working power
In the precious blood of the Lamb.
—LEWIS E. JONES, "WOULD YOU BE FREE," C. 1899

According to a dictum recorded in *Sipra*, the halakhic midrash on Leviticus, "there is no expiation except with blood" (*'yn kprh 'l' bdm*) (*Nedaba* 4:10). In the epistle to the Hebrews, an early Christian teacher writes, "Indeed, under the law almost everything is purified with blood, and without the shedding of blood there is no forgiveness of sins" (Heb 9:22 NRSV). Both the rabbinic sages and the author of Hebrews refer to a significant element in the cultic practice represented in the Pentateuch and elsewhere in the Hebrew Bible: manipulation—specialized handling and use—of the blood of sacrificial animals to achieve a variety of effects. We find, for example, references to the tossing of blood onto an altar or an assembly of people, to the pouring out of blood at the base of the altar or onto the ground, to daubing onto the altar's horns or parts of the human body, and to sprinkling onto or in front of appurtenances of sacred space. Biblical texts and their subsequent reader-interpreters attribute a variety of effects to these ritual blood manipulations: purification from impurity or sin, consecration, transformation of identity or status, and protection from a destructive force. Although the evangelical Protestant gospel song "Would You Be Free" refers explicitly and specifically to the salvific blood of Jesus Christ, its basic declaration is nonetheless applicable to the blood manipulation activity represented and interpreted in the Hebrew Bible: there is power in the blood.

This study explores the significance of the practice of cultic blood manipulation and the various ways in which power can be attributed to animal blood when it is manipulated in the ancient Israelite sacrificial cult represented in the Hebrew Bible. This exploration involves asking a variety of questions about how the practice of blood manipulation is represented in the biblical texts, how the texts interpret and explain blood manipulation, and how readers of these texts have understood the textual representations and interpretations. What kinds of power do the sources attribute to manipulated animal blood? What kinds of power do reader-interpreters of the texts identify? Do blood manipulation rituals function as communicative symbols? Does each mode of blood manipulation have only one symbolic "meaning," or is each ritual action a complexly multivalent symbol? Is thinking of ritual actions as symbols the best way to approach them? Did ancient Israelites attribute concrete instrumental effects to ritual actions? Is there a conceptual basis for cultic blood manipulation? Can that basis be located in the conceptualization of blood as the locus of "life"? What are we to make of the texts' evident preoccupation with the details of practice? What interpretive possibilities open up if one focuses on understanding what happens in the very doing of ritual activity?

The latter two questions reflect the influence on this study of the work of interpreters of ritual who have emphasized the importance of treating ritual as practice, as a type of human activity that must be understood in its relationship to all other types of activity.[1] Applying this perspective, I consider the ways in which blood manipulation activity both creates and enacts social-cultic relations between persons, with the god of Israel, and with the sacred space where the divine presence is manifest. I also note ways in which blood manipulation defines the sacred and distinguishes it from the common through the mapping of ordered patterns in physical space.

Blood Manipulation as Ritual: Ritual as Communicative Activity

Blood manipulation is one example of activity that can be identified as ritual. Hebrew lacks a term that we could translate as "ritual," and I could perhaps have written this study without employing the term. However, because scholars commonly identify blood manipulation as ritual activity, and because one's conception of ritual plays a significant role in how one understands the purpose and significance of blood manipulation, it is necessary to address how I define and understand the term.

Ritual has been defined in a number of ways, and what counts as ritual varies from interpreter to interpreter.[2] Nevertheless, many interpreters agree in identifying ritual activity as "pre-eminently a form of communication,"[3] and a number of these interpreters understand ritual communication to be accomplished through symbols.[4] Understanding ritual as communicative activity, however, does not limit it merely to transmitting messages about existing personal or social situations. Rather, as a number of theorists have suggested, the messages transmitted through ritual do not merely say something about the existing status or identity of the participants, or about the context in which they find themselves. These messages also affect status and identity, and the nature of the social context.[5] Thus, as Saul M. Olyan has affirmed in his study of biblical representations of ritual and social hierarchy, "Rites shape reality for participants; they do not simply reflect some preexisting set of social arrangements brought into being elsewhere."[6]

Although some biblical scholars have made sophisticated use of insights drawn from anthropological treatments of ritual as a form of communicative and constructive activity,[7] some work on ritual in the Hebrew Bible suffers from significant theoretical weaknesses. Whereas anthropologists and ritual theorists generally emphasize that ritual acts are characteristically multivocal symbols, with multiple levels of meaning,[8] many biblical scholars seem intent on identifying a single authoritative meaning, a one-to-one referent, for each discrete symbolic act or object. Moreover, they often appear to assume, with little or no critical reflection, that ancient Israelites interpreted their own activity in this way. The following examples illustrate this observation.

In his commentary on Leviticus 1–16, Jacob Milgrom writes that the reddish substances, "the surrogates of blood," used in certain purification rituals "symbolize the victory of the forces of life over death." Furthermore, "the blood of the purification offering symbolically purges the sanctuary by symbolically absorbing its impurities."[9] Milgrom fails to indicate what he intends by his use of the adverb "symbolically." What difference would there be if the term had been omitted? Although Milgrom has drawn on the work of anthropologists in his efforts to elucidate Priestly (P) ideas about purity and impurity, and when discussing rites of ordination to the priesthood,[10] his work on ritual and sacrifice lacks adequate theoretical reflection on the nature of ritual and its symbolic-communicative function. Milgrom seems, generally, to assume that ritual acts are univalent. [11]

In two articles on the symbolism of blood, Dennis J. McCarthy attempts to identify the singular and unique symbolic conception of blood that lies behind Israelite blood manipulation activity and the prohibitions on consuming blood.[12] Unfortunately, the articles lack reflection on the basic assumption that blood has a symbolic significance, and they work from the assumption that it can have but one meaning in each cultural context. Thus, in ancient Israel, McCarthy insists, blood symbolizes life, whereas in other societies it symbolizes only death.[13]

All symbols, however, including ritual symbols in the Hebrew Bible, characteristically possess the properties of "condensation of meaning, multivocality, and ambiguity."[14] *Condensation of meaning*, explains David I. Kertzer, "refers to the way in which individual symbols represent and unify a rich diversity of meanings. The symbol . . . somehow embodies and brings together diverse ideas." *Multivocality* refers to "the variety of different meanings attached to the same symbol. While condensation refers to the interaction of these different meanings and their synthesis into a new meaning for an individual, multivocality suggests another aspect, the fact that the same symbol may be understood by different people in different ways." *Ambiguity* means that "the symbol has no single precise meaning. Put in more positive terms, this means that symbols are not arcane ways of saying something that could be more precisely expressed in simple declarative form. The complexity and uncertainty of meaning of symbols are sources of their strength."[15]

To some extent, this approach is modeled in Frank H. Gorman's study of ritual in biblical texts, *The Ideology of Ritual*. Gorman draws on the work of the major exponents of a symbolic-communicative approach to ritual and reflects carefully on most of his theoretical presuppositions. Moreover, he provides a clear statement of his understanding of ritual, something that is lacking in the studies identified earlier. My debt to Gorman's study will be evident throughout this work, although I question some of Gorman's specific interpretations of blood manipulation activity, particularly those based on the assumption that blood functions as a ritual symbol and that its meaning as a symbol rests on its identification with the life-force animating the body. Also exercising a decisive influence on my study is the work of Saul M. Olyan on biblical representations of ritual. Olyan's monograph, *Rites and Rank: Hierarchy in Biblical Representations of Cult*[16] addresses many of the questions I raise in this study, although he makes only occasional references to the role of blood manipulation activity in the signaling and creation of social and cultic relations and status.

Problems in the Interpretation of Ritual

Although there is much to commend in an approach to ritual as symbolic-communicative activity, it is not lacking in theoretical and methodological problems. First, as Catherine Bell notes, "a distinction between technical practical and ritual symbolic activities often reflects categories rather alien to the peoples involved."[17] This criticism applies even to an approach to ritual that affirms that symbolic acts affect status and identity and shape reality, because ritual actors frequently describe only the instrumental effects achieved by their actions, with no reference to their supposed symbolic-communicative character. This is especially true of the authors of biblical ritual texts. Although scholars often treat ancient Israelite ritual activity as if the ancient Israelites themselves interpreted it symbolically, we actually find few, if any, symbolic explanations in the texts. Rather, we find declarations about the instrumental effects achieved by ritual actions. For example, biblical texts tell us that the sprinkling of blood onto candidates for the priesthood makes them holy, effecting a definite change in their status and identity (Exod 29:21; Lev 8:30), and that the daubing of blood onto the horns of an altar makes it pure, changing its condition (Lev 8:15).

If we give serious consideration to the nonsymbolic, instrumental explanations of ritual offered by "native" informants, however, we encounter further complications. First, relative to the number of textual representations of ritual practice, many of which are quite detailed, there are very few interpretive statements. Scholars have responded to this situation by applying explanations of blood manipulation that appear in specific contexts to uninterpreted activity represented in other contexts. In particular, many scholars have identified Lev 17:11 as providing the key to understanding all acts of cultic blood manipulation: "For the life of the flesh is in the blood; and I have given it to you for making atonement for your lives on the altar; for, as life, it is the blood that makes atonement" (NRSV). N. Kiuchi, for example, characterizes this as "the sole passage which explicitly refers to the meaning of blood manipulation," and he refers to "the consensus that Lev 17.11 should be applied to other animal sacrifices."[18] Interpreters have also sought to identify the conceptual basis of blood manipulation in more general terms by looking to those biblical texts that identify blood with the animation, the "life" (Heb. *nepeš*) of the body (Gen 9:4; Lev 17:11, 14; Deut 12:23). Thus, Jacob Milgrom writes that, "the identification of blood with life clarifies its function in the sacrificial system. . . . Impurity . . . is the realm of death. . . . Only its antonym, life, can be its antidote. Blood, then, as life is what purges the sanctuary."[19] However, if we do not assume that ritual actions are univalent, if we embrace the possibility that ritual symbols are characterized by condensation of meaning, multivocality, and ambiguity, we must question attempts to explain blood manipulation with reference to a single text or a single conceptual basis.

Anthropological research on ritual has indicated that a ritual performance is often experienced and explained differently by each participant.[20] How do we decide which of several competing "native" explanations to adopt? In the biblical texts we encounter what may be termed public interpretations—those made available in texts that are accessible to readers beyond the circles of ritual specialists. In many cases, these interpretations also seem to be official interpretations, promulgated by members of the social and cultic elite and presented as authoritative and binding explanations of the significance of ritual actions. However, public and official explanations of ritual performances do not exhaust their meanings. Individuals bring their own preconceptions and concerns to bear in making sense of ritual activity and formulate private interpretations.[21] If promulgated and adopted by others, these private interpretations become public interpretations and may be authorized as official interpretations. In this study, I identify and explicate the interpretations offered by some ancient Israelite and early Jewish tradents; however, I do not assume that these explanations were the only ones advanced or that they were necessarily widely embraced or officially enforced.

An Alternative Approach: Ritual as Practice

Biblical texts offer very little in the way of interpretation or explanation of ritual acts. Their obvious concern is with the details of practice, with telling the reader how ritual actions were enacted or in prescribing how to carry them out. Questions that focus on the symbolic meanings or instrumental effects of ritual acts are external to the purposes of most of the texts. They were not written to answer such questions. Rather, they invite questions about formal practice.

Catherine Bell has recently challenged the tendency in much scholarly discourse on ritual to create a dichotomy between thought and action in which thought becomes the privileged member of the pair.[22] Seeking to overcome this, Bell offers an alternative model and speaks of ritualization as a strategic mode of acting, whereby some actions are distinguished from, and privileged in relation to, other actions in their very execution.[23] For example, the Jewish Passover Seder is a ritualized meal, distinguished from all other meals by a number of characteristics, including the food served, the modes of its consumption, and the framework of elaborate verbal ritual, involving recitation of prayers and blessings and the reading of a variety of authoritative texts. Yet, because it is a meal and shares basic features with other meals, its privileged status in relation to those meals can be recognized. This very privileging shapes the identities and dispositions of those who participate in the meal, whether or not there is conceptual reflection on the rite and on the symbolic meaning of various elements of the meal. The *doing* of the acts is significant and effective for creating relations and status—not only in a ritual meal but in blood manipulation as well.

Highly compatible with Bell's identification of ritualization as a "strategic way of acting" is a proposal offered by Jonathan Z. Smith for understanding how ritual functions as activity in relation to other kinds of activity. Smith introduces his proposal by reflecting on what indigenous Siberian hunters say about how they hunt bears, as this compares with what they actually do, and by considering how what they say and what they do in practice connects with their ritual activity. He demonstrates that, although the hunters kill bears in a manner that is both expeditious and safest for them, they claim to follow a very precise set of rules. These rules, it turns out, are observed only in a ritual hunt, where all of the variables may be carefully controlled. He concludes by offering the following suggestion about ritual: "[A]mong other things, ritual represents the creation of a controlled environment where the variables (i.e., the accidents) of ordinary life may be displaced precisely because they are felt to be so overwhelmingly present and powerful. Ritual is a means of performing the way things ought to be in conscious tension to the way things are in such a way that this ritualized perfection is recollected in the ordinary, uncontrolled, course of things."[24]

This study draws on Smith's suggestions about the function of ritual activity and explores the ways in which the enacted order of ritual blood manipulation, as represented in the texts, functions to map order onto physical space, creating an ordered space that stands out in contrast to ordinary, unordered space. As Bell suggests, ritualized action "gives rise to (or creates) the sacred as such by virtue of its sheer differentiation from the profane."[25]

Finally—and most significantly for the overall theoretical thrust of this study—I apply Nancy Jay's approach to interpreting ritual activities as indexes.[26] Jay, drawing on the theoretical contribution of Charles Sanders Peirce, notes that signs function not only as symbols but also as indexes.[27] A *symbol* is a sign that is in a conventional relationship with its referent. For example, in India, China, and Japan the swastika refers conventionally to prosperity, well-being, and blessing. However, when the symbol was adopted by the National Socialist German Workers (Nazi) Party, it was given different conventional meanings, and after the Holocaust further conventional meanings have been attached to it. None of the many meanings attached to the swastika is inherent in the symbol itself. An *index*, however, is a sign that is connected with its referent as a matter of fact. It is in an existential relationship with it. The most basic example of an *index* is a pointing finger.[28] The finger is connected existentially, rather than conventionally, with the object it indicates. Jay applies Peirce's concept of indexes to sacrificial practice by noting the ways in which contact with a sacrificial animal and the parts into which it can be divided indicates and creates social relations:

> Sacrificial victims are given different symbolic meanings in different traditions, but sharing a victim's flesh puts participants in *existential* relation with the victim ("connected with it as a matter of fact"), and with one another. In unrelated traditions, participation in alimentary sacrifice both signifies and *causes* membership in the group with rights to participate. By indexing a social group, by indicating, "*this* group," alimentary sacrifice both identifies and constitutes it.[29]

In my exploration of the textual representations of blood manipulation, I consider how the "matter of fact," existential relationship between an individual or object and the blood of a sacrificial animal points to and creates various types of relations, and I show how blood manipulation accomplishes this effect, as an index, apart from any other communicative or instrumental effect that may be attributed to it. I also indicate that recognizing the indexical quality of blood manipulation contributes to a better understanding of other ways in which this activity may be interpreted.

Textually Represented Ritual

The emphasis on practice or action raises a problem for the focus of this study, which deals with textual representations of ritual activity. As Roy

Rappaport emphasizes, there is no ritual without performance, and the written account of a ritual is not itself a ritual.[30] Until quite recently, this important distinction between ritual as enacted and ritual as represented was accorded little attention by biblical scholars. For example, as Frank Gorman wonders, "are methods of interpretation used in the study of narrative texts equally useful in the study of ritual texts? More important is the methodological issue of whether the analysis of ritual texts should focus on *texts* or the ritual depicted in the texts."[31] Gorman concludes that the interpreter's focus should be on the ritual rather than on the text.

Although Gorman asks important questions, he fails to recognize that in dealing with a textual representation of a ritual performance one cannot get away from the text. Because one never achieves unmediated access to the ritual performance but experiences it only through the text, it is always a represented ritual. We are reading a text when we interpret a textual representation of a ritual. What is available for interpretation is what the text gives us. Thus, Gorman sets up an inappropriate dichotomy between the text and the ritual and fails to address how one goes about reading a ritual text in order to arrive at an adequate understanding of what is represented. Interpreting a textually represented ritual requires attention to the text as well as to the ritual. Both must be interpreted.[32] Moreover, because a ritual performance consists of a complex of actions carried out by human performers in a definite time and place, it is, in fact, appropriate that the methods applied to the study of narrative should be applied to textual representations of ritual activity. These are narrative representations that plot a sequence of ritual actions, which I refer to as a "ritual complex." Thus, in dealing with textual representations of ritual actions, I must give careful attention to the reading process through which I move from the text to an image of the enactment. Reader-oriented literary criticism is required, in addition to the analysis and interpretation of ritual.

Reading Texts: Theory and Method

The theoretical framework for my reading and reader-oriented analysis reflects the work of Stanley Fish.[33] Fish's key insights concern the situatedness of the reader, who reads and interprets as part of an "interpretive community," which both constitutes and is constituted by a specific body of rules and principles for identifying and making sense of a text. As a reader, my primary interpretive community consists of those biblical scholars who apply modern historical-critical interpretive methods to the texts. More broadly, I identify with communities of academic interpreters of ancient texts. I also give attention to the ways in which readers who are not part of this community have read the texts, recognizing, of course, that my reading of the literary records of these readers is itself a communally situated act. Thus, for example, I approach Ibn Ezra's medieval Jewish commentaries on the Torah from the standpoint of my own interpretive community, attempting to make sense of Ibn Ezra's readings as examples of the product of a different reading community.

On a practical level, I have found the insights of Wolfgang Iser particularly helpful.[34] According to Iser, readers inevitably experience "gaps" in the text before them and variously fill those gaps in order to arrive at a coherent understanding of the meaning of the text. The reader plays a vital role in constituting the "meaning" of any text. As long as a text remains unopened and unread, it has no meaning. Meaning comes into being only when the text is read, and the reader's contribution is irreplaceable. Thus, Iser emphasizes the process of reading, what readers do when they read.

All of my explanations of ancient texts throughout this study are expressions of a reading practice in which I attempt to determine what the texts communicate to me as a reader. What prevents my readings from being purely private and idiosyncratic is that they are informed and shaped by the concerns and methods of my interpretive community—the guild of modern, academic scholars of biblical literature and early Judaism. My readings are offered in dialogue and debate with other readings offered by modern scholars and, in some instances, also with premodern readers. At issue is what we, as readers, claim to find in the texts we read using shared conventions within the context of a reading community. My goal, as the goal of any scholar, is to produce persuasive readings. That is, my goal is to produce readings that are persuasive to readers who share my basic concerns and modes of reading. My reading only has value insofar as it convinces other readers of the biblical texts and comes to displace other readings. I must make a persuasive case for what I claim to find "in the text" and for what I add in the process of making sense of the text.

Although we have access to a textually represented ritual only through the text, in the reading of the text we may seek to construct an image of the living enactment of a ritual complex. This ritual enactment takes place in what may be termed "the world of the text," which is that image of a world constructed by the reader, in which the action of the narrative takes place. This world comes into being in the interaction of reader with text and is part of that "meaning" which can exist only through the process of reading. For this reason, we must distinguish carefully between the "world of the text" and a living, historical context in which ritual activity takes place. The latter context is not immediately accessible to the reader of the Bible. Only after we have developed a clear picture of the world of the text can we attempt to reconstruct an image of the real world in which ritual actions might have been carried out.[35]

Throughout this study, I speak of the world conveyed or constructed by a particular text and analyze the practical human activity of the people (the "characters") who inhabit this world. I search for patterns and structures in the observable action of these people. This is especially the case with the world created by Priestly (P) biblical texts, a world in which regular patterns of action play a central role. For heuristic purposes, to demonstrate the value of observing actions and seeing how they function as indexes, I also describe what the actions might look like if enacted according to the prescriptions set forth in the texts.

In doing so, I can show how rules are implicit in observed actions when consistent patterns of repetition and formality are observed. That is, actions carried out in consistent patterns present their own rules, without verbal expression, in the very enactments. Thus, for example, if every observed burnt offering involves the dashing of blood against the altar by priests, we may conclude that this action is required by the rules for that ceremony. These rules may not be stated explicitly. Indeed, the ritual actors may not even be able to explicate or present such rules, for their actions may not be governed by conscious desire to satisfy a known requirement but may simply express the enactment of a learned pattern. A priest may *never* have to be told, "Dash the blood of a burnt offering on the altar before you do anything else," if he knows he is to do this because he has seen countless other priests do it. It may seem the only "natural," the only possible course of action. Liturgies may be learned as much by observation and repetition as by verbal training. In this way, rules governing practice become internalized as habits. These ritual habits of the actors in the textual world are a major focus of my attention.

CHAPTER ONE

The Identification of Blood with "Life"

A Conceptual Foundation?

In scholarship on sacrifice in the Hebrew Bible a handful of biblical texts that identify blood with "life" (*nepeš*) have played a significant role in the interpretation of cultic blood manipulation, frequently being identified as revealing its conceptual basis. For example, Jacob Milgrom explains that "the identification of blood with life clarifies its function in the sacrificial system. . . . Impurity . . . is the realm of death. . . . Only its antonym, life, can be its antidote. Blood, then, as life is what purges the sanctuary."[1] Of particular significance for interpretations of cultic blood manipulation has been Lev 17:11: "For the life of the flesh is in the blood; and I have given it to you for making atonement for your lives on the altar; for, as life, it is the blood that makes atonement" (NRSV). In the Hebrew Bible *only* this text explicitly links the blood-"life" identification to the manipulation of the blood of sacrificial animals.

In this chapter I clarify what the texts tell us of some ancient Israelite conceptualizations of blood and introduce some preliminary reflections on how these conceptualizations may be related to the cultic-ritual uses of blood. Additionally, in an appendix to the chapter I introduce and discuss some of the Hebrew vocabulary associated with blood manipulation activity. Together, they constitute the foundation for the remaining chapters of this study, which examine Hebrew Bible representations and interpretations of cultic blood manipulation.

The texts treated in this chapter come from three of the source strata of the Pentateuch, the legal core of the book of Deuteronomy,[2] the Priestly source (P),[3] and the work of the Holiness school (H). Until quite recently, a majority of scholars believed that H consisted only of the "Holiness Code" (Lev 17–26)—so called because of its emphasis on the holiness of Yahweh and his demands that his people be holy—and that this was an older body of material incorporated by P.[4] Recently, however, Israel Knohl has argued that the H stratum is not older than P. Rather, the school that produced this material edited P in order to incorporate its own ideas and concerns into the Priestly texts.[5] Thus, H material is found not only in Leviticus 17–26 but is scattered throughout P. Early in his research, Knohl shared his ideas with Jacob Milgrom, who had independently identified evidence that H was secondary to P, and met with an immediately favorable response.[6] Together, Knohl and Milgrom make a persuasive case for regarding H as secondary to, and dependent upon, P. Consequently I have adopted this position as my own. Where both Knohl and Milgrom agree on the identification of H material, I simply refer the reader to their discussions of the text in question. Where only one of them supports an identification, I indicate where he defends this identification and note my reasons for being persuaded by the argument. In a few instances, I have adopted an identification that differs from those of both Milgrom and Knohl. The assumption that H is secondary to P has important implications for the way I read the sources and for how I shape my conclusions. Working with this assumption, I show how H interprets and develops P's sacrificial ideas and I adduce further evidence that both supports and refines the Knohl-Milgrom hypothesis.

My assumptions about the relative historical relationship of P and H have a central place in this study, since they play a key role in my arguments about the interpretive relevance of Lev 17:11. I have not, however, felt it necessary to take a position on the absolute dating of these source strata or on their relationship to other sources and traditions.[7] In particular, I do not engage the debates about the historical relationship between the legal materials in Deuteronomy and the P and H strata. Although the question of the historical relationship between the Deuteronomic identifications of blood with "life" (*nepeš*) and those that appear in P and H texts is certainly a significant one, it is not immediately germane to the central concerns of this study, and no major argument in this work depends on a decision about whether the Deuteronomic blood laws are older or later than those we find in P and H.[8]

Prohibitions of Consuming Blood in Deuteronomy

Deuteronomy 12 contains two prohibitions of eating blood (12:16 and 12:23–25).[9] Both appear in the context of provisions for noncultic slaughter of domestic livestock for food, within the larger framework of provisions for cult centralization.[10] A third prohibition that is clearly related to those in Deuteronomy 12 appears in Deut 15:23, at the end of laws about the consecration of the firstborn of livestock (15:19–22).

The first blood prohibition in Deuteronomy 12 is quite brief and appears in the third part of a threefold presentation of commandments directed toward cult centralization (12:13–19). Following a commandment not to offer up burnt offerings anywhere, save at "the place which Yahweh will choose in one of your tribes" (vv. 13–14), a limitation,[11] is placed on the decree on cult centralization: "Only, as much as you desire, you may slaughter and may eat flesh according to the blessing of Yahweh your god which he has given to you in all your towns; the impure and the pure may eat it, like the gazelle and like the deer" (v. 15).

This provision indicates that cult centralization does not limit the ability to consume meat. The fact that such a provision is set forth implies that the centralization program would make this an issue. Moreover, the statement that domestic animals may now be eaten "like the gazelle and like the deer" points to the existence of a prior contrast: formerly one could not simply slaughter a domestic animal for food wherever and whenever one wished; one could, however, hunt and eat game without restriction. This law establishes that the provision for game now applies also to domestic animals. All of this indicates that the permission of noncultic slaughter is an innovation.[12] According to the conceptualization of the text, prior to the institution of cult centralization in the land, and the corresponding permission of noncultic slaughter, slaughter of domestic animals was to be governed by unstated prescriptions. It may be going too far to affirm that all slaughter of domestic livestock was necessarily performed as sacrifice before the centralization of the cult.[13] However, it is difficult to escape the conclusion that this legal collection assumes that noncultic slaughter is an innovation, representing a loosening of control over the rules governing the slaughter and consumption of domestic livestock.

Against this background verse 16 commands, "Only [*raq*], the blood you shall not eat; upon the earth you shall pour it out like water [*'al-hā'āreṣ tišpĕkennû kammāyim*]" (cf. Deut 15:23). This verse establishes a limitation on the prior permission for noncultic slaughter. The introduction of the prohibition of eating blood in this context suggests that the permission to slaughter for food away from the central shrine would provoke a question. Apparently, one would know what to do with the blood if one slaughtered at the shrine; it would not be eaten. With noncultic slaughter the question arises, What is to be done with the blood? Deuteronomy 12:16 makes it clear that the permission to slaughter animals for food away from the central shrine and to eat the flesh does not include permission to consume the blood.

No explanation is given for the prohibition. We are simply told that an Israelite may not eat blood. It must be poured on the ground "like water." This specification seems to indicate that the blood is simply to be disposed of; it is not to be accorded the special treatment it would receive in the cult.[14] As von Rad puts it, "this pouring out of the blood is definitely denied the character of a sacrifice (it is to be like water)."[15] The prescription that the blood is to be poured out "like water" points to the possibility of an alternative way of dealing with the blood, that it could be treated other than "like water." Thus, the deliberate act of not doing anything with the blood except disposing of it by pouring it out on the ground is ritualized activity, since it is strategically distinguished from another assumed type of activity and a privileged opposition is established.

The second prohibition of eating blood is far more detailed. It appears in a second unit setting forth permission for noncultic slaughter. This provision (12:20–25) is rather complex and seems to be composed of at least two distinct layers of tradition. It also appears to represent the conceptual source of the much shorter provision in verse 15:

When Yahweh your god extends your border just as he has indicated to you, and you say, "I will eat flesh," because you desire to eat flesh, you may eat as much flesh as you desire. If the place where Yahweh your god will choose to place his name is far from you, you may slaughter some of your herd or some of your flock which Yahweh has given to you, just as I have commanded you, and you may eat in your towns as much as you desire. Indeed, just as the gazelle or the deer is eaten, so you may eat it; the impure and the pure together may eat it. (Deut 12:20–22)

This law sets forth the same general principles as we find in verse 15. An Israelite who desires to eat the flesh of one of his domestic animals need not bring it as a sacrifice. He may slaughter it at home and anyone may eat the flesh, regardless of his state of purity. Domestic livestock not designated for sacrifice are to be eaten just as one would eat game. Verses 23–25 then sets forth the prohibition of eating blood, limiting what has just been introduced: "Only [*raq*], take care not to consume the blood, for the blood is the life, and you shall not consume the life with the flesh. You shall not consume it; upon the earth you shall pour it out like water. You shall not consume it, so that it may go well for you and for your children after you when you do what is right in the sight of Yahweh."

Here we are told why eating blood with flesh is prohibited. It is the life, and one must not eat the life with the flesh. The text presents a direct equation. Blood *is* life. The reference to eating "the life with the flesh" (*hannepeš 'im-habbāśār*) indicates that the *eating* of the blood with the flesh is in view and not its separate consumption by drinking. The provisions, therefore, concern proper slaughter that results in the draining of the blood. That the eating of blood is a serious matter is indicated by the admonition to "take care" (*ḥăzaq*) and the fourfold iteration of the commandment not to eat the blood. Likewise, implicit in the positive promise that observance of this command will bring benefit is the warning that failure to obey will bring punishment.

Although the ban on consuming blood is based on the identification of blood with "life," it must be noted that the text does not indicate why "life" may not be consumed. This fact is overlooked by many interpreters, who apparently assume that the reason is obvious. Anthony Phillips, for example, explains that "all life was regarded as the gift of God to whom it belonged as of right. Since life was thought to be controlled by the blood, . . . in no circumstances could this be appropriated by man (Gen 9:4). Hence before the deuteronomic reform it was offered to God in the local sanctuary at the time of the slaughter of the animal for food. The new law in no way alters this attitude to blood: it must still be returned to God by being poured out on the ground in an irretrievable way."[16]

According to these interpretations, "life" may not be consumed because it belongs to Yahweh, the source of life, and must be returned to him. I would emphasize that this explanation is not explicitly articulated in Deuteronomy; it requires conceptual gap-filling. Thus, the reason for the ban on consuming blood is far from obvious. There is no necessary correlation between the belief that blood is life and a prohibition of eating it. Indeed, one might find good reason to base the consumption of blood on its identification with life, in the absence of some countervailing prohibition. As A. Noordtzij speculates, consumption of blood could be "motivated by the desire to appropriate the vital force of another creature."[17] While evidence is lacking for such a practice in the ancient Near East, ethnographic data demonstrate the reality of both the theory and the practice in human societies.[18] Moreover, it must be noted that the text itself nowhere affirms what Phillips and others assert, namely that life comes from Yahweh, belongs to him, and must be "returned" to him. What is missing, then, from the Deuteronomic law is any explicit indication of why Yahweh forbids his devotees to consume the life of an animal with its flesh.

The Primeval Blood Prohibition

Bearing a very close resemblance to Deuteronomy's blood prohibition is that found in the P narrative (Gen 9:4). This passage is P's only prohibition of eating blood and is not part of the cultic laws set forth in Exodus-Numbers.[19] Rather, P introduces the prohibition of eating blood after the narrative of the Flood. The context is the renewal of the creation blessings with the survivors of the Flood, Noah and his family (9:1–7). In this context, to the original blessing "be fruit-ful and multiply and fill the earth" (cf. Gen 1:28), God adds the extra condition that all living creatures will fear humankind (v. 2), and grants permission for human beings to consume animal flesh (v. 3). This is clearly a new provision, since Gen 1:29–30 had permitted humankind and animals to eat only plants.[20]

The permission to eat meat has a condition attached to it (Gen 9:4): "How-ever, flesh with its life, its blood, you may not eat" (*'ak-bāśār běnapšô dāmô lō' tō'kēlû*).[21] Because this qualification follows on the prior permission to consume living creatures, the word "flesh" (*bāśār*) must indicate those living creatures in the state of being food. "Flesh" is what may be eaten. However, the *nepeš* (life) that belongs to this flesh ("its life") may not be eaten. As in Deuteronomy 12, the *nepeš* (life) is directly identified with the blood: "its blood" (*dāmô*) stands in apposition to "its life" (*napšô*) and indicates what is intended by the term *nepeš*.[22] Blood is characterized as that which animates the flesh. Thus, the common rendering of *běnapšô dāmô* as "with its lifeblood" must be questioned.[23] It is misleading, since it suggests that a specific type of blood is at issue. Similarly, I can find no basis for following Benno Jacob and Claus Westermann in their insistence that the text refers to "rhythmic, pulsat-ing blood."[24] The text simply prohibits eating flesh with its life, which is iden-tified as its blood.

In both Deuteronomy and Gen 9:4, *nepeš* indicates the force of vitality, that which characterizes a body when it is alive. The vitality of the body is directly identified with the blood. In other words, blood is what keeps the body alive. As a number of interpreters have noted, the identification of life with blood apparently was based on simple empirical observation that life ebbs with the loss of blood.[25]

The prohibition of consuming flesh "with its life" indicates that the blood is understood to retain its identity as "life" even after the body ceases to be alive, when it becomes "flesh." As Vervenne correctly asserts, "In the ancient understanding, . . . blood remained menacing and potent, full of latent life."[26] Blood, therefore, is not a symbol of life, if by symbol one means something that merely stands for its referent. Blood really *is* life. Both Deuteronomy and Gen 9:4 attribute an inherent potency to blood by directly equating it with life.

The explicit identification of blood with life in Gen 9:4 and Deuteronomy establishes the reason why blood may not be consumed. The point is made especially clear in Deut 12:23: "Take care not to consume the blood, for the blood is the life, and you shall not consume the life with the flesh." However, although the identification of blood with life explains why blood may not be consumed, the explanation itself requires interpretation. Why may life not be consumed? For many interpreters the answer to this question is obvious. Life comes from God and, therefore, belongs to God.[27] Some go a step further and explain that since life comes from God, blood is "sacred."[28] However, because all created things have their source in God and belong to God, it is difficult to see why blood would necessarily be reserved to the deity. Those who identify blood as sacred make a more effective case, because it is clear that what is holy must be withdrawn from common use. However, the basic problem with this explanation is that the texts never explicitly declare that blood is "holy." Moreover, although Gen 9:4 and Deuteronomy prohibit the consumption of blood, it is not treated as something holy. It is not, in fact, "restored to God."[29] Indeed, Deuteronomy decrees that it is to be treated "like water."[30]

An alternative explanation, which does not rest on identifying life as coming from or belonging to God, is offered by U. Cassuto. He suggests that the ban on consuming blood was established "so as to do honour to the principle of life, . . . and to serve, at the same time, as a reminder that in truth all flesh should have been forbidden, and hence it behoves us to avoid eating one part of it in order to remember the former prohibition."[31] While this explanation is reasonable enough, like the others treated here it is based on conceptual gap-filling. The texts are silent about the reason for the ban on consuming blood (i.e., life).

At this juncture, some attention should be given to what follows the prohibition of consuming animal blood in the text. In Gen 9:5–6, God declares: "Moreover, your blood of your lives[32] I will require; from every wild animal I will require it, and from every human being—from every man's brother[33]—I will require human life. Whoever pours out human blood, by a human being his blood shall be poured out. For in the image of deity he made humankind."

In contrast to the permission to kill and eat animals, provided the blood is not eaten, God strictly prohibits the killing of a human being. Such killing is characterized as the pouring out of the blood (v. 6) and God's response is to "require" the blood or the "human life" (v. 5). Thus, God exercises control over life and promises to act against those who take human life. It should be noted, however, that God never makes an explicit proprietary claim to life.[34] He never declares that he is the source or owner of life. Rather, his authority or power over life is simply established in practice. First, he calls all living things into being (Gen 1:20–30). Then, he exercises the prerogative to destroy all living things (Gen 6:11–13, 17). It is against this background that God issues commandments about animal and human life.

Thus, it is possible to conclude that the prohibition of consuming blood in Gen 9:4 is based upon God's control over life. God grants lifeless animal flesh for human consumption but holds back the blood, the life itself. However, it must be stressed again that the rationale for the blood prohibition and the ideology behind it are implicit rather than explicit in the texts. The statement that P prohibits the consumption of blood because it is God's exclusive possession is the product of a process of textual interpretation and not a simple paraphrase of textual statements.

It must also be stressed that the text, in its present form, says nothing about what is to be done with the blood or about sacrificial slaughter. Von Rad proposes that the blood prohibition has its roots in the cult. Blood is claimed by Yahweh in sacrifice, and since it is his portion of the sacrifice, it may not be eaten.[35] There is, however, no mention of sacrifice in Genesis 9. In order to identify sacrifice as the background for Gen 9:4, one must assume that the connection Lev 17:11 draws between the identification of life with blood and its use in the cult was known to the tradent(s) who composed Gen 9:4. Furthermore, one must assume that the cultic reservation of blood to Yahweh antedated the ban on consuming blood and that there was a historical progression from devoting the blood of sacrificial animals to God to an outright ban on the consumption of any animal blood. Once it is recognized that H's statements are secondary to those of P, however, we can no longer be certain that they provide a background against which to understand P. It may still be true that the universal prohibition of eating blood is rooted in more specific cultic regulations, but because the evidence to support this conclusion is sparse to say the least, I believe it is best to avoid speculation on the matter and simply to deal with the texts as we have them. P, in the Genesis narrative, sets forth a prohibition of blood consumption that seems to apply to all of humankind. The cult is not mentioned. Indeed, according to P, there was no cult until Yahweh established it at Sinai. Read within P as a whole, Gen 9:4 has God set forth a prohibition of consuming blood long before animal sacrifice was practiced. Any attempt to interpret the cult in the light of this text will need to take these facts into consideration and emphasize the interpretive process engaged in to arrive at conclusions about the cultic manipulation of blood. Such conclusions, it must be acknowledged, are based on assumptions about what ideas were implicit in the Priestly tradents' interpretations of their own rituals and not on any explicit interpretation of those rituals by the tradents themselves. The only explicit interpretation of cultic blood manipulation in terms of the identification of blood with life is given by the H tradition in Leviticus 17. This interpretation seems to draw on P's identification of blood with life in Gen 9:4 and integrates rules about slaughter with provisions for sacrifice.

Blood Consumption and Conceptualization in H

I deal with H's prescriptions for, and interpretations of, sacrificial blood manipulation after I have examined P's treatments of sacrifice and blood manipulation. At this juncture I focus on H's identification of blood with life, and on those texts that ban the consumption of blood.

At the end of P's treatment of the sacrifice of well-being in Leviticus 3, H tradents added a prohibition of the consumption of fat and blood (Lev 3:16b–17):[36] "All fat is Yahweh's. It is a perpetual ordinance for your generations in all your settlements. You shall not consume any fat or any blood." The obvious focus of this short text is on fat. The ban on consuming blood is attached to and dependent on the teaching about fat. Indeed, it is introduced without explanation. The statement "all fat is Yahweh's" clearly provides the basis for the ban on consuming fat. However, the ban on consuming blood is not explained.

Are we to assume—to gap-fill—that consuming blood is forbidden because it *also* belongs to Yahweh? Certainly, in the preceding prescriptions for the sacrifice of well-being (Lev 3:1–16a), both blood and fat are identified as substances devoted to the altar, yet only the fat is characterized as an offering (see chapter 4). This short passage provokes as many questions as it answers. At this juncture, what should be noted is that blood is associated with fat and that there is an absolute ban on the consumption of either substance.

In Leviticus 7, H tradents added a further prohibition of consuming fat to P's instructions for the sacrifice of well-being (7:22–25),[37] which they followed with a prohibition of consuming blood (7:26–27):[38] "And you shall not consume any blood, of birds or of beasts, in all your settlements. As for any person who consumes any blood—that person shall be severed from his people." Although this ban on consuming blood follows on instructions about the sacrifice of well-being, its application to all blood is indicated by the use of the formula *kol-dām* (*any* blood), and, most clearly, by the reference to birds, which are not included as well-being offerings. Thus, it is clear that a general ban on eating blood can follow on a discussion of sacrifice.[39] Also, whereas the ban on consuming fat admits of some exceptions, the ban on consuming blood is absolute—and is not explained! [40]

Leviticus 17:10–12 is the third of the five units into which Leviticus 17 can be divided.[41] Structurally, it consists of two declarations of the ban on consuming blood (vv. 10, 12), which bracket, and thereby emphasize, the identification of the reason for the ban (v. 11).[42] Verse 10 reads: "Now as for any man from the house of Israel or any resident alien who resides among them who consumes any blood, I will set my face against the person who consumes blood and I will sever him from the midst of his people." Verse 12 repeats the prohibition of blood consumption and identifies verse 11 as providing its rationale: "Therefore ['al-kēn], I said to the children of Israel, 'No person from among you shall consume blood, and no resident alien who resides among you shall consume blood.'"

In verse 10, the ban on consuming blood is announced by first identifying the negative act, consumption of blood, and then threatening the negative consequence, being severed from the people.[43] The verse is constructed in such a way that it is the threat of severing that identifies the consumption of blood as a negative act. The solution to the threat of divine extirpation is to refrain from consuming blood. Thus, the threat-construction amounts to a prohibition of consuming blood. The rule against the consumption of "any blood" (*kol-dām*) applies to both Israelites and resident aliens and amounts to a general declaration against the consumption of any and all blood, regardless of its source.[44] In verse 12, as well, the rule against blood consumption applies both to Israelites and to resident aliens. Thus, in my view, Jacob Milgrom's claim that the verses refer only to the blood of the sacrifice of well-being must be rejected. As I noted with reference to Lev 7:26–27, it is characteristic of H to follow prescriptions on sacrifice with general declarations banning the consumption of any and all blood.

Standing between verses 10 and 12, verse 11 provides the reason for the prohibition of consuming blood. I provide here a preliminary translation: "For the life of the flesh is in the blood, and I myself have assigned it for you upon the altar to effect removal for your lives; for the blood itself effects removal by the life." In chapter 7, I offer a close reading and discussion of this verse in which I clarify what it says about the cultic use of blood and how this explanation may be applied to the blood manipulation as represented elsewhere in the corpus of P and H texts. At this juncture, I simply note some basic facts.

First, as a number of interpreters have noted, Lev 17:11 provides the *only* biblical explanation of how blood accomplishes the effects attributed to it. Specifically, this verse tells us what happens when blood is used to effect "removal" (*kipper*). This effect has something to do with the fact that blood is identified with life. It should be noted that the way in which the first clause of Lev 17:11 identifies blood with life differs from what we have seen in Gen 9:4 and Deut 12:23. Here the "life" (*nepeš*) is *baddām*. Most interpreters render the *bet* preposition with *dām* as *bet*-locative: the life is "*in* the blood."[45] This would mean that life is something distinct from blood, contained within it.[46] It is possible, however, that we have the *bet* preposition indicating identity (*beth essentiae*).[47] If the latter is the correct interpretation, then Lev 17:11 says essentially the same thing as the other sources I have identified. In either case, blood is identified with life, with the animation of the body. According to the final clause of the verse, it is the conceptual identification of blood with life that is the basis for the application of blood to the altar. Leviticus 17:11, I again note, is the only text in the entire Hebrew Bible that establishes this connection between the cultic blood manipulation and the identification of blood with life.

Following on Lev 17:10–12, we find further teachings on the proper treatment of blood, this time of wild animals killed in the hunt (Lev 17:13–14): "Now as for any man from the children of Israel or any resident alien who resides among them who hunts down a wild animal or a bird which may be eaten, he shall pour out its blood and cover it with dirt. For the life of all flesh is its blood, in that it is its life,[48] and I said to the children of Israel, 'You shall not consume the blood of any flesh. For the life of all flesh is its blood. Anyone who consumes it shall be severed.'" This unit provides a supplement to the previous rules, which have all dealt with domestic animals, and explains what is to be done by someone who hunts game for food—a legitimate activity whose legitimacy can be retained if a rule is observed.[49] When the animal is killed, its blood must be poured out and covered with dirt. Whereas in Gen 9:6 the idiom "pour out blood" (*šāpak dām*) refers to a negative act, murder, the illegitimate shedding of blood, here the pouring out of the blood is commanded by Yahweh. Additionally, the blood must be covered with dirt.

Verse 14 provides the reason for the rule set forth in verse 13 and its structure is like verse 11. First, we are told that blood is identified with the life of the flesh, then what practical principle follows from this—namely, that Yahweh prohibits the consumption of blood. There follows a repetition of the original statement identifying blood with life, which indicates clearly that the prohibition of consuming blood follows from the identification of blood and life. Thus, the reason why the blood of game animals and birds is to be poured out and covered with dirt is that it is identified with life and, as such, cannot be consumed. The specific provisions concerning game animals follow from, and reflect, a general ban on consuming blood, which is introduced in verses 10–12. Note the threefold repetition of "any flesh" (*kol-bāśār*) in verse 14. Verses 13–14 answers an implicit question about how to apply the ban on consuming blood when dealing with game animals.

We may wonder, however, why the blood must be both poured out *and* covered. Is it not enough simply to pour the blood on the ground? As we have seen, Deuteronomy merely prescribes that the blood of a domestic animal slaughtered for food be poured out on the ground "like water." H requires an additional act when a wild animal or bird is killed. It must be emphasized that the text does not, in fact, provide a precise explanation of the required procedure. Additionally, the text does not tell us how the identification of blood with life is related to the prohibition of consuming it and the requirement to pour it out and cover it with dirt. It is easy enough to conclude that the pouring out and covering are intended to dispose of the blood, which may not be consumed.[50] But why is the blood disposed of in this specific way? Clearly, we have to do with ritualized activity here[51]—that is, the text prescribes a definite mode of dealing with the blood, which differs from the normal and casual disposal of other waste products from a slaughtered animal, such as excrement in the digestive tract, or the bones. The special attention given to the blood indexes this substance as special, and this indexing reinforces the explicit emphasis on the identification of blood with the animal's life and the strict ban against its consumption.

Interpreters who attempt to explain why the blood is both to be poured out and covered identify three texts that can be used to fill in the conceptual gaps in Lev 17:13–14. The first text, Ezek 24:7–8, refers to shed blood being left exposed on a rock and not covered. Such blood provokes wrath and vengeance (for further discussion of this text, see chapter 6). In the second text, Job 16:18, Job cries out, "O earth, do not cover my blood; let my outcry find no resting place" (NRSV). Similarly, Isa 26:21 refers to the earth disclosing shed blood when Yahweh appears to execute judgment. These texts provide the basis for an argument that shed blood provokes vengeance against the one who shed it if it is left in view. Covering the blood, taking it from view, seems to eliminate the threat of vengeance being exacted.[52] However, it must be noted that each of the texts cited in support of this interpretation deals with human blood shed through unjust violence. Nevertheless, the first unit of Leviticus 17 suggests that animal blood could be regarded in the same way as human blood, with the same response expected when it is shed illegitimately.[53] Thus, there is some support provided by the immediate context of Lev 17:13–14 to interpret the covering of the blood as protecting the one who shed it from subsequent vengeance for having shed blood. Still, I would emphasize that this interpretation of the gesture is not given directly in the text but must be supplied on the basis of texts drawn from outside the context. The reader must engage in conceptual gap-filling. What is clear, nevertheless, is that the additional identification of blood with life in this text provides the basis for the ruling that the blood must not be eaten but must be poured out and covered with dirt. The fact that blood is identified with the animation of the body provides the basis for rules governing its treatment.

Conclusions

The conceptual linkage of blood with "life" (*nepeš*), the identification of blood as that which animates the body, is expressed in the legal core of Deuteronomy and in P and H texts, but is found nowhere else in the Hebrew Bible. This suggests the need for caution in drawing the conclusion that the identification of blood with life was a widespread phenomenon in ancient

Israel. Only H directly connects the conceptual linkage of blood with life to the use of blood in the cult, and this connection is expressed only in one text, Lev 17:11. Because I assume, on the basis of the recent work of Israel Knohl and Jacob Milgrom, that H is secondary to P, it is problematic, in my opinion, to identify Lev 17:11 as the key for unlocking the meaning of blood manipulation in P. However, as my treatment of P texts in chapters 3–5 will make clear, many interpreters, perhaps a majority, have identified Lev 17:11 in just this fashion. Indeed, the basic identification of blood with life has regularly been taken to provide the conceptual background for blood manipulation activity as it is represented throughout the Hebrew Bible. Having suggested why there are problems with this identification, in the chapters that follow I intend to explore the implications of referring to the blood-life identification when explaining blood manipulation activity and to further problematize this approach.

Appendix: Blood Manipulation Terminology

In order to clarify the basic meanings of the main terms for blood manipulation actions, I first explain my translation of each term, provide some relevant information on the history of its interpretation, and identify the sacrificial and other ritual complexes with which it is associated in the Hebrew Bible. Then I consider two verbs employed in some biblical texts to indicate the effects or purposes of blood manipulation activity—*kipper* (traditionally, "atone") and *ḥiṭṭēʾ* ("purify," "de-sin")—in order to establish a foundation on which to base my discussion of sacrificial procedures in subsequent chapters.

Blood Manipulation Verbs

zāraq (toss).[54] The root *zrq* appears thirty-four times in the Hebrew Bible, thirty-two times in the *qal* construction, and two times in the *qal* passive. It is used twenty-five times with sacrificial blood as its object, and nine times with other substances. On a basic level, it seems to indicate a scattering motion. It is used for the handling of both liquid and dry substances. By looking at the treatment of dry substances we can get a clear picture of the action indicated by the verb. According to Exod 9:8–10, Yahweh commands Moses and Aaron to take handfuls of soot from a kiln, which Moses casts (*zrq*) heavenward. Isaiah 28:25a speaks of scattering (*wĕhēpîṣ*) dill and tossing (*yizrōq*) cumin seed. The parallelism here and the fact that this mode of sowing seed is contrasted

with the planting of grain seed in neat rows (28:25b) indicate that a loose flinging motion with the arm is in view. In describing Josiah's reform of the cult, 2
Chron 34:4 says that he made dust of the Asherim and the various cult images
and scattered (*zrq*) the dust over the graves of those who had sacrificed to
them. Job 2:12 says that Job's friends cast dust heavenward onto their heads
(*wayyizrĕqû ʿāpār ʿal-roʾšêhem*). Finally, Ezek 10:2 states that the prophet was
instructed to fill his hands with coals of fire and to cast (*zrq*) these over the city.
From these various usages, it is evident that *zrq* indicates a scattering motion
by which loose, light substances are dispersed. Therefore, when the same verb
is used for liquids, we should understand an analogous motion by which the
liquid is caused to scatter over something. Clearly, the English rendering
"sprinkle" is incorrect.[55] Sprinkling is a finer and more precise gesture than is
indicated by the verb *zrq*, which should be rendered "toss," "throw," "fling," or
"scatter."[56] It is necessary to stress this distinction because some interpreters
have assimilated the gesture indicated by *zrq* with the gesture indicated by the
hiphil of *nzh* ("sprinkle") and have based interpretive conclusions on this incorrect move. Thus, commentators on 2 Kgs 16:12–15 have claimed that the
"sprinkling" of blood on the altar set up by Ahaz was an act that consecrated
the altar, apparently basing this interpretation on the fact that sprinkling is associated with consecration in other sources (Lev 16, 8; Exod 29).[57] The assumption that *zrq* means "sprinkle" allows for this conclusion. However, the
verb is never associated with consecration, and it is quite unlikely that it has
anything to do with consecration, even in 2 Kgs 16.[58]

In P's system of sacrifice, this manipulation of tossing or dashing blood
takes place in the burnt offering, the well-being sacrifice, and the reparation
offering. In H, Lev 17:6 indicates that the blood of the well-being sacrifice is to
be tossed onto the altar, and Num 18:17[59] indicates that the blood of a firstborn
clean animal taken by the priests as their due is to be dashed upon the altar.
Apparently, the animal is regarded as being offered by the priests as a well-
being sacrifice. There are no H references to the blood manipulation in the
case of the burnt or reparation offerings. The tossing of the blood of the well-
being offering is also mentioned in 2 Kgs 16:13, and that of the burnt offering
and the eaten sacrifice (*zebah*) in 2 Kgs 16:15. In 2 Chronicles we find reference
to the dashing of the blood of burnt offerings at Hezekiah's rededication of the
sanctuary (29:22). In all of these cases, the altar is the recipient of the gesture.
The blood is either tossed "on the altar" (*ʿal-hammizbēah*) or "altarward"
(*hammizbēhâ*). In most cases, there is further specification that this tossing on

the altar is "round about" (*sābîb*). Second Chronicles 30:16 and 35:11 state that the blood of Passover lambs was tossed, but these verses are notable in not indicating where the blood was tossed. In only one context, Exod 24:3–8, is another recipient of the gesture identified. Here, not only is blood tossed onto the altar (24:6) but also onto the people (*'al-hā 'ām*) (24:8).

hizzâ (sprinkle).[60] The verb *nzh* appears twenty-four times in the Hebrew Bible, four times in the *qal*, the rest in *hiphil*. The *qal* of this root means "splatter" or "spurt," and is transitive. The *hiphil,* being causative, would seem to indicate a controlled application that would have the same result as natural spurting. Thus, from "cause to spatter/cause to spurt," we arrive at the generally accepted translation, "sprinkle."

The verb is used for a blood manipulation only in priestly texts. In P's legislation for the sanctuary cult, the sprinkling of blood occurs in some versions of the *ḥaṭṭā't* sacrifice. A sprinkling manipulation also occurs in relation to the ordination of priests, although in this case, the sacrifice from which the blood is taken is the "ordination ram" (*'êl hammillu'îm*). In the rituals for the cleansing of a person healed of a skin disease and a house that had a fungal growth, the blood of a bird slaughtered over "living water" is sprinkled. In Numbers 19 a red cow is slaughtered and burned with a variety of substances, and the resulting ash, mixed with water, is sprinkled on those who have contracted death impurity. After the animal is slaughtered, the presiding chief priest is to sprinkle some of its blood toward the entrance of the Tent of Meeting. Besides blood, oil and water are also sprinkled in various ritual complexes, often in association with blood sprinkling, or even mixed with blood.

nātan (daub). The root *ntn* has a very large semantic range.[61] In ritual contexts, however, it indicates a gesture by which blood (or another substance) is placed, very deliberately, in a specific location. The action would involve daubing or smearing. It is used to refer to blood manipulation only in priestly texts (P, H, Ezekiel). In P's representation of the *ḥaṭṭā't, ntn* is used for the application of blood to the horns either of the altar of burnt offering or of the altar of spice incense inside the shrine building (see Exod 29:12; Lev 4:7, 18, 25, 30, 34; 8:15; 9:9; 16:18). In some instances, the instrument of the application is indicated to be a finger (Exod 29:12; Lev 4:25, 30, 34; 8:15; 9:9).

In Ezekiel's prescriptions for the consecration of a new altar, blood from a *ḥaṭṭā't,* is applied (*ntn*) to the four horns of the altar, as well as "to the four corners of the platform" and "to the border round about" (Ezek 43:20). In

Ezek 45:18–19 we find prescriptions for the annual purification of the shrine complex. Here, it is prescribed that blood from a *ḥaṭṭā't* be applied (*ntn*) to the doorposts of the temple building, to the four corners of the platform of the altar, and "to the doorposts of the gate of the inner courtyard" (Ezek 45:19).[62]

In the priestly ordination ceremony and the ceremony for purification of a person healed of a skin disease, blood is "put" (*ntn*) on the individual's right earlobe, right thumb, and right big toe.[63] In the instructions for the manipulation of the blood of the Passover sacrifice in Exodus 12, the priestly text (likely H; see chapter 2) indicates that the blood is to be placed (*ntn*) on the two doorposts and the lintel (12:7).[64]

šāpak and *yāṣaq* (pour out). Both of these verbs mean "pour out" and are used in P—apparently interchangeably—for the act by which the blood of the *ḥaṭṭā't* remaining after the manipulations of sprinkling and daubing is deposited at the "base" (*yĕsôd*) of the altar of burnt offering in the shrine courtyard (see Exod 29:12; Lev 4:7, 18, 25, 30, 34 [*špk*]; Lev 8:15; 9:9 [*yṣq*]).[65] Deuteronomy 12:27 states that the blood of eaten sacrifices (*zĕbāḥîm*) is to be poured out (*špk*) "on the altar of Yahweh" (*'al-mizbaḥ yhwh*). Whether this text prescribes a different gesture than that which P prescribes for "eaten sacrifices," or this is simply a different way of indicating the same gesture, is discussed in the following chapter. We also find that, in Deuteronomy's prescriptions for noncultic slaughter, the blood is to be poured out (*špk*) "like water" (Deut 12:16, 24; 15:23). Leviticus 17:13 (H) says that one who kills an animal in the hunt is to pour out (*špk*) the blood and cover it with earth. How these prescriptions for the treatment of blood relate to those concerned with the pouring of blood within the cult is discussed in subsequent chapters.

The Effects of Blood Manipulation Activity: *kipper and* ḥiṭṭē'

kipper.[66] There has been no lack of controversy over the meaning and significance of the verb *kipper* and related forms based on the root *kpr*. The older view was that this root had the basic meaning of "cover." On the basis of this explanation a theory about its meaning in relation to forgiveness of sin was developed, according to which sin was forgiven when it was covered, that is, taken out of Yahweh's sight.[67] It is clear, however, that this rendering and the theories based upon it cannot be maintained. The basic meaning of *kpr* is almost certainly "wipe." This identification of the root's meaning is based primarily on study of the usage of the Akkadian cognate in Babylonian and Assyrian texts.[68] As Milgrom notes in a brief discussion in his commentary on Leviticus 1–16, the G form (equivalent to the Hebrew *qal*) in Akkadian means "wipe," referring to the gesture by which something is applied to something else. The D form (equivalent to the Hebrew *piel*) means "wipe off" or "remove by wiping." A D-stem noun designates the instrument by which the wiping off or removal is effected.[69] In some cases, the best rendering of the D verb seems to be the more abstract translation "purify."[70] It is likely that the Hebrew root *kpr* has the same basic sense as the Akkadian cognate. However, because etymology does not determine diachronic meaning, identification of the etymological meaning of the root hardly settles the question of the precise meanings to be attributed to the verb *kipper* in the various textual contexts in which it appears. It should be noted, moreover, that controversy over the interpretation of *kipper* extends to the question of whether there is a single root *kpr* or two unrelated homographs. Baruch Levine maintains—correctly in my view—that the single root has developed two distinct meanings, "expiate" and "ransom," from a common base-meaning.[71] Baruch J. Schwartz, in contrast, maintains that *kpr* (expiate) and *kpr* (ransom) are "unrelated homographs."[72]

Because any translation of Hebrew terms reflects assumptions and ideas about what they mean conceptually, I have opted for a very literal etymological rendering, "effect removal," for the *piel* verb, and "removal" for the abstract noun *kippurîm*. By using these renderings I leave open the question of what is removed and how, so that in the course of this study I can nuance this basic rendering and indicate how context determines the precise meaning of *kipper*.

ḥiṭṭē'. The root *ḥṭ'* has the basic meaning "miss," "miss the mark," or "go off the path," as can be seen from the cognates in other Semitic languages and from a few instances in the Hebrew Bible.[73] In the Hebrew Bible, there are cases of the *qal* form being used with a literal meaning, "miss" (Prov 8:36; 19:2; Job 5:24). There is also one instance of a *hiphil* form with the obvious meaning "miss" (Judg 20:16). For the most part, however, the *qal* is used with a figurative meaning. In relation to human behavior as determined by divine commandments, it refers to engaging in behavior that "misses" Yahweh's standards. Thus, in most cases, it can be translated "sin."[74]

The *piel* construction of the root is a privative denominative,[75] which indicates the elimination or removal of the object noun ("sin" [*ḥēṭ'*]). Since *piel* privative denominatives "generally express a being occupied with the object expressed by the noun,"[76] *ḥiṭṭē'* apparently has the basic sense "to free from sin,"[77] "to de-sin," or "to unsin."[78] At this juncture, however, we would do well to recall James Barr's forceful critique of etymological explanations of Hebrew vocabulary. As Barr insists, etymology "cannot be a guide to the meaning of words in the contexts in which they are used."[79] Rather, "the semantic value of words in their current usage . . . has to be determined from the current usage and not from derivation."[80]

The *piel* verbal form *ḥiṭṭē'* appears fourteen times in the Massoretic text of the Hebrew canon.[81] These fourteen occurrences can be classified as follows. Two have a sacrificial animal offered as a *ḥaṭṭā't* sacrifice as their direct object (Lev 6:19; 9:15). One (2 Chron 29:24) has the blood of a *ḥaṭṭā't* as the direct object. The rest have direct objects that receive the effect indicated by the verb: a house with a fungal growth (Lev 14:49, 52), a person who has had contact with a corpse (Num 19:19), the sanctuary (*hammiqdāš*) (Ezek 45:18), the sacrificial altar (Lev 8:15; Ezek 43:20, 22 [bis], 23), and, in a figurative usage, a penitent sinner (Ps 51:9). Only once (Exod 29:36) does the verb take an indirect object with a preposition. In this case, the indirect object is the altar (*'al-hammizbēaḥ* [upon the altar]).

The first observation that can be made is that the verb can take a number of different objects, and clearly the object determines how the verb should be translated. It cannot mean exactly the same thing in Lev 6:19, 9:15, and 2 Chron 29:24 as it does in Lev 8:15 and other texts. In Lev 6:19 and 9:15 it indicates the act of offering an animal as a *ḥaṭṭā't* or using the animal in the rituals that define this sacrificial complex, and it can be rendered "offer as a *ḥaṭṭā't.*" In 2 Chron 29:24, where the blood of the *ḥaṭṭā't* is the object of the verb, it would mean "treat according to the usage for a *ḥaṭṭā't.*" The occurrence of the verb in Exod 29:36 is problematic. Some interpreters understand *wĕḥiṭṭē'tā 'al-hammizbēaḥ* in Exod 29:36 to mean "you shall offer a *ḥaṭṭā't* upon the altar," so that the verb has the same meaning as it does in Lev 6:19 and 9:15.[82] Unlike in Lev 6:19 and 9:15, however, the verb has the altar as its object and not the sacrificial animal. For this reason, I would argue that only when the object is the sacrifice itself (or a part of it, as in 2 Chron 29:24) should we translate it as "offer a *ḥaṭṭā't*" or with some similar rendering (for further discussion, see chapter 5).[83]

In Lev 8:15 and other texts, the verb indicates the effect of a ritual on an object. What is the ritual effect in these instances? How should we render the verb? Milgrom insists that the correct contextual rendering is "purify" and that the verb has no other meaning.[84] Other interpreters, as I have noted, appeal to the etymological meaning of the verb as "de-sin." My own study of the contextual usages leads me to basic agreement with Milgrom. "Purify" is an adequate translation, which may be employed as long as we do not make assumptions about what is purified or how. In my view, Milgrom goes too far, however, in insisting that "purify" is the only legitimate rendering, and that "sin" is never in view when *ḥiṭṭē'* is used for the effect of a ritual action. I elaborate on these points in my further treatment of the relevant texts (see, especially, chapter 5).

To end this discussion of the verb *ḥiṭṭē'*, a brief discussion is in order on the meaning of the etymologically related sacrificial name *ḥaṭṭā't,* which most standard translations render, in most of its occurrences, as "sin offering" (see, e.g., AV, RSV, NRSV, NIV, NJPS).[85] The name of the sacrifice is morphologically a *piel* construction. Thus, depending on how one renders the *piel* verb *ḥiṭṭē'*, the noun *ḥaṭṭā't* could be translated either "what de-sins" (de-sinning offering), or "what purifies" (purification offering).[86] The common rendering "sin offering" is at least as old as the Septuagint.[87] A noun that means "misstep" or "sin" is usually spelled in exactly the same manner as the name for the sacrifice, right down to the doubling of the middle root-letter: *ḥaṭṭā't.* Apparently, the LXX translators understood the sacrifice to be designated according to its object. Baruch Levine maintains, however, that the name of the sacrifice is not to be identified with this term for "sin," which, he asserts, was misvocalized by the Massoretes.[88] It follows, according to Levine, that there is no necessary connection between the offering designated *ḥaṭṭā't* and "sin" (*ḥaṭṭā't*).

According to Jacob Milgrom, who maintains that the verb *ḥiṭṭē'* means only "purify," the *ḥaṭṭā't* is a "purification offering" that deals with impurity from a variety of sources, including "sins," but not with the violations (sins) themselves.[89] This distinction is, of course, of immediate relevance to the explanation of the blood manipulations in the sacrifice, because the understanding of their significance depends, to a great extent, on understanding the purpose and focus of the sacrifice in which they play a role. Recently, Baruch J. Schwartz has advanced strong arguments in support of the view that the *ḥaṭṭā't* offering deals with the "sin" itself, removing it from the one who had violated one of Yahweh's commandments and from the sacred space where Yahweh's presence is manifest.[90] It should be noted, however, that Schwartz does not extend his argument to a criticism of Milgrom's insistence on rendering *ḥaṭṭā't* only as "purification offering" and never as "sin offering."

In my view, the *ḥaṭṭā 't* sacrifice, like all ritual performances, is a complex and multivalent phenomenon, and the sacrificial term itself is equivalently complex and multivalent. In some context, the *ḥaṭṭā 't* does seem to be a "purification offering," whose primary function is to eliminate impurity, which P treats as a miasmic force that attaches itself to sancta.[91] In other contexts, where its connection with "sin" (*ḥaṭṭā 't*) is emphasized (e.g., Lev 4),[92] it does seem to be a "sin offering," as the ancient LXX translators correctly recognized.[93] I have, therefore, opted to leave the term untranslated throughout this study.

CHAPTER TWO

Cultic Blood Manipulation

An Entry to the Textual Corpus

Outside of the P and H (priestly)[1] strata of the Pentateuch, there are relatively few representations of sacrificial practice and even fewer representations of blood manipulation activity. References to blood manipulation in Ezekiel and 2 Chronicles are treated in chapter 6, since the affinities of those works with the priestly tradition make it desirable to deal with them after the P texts have been examined. The remaining few nonpriestly references to cultic blood manipulation are the focus of this chapter. In addition, I deal with the priestly texts on the manipulation of the blood of the Passover sacrifice (Exod 12:7, 12–13) in connection with the parallel nonpriestly pericope (Exod 12:21–23). This is the only case of a true doublet of material on blood manipulation, and treating all of the textual materials together permits a more coherent and less repetitive exploration of the significance of the manipulation of the blood of the Passover than would result if the blocks of text were treated in separate chapters.

There are clearly not enough data from which to construct a comprehensive account of how any of the nonpriestly sources or traditions conceived of blood manipulation. Therefore, my primary concern is to make sense of each individual text on its own terms. Whenever possible, however, I address questions about how texts may be interrelated, and how the understanding of blood manipulation obtained from one text might be applied in understanding another. I also explore how the conceptual identification of blood with life might provide a basis for explaining the meaning or effect of blood manipulation activity. The basic purpose of this chapter is to develop, through practical examples, the questions and methodology that I direct to the far more extensive body of P materials treated in subsequent chapters (chapters 3–5). The eclectic group of texts treated here serves that purpose.

"The Blood of My Eaten Sacrifice"

In Exod 23:18a and 34:25a, we find two nearly identical commandments. The first is in the legal collection commonly referred to as the Book of the Covenant,[2] and the second is in a short legal collection incorporated into covenant narrative of the "Yahwist" (J) source.[3] Exodus 23:18a reads: "You shall not sacrifice [*lō'-tizbaḥ*][4] with leaven the blood of my eaten sacrifice [*dam-zibḥî*]," while Exod 34:25a states: "You shall not slaughter [*lō'-tišḥaṭ*] with leaven the blood of my eaten sacrifice."[5] It is far from clear what is prohibited by these two commandments.

Normally the verb *zbḥ* means "slaughter as a sacrifice," but in Exod 23:18a blood is the grammatical object of the verb, not the animal from which the blood is taken. Nowhere else in the Hebrew Bible is blood the object of the verb, a fact noted by commentators.[6] U. Cassuto asserts that *dam-zibḥî* should be construed as "my bloody sacrifice," identifying *dām* as an adjectival modifier of *zebaḥ* (eaten sacrifice).[7] In support of this interpretation he notes that *rōa' ma'allêkem* (evil of your deeds) (Isa 1:16) can be rendered "your evil deeds" and that *qômat 'ărāzāyw* (height of its cedars) (Isa 37:24) can be translated "its tall cedars." However, several observations speak against Cassuto's interpretation. In the two examples he cites, "evil" and "height" are abstract nouns. In contrast, *dām* is a concrete noun, and concrete nouns are not employed in this construction.[8] Furthermore, it is possible to render both formulations literally, so that "evil" and "height" remain the objects of the verbs in each case. NRSV, for example, renders *rōa' ma'allêkem* as "the evil of your doings." In Isa 37:24, "height" actually functions as a superlative, designating which cedars were felled.[9] Thus, "the tallest (of cedars)" can be construed as the object of the verb. In fact, whether we take the first noun as the primary object of the verb, or as an adjectival modifier of the verb it precedes, this noun is of crucial importance for the meaning of the combination. In Isa 1:16, it is not simply "deeds" that are removed but deeds that are characterized by their evilness. Similarly, Isa 37:24 refers not to any and all cedars but to the tallest of them. Thus, even were we to adopt Cassuto's interpretation, we would still need to ask why the text emphasizes the blood. Why is the bloodiness of the eaten sacrifice at issue?

The verb *šḥṭ* clearly means "slaughter" and must in Exod 34:25a refer to sacrificial slaughter. The verb "can hardly have blood as its object."[10] However, most translations, taking blood as the object of the verbs, render both as "offer."[11] On the basis of this interpretation of the verbs, many interpreters understand the commandments to refer to the application of blood to the altar and to prohibit the burning of a leavened cereal offering on this altar.[12] A significant problem with this interpretation, however, is its failure to come to terms with the unusual verbs, especially *šḥṭ* in Exod 34:25a.

A solution to the problem is suggested by the explanation offered by several of the medieval Jewish commentators. For example, Nachmanides (on Exod 23:18a), noting that it is strange to have blood as the object of *zbḥ*, draws on the rabbinic explanation of the verse recorded in *Mekilta de-Rabbi Ishmael* (*Mishpatim* 20), which holds that the unusual construction refers simultaneously to the slaughter of the animal and to the subsequent tossing of its blood on the altar. According to Nachmanides, the language of the verse is elliptical. Similarly, Noth comments on Exod 34:25a that "the slaying of the victim and the offering of the blood are here combined in one sentence."[13] The virtue of this explanation is that it allows us to recognize that treatment of the blood is at issue while disassociating this treatment from the verbs. Thus, with Nachmanides and Noth, I understand the verse to refer elliptically to the manipulation of the blood following the slaughter.

However, there is no explicit indication of what is to be done with the blood. It is also far from clear what leaven is at issue. Is it, as many modern interpreters maintain, leaven in a cereal offering devoted to the altar? The commandment, in both versions, is cryptic, and the interpreter must fill gaps with information derived from other sources in order to make sense of it.

The classic Jewish interpretive tradition understands the commandments to deal with the Passover sacrifice and to mandate that those who participate in the sacrificial rites must have eliminated all leaven from their possession before the sacrifices are slaughtered.[14] According to this interpretation, direct association of blood and leaven is not in view. Rather, the rules express concern about the invalidation of the Passover sacrifice itself. The blood manipulation assumed by this interpretation is the tossing of the blood onto the altar (see 2 Chron 30:16; 35:11). The leaven would not be in a cereal offering for the altar, but the leaven that may not be eaten during the festival. Martin Noth offers a similar explanation, suggesting that Exod 23:18a "means that leavened bread may not be eaten at a sacrificial meal."[15] Thus, for Noth, the law is concerned with the validity of the sacrificial meal, although he denies that the Passover festival is in view.

As I noted, most modern interpreters understand the laws to prohibit the offering of leavened bread on the altar where the blood has been placed. This interpretation requires, first, the assumption that *dam-zibḥî* refers to blood placed on the altar. The conception of sacrificial blood being applied to the altar is necessarily drawn from other sources that refer to the practice. Second, interpreters must draw on other sources, which refer to the burning of cereal offerings in the altar fire. Again, Exod 23:18a and 34:25a do not clearly refer to this practice. Having established this identification of the practice addressed by the laws, these interpreters then consider why the laws prohibit the offering of a leavened cereal offering on the altar. G. Henton Davies offers a concise explanation: "Leavened bread and sacrificial blood are not to be offered together, lest the leavened, fermented bread contaminate the blood."[16] Behind this explanation is the assumption that leaven was seen in some sense as impure and capable of communicating its impurity to the sacrificial blood on the altar. Once again, however, Exod 23:18 and 34:25 are silent about this conception of leaven.

Finally, it should be noted that some interpreters refer to the conceptual connection of blood with life to explain the strictures concerning its treatment. John I. Durham writes, for example: "The prohibition of any combination of leaven with the blood of a sacrifice offered to Yahweh . . . [is] linked to the association of blood . . . with the very essence of the life that is Yahweh's gift to all his creatures."[17] Clearly, the association of blood with life is not expressed explicitly in this text, and the interpreter who refers to it must assume that it lies behind the commandment set forth in Exod 23:18a and 34:25a.

The following conclusions may be drawn from the foregoing discussion of Exod 23:18a and 34:25a. First, both texts evidence concern with the proper treatment of the blood of an animal slaughtered as an eaten sacrifice (*zebaḥ*). However, the verses do not tell us what was to be done with the blood, nor do they tell us anything about how blood itself was conceptualized. Second, the two verses indicate that the presence of leaven is, in some fashion, incompatible with valid sacrificial practice. Again, however, it is unclear whether leaven itself is understood to pose some danger to the purity or potency of the blood of the victim. On a methodological level, I have emphasized the importance of gap-filling for constituting textual meaning. I have indicated that all interpretations of Exod 23:18a and 34:25a, both ancient and modern, reflect specific assumptions about conceptions and principles lying behind the cryptic words of these verses. As I deal with other texts in this chapter, and in subsequent ones, further attention is given to this important methodological point.

Blood and the Covenant

In Exod 24:3–8 we find a narrative of a covenant-making ceremony at Mount Sinai.[18] Prior to the ceremony proper, Moses recounted all the words and decrees of Yahweh to the people, who responded that they would do all that Yahweh demanded (Exod 24:3). Moses then wrote out the words of Yahweh. The next morning, he built an altar at the foot of the mountain along with twelve standing stones for the twelve tribes of Israel (v. 4). He sent "the youths of the children of Israel," who "offered up burnt offerings" (*wayya'ălû 'ōlōt*) and "sacrificed eaten sacrifices which are well-being offerings" (*wayyizbĕḥû zĕbāḥîm šĕlāmîm*) (v. 5).[19] The text then states (v. 6): "Then Moses took half the blood and put (it) in bowls and half the blood he tossed on the altar."

Following this blood manipulation, Moses took the Book of the Covenant, the written record of the commandments he had recited orally the previous day, and read it aloud to the people, who formally announced their willingness to obey "all that Yahweh has spoken" (v. 7). The narrative continues (v. 8): "Then Moses took the blood and tossed [it] upon the people and said, 'Here is the blood of the covenant that Yahweh cut with you concerning all these words.'"

My treatment of this pericope exemplifies and establishes the approach to be taken with other textual representations of cultic blood manipulation activity within a ritual complex. Here, my first questions focus on determining how to envisage what is represented in the text, while also noting some instances of the indexical qualities of ritual activities. The ceremony begins with the building of the altar and the erection of the standing stones. This activity is attributed to Moses. Although we might imagine Moses being assisted in these activities, I note that the text identifies Moses alone as the actor. It is *he* who creates a ritual space marked by the altar and the standing stones. Moses continues to function as the primary actor by sending—that is, delegating— the "youths" of Israel to offer sacrifices. They act under Moses' authority. Thus, Moses' activity indexes him as a ritual specialist who creates a ritual space and directs the activities of others who participate in the execution of a ritual complex. It may be added that the designation "youths" for those whose cultic activity is directed by Moses further marks their subordination and Moses' higher status. This is also true if, as E. W. Nicholson argues, *ně'ārîm* is understood not as "youths" but as a technical term for low-ranking cultic officials, the assistants or "servants" of the priests (see 1 Sam 2:13–17).[20]

According to the text, the young men "offer up" the burnt offerings and "slaughter" the sacrifices of well-being. It is not entirely clear which specific components of the ritual complexes we should envisage them carrying out. However, it is clear that the "young men" do not perform the blood manipulations. Moses deals with the blood. Thus, the text distinguishes between Moses and the young men in terms of their cultic activity.

Moses' manipulation of the blood begins when he takes half of it and puts it in the bowls. The textual representation is quite basic here. Are we to envisage that Moses himself collected the blood when the animals were slaughtered, as Nahmanides suggests (ad loc.), or should we think of the young men collecting all of the blood, which Moses then divided up for the two applications? In either case, what is significant is that all of the verbs that have the blood as their object have Moses as subject. Moses is identified by the text as the one who deals with the blood. This ritual action is indexed, therefore, as the prerogative of the ritual specialist who presides over the complex. It is an elite activity. The immolation of the animals, on the other hand, is subordinate activity carried out by subordinate cultic actors.[21]

After Moses divides the blood, placing half of it into bowls, he tosses the other half onto the altar. The reader must envisage Moses tossing the blood from vessels, probably of the same type he used to hold the blood that was reserved for later use. It is noteworthy, however, that the bowls are only indicated with reference to storing blood and not with reference to tossing it. We might conclude that the author assumed that the reader would understand that Moses tossed the blood from vessels of some kind. The explicit reference to the bowls used to store the reserved blood is required by the need to make it clear that the two manipulations did not take place at the same time. In order to represent the sequence of actions successfully, the author has to tell us that Moses set aside half the blood in containers.

Having performed the first blood manipulation, Moses reads the Book of the Covenant to the people. When they affirm that they will give active obedience to Yahweh's commandments, Moses takes the reserved blood and tosses it "on the people" (*'al-hā'ām*) just as he tossed blood on the altar. Because the verb *zrq* indicates a flinging motion, we may envisage Moses standing before the people, perhaps elevated above them, and tossing blood out of a vessel of some sort—perhaps the "bowls" in which it was stored, if these could be picked up and handled—so that it fell down on the people. This is, to say the least, a striking ritual act.

What is the significance of the two-part blood manipulation complex? How should we understand and make sense of it? Some interpreters have suggested that the blood applied to the people functions as a negative sign, a warning that their blood will be spilled if they break the covenant.[22] Had Moses tossed blood only on the people, this interpretation might be accepted. However, because Moses also tossed blood on the altar, it is unlikely that this act refers to a blood curse.

Ibn Ezra (on Exod 24:7) refers to the sprinkling of blood on Aaron and on his garments to consecrate him when he is ordained to the priesthood (Lev 8:30). Analogously, the blood tossed on the people would sanctify them. In the priestly ordination ceremony, blood is tossed on the altar, and then some is removed from it and sprinkled on Aaron and on his garments. Ibn Ezra apparently sees the initial tossing of blood on the altar here as analogous, preparing the rest of the blood to sanctify the people.[23] This explanation of the blood manipulations makes better sense of what is represented than the previous suggestion, but it is not without problems. The two ritual enactments are by no means identical, either in form or in purpose. Furthermore, they appear in different pentateuchal sources. It is methodologically problematic to draw on the interpretation of a ritual act in one context to explain another in a very different context.

Many commentators suggest that the tossing of blood on the altar (understood to represent Yahweh) and on the people functions to establish a bond between the two parties to the covenant,[24] an explanation I find compelling. G. Henton Davies offers an especially eloquent and sophisticated expression of this interpretation of the blood rites, which merits quoting in full:

> Moses' reading of the law and the promise of the people takes place between the two halves of the blood ritual. The divine offer and the people's acceptance takes place together in a space of time and experience bounded at each end by sacri-

ficial blood and life. Within that span is the union of will and purpose, decided upon and achieved in the covenant. Even more conclusively the divine offer and the people's acceptance are not merely contained within that span, they are covered and embraced by a third factor common to both—the blood covering the altar and the people (though not the twelve pillars). Both partners, divine and human, are joined and united so far as the matter in hand is concerned—the giving and acceptance of the words of the Lord—in the blood of the animals which have been slaughtered. Whereas in the giving and accepting of the law the Lord and people stand over against each other as contracting partners, in the blood ritual they are organically related and become united. This is the sacramental at-one-ment of the covenant relationship.[25]

Davies's identification of the manner in which the blood manipulation complex structures the covenant-making process merits attention. One blood manipulation stands before the reading of the Book of the Covenant, and the other stands after it. In both its literary form and as we envisage the ritual complex being enacted in the world of the text, this bracketing serves to emphasize the central element, the reading of the book and the people's solemn affirmation that they will actively obey Yahweh's words. As Davies notes, the two acts of blood manipulation serve to mark the bounds of a time in which Yahweh's words are offered to the people in a concrete written form and the people express their acceptance of Yahweh as suzerain.

In these blood manipulations we encounter ritualization, which Bell defines as "a way of acting that is designed and orchestrated to distinguish and privilege what is being done in comparison to other, usually more quotidian, activities."[26] As a strategic way of acting that distinguishes special actions from ordinary ones, ritualization "gives rise to (or creates) the sacred as such by virtue of its sheer differentiation from the profane."[27] Of particular relevance here are Bell's observations on the ways in which ritualized activities construct "an environment organized according to schemes of privileged opposition,"[28] an environment in which these schemes act upon the bodies of ritual participants.[29] The result is a "ritualized body."[30]

If we reflect on the ritual complex represented in Exod 24:3–8 in light of Bell's concept of ritualization, we may note that the blood manipulations construct "an environment organized according to schemes of privileged opposition." The altar—the locus at which, in this cultural system, sacrifice is offered to Yahweh—receives the first blood manipulation. Then Moses reads Yahweh's words to the people. The privileging of Yahweh by the application of blood to the altar is subsequently reflected in the fact that Yahweh speaks first, placing demands on the people. The people then respond by affirming that they accept Yahweh's demands. After this, they are the objects of a blood manipulation. Within the framework of the two blood manipulations the people are constructed as Yahweh's vassals. The people's simple affirmation of their willingness to obey Yahweh's words transmitted verbally by Moses (v. 3) is not sufficient to establish a covenant. The words must be written down and there must be a ritual complex for a covenantal relationship to be created.

The identification of the blood manipulations as forging a bond between Yahweh and the people may also be related to the conception of ritual actions as indexical signs. This interpretation rests on an implicit recognition of the indexing function of the blood manipulations. Blood from the animals is divided into two parts and applied in an identical manner to the altar and to the people. Clearly, an existential relationship is established in this way between the altar and the people. As I have noted, many interpreters understand the altar to represent Yahweh. Thus, we may speak of a relationship between Yahweh and the people being indexed by the blood manipulations.

Further elaboration on the nature of this relationship requires reflection on how blood, the ritual material that marks the relationship, might have been conceptualized. Several scholars, not surprisingly, refer to the identification of blood with life. Nahum Sarna, for example, refers to "the prevailing notion in Israel . . . that the blood, the vital bodily fluid, constituted the life-force." He then suggests that, in the covenant ceremony, "the blood functions mysteriously to cement the bond between the involved parties. Through God's sharing, as it were, of the vital fluid with Israel . . . ,the life of the recipient is thought to take on a new dimension and to be elevated to a higher level of intimate relationship with the Deity."[31] Clements cites Lev 17:10–13 on the connection of blood with life and suggests that "the flinging of half the blood over the people established a solemn community of life between them and God. Thus the sharing of life in the covenant between God and Israel was symbolized by the sharing of life in the form of blood."[32] It must be emphasized, however, that the blood manipulations are not interpreted in Exod 24:3–8 in terms of the identification of blood with life. To arrive at such an interpretation, readers must supply information from another context, filling a conceptual gap. They must make assumptions about the conceptual information assumed by the author, and which an ancient reader might have brought to the text. If we limit ourselves to the information supplied by Exod 24:3–8, we can speak only of an indexed relationship between the people and the altar. Indeed, we cannot be certain that the altar represents Yahweh. This conceptualization of the altar is something else that must be supplied by the reader.[33]

The question of the symbolic or instrumental qualities of the activity represented in the text requires some attention. Interpreters have characterized in different ways what was accomplished by the blood rites. Cassuto, for example, says that the ritual "signifies a joining together of the two contracting parties (*communio*), and symbolized the execution of the deed of covenant between them."[34] For Cassuto, there is evidently a distinction between the actual establishment of a bond between Yahweh and Israel and the ritual action that refers to the establishment of that bond. In other words, the blood ritual does not create the bond; it simply indicates that it has been established. Noth, on the other hand, says that "the blood of the communal sacrifice applied to the partners in the covenant joins them together."[35] Hyatt wavers between these two approaches: "The common blood upon the altar, representing Yahweh, and upon the people creates (or signalizes) their union."[36] As Bell notes, the question whether ritual acts communicate a message about a state of being or actually generate such a state is of great importance to students of ritual. She cites as an example the act of kneeling. This act, Bell writes, "does not so much communicate a message about subordination as it generates a body identified with subordination. In other words, the molding of the body within a highly structured environment does not simply express inner states. Rather, it primarily acts to restructure bodies in the very doing of the acts themselves. Hence, required kneeling does not merely *communicate* subordination to the kneeler. For all intents and purposes, kneeling produces a subordinate kneeler in and through the act itself."[37]

Exodus 24:3–8 does not itself offer an interpretation of the ritual actions. Moses' words, "Here is the blood of the covenant which Yahweh cut with you concerning all these words," simply identify the blood. They do not identify the significance of what is done with it. Therefore, the interpretation of the ritual acts—symbolically or instrumentally—is something the reader brings to the text. To the extent that modern readers are attempting to identify the interpretations of the author or original readers, they will make assumptions about their conceptualization of ritual activity. Here, therefore, I raise again the question whether ancient Israelites conceived of ritual activity as expressive-symbolic or instrumental, or whether their understanding of ritual blurred such distinctions. The question cannot yet be answered because any conclusions require reflection on other texts. Based on the evidence presented thus far, we simply do not know how ancient Israelites understood ritual activity.

Passover Blood Manipulation

The account of the first Passover in Exodus 12 seems to be made up of material from at least three traditions.[38] There are two accounts of the manipulation of the blood of the Passover lamb, each with an accompanying explanation of the effect of the rite. Critical scholarship commonly attributes the second account (Exod 12:21–23) to J.[39] The first (Exod 12:6–7) is usually assigned to P. According to Israel Knohl, however, the whole of Exod 12:1–20 is an H composition.[40] Knohl notes the presence of a number of "linguistic and ideational indicators" of the pericope's H provenance.[41] Although the evidence cited by Knohl is persuasive, there are also indications of a P stratum in this pericope, suggesting that Exod 12:1–20 was composed by H tradents who drew on earlier P materials.

Since J's version of the blood manipulation is more detailed, I begin my analysis with it, and then turn back to the P/H account. The J passage reads as follows: "Moses called to all the elders of Israel and said to them, 'Proceed and take sheep for your clans, and slaughter the Passover. Then you shall take a bundle of hyssop, shall dip [it] in the blood which is in the basin (*bassap*), and shall touch some of the blood which is in the basin to the lintel and to the two doorposts. None of you shall go out of the entrance of his house until morning'" (Exod 12:21–22).

In Moses' instructions, after the sheep have been slaughtered, a bundle of hyssop is to be used as a brush to apply the blood to the lintel and the doorposts of each house. According to most standard translations the bundle of hyssop is to be dipped into the blood, which is "in the basin" (*bassap*). However, the word *sap* has two meanings, "basin" (goblet) or "threshold,"[42] and Bernard M. Levinson maintains that here "threshold" is the correct rendering. According to his interpretation, the sheep is slaughtered on the threshold, where its blood flows out. Then the bundle of hyssop is dipped in the blood on the threshold and applied to the lintel and doorposts.[43] According to Levinson, the rendering threshold "is the only logical one: the stipulation intends that the entire doorway—top, sides, and bottom—be framed with blood."[44] It is not at all clear to me how Levinson knows what the "stipulation intends." It appears that his understanding of the *purpose* of the blood manipulation ultimately decides how the action is to be envisaged.

A proper evaluation of Levinson's interpretation requires careful attention to the text's representation of the blood manipulation practice as well as to what it says about its purpose. Although the text does not specify the locus of slaughter, it seems reasonable to envisage the slaughter taking place at the entrance to the house. As the text now stands, there is no prior reference to the *sap* where the blood is located. Its introduction is somewhat jarring, whether we identify it as a basin or as the threshold. In the first case, we would observe that there was no prior indication that the blood was to be collected. In the second case, we would note that no information was provided about the precise locus of slaughter. The text is clear, however, in its specification that blood is to be applied from the *sap* to the lintel and doorposts (v. 22).

The following verse (v. 23) indicates the purpose of the blood manipulation: "Then Yahweh will pass through to strike Egypt with a plague. He will see the blood upon the lintel and upon the two doorposts, and Yahweh will pass over the entrance, and will not permit the destroyer to enter into your houses to strike with a plague." Here we are told that Yahweh sees the blood that was deliberately applied to the lintel and doorposts. There is no reference, however, to Yahweh seeing the blood that is *bassap* ("in the basin" or "on the threshold"). The text's silence about the *sap* speaks eloquently against Levinson's claim that we should picture the door as framed with blood. Such a framing is accorded no significance by the text.

As he passes through, verse 23 tells us, Yahweh sees the blood, restrains "the destroyer" (*hammašḥît*), and does not allow the inhabitants of the house to be struck down. The blood is identified as an apotropaic agent. It achieves an instrumental effect, warding off destruction, because Yahweh sees it. Yahweh determines whether the "destroyer" will enter the house, and Yahweh makes this determination on the basis of the presence or absence of the blood markings.

These textual facts must serve as a starting point for any attempt to elucidate how the Passover blood manipulation was conceptualized. It is necessary, too, to clarify whether one is elaborating on the textual interpretation of the represented ritual, or attempting to explain the meaning of the rite in actual practice. Often, it is difficult to tell which course an interpreter is following, and it appears that there is some confusion about the necessary distinction. Levinson, for example, explains that the marking of the door with blood "protects the household from the demonic agent of destruction, barring his entrance," and cites Exod 12:23.[45] He adds that the framing of the door with blood "establishes a liminal barrier between 'within the house'—as a refuge—and . . . 'outside the door of his house' (Exod 12:22)—as the realm of otherwise uncontrolled demonic energies. The ritual works by the magic of sympathetic substitution: the token of the lamb's blood on the doorway averts the spilling of further blood—that of the house's occupants."[46]

From Levinson's references to Exod 12:22–23, one gets the impression that he regards these verses as providing the basis for his explanation of the effect of the blood manipulation. However, it is difficult to find in them much support for Levinson's explanation. First, verse 23 indicates quite clearly that Yahweh sees the blood and responds by not allowing "the destroyer" to enter the house. The blood has an effect not on the destroyer but on Yahweh, who controls the destroyer. Thus, it is incorrect to speak of "otherwise uncontrolled demonic energies." Furthermore, there is little evidence for "the magic of sympathetic substitution." The text never indicates that the blood substitutes for the blood of those in the house.

These criticisms do not, however, require a complete rejection of Levinson's identification of the significance of the blood manipulation. It is certainly possible that the Passover blood manipulation ritual was conceptualized, in some context, just as Levinson interprets it. However, this is not the interpretation of the rite suggested by Exod 12:23. The official interpretation articulated by the text is not the same as the private interpretation developed by Levinson.

Baruch Levine also offers an interpretation of the Passover blood manipulation that essentially ignores the explicit explanation provided by the text.[47] According to Levine, the application of the blood to the lintel and doorposts had a "magical objective of 'washing off' impurity."[48] However, the text says nothing about the blood washing away impurity. Indeed, the text actually says nothing about how the blood does what it does, except to indicate that Yahweh sees it. Again, the problem is a failure to distinguish between speculation about a possible earlier purpose or meaning of the rite, or some purpose or meaning lying behind what is stated explicitly, and the explicit statements of the text. Levine writes, for example, "In the account, as we have it, the identities of Yahweh and the *mašḥît,* a destructive force, are somewhat muddled, but it is clear, nevertheless, that the *mašḥît* was conceived as a distinct force which, once unleashed, was not controllable, even by Yahweh, himself."[49] In my opinion, it is anything but clear that the *mašḥît* is represented by J as beyond Yahweh's control! In Exod 12:23, Moses says that when *Yahweh* sees the blood *he* will *restrain* the "destroyer." The destroyer is clearly not beyond Yahweh's control. Furthermore, the distinction between Yahweh and the destroyer is quite clear in the J materials.

Although it is possible to get a basic sense of the official interpretation of the blood manipulation advanced in Exod 12:23, certain obvious gaps may be noted. First, as I noted, there is no explanation of why the blood, and not something else, serves as a marker. Second, it is not clear what the significance is of the specific manipulation, that is, why the blood is placed where it is placed.

Not surprisingly, attempts have been made to explain the ritual with reference to the conceptual connection of blood with life. There are two variations to this explanation. One takes the blood as a positive force, which repulses death and destruction. The second approach identifies the blood as symbolic of death, representing life terminated. This latter explanation is frequently connected to an interpretation of Israelite sacrifice heavily dependent on the Western Christian doctrine of "substitutionary atonement." The lamb dies in the place of the firstborn of Israel and its substitutionary death is indicated by the blood on the doorposts and lintel. Interpreted in this fashion, the blood manipulation may be identified as effecting atonement, that is, as ransoming the lives of the Israelites.[50] An interesting variation on this interpretation is offered by Ibn Ezra, who claims that the blood on the lintel and doorposts is a *kōper* (ransom), a sign for the "destroyer" to spare those in the house.[51] Although Ibn Ezra does not refer explicitly to Lev 17:11, it is evident that his understanding of the use of animal blood as a *kōper* (ransom) depends on his interpretation of that text.[52] In his commentary on Lev 17:11, Ibn Ezra explains that blood serves as a ransom, "life in place of life" (*npš tḥt npš*). In his commentary on Exod 12:7, he seems to understand the blood of the Passover sacrifice to substitute, as "life," for the lives of the firstborn of Israel.

There is a serious problem, however, with applying the general conceptualization of blood as life, and H's specific explanation of the working of sacrificial blood manipulation, to this text. There is simply no way of knowing if the J tradent(s) viewed blood as life and explained blood manipulation on the basis of this conceptualization. The text offers no explanation except that Yahweh sees the blood and restrains the "destroyer." Thus, while the explanations discussed here do not actually contradict the evidence, they remain speculative. The interpretation of the Passover blood manipulation in this context with reference to the identification of blood as life requires conceptual gapfilling.

To conclude this discussion, I note how the blood manipulation activity represented in Exod 12:22 functions as a status index. As in Exod 24:3–8, the assignment of the central ritual action—which, again, is blood manipulation—to a specific leadership group functions to reinforce their status. The status of the elders is ritually inscribed through the special role they play. They are marked as those who act to make possible the Israelites' survival. Like Moses, they mediate between Yahweh and his people by marking what Levinson correctly identifies as "a liminal barrier." At the same time, the assignment of the blood manipulation activity to a status-marked group[53] functions to highlight its importance. It is indexed as elite activity.

Saul M. Olyan suggests that the elders' application of blood to the lintels and doorposts "recalls priestly blood manipulation at the altar and so underscores elder privilege in yet another way, by allowing the head of household to play a priest-like role in the context of his household's celebration of the Passover."[54] In my opinion, this suggestion about the indexing function of the elders' blood manipulation activity is valid if Exod 12:21–22 is read in the light of those texts that represent blood manipulation activity as a priestly prerogative.[55] In the absence of any other J representations of blood manipulation, however, some caution should be exercised in assuming that the J tradent(s) identified blood manipulation as a priestly prerogative and thus understood the elders to be acting in a specifically *priestly* capacity.

I now turn to the P/H instructions for the slaughter of the Passover lamb and the performance of the blood manipulation complex, which appear in Exod 12:6–7. The people are addressed in the second-person, masculine plural at the beginning of verse 6, which is a characteristic of H.[56] However, the instructions for slaughter and blood manipulation employ third-person plural verbs. In verse 7 there are no H characteristics. The cultic terminology is typical of P: "They shall take some of the blood and shall daub (it) onto the two doorposts and onto the lintel upon the houses in which they shall eat it." These instructions invite several gap-filling moves on the part of readers. The primary source of information that may be supplied is the J version of the blood manipulation prescriptions (v. 22). We may also draw on other representations of blood manipulation in P. It seems reasonable to envisage the collection of the blood in some kind of vessel.[57] We are told that the blood is to be daubed onto the doorposts and lintel, but we are not told how this daubing is to be accomplished. From verse 22 a reader may supply the use of a bundle of hyssop, which is dipped into the blood. Whereas verse 22 indicates that the blood is to be applied first to the lintel, verse 7 prescribes that the blood be applied to the doorposts first.[58] Unlike in verse 22, there is not even a hint in verses 6–7 that blood was applied to the threshold.

Who performs the blood manipulations? According to verse 3, Moses is to address his instructions to "the whole congregation of Israel." In verse 6, we are told that "the whole assembly of the congregation of Israel" is to slaughter the lamb. Since no other subject is specified for the blood manipulation verbs, it seems that "the whole assembly of the congregation of Israel" should be identified as the subjects of those verbs. Thus, the whole national-cultic assembly is to perform the blood manipulations. Uncharacteristically for P and H, blood manipulation is not identified as a priestly prerogative. The reason for this is clear enough: for P and H there can be no priestly ritual activity until the tent-shrine has been constructed and consecrated, and Aaron and his sons have been ordained to the priesthood. In the absence of the priesthood, this quasi-cultic ritual performance is carried out by the whole people. In the light of other P and H representations of sacrifice and blood manipulation, we might say that the blood manipulation activity of the assembled congregation indexes their special priestly status on this occasion. However, the P and H tradents would doubtless have emphasized the differences between the present context and the context of priestly cultic activity. There is no tent-shrine, no altar, and no consecrated sphere of holiness. It seems that the assigning of priestly functions to the whole congregation is possible in this context precisely because there is no tent-shrine, and no need to index priestly access to, and lay and Levite exclusion from, its sancta. It is also worth noting that there is no clear indication in the pericope that the blood manipulation is to be repeated. Indeed, the text's emphasis on the special function of the blood manipulation strongly suggests that the rite was not to be performed again.

Following the prescriptions for the eating of the flesh of the animal, we find the account of the effect of the blood manipulation in verses 12–13: "I will pass through in the land of Egypt during this night, and I will strike down every firstborn in the land of Egypt, of human beings as well as of livestock, and upon all the deities of Egypt I will execute judgment. I am Yahweh. The blood shall be a sign for you upon the houses where you are. When I see the blood I will skip over you and no plague will be a destroyer among you when I strike down in the land of Egypt."

Like verse 23, verse 12 indicates that Yahweh himself will pass through the land of Egypt and strike down the firstborn. Verse 13 characterizes the blood as a "sign" (*'ōt*). The significance of "for you" (*lākem*) has been discussed by interpreters since antiquity. Does it indicate that the blood functions as a symbol to convey a message to the Israelites? Or does it indicate that the sign is for the benefit of the Israelites? The specification that the blood is a sign "on the houses where you are," and the subsequent declaration by Yahweh that he will see the blood and skip over the people, led to the conclusion that the blood is a sign that functions on behalf of the people. That is, the blood signals the presence of the Israelites in the houses and benefits them by keeping Yahweh from striking their firstborn. As in verse 23, it is Yahweh's response to the blood that saves the Israelite firstborn. However, while verse 23 refers to a destructive force that is controlled by Yahweh, verse 13 indicates that Yahweh controls a plague that would function as a destroyer. The text does not identify the blood as warding off an otherwise uncontrollable destructive force unleashed by Yahweh. Rather, Yahweh is the one who acts and remains in immediate control throughout.

I turn now from the explicit "official" or "public" interpretations to some further reflection on how the blood manipulation actions function as ritualized actions in the world of the text. First, the blood manipulation actions establish a boundary and construct a sphere for subsequent ritualized activity, the specialized eating of the lambs, which is characterized by precise and unusual instructions (Exod 12:8–11). Furthermore, the blood manipulation indexes access to the subsequent rites. Those who are part of the community that manipulates blood are able to participate in the meal inside the marked houses. Finally the precise and ordered placement of the blood indexes order, defining the marked homes as ordered space, which is marked off from chaotic space. Inside the blood-marked houses, life is preserved, while outside the houses, life is lost. In my treatment of P texts in subsequent chapters, I identify further examples of these functions and effects of blood manipulation activity and elaborate on the theoretical significance of these observations.

Applying Blood to the Altar in Deuteronomy

Only one reference to cultic blood manipulation appears in the book of Deuteronomy, in the context of the laws for the centralization of the cult. As I noted in the preceding chapter, Deut 12:20–25 permits noncultic slaughter but forbids the consumption of blood (equated with life) with the flesh. Following these provisions, the text repeats the commandment for cult centralization, indicating that all offerings must be taken to the place Yahweh chooses (v. 26). Then, the text indicates, in general terms, how the offerings are to be made (v. 27): "And you shall make your burnt offerings—the flesh and the blood—upon the altar of Yahweh your god, and the blood of your eaten sacrifices shall be poured out upon the altar of Yahweh your god, while the flesh you may eat."

The structure of this law is chiastic, with flesh and blood in the first half standing against blood and flesh in the second half. The point is clearly to spell out the distinction between a burnt offering and an eaten sacrifice in terms of their altar rituals. The burnt offering is made on the altar, both the blood and the flesh. In contrast, in the eaten sacrifice the blood is "poured out on the altar" while the flesh is eaten by the sacrificer. Thus, the two sacrifices are linked by the treatment of the blood and distinguished by the treatment of the flesh. There is no reference to the treatment of the fat of the eaten sacrifice; rather, the pouring of the blood on the altar seems to be of primary concern. The reason for this seems to be contextual. The previous declarations about noncultic slaughter have been concerned with two issues: the ability of Israelites to eat meat whenever they desire, and the necessity of abstaining from the blood. In this short instruction about sacrifice, the focus remains on flesh and blood. The text makes clear that both the flesh and the blood of the burnt offering go to the altar. In contrast, only the blood of the eaten sacrifice goes to the altar, while the flesh may be eaten.

What kind of manipulation or disposition is indicated in Deut 12:27? Rendtorff has argued that *'al-mizbaḥ yhwh* in this verse should be rendered "*by* the altar of Yahweh" and maintains that there was no distinct blood manipulation for the *zebaḥ* (eaten sacrifice). The blood was simply disposed of by being poured out in the sacred sphere, just as blood in noncultic slaughter was disposed of by being poured out "upon the earth like water." This requires, first, the assumption that the burning of the fat was the primary altar rite of the *zebaḥ*, even though such a rite is not even mentioned here. It also requires ignoring the clear parallelism between the two parts of the verse. In the first half of the verse, *'al* clearly means "upon." I would argue, then, that it must mean "upon" in the second half of the verse. What is at issue, after all, is not a distinction between the treatment of the blood in the two sacrifices but between the treatment of the flesh. In the first half of the verse, the general verb "make" (*'śh*) is used to indicate the treatment of both the blood and flesh. In the second half, however, different verbs must be used to indicate that the blood is placed on the altar while the flesh is eaten.

It is noteworthy, nevertheless, that "pour out" is used here rather than "toss" (*zrq*), which is found in all other texts that deal with the treatment of the blood of eaten sacrifices.[59] While the tradent who composed this text may have envisaged a different mode of blood manipulation than we find represented in other texts, it is also possible that the choice of the verb *špk* was determined by literary considerations, that is, the intention to highlight the contrast between the treatment of the blood of animals slaughtered noncultically and those slaughtered as sacrifices. The blood is to be poured out on the ground "like water" in the former case, but on the altar in the latter.[60] Thus, we must exercise caution in drawing conclusions about living practice from literary representations. Deuteronomy 12:27 may, in fact, tell us nothing about how an ancient Israelite believed blood was to be applied to the altar.

From Deut 12:27 we learn what is done with the blood of a sacrificial animal but not *why* it is done; there is no conceptual explanation of the prescribed practice. Many of the interpreters who attempt to fill in the missing explanation begin with the identification of blood as "life." We know from Deut 12:23 that blood is the *nepeš* (life). Thus, the blood that is applied to the altar is the animal's "life." What, then, is the significance of applying animal life to Yahweh's altar? If one begins with the idea that life has its source in and belongs to Yahweh, and if one identifies the altar as the locus of Yahweh's presence, one may draw the conclusion that the application of blood to the altar accomplishes the return of the animal's life to Yahweh.[61]

Other interpreters go further. Taking a holistic approach to the Hebrew Bible, they look to Lev 17:11, the one text that seems to explain why blood is applied to the altar. Thus, for example, J. Ridderbos writes: "Man may eat the meat, but the soul or life belongs to God, and in the blood He gives this life to man on the altar 'to make atonement . . . on the altar; it is the blood that makes atonement for one's life' (Lev. 17:11)."[62] Clearly, an explanation of this kind is unpersuasive to an interpreter who does not assume that the interpretation of blood manipulation advanced in an H text can be employed to explain blood manipulation activity as represented in other sources.

Deuteronomy 12:27 tells us in general terms what is to be done with the blood of sacrificial animals. It is to be applied to the altar. This is the case both with the blood of burnt offerings and with the blood of eaten sacrifices. In the case of eaten sacrifices, the verb *špk* is employed to emphasize the contrast between what is done with the blood of an animal slaughtered for food away from the shrine and of one slaughtered as a sacrifice at the shrine. In both cases, the blood is poured out (*špk*). However, in noncultic slaughter, the blood is poured "on the ground," whereas in cultic slaughter it is poured on the altar. The gesture is the same, but the loci where it is performed are different. The latter gesture indexes the altar and, by extension, Yahweh, indicating that the sacrificial rite is one in which he has a direct involvement. In contrast, the pouring of blood onto the ground indexes away from Yahweh and by an act of ritualization—action that is distinguished from other action—establishes noncultic slaughter as substantively different from cultic slaughter. Finally, it is noteworthy that the identification of blood with life, which is adduced to explain the ban on consuming blood, is not invoked by the author of Deut 12:27 to explain the application of blood to the altar. Modern scholars who wish to reconstruct the author's interpretation of cultic blood manipulation must gap-fill not only the blood-life identification in the cultic context but also an explanation of why blood, as life, is applied to the altar.

Blood Manipulation on Ahaz's Altar

In the Deuteronomistic History outside of the book of Deuteronomy, only 2 Kgs 16:10–18 deals explicitly with cultic blood manipulation.[63] This text is concerned with Ahaz's activities in relation to the temple in Jerusalem—in particular, his construction of an altar based on one he saw in Damascus. It has been closely analyzed by many commentators but with little agreement about its origins or composition history.[64] Many scholars, however, affirm that 2 Kgs 16:10–18 is drawn from priestly source materials.[65] Verses 12–13 describes Ahaz's sacrificial activity following the construction of the new altar: "When the king arrived from Damascus, the king saw the altar, and the king drew near to the altar, and he went up upon it. He turned his burnt offering and his cereal offering into smoke, he poured out his drink offering, and he tossed the blood of his well-being offering upon the altar."

Verse 13 describes the inaugural ritual complex for the new altar[66] and seems to indicate that Ahaz himself carries out the sacrificial rites,[67] acting as a priest.[68] At the very least, we may say that he presides over the inaugural rites. He goes up onto the altar, an act that indexes his authority over rites. If he is also envisaged as performing the altar rites of burning offerings and tossing blood, his special cultic status in this context is further indexed. This is especially the case if we read the text in the light of P's representations of the cult, in which altar rites are an exclusive preserve of the Aaronid priesthood (see chapters 3–5).

Two types of sacrificial offerings are mentioned, the burnt offering, which is accompanied by a cereal offering and a libation, and the well-being offering. This verse refers to the incineration of the burnt offering, without indicating what was done with the blood. It then indicates that the blood of the well-being offering was applied to the altar, without referring to the burning of a portion in the altar fire. Does the text's failure to mention the manipulation of the blood of the burnt offering indicate that it was not applied to the altar? This seems unlikely. Rather, the act seems to be assumed. On the other hand, the act of burning a portion of the well-being offering may also be assumed. Still, we may wonder why the author leaves the particular gaps we encounter. Why is the manipulation of the blood of the burnt offering not mentioned, while the manipulation of the blood of the well-being offering is described?

Whereas verse 13 seems to represent the inaugural service for the altar, verse 15 records the king's instructions to the chief priest concerning the regular use to be made of the new altar, as well as of the old bronze altar, which Ahaz had moved to a location north of the new altar (v. 14): "Then King Ahaz commanded Uriah the priest, 'On the large altar, turn the morning burnt offering into smoke, as well as the evening cereal offering, the king's burnt offering, his cereal offering, the burnt offering of all the people of the land, their cereal offering, and their drink offerings; and all the blood of burnt offerings, and all the blood of eaten sacrifices, you shall toss upon it. But the bronze altar shall be mine for inquiring.'"

In this verse, as in verse 13, the turning into smoke of burnt offerings is referred to first. Then, blood manipulation is mentioned. In this instance, the verse refers to the tossing onto the altar of the blood of both burnt offerings and eaten sacrifices. Clearly, there are subtle differences in terminology and emphasis between the two verses. According to Rendtorff, the most significant distinction between verses 13 and 15 lies in the fact that the former verse refers only to "the blood of the well-being offering" whereas the latter verse mentions "the blood of burnt offerings" along with "the blood of eaten sacrifices."[69] Rendtorff argues that the well-being offering (*šĕlāmîm*) was originally distinct from the eaten sacrifice (*zebaḥ*) and was distinguished from all other sacrifices by its blood rite. The eaten sacrifice, he claims, referring to Deut 12:27, had no specific blood rite. The burnt offering adopted the blood rite from the well-being offering, and then the eaten sacrifice did as well, once the well-being offering had come to be identified with the eaten sacrifice. He concludes that verse 13 bears witness to the original distinction, whereas verse 15 reflects the later development. In other words, according to Rendtorff, the blood manipulation of the burnt offering is not mentioned in verse 13 because the manipulation did not exist when the verse was composed. Verse 15, on the other hand, is related to the P tradition reflected in Leviticus 1 and 3. Rendtorff bases an elaborate historical reconstruction on very weak evidence. He simply assumes that the lack of reference to the tossing of the blood of the burnt offering in verse 13 is significant, without considering that the performance of the act may be assumed by the tradent. Moreover, his interpretation of Deut 12:27 is questionable, as I demonstrated earlier. Certainly, as the text stands in its present form, a sharp distinction is not drawn between the blood rites of the various sacrifices, although it is possible that some added emphasis is given to the blood rite in the case of the well-being offering. The well-being offering and the eaten sacrifice seem to be closely associated in a variety of sources. In verse 13, *šělāmîm* can be understood to refer to an official or public eaten sacrifice, whereas *zebaḥ* in verse 15 refers to all eaten sacrifices. Taken together, the two verses indicate that the blood of well-being offerings, eaten sacrifices, and burnt offerings was tossed on the altar.

It should be noted that none of the represented ritual actions is explained in either verse. Some interpreters have suggested that the application of the blood of the well-being offering to the altar should be understood as an act that consecrated the altar.[70] This interpretation must, however, be questioned. First, I would note that the Deuteronomistic tradition knows nothing of consecration through the application of blood to sancta. Second, if the verses in question are traced to a Priestly source, it must be stressed that the Priestly tradition does not link the tossing of blood with consecration. Rather, sprinkling, in one instance only, is interpreted as an act that sanctifies (Lev 16:19).[71] As I noted in the discussion of terminology, this attempt to interpret blood tossing as consecratory is based on a failure to distinguish the verb *zrq* (toss), which appears in 2 Kgs 16:13, from the *hiphil* of *hzh* (sprinkle). This can be seen in the English translations of the verses offered in the commentaries that make the claim.[72]

An Ambiguous Reference to Blood Manipulation

According to 1 Sam 14:24, in the midst of a campaign against the Philistines, Saul commanded his troops to abstain from food until evening and the enemy had been defeated.[73] First Samuel 14:31–35 describes what happened at the end of the day, when the Israelites had defeated the Philistines and were overcome with hunger:

> On that day, they struck down the Philistines from Mikhmash to Aijalon, and the people became very faint. Then the people fell greedily upon the spoil and took flock animals, herd animals, and calves. They slaughtered groundward [or, "on the ground"; 'āreṣâ] and the people ate with [or "upon"] the blood [*wayyō-'kal hā'ām 'al-haddām*]. It was reported to Saul, "Look, the people are sinning against Yahweh by eating with the blood." Then he said, "You have behaved treacherously; roll to me here[74] a large stone!" Then Saul said, "Disperse among the people and say to them, 'Bring before me, each man, his ox, and each man, his sheep, and you shall slaughter them in this way and you shall eat and shall not sin against Yahweh by eating with the blood.'" So all the people brought, each man, his ox by his own hand that night and they slaughtered there. Then Saul built an altar for Yahweh; it was the first of the altars he built for Yahweh.

Our first concern, in trying to make sense of this pericope, must be with the meaning of the idiom *'al-haddām,* which appears only two other times in the Hebrew Bible (Lev 19:26; Ezek 33:25). Many interpreters, rendering *'al-haddām* as "with the blood," understand the text to indicate that the slaughter of the animals "groundward" or "on the ground" resulted in inadequate drainage of the blood from the flesh, leading to the consumption of flesh "along with the blood." Thus, according to this interpretation, the people violated a commandment against the consumption of blood. The large stone was employed so that the blood could be properly separated from the flesh and removed from human consumption.[75]

Some interpreters go a step further and identify the stone as an altar to which the blood was applied so that it could be devoted to Yahweh.[76] This interpretation of the text rests on the assumption that the consumption of blood is prohibited because blood, as life, belongs to Yahweh, and must be returned to him at the altar. Most interpreters who identify the stone as an altar understand 1 Sam 14:32–35 to reflect the ideology of a period when all slaughter of domestic animals had to be sacrificial.[77]

There is, however, a basic problem with the identification of the people's offense as the eating of blood. As Hans W. Hertzberg notes, *'al-haddām* is an unusual way of referring to the consumption of blood.[78] In other texts, *dām* is the direct object of the verb "eat" (Deut 12:16, 23; 15:23), or we find references to the consumption of flesh "with its life" (Gen 9:4), or to the consumption of the life with the flesh (Deut 12:23). To Hertzberg's observations, I would add that the examples commonly cited by scholars of *'ākal 'al,* with the meaning "eat with," all involve the specific identification of the primary food item, which is accompanied by something. Thus, in Exod 12:8, we read, "They shall eat the flesh this night fire-roasted; with unleavened bread accompanied by [*'al*] bitter herbs they shall eat it" (see also Num 9:11b). In 1 Sam 14:32, 33, 34 we do not have *bāśar 'al-haddām* (meat accompanied by the blood) but simply *'al-haddām,* although a number of translators insert the words "meat" or "them" (the animals).[79] Thus, the rendering "with the blood" is not beyond dispute. Furthermore, as Karl Budde notes, it is difficult to understand how slaughter on the stone would automatically prevent consumption of the blood.[80] The fact that Saul commands the use of a stone as the alternative to slaughtering "groundward" and eating *'al-haddām* suggests that something other than the consumption of blood is in view. This is recognized by those interpreters who identify the stone as an altar, and who refer to the devotion of the blood to Yahweh.

Recognizing these problems with the common explanation, Hertzberg proposes that we render *'al-haddām* as "upon the blood," understanding the preposition in a locative sense. According to Hertzberg's explanation, "they prepared the meal 'on' the blood. The blood did not go, as we are to see later, to the place that belonged to Yahweh, and thus the spatial and, as a result, the actual separation between God's due and man's due was lacking."[81] Thus, the people's offense was not the consumption of blood but their failure to devote the blood to Yahweh by placing it on an altar.[82] According to Hertzberg, the large stone Saul ordered rolled before him was used as an altar.[83]

Thus, so far we have three explanations of the people's offense. According to the first explanation, the people sinned against Yahweh by eating meat with the blood. The second explanation holds that the sin involved both the eating of meat with blood and the attendant failure to place it on the altar in a sacrificial rite. The third interpretation identifies the sin as involving the eating of a meal on the ground where the blood had been poured out, again with the attendant failure to place the blood on the altar stone and thereby devote it to Yahweh.

A fourth explanation looks to Lev 19:26, in which the prohibition against eating *'al-haddām* is followed by prohibitions of divinatory activities. According to several medieval Jewish interpreters, this linkage indicates that the former act is also a type of magic or sorcery.[84] Understood as directed against a type of sorcery or divination, the prohibitive commandment in Lev 19:26 can be applied to 1 Sam 14:32–35, and the people's offense identified as an attempt to engage in divination. Thus, Jehoshua M. Grintz argues that the people slaughtered animals on the ground, and ate where the blood had been absorbed into the earth, in the hope of receiving communications from underworld spirits or demons.[85] Grintz attempts to shore up an argument based on the explanations of medieval Jewish commentators by referring to alleged evidence for the Greek practice of making offerings to chthonic deities. He emphasizes the fact that such offerings were made at night and notes the reference to night in 1 Sam 14:34. Ziony Zevit accepts the common translation "with the blood" but argues that a specific cultic offense is in view. The blood is eaten for divinatory purposes.[86] His evidence for this is that Lev 19:26 couples a prohibition of "augury and witchcraft" with the prohibition of eating *'al-haddām*.

While Zevit's suggestion makes a certain amount of sense for Lev 19:26, his attempt to apply this interpretation to 1 Sam 14:31–35 and to argue that the soldiers ate the blood in order to facilitate divination concerning the future of their war with the Philistines is unpersuasive.[87] The same criticisms apply to Grintz's interpretation. In addition, one may question Grintz's claim that legitimate Yahwistic sacrifices could not be offered at night. His argument is based on an uncritical citation of rabbinic halakha that bans sacrifice after sunset. Moreover, Grintz ignores the fact that the people had fasted until nightfall because Saul had commanded it. The fact that they slaughtered animals at night follows naturally from this. There is no indication that the people were attempting to engage in divination about the course of the war. Rather, verse 31 indicates that the people were faint from hunger, and the use of the expression "they fell greedily upon the spoil" suggests that ravenous hunger is the motivation for the way they slaughtered the animals. Saul's subsequent attempt to inquire of Yahweh about the war stands apart from the incident with the animals and can only be linked with it on the assumption, otherwise unsupported, that the people were attempting to engage in divination when they slaughtered animals. Furthermore, the overall context of the text establishes as a key theme the problems resulting from Saul's rash decree commanding fasting. First, the people sin against Yahweh because of the extreme hunger caused by fighting while fasting. Then, Jonathan is discovered to have violated the command (see 1 Sam 14:25–30, 36–46). I conclude, therefore, that eating "upon the blood" is not a divinatory practice, at least in 1 Sam 14:31–32, and that one of the other three explanations must be adopted. However, it is far from clear which of these is to be preferred.

This text highlights the vital role of the reader in producing textual meaning. Although it is clear that eating "upon the blood" is an offense against Yahweh, and that the use of a stone in connection with slaughter prevents the offense, readers have been unable to agree about the precise meaning of "upon the blood" and the significance of the stone. I would add that the text requires gap-filling to produce a picture of what activity is carried out in relation to the stone, although most readers apparently agree in understanding the stone as the locus of slaughter. The blood is drained out upon it. Although I find Hertzberg's explanation most persuasive, namely that the stone is used as an altar so that the blood can be devoted to Yahweh, I must affirm that the textual evidence is quite ambiguous. First Samuel 14:31–35 is a text that requires explanation rather than one that provides unambiguous information about Israelite conceptions of blood manipulation.

Conclusions

The texts treated in this chapter provide mostly representations of blood manipulation activity. There is very little in the way of conceptual interpretation. The texts do not usually tell us why blood is manipulated. Even when they do, the explanations are not what many modern readers seem to want. All attempts to identify the meaning or purpose of the blood manipulations require the interpreter to bring concepts from outside the immediate context. Some interpreters attempt to fill conceptual gaps by drawing on texts from the same source or tradition. Others follow a holistic approach to the Bible and draw on any available textual data. Thus, many interpreters look to Lev 17:11 as a key text for understanding almost all types of blood manipulation activity.

As an alternative to the quest for a conceptual interpretation of blood manipulation, a quest limited both by the lack of textual data and by the fact that ritual acts are characteristically subject to a bewildering variety of interpretations, I have drawn on approaches to ritual activity that emphasize practice. In this chapter, I have offered an initial application of Bell's concept of ritualization and Jay's approach to the identification of ritual acts as indexes. In some specific cases, the application of these perspectives has proved fruitful. For example, Jay's approach works well when applied to Exod 24:3–8 and happens to reinforce the interpretation of a majority of scholars who recognize the indexical effect of the double application of blood to the altar and to the people. This unique manipulation indexes a bond between the altar and the people. If the altar is understood to represent Yahweh, then we may speak of an indexed bond between Yahweh and the people.

I have also noted how blood manipulation functions to index status. In Exod 24:3–8, Moses manipulates blood, whereas the young men of Israel perform other sacrificial functions. The reservation of blood manipulation to Moses marks it as a status activity. As I demonstrate in the next three chapters, this identification of blood manipulation as a status marker is fully in line with Priestly representations of blood manipulation, in which only Aaronids may deal with blood and apply it to sancta. It should be noted, however, that there are no representations of priests manipulating blood in the nonpriestly pentateuchal texts, and but one somewhat ambiguous representation in the Deuteronomistic History (2 Kgs 16:15, where Ahaz instructs the high priest to burn altar offerings and manipulate blood). In Exod 12:21–22 (J), the elders of Israel, the heads of households, seem to be assigned the task of manipulating the blood of the Passover sacrifice. If this representation is interpreted in the light of later Priestly representations of blood manipulation activity, it is possible to speak of the elders acting in a priestly capacity. However, since J itself lacks any representations of priestly activity, it is difficult to determine if the J tradents would have understood the elders as performing a priestly duty. Nevertheless, it is certainly the case that they are assigned special ritual duties, and that these index high status, even if we cannot speak of a priestly identity or role.

In my treatment of Exod 12:1–13, I noted that the assignment of blood manipulation activity to the whole cultic-national community indexed both its special status on that occasion and the special character of the event. Moreover, the precise and ordered blood manipulation activity created an ordered space in which other ritualized activities could be performed. Also, participation in the ritual actions, and being subsequently located inside a blood-marked house, function to define membership in the community of those whose lives are preserved by Yahweh. All of these observations provide an important supplement to what the texts tell us explicitly about the purpose of applying the blood of the Passover to the lintels and doorposts.

The problems I identified with evaluating the representation in Exod 12:21–22 exemplify the general difficulty we have with the nonpriestly materials—namely, the relative lack of clear representations. We do not have enough textual data upon which to base a clear image of practice. Thus, since reflection on the indexical function of ritual acts, and on the ways in which ritualization distinguishes specialized activity from more mundane activity, requires access to practice, there are definite limitations on our ability to draw firm conclusions about indexing and ritualization.

In the following chapters, the relative abundance of textual material allows for more comprehensive construction of images of practice and, correspondingly, more sophisticated elaborations on the ways in which blood manipulation activity functions to index relationships and status. At the same time, we must not lose sight of the fact that we are dealing with textual representations and not with living practice. Textual representations reflect ideological and literary considerations and do not provide direct access to living practice.

CHAPTER THREE

The Blood of the Burnt Offering

This chapter, and the two that follow, will deal with Priestly (P) representations and interpretations of cultic blood manipulation. I have structured my treatment according to the types of sacrificial offerings represented in that source, beginning with the burnt offering (*'ōlâ*) since P's manual of prescriptions for sacrifice (Lev 1–7) begins with this offering.[1]

In contrast to the preceding chapter, a wealth of textual representation is available to construct a far more complete image of practical activity to which we can then apply our theoretical perspectives. I begin the chapter by clarifying what is represented in the texts and by constructing a picture of practical activity in the world of the text; then reflect on the significance of the manipulation of the blood of burnt offering animals, giving particular attention to the variety of roles Lev 17:11 plays in interpreters' attempts to explain the blood manipulations; and, finally, consider what can be said about the burnt offering blood manipulations if we consider their functionality as indexical signs. In sum, the chapter attempts to determine how the manipulation of blood marks, defines, enacts, and reinforces relationships and status within the context of the cult as it is represented in the textual corpus.

Prescriptions for the Burnt Offering

In P, the primary and most detailed treatment of the burnt offering is found in Lev 1:3–17. This text presents general instructions for carrying out the ritual complex when an individual brings a burnt offering (Lev 1:3). In addition, Exod 29:15–18 sets forth detailed prescriptions for a burnt offering as part of the rites for ordaining Aaron and his sons to the priesthood, Lev 8:18–21 describes the execution of these instructions, and Lev 9:12–14 describes the offering of a burnt offering on the day Aaron and his sons began to officiate as priests. Other texts simply refer to the making of a burnt offering, without presenting the procedure (e.g., Lev 5:10; 9:16; 12:6–8; 14:20, 31; 15:15, 30; 16:24).

Leviticus 1:3–17 is subdivided into three sections.[2] Each section presents the procedure for offering a particular type of victim as a burnt offering. The first section (vv. 3–9) treats the burnt offering of a herd animal. The second (vv. 10–13) deals with the offering of a flock animal. The third (vv. 14–17) is concerned with the offering of a bird. The first two sections are very similar in detail, given the basic physical similarity of the sacrificial animals. The third section differs from the previous two in a number of significant details apparently related to the physical differences between a bird and a domestic quadruped.[3]

The second section seems to have been composed with the first in view, assuming it and giving a more abbreviated outline of the ritual complex. Consequently, I focus on the first section but note where it is significantly different from the second. After treating the two quadruped offerings in some detail, I discuss the third section on the burnt offering of a bird.

Division of Labor in the Ritual Complex

Leviticus 1:3–17 focuses on ritual praxis, on actions rather than on conceptual matters. In order to clarify the place of blood manipulation within the sacrificial complex of the burnt offering, it is necessary to give some attention to how the text identifies the subjects of the various ritual actions that make up the complex.

In the general preface to the offering prescriptions of Leviticus 1–3 (Lev 1:1–2), verse 2 refers to a "person" (*'ādām*) who chooses to present an offering. This individual subject is characterized as being "from you" (*mikkem*), and in the second half of verse 2, the subject shifts to second-person, masculine plural.[4]

Then, in verse 3, we return to third-person, masculine singular verbs and reference to "his offering" (*qorbānô*) (cf. v. 10). The subject throughout verse 3 is clearly the individual mentioned in verse 2. Likewise, the individual who brings the offering is the subject of the verb "press" in verse 4. Verse 5 begins, "and he shall slaughter the bull" (v. 11 reads, "and he shall slaughter it"; i.e., the flock animal). Contextually, we are led to identify the subject of the verb here as the individual offerer. No other subject has been introduced, and the third-person, masculine singular verb follows on a sequence of third-person, masculine singular verbs with the offerer as subject.[5] The Greek translation, however, has a plural here and in verse 11, which suggests a change of subject. The plural verb seems to look ahead to the plural verbs used for the priests' blood manipulation activity in the second half of the verse.[6] It appears that the Greek translation reflects a tradition according to which priests or Levites slaughtered animals for offerers.[7] The Massoretic Text (MT), in contrast, treats the offerer as capable of slaughtering his own offering.[8] He wields the sacrificial knife and cuts the animal's throat.

With the next action in the complex, a change of subject occurs: "the sons of Aaron, the priests" are introduced. According to verse 5, they perform two acts with the blood. First, they bring the blood forward (*wĕhiqrîbû*); then they dash it (*wĕzārĕqû*) round about (*sābîb*) on the altar that is before the Tent of Meeting. In verse 5, these two acts constitute the blood rite of the burnt offering. In the parallel section on the burnt offering of a flock animal, only the second act is mentioned (v. 11). This omission seems simply to be a result of the more succinct quality of the second section.

In verse 6 in the MT, the first two verbs are third-person, masculine singular, reflecting a reversion to the prior subject, the offerer, who flays and divides the animal into pieces.[9] Likewise, verse 12 begins with a third-person, masculine singular verb ("he shall divide up"), equivalent to the second verb in verse 6, verse 12 lacking the reference to the flaying of the animal. In these instances, both the Greek translation and the Samaritan version have plural verbs, which seem to indicate the previously mentioned priests as subjects.[10] Thus, the MT conveys one particular image of the activity involved in carrying out a burnt offering rite, while the Greek and Samaritan texts convey a different image. In the MT, the offerer slaughters the animal. The priests then present the blood and toss it on the altar. The offerer skins and dismembers the animal. In contrast, the Greek translation represents the priests as slaughtering the animal, performing the blood manipulations, and skinning and dismembering the carcass. The Samaritan text presents a similar image, except that it apparently does not assign the slaughtering of the animal to the priests. In both the Greek translation and the Samaritan version, all ritual actions from the blood manipulation on are performed by priests.[11] The MT has a far more active and engaged layperson.

Verse 7, which lacks a parallel in the second section, reintroduces the priests as subjects of plural verbs. The formulation in MT is somewhat odd, however. The standard MT text has, literally, "the sons of Aaron [pl.], the priest [sg.]."[12] It is possible to construe "the priest" here as standing in apposition only to "Aaron," and to render the formulation as "the sons of Aaron the priest."[13] However, this formula is not otherwise attested in P and stands out in comparison to the formulation "the sons of Aaron, the priests" that occurs elsewhere in this chapter. Thus, it is possible that the text is disturbed or has been edited unevenly.[14] In any event, this verse clearly assigns priests the duty of stoking the altar fire and placing wood on it. Verse 8 continues with verbs in the plural, with the subjects identified as "the sons of Aaron, the priests." According to this verse, the priests are to arrange the pieces of the animal's carcass, with the head and the suet, on the altar fire.

In verse 9, in the MT the first verb is third-person masculine singular, and no subject is specified (cf. v. 13). The reintroduction of a singular verb in this manner suggests a change of subject back to the offerer. He washes the entrails and hind legs. Again, the Greek and Samaritan texts have a plural verb, which stands in continuity with the plural verbs in verses 7–8, where the priests are explicitly identified as the subjects.

The next act is the burning of the animal (v. 9b). In this case, the MT has "the priest" and a corresponding verb in the third-person, masculine singular ("he shall send up as smoke"). The Greek version (with the exception of Codex Alexandrinus, which corresponds to the MT) has "the priests" and a plural verb. The parallel in verse 13 also has a single priest as subject. In this case, the Greek version corresponds to the MT. Verse 13 has the added detail that "the priest shall present the whole" before the mention of the burning.

In his *Studien zur Geschichte des Opfers im Alten Israel,* Rolf Rendtorff asserted that the changes of subject in verses 3–9 reflected no consistent pattern.[15] In my opinion, however, one can be identified with little difficulty. If we consider those instances where the priests are explicitly identified as the subjects of a ritual act, we see that all of these actions are directed at or take place on the altar. In contrast, when the priests are not identified as subjects, the actions take place away from the altar. Thus, the text makes clear that priests perform all altar rituals. The text may also be understood as identifying those actions that can be carried out by the offerer,[16] but the fact that it does not specify a subject in these instances may indicate that making this point is less important. Behind the formal features of this text, therefore, seems to lie a concern to highlight those acts that are reserved for the priests—namely, altar rituals. Some interpreters have noted that the text reserves altar rituals to the priests[17] and that the blood manipulations are their first ritual actions.[18] However, very little consideration has been given to how the blood manipulations, as the first acts carried out by the priests, relate to the other altar rites, and to the conception of altar rites as reserved to the priesthood, which I have identified here. Before pursuing these matters, however, more attention needs to be given to the manner in which the texts represent blood manipulation activity and to scholarly efforts to identify its significance.

The Blood Manipulation in the Burnt Offering of a Quadruped

As noted earlier, verse 5 represents a twofold blood rite. The blood is first presented and then dashed on the altar. Some commentators have attempted to fill out the picture of the activity represented here, either by logical inference or by drawing on later liturgical tradition. Thus, some note that the blood would have been collected in some kind of vessel,[19] a logical enough inference. One may also note that Exod 24:6 specifies that Moses put half the blood of the covenant sacrifices in basins and that the J Passover text mentions the use of a dish to hold the blood of the Passover lamb (Exod 12:22). Finally, there is the telling existence of a cultic vessel called a *mizrāq*, which we might render "tossing vessel" (Exod 27:3; 38:3; Num 4:14). The noun is clearly based on the same root as the verb that designates the blood manipulation in the burnt offering.[20] Yet, surprisingly, the noun never appears anywhere in the Hebrew canon in connection with blood manipulation. Nevertheless, Hartley confidently asserts that the priest caught the blood in a *mizrāq*, adding that he stirred the blood in the bowl to prevent it coagulating.[21] This latter detail is apparently drawn from the Mishnah (see *m. Yoma* 4:3).

After the blood had been collected, it had to be transferred to the altar, an act perhaps indicated with the statement "and the sons of Aaron the priests shall present [*wĕhiqrîbû*] the blood." Milgrom comments: "This protean verb, whose subject is the priest, clearly refers to a specific rite. . . . Perhaps it was executed with the priests carrying the blood, collected in special bowls, . . . in solemn, dignified procession."[22] Wenham notes that "what was involved in 'offering the blood' is not made clear in this passage." He then speculates, "Perhaps the priest lifted it up and said a prayer." Wenham also specifies that the blood was offered "to God."[23] There are other occurrences in Leviticus 1 of the verb "present" with priests as subjects. In Lev 1:13, for example, in the instructions for the burnt offering of a flock animal, the priest presents "everything" (*'et-hakkōl*) before turning it into smoke. In Lev 1:15, the priest brings ("presents") the burnt offering bird to the altar before killing it.[24] The presentation of the blood is not mentioned in the parallel account of the offering of the flock animal (Lev 1:11). It is probably simply assumed in the abbreviated second section.[25]

Following the presentation of the blood, the priests dash or toss the blood "on the altar round about" (vv. 5 and 11). Where, precisely, are we to envisage the blood being tossed? There is a strong scholarly consensus for envisaging the blood being tossed onto the sides or walls of the altar and not onto its top.[26] This understanding of the character of the gesture is strongly dependent on the appearance of the adverb *sābîb* (round about). Blood that is tossed round about could not be tossed onto the top of the altar. "Round about" implies the sides.

How was this tossing of the blood round about on the sides of the altar executed? One might envisage a priest carrying a vessel filled with blood, splashing small amounts from it as he circumambulated the altar, with a solid application running all the way around.[27] David Hoffmann, however, declares such an application of blood practically impossible, arguing that a flock animal would not provide sufficient blood for it.[28] Hoffmann then notes that we could envisage the priest circumambulating the altar and tossing blood from a vessel once onto each of the four sides.[29] He rejects this possibility, however, by noting later rabbinic traditions about the construction of the altar and the importance of the "base" or "foundation" (*yĕsôd*). According to the Mishnah, the "base" did not extend fully around the altar. It was interrupted at the point where a ramp extended up to the top of the altar. Blood had to be tossed on the sides toward (*kngd*) the base. Where there was no base, there could be no tossing of blood. Hoffmann, therefore, adopts the Mishnah's representation of a twofold dashing of blood onto opposite corners of the altar. This twofold tossing put blood on part of each side.[30] However, since this explanation depends on the Tannaitic representation of the altar, and the altar described in P differs significantly from the Mishnaic altar, it seems unnecessary to assume the Mishnaic practice. Still, Hoffmann's suggestion about the practical difficulty of a continuous dashing is persuasive. It is likely, therefore, that we should envisage the application of blood in four individual applications to each of the four sides.[31] While such an effort to determine what to envisage may seem unnecessary, it is a reasonable exercise, given the normal tendency of readers to fill in gaps in a textual description and construct a mental picture of what is described. Consequently, I propose to envisage, within the world of the text, a priestly circumambulation of the altar accompanied by the dashing of blood from a vessel one time on each side of the altar.

Besides Lev 1:5 and 11, a few other texts also represent how the blood of a quadruped offered as a burnt offering was handled. Leviticus 8:19 describes how Moses performed the blood rite when he offered the burnt offering during the rites consecrating Aaron and his sons as priests (for a discussion of the context, see chapter 4). The verse reads: "Then he slaughtered (it), and Moses tossed the blood onto the altar round about." Moses is clearly identified as the one who manipulates the blood in this unique situation. Since Aaron and his sons are not yet consecrated as priests, Moses, by benefit of his special status as mediator between Yahweh and Israel, can and must function as a priest.[32] He dashes the blood against the altar in the same manner as indicated in Leviticus 1. The rest of the ritual also corresponds with the prescriptions in Lev 1:3–9. Thus, according to the representation of P, the first burnt offering performed at the new tent-shrine complex was performed as mandated in the general prescriptions of Leviticus 1. Exodus 29:16, the parallel to Lev 8:19, and its probable basis (see chapter 4), reads: "Then you shall slaughter the ram, take its blood, and toss (it) on the altar round about." Here, Moses is instructed to slaughter the animal. Thus, we have an unusual variation from the model presented in Leviticus 1. As the offerers, Aaron and his sons press their hands on the head of the animal (Lev 8:18), but they do not slaughter it as we would expect. Moses is instructed to "take" the blood and dash it on the altar. As in Lev 1:5, a two-act process is indicated. This implies that blood was not to be dashed straightaway. It had to be collected and brought to the altar.

Likewise, in the account of Aaron's first liturgical celebration, Lev 9:12 states: "He slaughtered the burnt offering, and the sons of Aaron presented [*wayyamṣi'û*] the blood to him, and he dashed it on the altar round about."

Following the slaughter, the sons of Aaron presented the blood to Aaron. Quite literally, "the sons of Aaron caused the blood to attain to him."[33] That is, they brought it directly to him and handed it over for use.[34] Aaron then dashed the blood on the altar round about. In this account, the two acts have two distinct subjects. Aaron's sons brought him the blood. Aaron dashed it. Again, the gesture is performed by Aaron in the same manner as that indicated in Leviticus 1.

From all of this evidence, we can conclude that P assumes a standard pattern of blood handling. The animal is slaughtered, generally by the one who brings it as an offering (although textual ambiguity suggests that identification of the subject of the slaughtering is relatively insignificant). The blood is collected, although the act of collection seems not to have been of particular interest to the tradents who produced the literary representations. The blood is transferred to the altar. This is a priestly act. The blood is dashed on each of the four sides of the altar. This is also a priestly act.

The Burnt Offering of a Bird

Having treated the blood manipulation represented in the first two sections, I can now examine its representation in the case of a burnt offering of a bird. Like the first two sections, the third section begins with a prescription about what the offerer should bring (v. 14). In this ritual complex, however, no hand-pressing is prescribed, and the offerer does not slaughter his offering away from the altar. Verse 15 prescribes that the priest (sg.) should convey the bird to the altar, wring off its head, and turn it into smoke on the altar. Then he is to let the blood drain out on the side of the altar. Verse 16 prescribes activities for the disposal of parts of the bird that cannot be offered on the altar. Verse 17 prescribes that "he shall tear it asunder by its wings, but not split it, and the priest shall turn it into smoke on the altar upon the wood which is upon the fire."

In this section, we are faced with some ambiguity with respect to the subject of the verbs. Twice, the priest is explicitly mentioned. In verse 15, he clearly is the one who conveys the bird to the altar. Logically, he would also be the subject of the following series of acts (wringing off the head, turning it into smoke, draining out the blood). Is he still the subject of the activity in verse 16? A number of interpreters regard the priest as the subject of all the verbs from verses 15 through 17.[35] According to Martin Noth, on the other hand, the text assigns the disposal of waste portions (v. 16) and the tearing open (v. 17a) to the offerer.[36] He assumes the same division of labor prescribed in the previous sections: the priest performs the altar rites, while the offerer prepares the body for burning.

It is clear, however, that the ritual presented in this section is distinct from what is presented in verses 3–13. First of all, the offerer does not kill the bird himself. This is done by the priest at the altar. There is nothing in the text to indicate that we should envisage the offerer accompanying the priest to the altar, or the priest returning from the altar so that the offerer could clean and dismember the bird. The first interpretation, therefore, seems more logical. The priest conveys the bird to the altar and then performs all the prescribed tasks at the altar. As I demonstrate shortly, this fits with the presuppositions behind the division of labor in the case of all three types of burnt offering.

I turn now to an examination of the blood manipulation prescribed in this section. Rather than cut the bird's throat with a knife, the text prescribes that the priest wring off the head, apparently with his bare hand.[37] If the text is understood as presenting an actual sequence of events, the next step is the burning of the head. We can envisage the priest tossing it into the fire on the altar as soon as he has decapitated the bird.[38] Alternatively, the reference to the burning of the head can be understood to anticipate its consignment to the altar fire after the blood manipulation has been carried out.[39]

The blood manipulation itself involves the draining out (*mṣh*) of the blood.[40] As Milgrom notes, the verb *mṣh* is used for squeezing water out of a wet fleece (Judg 6:38) and draining a cup of wine (Isa 51:17; Ezek 23:34; Ps 75:9).[41] There is apparently too little blood to collect in a vessel and toss.[42] Note, also, that the blood is drained out "on the side of the altar" (*'al qîr hammizbēaḥ*).[43] Where are we to envisage the priest standing when he does this? Altars described in other sources can be mounted by ramp or steps. We might, then, think of the priest standing atop the altar and draining out the blood downward over one of the sides. However, P does not represent such an altar. Rather, P's altar is a relatively low structure, and there is neither necessity nor provision for someone to stand atop it. We should picture, then, a priest standing next to the altar and draining out the blood. Rashi (ad loc.) suggests that, because *mṣh* can mean "squeeze," the blood was applied to the altar by the priest pressing the bird against the side of the altar.[44] This act is clearly the equivalent of the blood tossing in the previous two sections.[45] We may conclude from this that the specific act of tossing is not itself important. What matters is that all of the blood of the offering is applied in its liquid state to the side of the altar. In the case of a burnt offering of a bird there is no requirement that the blood be applied "round about." It is to be applied only to one side.

The blood manipulation clearly precedes the burning of the body of the bird. Are we also to see it as preceding the burning of the head, as Hoffmann maintains following rabbinic tradition? Since there would be some blood flowing from the severed head, it seems reasonable to envisage the draining of blood from head and body taking place at the same time. Then, with all the blood drained, the head could be thrown into the fire. If this is a correct understanding of the prescribed ritual, we need to read the reference to the burning of the head as out of sequence.[46] It is possible, however, to read the text as indicating that no blood is drained from the head, which is simply tossed into the fire as soon as the bird has been decapitated. Following this procedure would free up both of the hands of the priest for applying blood from the body to the altar.[47]

The Significance of the Blood Manipulation

What effect, then, is achieved by the blood manipulation? Does the act communicate symbolically? If so, what does it communicate? Or, should we think in terms of an instrumental effect? More than one interpreter has noted that the blood ritual in the burnt offering is not explained for us.[48] Thus, we must note, first of all, that no scholarly interpretation of the action is a simple paraphrase or expansion upon an explanation given in the texts. Rather, every explanation is a construction produced by a reader. (Although this section focuses on the dashing of the blood of the quadruped burnt offerings, the primary form of the rite, nevertheless the observations apply generally to the blood manipulation for the burnt offering of a bird.)

Some scholars characterize the dashing of the blood as an act of ritualized disposal. For example, Martin Noth writes "This blood-rite originates from the notion that the life of the sacrificial animal resides in its blood (cf. 17.11), and that the life as such belongs to God and can therefore form no part of the human gift presented for sacrifice. It is therefore, before the offering of the sacrifice, applied to the altar, the place belonging to God and devoted to God."[49]

Clearly, Noth's explanation of the blood manipulation depends on a particular interpretation of Lev 17:11 and a specific conception of its relevance for understanding cultic blood manipulation. As I noted in chapter 1, no text identifies blood as "holy" or explicitly identifies it as Yahweh's special property. Moreover, no P text connects blood manipulation with the conceptual identification of blood with life. Only the H text Lev 17:11 does this, and it does not explain blood manipulation as effecting the return of life to its source.

Rolf Knierim notes perceptively that the "meaning of the blood itself," that is its ontological identification as the seat of life, does not itself explain the gesture of tossing it on the altar.[50] Nor, he continues, does the fact of the prohibition of consuming blood, which Rolf Rendtorff identifies as the key to understanding the action.[51] Knierim argues that if prevention of human consumption is the only concern, "the blood might as well be spilled at the place of slaughter in order to comply with the prohibition against eating it." Thus, he asserts, "the blood-rite is governed by where the blood goes, not from whom it is withheld." He quotes with approval Karl Elliger's pregnant suggestion that "die schwerlich noch verstandene Sitte des Rundumgießens hat ihren Ursprung vermutlich in der Vorstellung vom 'Altar' als dem Ort der besonderen Gegenwart der Gottheit."[52] Knierim observes, however, that Elliger "does not explain why the blood is to be tossed against the altar rather than burned upon it with the animal."[53] Knierim concludes that Noth most successfully explains why the blood is tossed on the altar. Like Noth, Knierim asserts that the blood belongs a priori to Yahweh. For this reason, "it cannot be part of the offerer's sacrificial gift burnt with his gift upon the altar. It must instead in a separate act be surrendered to Yahweh at his altar and—quite consistently with Yahweh's a priori ownership of it—before the offerer's own sacrifice is spent by the priest upon the altar as a gift to Yahweh in the sacrifice proper!"[54]

To summarize: it is possible to note that blood is identified as life or as the locus of life in priestly literature and that the human consumption of blood is prohibited (Gen 9:4; Lev 17:11). On this basis, some interpreters, such as Rendtorff, have suggested that tossing the blood on the altar is a reflex of the prohibition against human consumption. Others—Noth and Knierim—go further, however, and argue that more is involved than simply preventing human consumption of the blood. Because Yahweh is the source of life and its ultimate owner, the tossing of the blood on the altar, the locus of his presence, effects its return to him. On both accounts, the tossing of the blood does not constitute an "offering" or "gift" of the blood to Yahweh. Human beings cannot give to Yahweh what he already owns.

In response to the argument that what belongs a priori to Yahweh cannot be given to him as a gift, I would note that Yahweh is not only the source of life, and the owner of life; he is the source and owner of the animal itself—its flesh as well as its blood. Human beings may give to Yahweh gifts from what is really already his property, and receive back portions for their own use. Thus, it does not necessarily follow that blood—as Yahweh's property—cannot be given to him as a gift. Certain texts do in fact treat the blood as if it were food or drink given to Yahweh, even if some of these texts reject the possibility that Yahweh would need or want food or drink (for example, Ezek 44:7; Ps 50:13). Furthermore, it should be observed that, according to the H tradents, "All fat [*ḥēleb*]) is Yahweh's" (Lev 3:16b); it belongs to Yahweh a priori.[55] Yet, the fat portions are given to Yahweh as a gift on the altar and burned. In addition, it should be noted that P never refers to blood as belonging to Yahweh. Even H, which identifies fat as Yahweh's, fails to make the same claim for blood. Thus, the claim that the blood is not a "gift" or "offering," and not "sacrificial," is not entirely compelling.

In support of the argument that the blood is an offering or gift, one might note that the act of "offering" the blood (from the root *qrb*, from which the noun *qorbān* is derived) suggests that it is a "gift" or "offering."[56] We might see the offering of the blood as the primary offering, the act by which the animal is devoted to the altar *pars pro toto*. By the act, the offerer would testify that the animal did belong to Yahweh, that its life was his, and that the ultimate disposition of the animal rested with the deity. This is, of course, a speculative reconstruction of the underlying rationale of the action. It is, however, no more speculative than the reconstructions I have already discussed. This observation highlights once again the fact that the blood rite, like almost all ritualized actions represented in the Bible, is not explained or interpreted for us. Readers of the texts must interpret the actions based on evidence provided by the text and from their own background, experience, and theoretical presuppositions.

Up to this juncture, I have not directly addressed how general interpretations of the nature and purpose of the burnt offering help to shape explanations of the blood manipulation. It should already be evident, however, that such interpretations do play an important role. Noth, Rendtorff, Knierim, and others root their discussions of the blood manipulation in an understanding of the burnt offering as a gift offered to the deity. For them, the question to be answered is whether the blood can be offered as part of this gift. They answer in the negative and maintain that it is disposed of ritually before the offering proper is made.

Other interpreters note that Lev 1:4 apparently identifies "removal" (*kipper*) as an anticipated effect of the offering. At the end of the verse (4b), following the prescription that the offerer is to press his hand on the head of the animal (4a), this declaration appears: "And it will be accepted with favor for him to effect removal on his behalf." There is considerable disagreement about the translation and interpretation of these clauses.[57] For our present purposes, it suffices to note that many interpreters understand Lev 1:4b to attribute an atoning or expiatory effect to the burnt offering. In addition to this verse, a handful of other texts also seem to ascribe a "removal" effect to the burnt offering (Lev 5:10; 9:7; 12:7, 8; 14:20, 31; 15:15, 30; 16:24). It should be noted that in all of these texts the burnt offering is sacrificed in connection with a *ḥaṭṭā't* offering.

What does the verb *kipper* mean in connection with the burnt offering, and what relationship does the blood manipulation have to the effect indicated with this verb? Many interpreters take their cue from Lev 17:11 and its declaration that the blood applied to the altar is "to effect removal for your lives" (*lĕkappēr 'al-napšōtêkem*), which is understood to identify the purpose to the burnt offering blood manipulation. An early example of this approach appears in *Sipra* (*Nedaba* 4:9), which comments on Lev 1:4 and identifies the agent of "removal" as the blood, citing the final clause of Lev 17:11 in support of this identification: "'And it will be accepted with favor for him to effect removal': (This means) by means of the agent of removal. What is the agent of removal? It is the blood, as it is said, 'For the blood itself by means of the life effects removal.'"[58] Ibn Ezra, who argues that the verb *kipper* means "serve as a ransom" (on Lev 1:1), explains that the blood of the burnt offering is tossed onto the altar "to be a ransom payment [*kōper*] for whatever punishment he [the offerer] deserves" (on Lev 1:4).[59] Although Ibn Ezra does not refer explicitly to Lev 17:11 in this context, his references to that verse elsewhere in his commentaries indicate that he understood it to provide an explanation of the workings of almost all modes of blood manipulation.

According to David Hoffmann, the fact that the burnt offering is associated with "removal" indicates that it deals with some sin.[60] Traditional Jewish sources explain that the burnt offering deals with sins of omission.[61] Hoffmann accepts this tradition but suggests that the burnt offering might also deal with any human failing that otherwise lacks a penalty. He explains the significance of the blood manipulation and its connection with "removal" by referring to Lev 17:10–12.[62] Reflecting nineteenth-century Jewish neotraditionalism, Hoffmann proposes a noninstrumental symbolic explanation of how the blood rite effects atonement.[63] According to Hoffmann, the tossing of blood on the altar is a symbolic affirmation of devotion to God. The blood is the animal's life and, on the altar, the animal's life "versinnbildichte . . . die Menschenseele." It is designated as a symbol of human life "vom göttlichen Gesetze." The tossing of the blood, its surrender to God, represents "symbolisch die Hingabe der Menschenseele an Gott."[64] In Hoffmann's view, the act of dashing blood achieves its atoning effect through the symbolic identification of the animal's blood as representative of the life of the individual being devoted or surrendered to God. Hoffmann understands the process indicated with *kipper* as a genuine "at-one-ment." The blood is given to God as a symbol of human life, the God-like part of the human being.[65] By accepting it, God conveys his acceptance of the individual, and his willingness to overlook sin.[66]

Hoffmann asserts that the blood manipulation can achieve the effect he attributes to it, because another ritual action has rendered the animal capable of functioning as the representative or substitute for the offerer. This action is the hand-pressing on the head of the animal.[67] This act is prescribed for the burnt offering in Lev 1:4 (as well as Exod 29:15 and Lev 8:18). It immediately precedes the slaughter of the animal. The significance of this gesture has been the subject of considerable scholarly discussion, and diverse explanations have been offered.[68] For the purpose of the present discussion, explanations may be categorized according to whether they understand the hand-pressing to prepare the animal to be used to deal in some fashion with the offerer's sin. Some interpreters, Hoffmann among them, argue that the hand-pressing effects an identification between the offerer and his offering. This identification allows the animal to be offered to Yahweh as a substitute or representative for the offerer.[69] Its blood, as its life, substitutes for or represents the life of the offerer. This representation or substitution has an essentially positive character, since the blood comes to Yahweh as a symbol of the self-devotion of the offerer to Yahweh.

According to other interpreters, the hand-pressing gesture in the case of *all* sacrifices effects the transfer of sin and guilt to the animal, which bears them on behalf of the offerer. This interpretation is rooted in understanding the hand-pressing on the scapegoat represented in Lev 16:21 as providing the key for understanding the hand-leaning gesture in the case of all sacrifices. Lev 16:21 seems to indicate the hand-pressing gesture as effecting the transfer of Israel's sins to the scapegoat.[70] Bearing his sins, the animal dies in place of the offerer. A. Noordtzij's explanation of the relationship between the hand-pressing, slaughter, and blood manipulation in the burnt offering complex may be taken as representative of this interpretation: "The laying on of hands in a sense made the animal into the successor of the person who presented it. It came to stand in his place, so that when the life or 'soul' of the sacrificial animal was poured out with its flowing blood and sank into death, it was just as if the soul of the person who brought it departed from him and likewise died away."[71] Referring to Lev 17:11, Noordtzij explains that "in the offering, soul was substituted for soul, or life for life."[72] This substitution is of a more negative character. Laden with sin, the animal dies in place of the sinner, who merits death because of his sins.[73] If the blood of the sinner were applied to the altar, it would indicate his death. The animal blood substitutes for the blood of the sinner.

Other interpretations of the hand-pressing gesture involve neither transfer of sin nor substitution of the animal for a sinner. Jacob Milgrom, for example, argues that the hand-pressing gesture indicates ownership of the animal by the offerer.[74] Milgrom does not clearly explain why the offerer needs to identify the animal as his property. Presumably, ownership is necessary if the offerer is to receive the benefits that follow from the performance of the sacrificial rite.

The great variety of explanations of the hand-pressing gesture again indicates the problem of trying to interpret an uninterpreted gesture. Most interpreters are obviously interested in the "meaning" of the gesture. Gerhard von Rad, for example, writes, "We would give much to know the special significance which was attached to the laying on of hands upon the head of the victim."[75] N. Kiuchi speaks repeatedly of seeking the "symbolic meaning" of the gesture.[76] However, an interpretation of the hand-pressing action in terms of its "meaning" is not all we need to seek, and it may not ultimately turn out to be the most important thing to be sought. Knierim seems, in part, to have understood this. He examines the hand-pressing gesture in the burnt offering in terms of its relationship to the other actions of the sacrifice. He notes that the slaughter of the animal follows the hand-pressing immediately, and suggests that the gesture is related to the death of the animal. He then resorts, however, to the usual quest for a symbolic meaning and concludes that the gesture "is a distinct act by which the animal is officially surrendered to its subsequent sacrificial death."[77] It may be true that the action is somehow related to the death of the animal, but the problem remains that we do not know what it might "mean" or "symbolize" or whether such an explanation was ever articulated by ancient Israelites. Such an explanation is not articulated in the Priestly texts.[78]

Furthermore, it is by no means the case that an explanation of the hand-pressing gesture necessarily amounts to an explanation of the meaning or purpose of the burnt offering itself. It is possible, for example, to accept Milgrom's argument that the hand-pressing gesture marks ownership, without thereby rejecting the thesis that the animal serves as a substitute for the offerer. Declaration of ownership may be a prerequisite for such substitution. It is even possible to propose that transfer of sin takes place by some mechanism other than hand-pressing. Likewise, understanding the hand-pressing gesture as effecting an identification of the offerer with the animal does not serve to explain the effect achieved for the offerer by the sacrificial process. The offerer need not be seen merely as a sinner in his identification with the animal.

It follows, then, that an interpretation of the hand-pressing gesture does not explain the burnt offering, nor, in turn, is the blood manipulation thereby explained. All we can do is suggest possible interpretations of the significance of the burnt offering and explain the blood manipulation in accordance with each of them. If the burnt offering deals with "sin," then the blood manipulation may have something to do with elimination of this sin and the forgiveness of the sinner. How was this elimination and forgiveness of sin achieved?

For many interpreters, Lev 17:11 provides the answer to this question. We have already seen how Hoffmann and Noordtzij turn to that text to explain blood manipulation. According to each, the animal's blood, as life, substitutes for or represents the offerer's life. Noordtzij thinks in terms of the offerer's life being demanded because of his sin. Hoffmann thinks of the offerer symbolically devoting his life to God, asserting that the placing of blood on the altar represents "symbolisch die Hingabe der Menschenseele an Gott."[79] Offering a very similar characterization of the meaning of the blood manipulation, also drawing on Lev 17:11, Bernd Janowski characterizes the blood manipulation as "eine zeichenhaftreale Lebenshingabe des Opfernden an das Heiligtum Gottes."[80] Since these explanations of blood manipulation are based on an interpretation of Lev 17:11, a full evaluation of their adequacy for explaining the blood manipulation in the burnt offering must await my detailed treatment of that text in chapter 7.

Baruch Levine also appeals to an interpretation of Lev 17:11 in explaining the role of the blood tossing in the burnt offering, but his interpretation of that text differs from Hoffmann's and Janowski's. He roots his interpretation of Lev 17:11 and his explanation of the blood rite in the burnt offering in the claim that there are, in fact, two distinct *piel* constructions of the root *kpr*, the "primary" *piel*, which is to be rendered as "purgate, expunge, efface, purify, expiate" depending on context, and a "secondary denominative" form derived from the noun *kōper*, "ransom, expiation gift."[81] This secondary form, according to Levine, appears normally in the formulation, *kipper ʿal-nepeš*, "ransom for a life."[82] This formula appears twice in contexts where something other than blood serves as the ransom (Exod 30:15–16; Num 31:50),[83] and once in connection with blood—in Lev 17:11. According to Levine, the blood tossed on the altar functions as a ransom for the lives of those who present an offering. It is the concept of blood as a ransom that, according to Levine, is the key to understanding the "blood libation."[84] Levine asserts that entry into the presence of the deity is inherently dangerous. Yahweh's wrath may strike out against anyone who causes him displeasure. Human beings, because they tend to become impure, and to make mistakes in their ritual activity, are in constant danger. Yet, in his compassion, Yahweh allows them to offer animal blood to ward off his wrath. Rather than striking out and taking human lives, Yahweh accepts animal life—in the blood—as a ransom, a substitute, for human life.[85]

Levine's theory faces a problem, however, in that the idiom *kipper ʿal-nepeš* does not appear in Lev 1:4, or in any of the other texts where *kipper* is associated with the burnt offering. Rather, the idiom is simply *kipper ʿal*, with a noun or pronoun indicating the human object of the effect. This is the idiom that Levine claims has to do with purification and expiation, effects that, he asserts, are not to be attributed to the dashing of the blood of the burnt offering. Levine has responded to this problem in two ways. In his earlier treatment of the question in *In the Presence of the Lord*, he argued that Lev 1:4 did not actually deal with the burnt offering itself but with the "purification offering" (*ḥaṭṭāʾt*), which is in the general category of burnt offering.[86] This argument is not especially persuasive, since it is clear that the attribution of "removal" power in Lev 1:4, whatever this power is, is directed at the burnt offering being described in Leviticus 1. The *ḥaṭṭāʾt* is not in view. Levine must have recognized the weakness of his argument, for in his recent commentary on Leviticus, he offers a different explanation, asserting that *kipper ʿal* is an abbreviation for the standard formulation *kipper ʿal-nepeš*.[87] This explanation is no better than his earlier effort. It requires us to believe that a formula, which appears repeatedly throughout priestly (P and H) texts, has a different meaning in one verse from its meaning everywhere else. While certainly possible, one expects some kind of sustained argument for the position. Such an argument is not provided by Levine. A great deal more could be said about Levine's interpretation of the burnt offering blood manipulation. At this juncture, however, I simply emphasize that this interpretation rests on a particular reading of Lev 17:11, just like the others we have considered. Thus, further discussion must await my treatment of that text.

Jacob Milgrom also draws on Lev 17:11 to explain the burnt offering blood manipulation. According to Milgrom, the tossing of the blood on the altar is a means of returning to God what is rightfully his. At the same time, Milgrom asserts that this action has a profound effect. It saves the one who slaughters an animal from being classed as a murderer, one who has taken life.[88] Milgrom bases this explanation on his understanding of the role of the blood rite in the well-being sacrifice. This understanding depends heavily on Milgrom's interpretation of Lev 17:11. He claims that the effect of the blood rite in the well-being sacrifice is also realized in the same manipulation in the burnt offering. To evaluate the theory, I need to deal with the well-being offering and with Lev 17:11, so I leave discussion of Milgrom's theory until that juncture.

Since the explanations of the burnt offering blood manipulation of Hoffmann, Noordtzij, Janowski, Levine, and Milgrom—not to mention many other scholars—depend, each in its own way, on their interpretations of Lev 17:11, they can be properly evaluated only when that text has been treated in detail. Although this single text plays a crucial role in the interpretation of the blood manipulation activity represented in Leviticus 1, there is still no consensus on what that text actually says about the significance of blood manipulation.

An Alternative Approach: Blood Manipulation as an Indexical Sign

A further conclusion can be drawn from the preceding discussion. It is clear that the "meaning" of the blood manipulation is not inherent in the act itself. Our understanding of the blood rite is shaped by our understanding of the significance and purpose of the burnt offering as a whole. This understanding, in turn, rests on analysis of the component parts of the ritual complex, and its contextual execution within the cultic system. In effect, interpretation of the uninterpreted blood rite relies on interpretation of other uninterpreted ritualized actions. This interpretive process, in turn, relies on assumptions of various kinds—historical, textual, and methodological-theoretical.

As I have noted, many interpreters of biblical ritual deal with the question of "meaning" by attributing *symbolic* meanings to ritual acts. This approach takes "symbol" as the key significance of a sign. That is, the ritual action, as "sign," may be understood to communicate some concept. However, as I noted in the introduction to this study, a sign may be understood as an index. The index is in an existential relationship with its object and indicates rather than represents it. Thus, the relationship between the sign and its object is not conventional but can be observed and understood across cultural and linguistic boundaries.[89]

I propose to consider here how the burnt offering blood manipulation functions as an index of relationships in the cultic sphere. My focus is on the ritual complex for the offering of quadrupeds, since, as I have noted, this is the primary form of the rite. I begin by noting again the distinctions of subject obtaining in the MT of the P texts I have examined. The key point to be made here is that nonaltar acts do not specify the priest(s) as subject(s); we are simply told that "he" shall do such-and-such. I have suggested that this indicates that the one who makes the offering is to do the acts, or that it does not matter who does them. Altar acts in every case specify the priest(s) as subject(s). They are to do certain specified tasks, all of which involve contact or some close relation to the altar. The first of these altar acts is the dashing of the blood.

If we visualize the practices described in Lev 1:3–13, we get a clear sense of the indexing quality of the actions. The one who brings the offering selects it according to the specified rules and conveys it to the entrance of the Tent of Meeting—that is, he brings it to the locus of the singular presence of Yahweh, as defined in the Priestly ideology. Yahweh is at once implicated in the activity and remains implicated until its culmination, which indicates that the goal of the whole operation is to establish a particular mode of contact between the offerer and Yahweh.

The one who brings the offering presses his hand on the animal's head and then slaughters it. Following the slaughter, the priests come to the foreground, whereas previous to this moment their role in the act of making an offering had been undefined. They take the blood and bring it to the altar. Note that the one who makes the offering brings (*hiqrîb*) the animal to the entrance of the Tent of Meeting. After he has slaughtered it, the priests bring (*hiqrîb*) the blood. Their act of offering takes them to a different location within the sphere of holiness. The text does not specify that nonpriests are prohibited access to the altar, but the division of labor seems to be rooted in such a restriction. The act itself serves to index this restriction. The priests, who have taken the blood and brought it to the altar, dash it on the altar round about. Apparently, while they are doing this, the one who brought the offering is dressing the carcass. He skins it, divides it into parts, and washes the entrails and hind legs. The priests stoke the fire on the altar and place wood on the fire. They place the parts of the animal, prepared by the one who brought the offering, on the fire.

Note that the priests' activity in relation to the altar begins with the blood manipulation. Only after the blood has been dashed, according to the structure of the account, do they stoke the fire and place the wood. Blood manipulation marks the moment when the priests enter into their role vis-à-vis the altar. Like signs, these acts communicate multiple messages. The text tells us what the priests do, and the acts that the priests perform in the world of the text communicate to the characters inhabiting that world. The blood marks this-space-and-not-that-space. It also marks this-actor-and-not-that-actor. All else follows from the pattern that is established with the blood manipulation. The picture is consistent: priests perform acts connected with the altar; the one who brought the offering performs acts not connected with the altar. Relationships between person and place in holy space are defined and enacted. This basic point may serve to explain the sequence of actions represented in the case of the bird burnt offering. The priest is represented as carrying the bird to the altar. Everything he does is an altar rite. It follows, therefore, that the blood draining does not need to be stressed as the primary act. On the other hand, if the removal of the head presupposes the draining of the blood, there would be a blood application prior to the burning of the head. Nevertheless, this act of blood draining is not mentioned, and the sequence of represented actions differs from the sequence in the previous two sections.

Furthermore, we are informed by the text's lack of specificity that anyone who is one of "the sons of Aaron" and designated "priest" may carry out the acts that are connected with the altar. Thus, implicit in the actions is a message about distinctions within the group designated "priests, sons of Aaron." In this case, the message is that there are no distinctions. Each enactment, within the world of the text, communicates this principle to the inhabitants of that world. The key observation to stress at this juncture is that blood manipulation indexes not only relationships between priests and nonpriests but also relationships between priests. If we ask who may perform what act in what place, we are given the answer not by an explicit instruction but by the action itself. By watching the actions repeated in the self-sustaining world of the text, we can deduce what the rule is without having it presented in a linguistic form.

To clarify this point, I suggest an analogy. In most armed forces, subordinates salute commissioned officers. Superior commissioned officers return the salutes of subordinates. Noncommissioned officers salute commissioned officers, but the subordinates of noncommissioned officers do not salute noncommissioned officers. All of this may be explained to us verbally. However, if we observe the self-contained world of a military base, we can begin to note patterns of behavior and to define what the rules are simply on the basis of activity. The same applies to the system we observe at work in P. Although the patterns of relationships are not set forth in explicit instructions, the principles that govern those relationships may be accurately deduced from the pattern of behavior. As Jay stresses, the relationship of sign to what is signified is clear in cases where the sign is an index. This is so because "the relationship of sign to signified is not conventional." Therefore, "indices can be understood across cultural and linguistic boundaries. They *indicate* their object rather than represent it."[90] Thus, while the *meaning* of blood, understood as a symbol, is not apparent simply by observing it, the meaning of blood as an index is immediately evident to the observer who watches for patterns of existential relationship that are marked, indexed, by the handling of the blood.

Because I discussed the hand-pressing gesture earlier, I address here its indexing quality and its relationship, in these terms, to the blood rite. The hand-pressing indexes a relationship between offerer and animal. It is the one who offers the animal who presses his hand on its head. With this relationship indexed, the immediately following slaughter may be indexed backward to the offerer. The slaughter of the animal in the cultic setting is somehow related to the person of the offerer. There is an indexed relationship between the offerer and the animal that is slaughtered. The slaughter makes the blood available. The blood manipulation follows. At a basic level, it indexes a relationship between the blood and the altar. The indexed relationship between offerer and animal is then mediated forward to the altar and backward to the offerer through the blood. That is, the application of blood to the altar indexes a relationship between the offerer and the altar, a relationship mediated by the animal and its blood.

When we move from simple observation of activity within the world of the text to the explicit conventional articulations about what is happening in this world, we are able to develop a fuller understanding of what transpires in the ritual activity we have witnessed. The altar is a locus of the divine presence. The application of blood to it has indexed a relationship between the offerer and the altar. This relationship between offerer and altar must involve a relationship between the deity whose altar it is and the offerer. Thus, apart from any explicit theorizing about what is achieved by the application of blood from the burnt offering to the altar, we can identify an existential linkage, an indexing of a relationship, achieved through the gesture. The offerer, whose relationship with the animal was indexed by the hand-pressing gesture, is linked to the altar, and to Yahweh, whose presence is manifested at the altar, by the transfer of the animal's blood to the altar. This is true whether the blood conveys the worshiper's life to Yahweh, whether it serves the purpose of warding off Yahweh's lethal wrath as a substitute for the worshiper's life, or whether it is simply the animal's life being restored to Yahweh before the animal's flesh is offered as the worshiper's gift. Through the blood rite, the offerer is connected in some fashion with Yahweh. This connection is reinforced by the subsequent offering of the animal's flesh in the altar fire. However, the first index of the relationship is the blood manipulation.

Because the blood manipulation is carried out by the priests, it also serves to index their relationship to the altar. The priests mediate the offerer's access. The offerer is indexed to the animal by the hand-pressing gesture. The blood comes from this animal and is handled by the priests. Thus, we have a triangular relationship established between the offer, the altar (Yahweh), and the priests. This relationship is established by the blood manipulation. The subsequent burning of the animal's body reinforces the relationship.

Conclusions

Although only a handful of texts prescribes or describes the manipulation of the blood from a burnt offering animal or bird, there is nevertheless sufficient textual data from which to construct an image of living practice in the textual world. In the case of quadrupeds offered as burnt offerings, the represented action involves slaughter of the animal, transfer of blood from the place of slaughter to the altar (which assumes its prior collection), and the tossing of the blood against the four sides of the altar. The blood is applied to the altar in its fresh, liquid state. The blood manipulation precedes any other priestly action at the altar. The represented procedure for the offering of a bird as a burnt offering differs from that for a quadruped. The first priestly duty is conveying the bird to the altar, where the priest kills it and drains out its blood against one side of the altar. Consequently, unlike in the case of the quadruped, the blood manipulation cannot be the first altar rite. Nevertheless, this variation indicates an underlying principle—only priests ("the sons of Aaron") have access to the altar, and only they may perform ritual actions there.

The blood manipulation in the burnt offering ritual complex is never explicitly interpreted in any of the P texts where it is prescribed. A survey of scholarly efforts to explain the manipulation reveals the extent to which such explanations rely upon prior identifications of the nature and function of the burnt offering, and upon the particular use of Lev 17:11 as a key to understanding blood manipulation in the cult. The "meaning" of the manipulation is not inherent in the action itself. It must be constructed by scholars. It is clear that no firm conclusion can be reached without careful analysis of Lev 17:11 and of the various attempts that have been made to explain it.

As an alternative to the exclusive quest to identify symbolic "meanings" or instrumental effects of the act of dashing blood on the altar, I have proposed looking at the rite as an indexing sign that points to existential relationships within the cultic sphere. Specifically, I noted how the blood manipulation serves to distinguish between the realm of responsibility of the priesthood and that of the laity in the MT version of the Priestly texts. I also noted that the blood indexes a three-way relationship between priests, lay offerers, and Yahweh, joined at the nexus of the altar. Of particular importance is the relationship between the offerer and Yahweh, first indexed through the manipulation of blood, and then reindexed through the offering of the animal's body in the altar fire. This relationship is mediated by the priests, whose special access to the altar, the locus of contact with Yahweh, is indexed by their act of conveying blood to the altar and manipulating it there in each enactment of the ritual complex for the burnt offering of a quadruped. Status within the priesthood is indexed through blood manipulation at the inaugural ritual complex for the cult as it is represented in Leviticus 9. There, Aaron's sons perform the subordinate task of making blood available to their father, while Aaron carries out the primary priestly duty in a sacrificial complex, the application of the blood to the altar. This distinction indexes Aaron's higher status relative to his sons.

It is certainly legitimate and desirable for scholars to engage in conceptual reflection on possible symbolic meanings or instrumental effects of a ritual action such as blood manipulation and to seek to recover a public or official "native" interpretation. However, a singular focus on such a project, especially in the absence of clear textual data, leaves much ground unexplored. The virtue of the alternative approach that I have developed in this chapter is that it focuses on the *activity* of ritual, which is a focus of the texts themselves. By focusing on praxis, we are able to bring to light the ways in which blood manipulation functions to index and thereby to create, and to reinforce, relationships and status identity within the cultural sphere. Recognizing these functions represents a definite advance in our understanding of the workings of cultic blood manipulation as ritualized activity.

Blood Manipulation in the Sacrifice of Well-Being, the Ordination Offering, and the Reparation Offering

In Priestly texts, three sacrificial complexes—the sacrifice of well-being (*zebaḥ šĕlāmîm*),[1] the ordination ram (*'êl hammillu'îm*), and the reparation offering (*'āšām*)[2]—have in common the manipulation of dashing or tossing (*zrq*) the animal's blood onto the altar and the fact that most of the flesh is eaten rather than burned on the altar. The discussion of these three sacrifices, follows on my treatment of blood tossing in the preceding chapter and develops the major points raised there. I give further attention to the purposes or effects that can be attributed to the gesture of tossing blood and also continue to explore how blood manipulation activity indexes relations and status within the cultic sphere.

In addition to the tossing of the blood onto the altar, P texts represent other forms of manipulation using the blood of the ram of ordination and, in one instance, the reparation offering. Treating these manipulations in this chapter, I again ask two basic questions: what meaning or instrumental effect might be attributed to these blood-tossing manipulations; and what kinds of relations and status are indexed by these uses of the blood of sacrificial animals?

The Sacrifice of Well-Being

Leviticus 3 provides the basic instructions for the sacrifice of well-being, while supplementary instructions in Leviticus 7 indicate some differences between the subtypes of the sacrifice in the course of prescribing what is to be done with the flesh. The "ordination ram" (Exod 29:19–33; Lev 8:22–31), offered as part of the ritual complex for the consecration of Aaron and his sons as priests, should be treated with the sacrifice of well-being, since it is represented in Exod 29:28 as the paradigm for the distribution of priestly prebends from the well-being sacrifices of the Israelites. Like the blood of the well-being sacrifice, the blood of the ordination ram is tossed onto the altar (Exod 29:20; Lev 8:24).[3]

According to Leviticus 3, a herd animal, a sheep, or a goat may be offered as a sacrifice of well-being. A complete set of prescriptions is presented for each of the three types of animal. Sheep and goats are distinguished because the sheep envisaged by the laws have a "broad tail," which is burned on the altar along with other fat portions, and this fact must be noted in the instructions.[4] The three units present a common ritual procedure. In each case, the ritual begins with the offerer bringing the animal to the shrine complex, "before Yahweh" (Lev 3:1, 7, 12). The offerer first presses a hand on the head of the offering and then slaughters the animal (3:2, 8, 13). As in Leviticus 1, the verb is third-person, masculine singular in each unit, and the subject is most reasonably identified as the offerer. The Greek translation has a singular verb in verses 2 and 8, in line with MT, but a plural in verse 13, in line with its renderings in Lev 1:5, 11. It is difficult to account for this inconsistent use of a singular verb in two verses and a plural in the third.

The blood manipulation follows immediately on the slaughter. As in Leviticus 1, the priests appear for the first time at this juncture and are explicitly identified as the subjects of the activity. The blood manipulation is identical to that for the burnt offering. The priests toss the blood "on the altar round about" (*'al-hammizbēaḥ sābîb*). A number of scholars base their explanations of the blood manipulation on the assumption that identity of form reflects identity of "meaning" or effect. Thus, they attribute the same meaning or effect to the blood rite of the well-being sacrifice as they attribute to the same rite in the case of the burnt offering.[5] This logical approach is supported by an analysis based on considering the indexing quality of the action. Because the blood manipulation in the sacrifice of well-being is identical to the burnt offering blood manipulation, it indexes the same kinds of sociocultic relationships as the latter manipulation. Furthermore, we may suggest that the identity of ritual procedure is an index pointing to some sort of basic connection between the two offerings. This having been noted, we must still recognize that the blood manipulation in the well-being sacrifice is given no explicit interpretation by P, and it is at least a possibility that the blood manipulations in the burnt offering and well-being sacrifice—although identical in form— could be explained differently in terms of the meanings or effects attributed to them.[6]

It is not only the blood manipulation that the burnt offering and well-being sacrifice have in common. The other procedures for the two offerings are basically the same until after the blood manipulation, when attention turns to the carcass.[7] Within the world of the text, as we observe the initial ritual procedures being carried out, we are provided few clues that would help us to determine which sacrificial complex is being executed. Only the sex of the animal gives some hint. We know that a female animal cannot be brought as a burnt offering.

Following the blood manipulation, attention turns to the carcass of the animal. At this juncture we can clearly distinguish the well-being sacrifice from the burnt offering. The carcass of the well-being sacrifice is not divided into pieces and burned on the altar. Rather, portions of fat from the internal cavity, some internal organs (the kidneys and the caudate lobe of the liver), and, in the case of a sheep, the broad tail are removed from the animal and offered (vv. 3–4, 9–10, 14–15).[8] The removal and offering of these portions is the task of the offerer. The verb is in the singular, and no specific subject is identified. Because the priests have been explicitly mentioned in the plural in the preceding sentence, it does not seem that a priest should be identified as the subject here. As I affirmed in the previous chapter, this usage of a singular verb without specification of a subject indicates activity that may be performed by a nonpriest.[9] The selected portions are designated "a food gift for Yahweh" (vv. 3, 9, 14; cf. 7:30)[10] and are turned into smoke on the altar by the priests (vv. 5, 11, 16; cf. 7:31). These burned portions are identified explicitly as "food" (*leḥem*) (vv. 11 and 16), and burning them produces a "soothing odor" (vv. 5 and 16).

Thus, one part of the ritual complex is interpreted for us, and another is left without explanation. We are not told why the blood is tossed onto the altar. However, we know that the fat portions are an offering, that they are "food," and that their burning produces a "soothing odor." It seems clear, moreover, that the interpretation of the treatment of the fat portions cannot be applied to the blood manipulation. The blood dashed on the altar is distinct from the fat and organs. It is not designated as "food gift." The extraction of the "food gift" takes place after the blood dashing.

These observations require us to return to the question of the place of the blood manipulation in the execution of the burnt offering. In Leviticus 1, the burning of the whole body is termed "a food gift of soothing odor for Yahweh" (Lev 1:9, 13, 17). In each instance, this declaration about the significance of the burning is preceded by the notice, "it is a burnt offering," which seems to explain the fact that the whole carcass is burned. In turn, the declaration about the significance of the burning serves to characterize the essential significance of the burnt offering. What matters, what constitutes a burnt offering as such, is the burning of the carcass on the altar. The burning makes of the carcass "a food gift of soothing odor for Yahweh." In the light of this fact, the blood manipulation appears to play a subordinate role. It is carried out preliminary to the actions that constitute the essential core of the ritual complex. The same is true for the well-being sacrifice, which differs from the burnt offering only in the smaller size of the "food gift" that is offered. In both cases, the blood is distinct from the "food gift." It is not burned and, consequently, does not produce a soothing odor. It does not serve to define the well-being offering as such.

In Leviticus 3, neither of the terms "food gift" or "offering" is used to characterize the blood. Furthermore, unlike in Leviticus 1, the root *qrb* never appears in connection with the blood. In Leviticus 1, it appears once, in the prescriptions for the offering of a herd animal. The priests are to "offer" the blood. In Leviticus 3, the root is used of activity of the offerer. There is a distinction evident here. The offerer does not "offer" the blood—the priests dash it on the altar—but he does offer the fat portions. In Leviticus 1, however, the clean distinction is not maintained. There, the priests "offer" both the blood and the whole animal. It is much easier to draw careful distinctions on the basis of the formulation of the prescriptions in Leviticus 3 than on the basis of those in Leviticus 1. Still, overall, it appears that the blood is not part of the offerer's offering. It is taken by the priests when the offerer slaughters the animal. The priests exercise proprietary control over the blood.

We must consider whether the conclusions drawn here can help us to understand the significance of the blood manipulation, first in the case of the well-being sacrifice, and then in the case of the burnt offering. I suggested, in my treatment of the burnt offering, that the identification of the blood as an offering was uncertain but possible. In the case of the well-being offering, however, the possibility that the blood constitutes an offering in any way like the fat seems unlikely. It is not treated by the text as if the offerer has any proprietary claim on it. Does this fact require us to understand the blood of the burnt offering in the same way? This is a reasonable conclusion. The same blood manipulation appears in the two offerings, linking them at the beginning of their execution. Furthermore, although the two offerings differ in the actual treatment of the animal's carcass, the text provides the same explanation for the actions of placing the whole carcass or the fat parts into the altar fire. Thus, the suggestion that the blood constituted some sort of offering cannot be sustained. It is not simply a matter of an argument from silence, that the blood is never called an offering. It is also the fact that the relationship of the offerer to the blood is different. In the representations of the texts, he has nothing to do with the blood, except that he lets it flow when he cuts the animal's throat. The blood is then taken away by the priests. In contrast, the offerer dismembers the burnt offering animal and washes those portions that require washing, and it is prescribed that he "offer" the fat portions extracted from the well-being sacrifice.

If, then, we set aside the possibility that the blood is an element of the offering, we are left with two broad categories of alternatives. We may understand the dashing of the blood as a mode of sacral disposal. The blood is dashed on the altar in order both to remove it from the possibility of human consumption and to return it, as the medium of life, to Yahweh, the source of life. We may assume that performance of the rite has benefits for the offerer and the priests, but these would only be the general rewards attendant on obedient performance of Yahweh's commands. Other interpreters, however, suggest that more specific benefits stem from the blood rite. For Rudolf Schmid, the key to understanding the blood manipulation for the well-being sacrifice is provided by Exod 24:3–8.[11] Schmid asserts that Lev 17:11 should not be used to explain the significance of the blood manipulation of the well-being sacrifice, and that the blood manipulation should not, therefore, be understood to have an expiatory effect. There are, he maintains, two alternative ways of understanding blood manipulation: first, since blood is life, it belongs to God and must be returned to him; second, blood can effect a covenantal bond that corresponds to blood kinship. Schmid points to Exod 24:6–8 as providing an example of the use of the blood of the well-being sacrifice to effect such a bond and suggests that this text be employed to illuminate the significance of the blood manipulation for the well-being sacrifice in Leviticus 3.

Baruch Levine notes that Schmid's treatment of the blood ritual represented in Exod 24:6–8 as "the paradigm for the use of blood in sacrifices" follows from William Robertson Smith's interpretation of the role of sacrifice in covenant making.[12] Levine's critique of Schmid's position is rooted in this recognition of its connection to Robertson Smith's explanation of the relationship between sacrifice and covenant making. Levine emphasizes that, in the covenant-making context, blood is applied to both parties, the people and Yahweh (represented by the altar), whereas in the normal sacrificial ritual blood is applied only to the altar. In Levine's view, "the activity at Sinai represents a different phenomenon from sacrifice as such, and the blood had a different function."[13] Levine's emphasis on the different forms of the ritual is a particularly strong point against Schmid's interpretation. As I noted in chapter 2, the application of blood to *both* the altar and the people indexes a bond between the covenant parties. In Leviticus 3, since blood is not applied to the offerer, an index of this type is absent.

Further criticisms of Schmid's interpretation may be adduced. First, it should be noted that Exod 24:3–8 is not a P text. P assumes a very different conception of covenant. Since P insists that there was no sacrificial cult until the Tabernacle and its appurtenances had been constructed and consecrated, and Aaron and his sons had been ordained as priests, it is unlikely that P would have assumed a sacrificially constituted covenant. Second, it is methodologically problematic to refer to the representation of an uninterpreted ritual in one source in order to explain an uninterpreted ritual in another. Finally, since the blood manipulation of the well-being sacrifice is identical to that of the burnt offering, we may question whether a different significance should be attributed to the act of blood manipulation in the case of the well-being sacrifice than is attributed to it in the case of the burnt offering. As I noted in chapter 2, the mixed blood of both burnt offerings and well-being sacrifices is applied to the altar and the people in Exod 24:3–8. Thus, if the manipulation of the blood of the well-being sacrifice is to be understood to renew the covenant bond, the same interpretation should be applied to the manipulation of the blood of the burnt offering. However, Schmid rejects this conclusion. Given this range of objections, Schmid's theory must be rejected.

For other interpreters, probably the majority, Lev 17:11 plays a key role in the formulation of their explanations. Levine attributes the same significance to the tossing of blood in both the burnt offering and the well-being sacrifice, arguing that "the blood libation" served in every case to ward off Yahweh's wrath. Yahweh accepted the blood in lieu of human life whenever human beings entered his realm. The blood protected human beings from the danger attendant on the entry of the profane and potentially unclean into the realm of the utterly holy and utterly pure.

While Levine understands Lev 17:11 to employ *kipper* with a distinct meaning ("ransom"), and to apply only to the tossing of blood on the altar, a number of interpreters understand the verse to refer to the blood manipulations in all sacrificial complexes—including that of the well-being sacrifice—and to attribute to them a common expiatory function. From this understanding, it follows that sin and impurity are in view when the well-being sacrifice is offered, even if only in a quite general way. For example, J. H. Kurtz, making the case for the expiatory character of the well-being sacrifice, writes, "The question is settled already in Lev. xvii. 11. If all blood placed upon the altar was atoning blood, this must have applied to the blood of the peace-offering also."[14] David Hoffmann, likewise, maintains that the blood rite is expiatory in a general sense and is observed because a worshiper *always* becomes conscious of his sinfulness when he stands in the presence of Yahweh.[15] Noting that the offerer feasts on the well-being sacrifice as a guest at Yahweh's table, Hoffmann asserts that the offerer enters Yahweh's presence with a sense of his unworthiness to enjoy such a benefit. As he does in the case of the burnt offering, Hoffmann understands the hand-pressing gesture to effect a symbolic identification of the offerer with the offering, so that it may take his place. The subsequent blood manipulation is, like all blood manipulations, an expiatory act. Hoffmann justifies his attribution of an expiatory effect to the blood manipulation in the well-being sacrifice by appealing to Lev 17:11, which he understands to declare that *all* sacrificial blood effects expiation.[16] As I noted in chapter 3, Hoffmann explains that the blood manipulation covers sin and impurity because God accepts the self-surrender of the offerer's life and soul symbolized by the offering of the blood. According to Hoffmann, "atonement" is an essentially positive process, wherein the offerer enters into communion with God through the symbolic medium of the blood.

Jacob Milgrom also posits that the blood manipulation in the case of the well-being offering makes possible the joyful feasting that follows it and roots his thesis in an interpretation of Lev 17:11. Unlike the other interpreters, however, Milgrom offers a very specific explanation of what the blood manipulation does and denies that it has to do with sin and impurity in general. According to Milgrom, the blood manipulation legitimizes the killing of the animal. More specifically, the killing of the animal is an offense against Yahweh, the source and guardian of life. It would be counted as murder if the blood was not given to Yahweh as a ransom for the life of the one who slaughtered the animal.[17] Like the other explanations of the blood manipulation, the ultimate validity of Milgrom's thesis rests on his interpretation of Lev 17:11, which is evaluated fully in chapter 7. Nevertheless, some preliminary matters can be addressed at this point.

Milgrom maintains that P's prescriptions concerning the well-being sacrifice serve to emphasize the blood manipulation, allowing us to identify it as the "quintessential element," which is of "quintessential significance" within the ritual complex.[18] In Leviticus 6–7, priestly prebends are distributed according to tasks performed by priests. The hide of the burnt offering goes to the priest "who offers a man's burnt offering" (7:8). The extracted portion of a cereal offering also goes "to the priest who offers it" (7:9). The flesh of the reparation offering goes to the priest "who shall effect removal with it" (*'ăšer yěkapper bô*) (7:7). The flesh of the *ḥaṭṭā't* goes to the priest "who offers it as a *ḥaṭṭā't*" (*haměḥaṭṭē' 'ōtāh*) (6:19).[19] Only in the case of the well-being sacrifice do we find explicit mention of blood manipulation in connection with the distribution of prebends.

Leviticus 7:14 indicates that one of each type of bread brought with the well-being sacrifice offered for thanksgiving (*tôdâ*) goes "to the priest who tosses [*hazzōrēq*] the blood of the well-being offering [*dam haššělāmîm*]." Milgrom asserts that the use of the expression "the blood of the well-being offering," and the omission of "thanksgiving," "is no accident; its intention is to apply this rule to every well-being offering."[20] How Milgrom is able to deduce the "intention" of the textual formulation is unclear. Apparently, he believes that intention is inherent in the text itself and can be deduced by a careful reading. Here, Milgrom seems to be applying a classic principle of rabbinic midrash: linguistic variations carry significant meaning. However, the problem with the application of this approach here is that it ignores the overall context. It is true that 7:14 refers to the priest who tosses "the blood of the well-being offering" rather than "the blood of the thanksgiving offering." However, the prebend, which is assigned to this priest, is derived from the bread offering that specifically accompanies the thanksgiving offering (7:12–13). According to the context, the prescription in verse 14 can only be observed when the prebend exists to be given. There is no mandatory bread offering to give to a priest in any other type of well-being sacrifice, as Milgrom himself notes.[21] In addition, the verse that immediately follows (v. 15) spells out rules for the consumption of the flesh of the thanksgiving well-being sacrifice, further emphasizing that the prescriptions about the blood manipulation refer to the blood of the "thanksgiving." It follows, therefore, that verse 14 cannot refer to all well-being sacrifices.

Leviticus 7:33 also deals with the distribution of prebends.[22] In this case, the context is a set of general prescriptions about the division of the carcass into portions to be offered on the altar, given to priests, and consumed by the offerer. Two portions of flesh—the breast and the right shoulder—are designated as priestly prebends. The breast goes "to Aaron and to his sons," that is, to all members of the Aaronid priesthood (v. 31). In contrast, the right shoulder, taken from all well-being sacrifices (v. 32), goes to the priest "who offers the blood of the well-being offering and the fat" (*hammaqrîb 'et-dam haššĕlā-mîm wĕ'et-haḥēleb*) (v. 33). In citing this verse as evidence for his position on the quintessential character of the blood, Milgrom omits the reference to fat.[23] This omission seriously distorts the evidence. Whereas Milgrom asserts, "Only in the case of the well-being offering . . . is the rite with the blood singled out,"[24] the fact is that only in the case of the well-being sacrifice is the offering of the fat also emphasized. Leviticus 7:33 indicates both priestly duties—the tossing of the blood and the burning of the fat—listing them in the order of their execution.[25] The implication is that a single priest carries out both tasks. Thus, the shoulder prebend goes to the priest who carries out the priestly altar rites.

It is true that the blood manipulation is emphasized in these verses (7:14, 33) in a way that it is not in other contexts. However, the burning of fat is also emphasized (in 7:33). Thus, we need to ask why the specific acts were emphasized in the case of the well-being sacrifice, while in other cases a more general characterization of the ritual activity was employed. As I have noted, Milgrom does attempt to explain the emphasis on the blood. He argues that the offering of the blood is of quintessential significance because it ransoms the life of the offerer, who would otherwise be liable for having taken the animal's life. However, Milgrom's explanation does not follow from the P texts we have examined here but rather from his interpretation of Lev 17:11. Without Lev 17:11, Milgrom could only assert that the Priestly texts emphasize the blood manipulation. The fact of emphasis, however, does not amount to an explanation of the significance of the rite.

I return to Milgrom's interpretation of Lev 17:11 in chapter 7. At this juncture, I consider how we might explain the emphasis on the blood of the well-being sacrifice in Lev 7:14 and 7:33 without recourse to Lev 17:11. First, I note that Lev 7:33 refers to both the blood *and* the fat. In the overall structure of the well-being sacrifice ritual complex, the two acts—dashing blood and burning fat—are the altar rites. They define the priestly role in the complex. But why would the text not simply refer to "the priest who offers the well-being sacrifice," just as it refers to "the priest who offers a man's burnt offering" (Lev 7:8)? The answer seems to be that the whole well-being sacrifice cannot be the object of the verb "offer" as the whole burnt offering animal can be. In the case of the well-being sacrifice, there is a clear distinction between what is taken from the well-being sacrifice as an offering and what remains (Lev 3:3, 9, 14; 7:29).

There is an apparent problem, however, with this explanation. The "reparation offering" (*'āšām*) and the "sin offering" or "purification offering" (*ḥaṭṭā't*), like the well-being sacrifice, are subdivided into parts that go to the altar and parts that are eaten. Yet, in describing what happens to the flesh, verbs are used with the whole animal as subject, as if even the eaten parts were subject to the ritual activity. This problem can be resolved. In the case of the two expiatory sacrifices—as with the burnt offering—the whole animal is devoted to the cultic realm. It is designated "most holy." Thus, even though the flesh is eaten by the priests, this flesh is like the burnt offering flesh. It follows that the verbal formulations employed with the three "most holy" offerings reflect their common quality, while the careful distinction drawn in the case of the well-being sacrifice reflects the significant distinction between those portions handled by the priests and offered on the altar, and those portions that do not belong to the cultic realm. In other words, the emphasis on the blood and fat is a reflex of the distinction between the well-being sacrifice as a whole and those portions extracted from it as altar offerings. In the case of no other offering is this distinction as significant as it is in this offering, for in no other offering can a lay person take part of the animal out of the cultic realm and consume it. None of this explains why the blood is dashed on the altar, of course. It does suggest, however, that Milgrom is finding a special emphasis on the blood that is simply not present in the texts we have examined.

I turn now from prescriptive texts to the single description in P of the execution of a well-being sacrifice. This description appears in the account of Aaron's first liturgical activity at the Tent of Meeting (Lev 9). The text prescribes that the people are to provide an ox and a ram "as a well-being (offering) to sacrifice before Yahweh" (*lišĕlāmîm lizbōaḥ lipnê yhwh*) (9:4). These animals are offered after Aaron has offered all the other animal offerings of the day. Aaron's activity is described in 9:18–21: "Then the ox and ram were slaughtered [*wayyišḥaṭ*] as the well-being sacrifice which belonged to the people. The sons of Aaron conveyed the blood to him, and he dashed it on the altar round about. As for the fat from the ox and from the ram, the fat tail, the covering [fat], and the kidneys, and the lobe of the liver, they [the sons of Aaron] set the fat upon the breasts, and then he [Aaron] turned the fat into smoke on the altar. As for the breasts and the right shoulder, Aaron elevated [them] as an elevation offering before Yahweh, just as Moses commanded."

As in the account of Aaron's performance of the rites for the burnt offering, this account spells out a division of labor. The slaughter is indicated generally. For this reason, I have translated *wayyišḥaṭ* with a passive formulation. Aaron may be the subject of the verb, but the actual actor in this case seems unimportant. After the slaughter, Aaron's sons convey the blood to him (cf. 9:12), and Aaron dashes the blood on the altar in the manner prescribed in Leviticus 3. Afterward, the sons of Aaron prepare the fat portions and the prebend pieces, and Aaron turns the fat into smoke and then performs the elevation ritual.[26]

In this description, as in the description of the burnt offering, there are two fundamental acts: the blood manipulation and the burning on the altar. In both descriptions, the burning rite is given as much attention as the blood rite. Thus, we find the same emphases here as in Lev 7:33. The blood manipulation and the burning of fat together constitute the essential priestly rites. As in Leviticus 3, the consumption of the flesh by the offerers is not even mentioned. The emphasis is on the shrine rituals, and on the priestly functionaries who carry these out. Indeed, except for the notice in verse 18 that the well-being sacrifice belongs to the people, they play no role in the ritual. The hand-pressing, the one crucial lay act, is not even mentioned. Thus, when we reflect on how the ritual acts serve as indexes, we find relationships indexed only between the priesthood and the altar, and within the priesthood itself. The relationship of the lay offerers to the offering, to the altar, to Yahweh, and to the priesthood is hardly indexed at all in the ritual represented here. In this representation of the inaugural priestly service, the emphasis is placed firmly on the activities of the priests and on identifying status distinctions within the priesthood.

The indexing accomplished in the rituals begins with the blood manipulation. Aaron's sons convey the blood to him, an act that points to a connection between Aaron and his sons. Aaron then dashes the blood on the altar, which serves to index a relationship between Aaron and the altar. His sons' relationship to the altar is mediated through Aaron's action. To the extent that the conveying of the blood can clearly be identified as an act subordinate to the tossing of the blood, we can identify a status distinction enacted by the distinction in ritual duties. Within the world of the text it is easy to see that the altar is special and that access to the altar indicates special status. Thus, it follows that Aaron's immediate connection with the altar, enacted by the blood dashing, indicates his higher status relative to that of his sons. This status distinction is then carried through in the rest of the ritual. Aaron's sons perform the subordinate rite of preparing the fat pieces and prebend portions, whereas Aaron burns the fat on the altar and conducts the elevation rite.[27] The lay Israelites, as I noted, play no role in the ritual complex. Their lack of cultic status is strikingly indexed by their absence from the representation of ritual activity.

The Ram of Ordination

Two texts deal with the ceremonial complex for the ordination of Aaron and his sons as priests, Exodus 29 and Leviticus 8. There is clearly a close relationship between the two texts, and it is most likely that Leviticus 8 was composed in the light of Exodus 29 to explain, amplify, and clarify the latter passage.[28] It remains an open question, however, whether the two texts come from the same tradent(s) and should be taken simply as two parts of a single composition, or whether Exodus 29 was composed and transmitted independently and then subjected to interpretation by the author(s) of Leviticus 8.[29] For this reason, I treat the two texts together as accounts of a single sacrificial complex but also note where they seem to differ in emphasis and perspective.

According to Exodus 29 and Leviticus 8, among the animals to be collected for the rituals for the ordination of Aaron and his sons, there was to be a ram, designated "the ram of filling" ("ram of ordination"; *'êl hammillû'îm*) (Exod 29:22, 26; Lev 8:22, 29).[30] In the representations we find in Exodus 29 and Leviticus 8, after the ordination ram is slaughtered, Moses takes some of its blood and daubs (*ntn*) it onto the right earlobes, the right thumbs, and the right big toes of Aaron and his sons. Moses then tosses the rest of the blood "onto the altar round about" in the same manner as the blood from the preceding burnt offering and the well-being offering was tossed (Exod 29:20; Lev 8:23–24).

Again, we are confronted with an uninterpreted ritual action. The texts do not tell us what effect this act achieves, or if it has some symbolic significance. Scholars have, of course, attempted to determine the "meaning."[31] According to some interpreters, the daubing of blood on the earlobe dedicates the ear to hear Yahweh's instructions, while the applications to the thumb and big toe dedicate the hand and the foot to carry out those instructions.[32] In this interpretation, the daubed parts of the body are selected because of their functional significance. The identification of functional significance is brought by the reader from outside the text but is assumed to be the implicit conceptual basis for the selection of the ear, thumb, and big toe as the objects of the application of blood. Furthermore, the identification of the blood as an agent of consecration must be supplied by the reader.

Cornelis Houtman understands the blood manipulation to be a rite of consecration but offers a different explanation of why the blood is applied to the ear, thumb, and big toe. He sees the process of application from earlobe to big toe as effecting a "top-to-bottom" sanctification. Thus, the organs are not selected on the basis of their functional significance but due to their anatomical location. They represent the top, middle, and bottom of the body, and the blood daubing effects a complete consecration.[33] According to Houtman, this explanation also applies to the nearly identical rite performed for the person healed of a skin disease (Lev 14:14, 25). Houtman maintains that the two rites must have the same meaning or effect and that the idea of consecration to obedient action would not make sense for the latter ritual. As I have noted, however, it remains an open question whether identity of form indicates identity of "meaning."[34]

Ibn Ezra explains the daubing of the blood by referring to Lev 17:11 and the conceptual identification of blood with life. Commenting on Lev 8:23, he explains that "the blood effects a ransom [*ykpr*][35] for Aaron's life." He then cites the final clause of Lev 17:11 (for the blood effects ransom by means of the life) and explains that the clause means that the blood effects a ransom by means of the life contained in it, "life in place of life." Then, strikingly, he cites Exod 4:25, which refers to Zipporah touching her son's foreskin to Moses' feet. Ibn Ezra evidently believes the blood applied to Aaron has an apotropaic effect. Just as the blood of the foreskin applied to Moses' feet protected him, so the blood applied to Aaron's body protects him from harm, the life of the animal taking the place of Aaron's life. Ibn Ezra's explanation rests on a basic understanding that conceptual gaps can be filled with information drawn from other biblical textual contexts.

Jacob Milgrom approaches the question by looking to two sources for help in explaining the ritual action. He first notes examples of ritual daubing in ancient Near Eastern literature, especially Hittite texts. The purpose of these rites is "purificatory and apotropaic: to wipe off and ward off the incursions of menacing demonic forces. Always it is the *vulnerable* parts of bodies (extremities) and structures (corners, entrances) that are smeared with magical substances."[36] Having suggested that the Israelite rite be interpreted in the light of its wider cultural context, Milgrom then turns to the evidence provided by another Israelite source, the account of the dedication of Ezekiel's altar (Ezek 43:20) (see chapter 6 for further discussion). In the ritual represented in Ezekiel, blood from a *ḥaṭṭāʾt* is daubed on the horns of the altar, as well as on other projections. According to Milgrom, "These points correspond to a person's earlobe, thumb, and big toe. It is safe then to conclude that these two congruent rites share the same purpose, which in the case of Ezekiel's altar is made explicit."[37] According to Ezek 43:20, by means of this ritual action "you shall purify it and effect removal to it" (*wĕḥiṭṭēʾtā ʾôtô wĕkippartāhû*) (see also Ezek 43:26). Milgrom concludes that the same goal must be in view in the case of the priests: the blood manipulation purifies them.[38]

Milgrom's approach is based on seeking analogous rituals to which explicit interpretations are attached and applying the explanations given for them to the unexplained ritual. This approach has a great deal of logical force behind it. Furthermore, it allows us to adopt something that can be represented as a "native" explanation. Yet, there are also problems with the approach. First, one must assume that ritual actions have or require a "meaning." Second, one must assume that the same action always means the same thing to those who perform it or who observe it being performed. Third, one must assume that the search for an "official" or "public" explanation of a ritual action is our primary responsibility. All of these assumptions may be questioned.

The very fact that the ritual action is not explained by our source should give us pause. As I have noted, P seems remarkably unconcerned with explaining or interpreting ritual actions. P's concern is with the actual execution of the rites, which is typical of ritual specialists in a variety of cultures, for whom it is the correct performance of the rite itself that is "meaningful." The very success of the execution serves to enact the order and structure to which the ritual complex is directed. Thus, we may ask if we are doing justice to the concerns of the tradents who produced the texts when we seek to explain a ritual act, when they themselves seem minimally interested in such explanation.

Furthermore, we may question whether the use of analogical reasoning and comparison can truly provide access to an explanation. While it is certainly possible, and even probable, that the same action is expected to have the same effect when executed in different contexts, a hint of doubt must remain. We may also note that the ritual represented by Ezekiel is not strictly identical to that represented in Exodus 29 and Leviticus 8. In one instance an altar is daubed with blood from a *ḥaṭṭā't*, whereas in the other people are daubed with blood from a "ram of ordination." Milgrom recognizes the problem here and addresses possible objections. He explains why the source of the blood is not the same by noting that P does not allow for the possibility that *ḥaṭṭā't* blood could be used to purify people.[39] It follows, argues Milgrom, that another sacrifice must provide blood for the purification of human beings. In this connection, he notes that the identical ritual action is employed in the rites for the purification of a person recovered from a skin disease. In this case, blood from a "reparation offering" is employed. Milgrom notes that the ritual seems to have the effect of "purgation" attributed to it (Lev 14:18, 29). This response, however, begs the question. The fact is that blood from two different sacrifices is employed in an identical manner. Blood from yet a third is employed in an analogous fashion in a text from another tradition. Does not the fact that different sacrifices are involved allow some question to be raised about the alleged common meaning of the rite? Might not the different qualities of the different sacrificial offerings have an impact on the quality and significance of the blood manipulations? Does blood from a reparation offering do the same thing that blood from an "ordination ram" does? The unstated assumptions behind Milgrom's argument seem to be that blood is a univalent ritual material and that the source of the blood is immaterial. Yet Milgrom argues that different applications define different functions. It appears, then, that Milgrom privileges the manipulatory act in drawing distinctions, rather than the sacrificial complex in which it is situated. Although this choice may be valid, it is hardly necessary, as Milgrom himself concedes when he examines other blood manipulations. Sprinkling of blood, for example, need not have the same significance even when the blood is drawn from the same type of sacrifice. According to Milgrom, sprinkling of *ḥaṭṭā't* blood can either purgate or consecrate that upon which it is sprinkled. Indeed, Milgrom even argues that sprinkling can, in a unique instance—the "red cow" of Numbers 19—consecrate the blood rather than the thing toward which it is sprinkled.[40]

Finally, it must be stressed that an "official" or "public" explanation of a ritual action does not exhaust its significance within a culture. It is certainly legitimate to attempt to clarify how ritual specialists understand the ritual activities they perform. It is also worthwhile to examine what they tell non-specialists about the rituals, and how nonspecialists as a group articulate the meaning or significance of the acts they witness or in which they may be participants. However, "public" and "official" explanations are not all that we can find. Various individuals in a society may have their own idiosyncratic understandings of a ritual act. Indeed, even specialists may not be able to agree about what a ritual "means" or "does." Explanations of all types may be secondary to the ritual action itself. William Robertson Smith, for example, insisted that interpretation of ritual came after the emergence of ritual activity. The relationship between ritual, as action, and the explanation of ritual, the conceptual, is highly problematic, as Catherine Bell has demonstrated.[41]

Again, we may turn from the quest for "meaning" and "significance," in terms of either symbolism or instrumental effect, to consideration of the indexing quality of the action. If we examine the ritual action within its larger context, and attempt to visualize its enactment in the world of the text, a number of significant facts come into view. We may note, first, how the total ritual complex begins with a focus on Aaron and his sons. After the ritual elements have been gathered, Aaron and his sons are the objects of the first ritual activity. They are washed, dressed in special garments, and Aaron is anointed with oil. According to the representation of Leviticus 8, Aaron is anointed at the same time as the various sancta in the shrine complex, but his sons are not. This distinction serves both to index a special connection between Aaron and the shrine complex and to emphasize his difference from his sons, already indexed by the distinction in his garments. The focus then shifts from Aaron and his sons to the altar. Aaron and his sons continue to be significant to the ritual process, in that they press their hands on the heads of the sacrificial animals. Yet they are not the objects of ritual action for a considerable length of time within the framework of the ritual complex. First, a *ḥaṭṭā't* is offered, and one of the standard blood manipulations is performed. Next, a burnt offering is made. Again, the standard blood manipulation is carried out. Moses is the ritual actor, and his special status is indexed by his activity.

After these two sacrifices have been made, the ordination ram is presented. The rite begins as the others did, with the hand-pressing. This act serves to link the three sacrifices, and to indicate, as usual, the relationship between the offerers (Aaron and his sons, in this case) and the animal to be sacrificed. The animal is slaughtered. Then, at the moment of the blood manipulation, a dramatic variation from normal procedure occurs. If we view the liturgical performance as analogous to a dramatic performance, or if we think of the plot of a literary work, we may speak of a "plot twist." The "audience," like the audience of a play or the readers of a literary work, has been prepared to expect a particular course of events. The "plot twist" at this juncture serves to emphasize and highlight the action. The normal procedure, already encountered twice, is the application of blood to the altar. Instead of this, blood is applied to Aaron and his sons. They receive what we might expect the altar to receive. At a general level, the action points to a relationship between Aaron and his sons and the altar. To the extent that the altar is a locus where the presence of the deity is manifested, the blood manipulation also indicates a relationship between the Aaronids and Yahweh.[42]

More specifically, since the manipulation of which the Aaronids are the object bears a striking resemblance to the manipulation in the case of the *ḥaṭṭā't*, the action seems to index a connection with the altar as the recipient of the analogous ritual action. Obviously, we are close to Milgrom's argument about the meaning of the ritual action. However, I am approaching the issue from a different direction. Rather than seek for conceptual explanations outside the framework of the world of the text through the use of analogical reasoning, I am attempting to understand how observers of the ritual enactment within the world of the text might experience the indexing quality of the actions. As we observe the ritual enactments, we cannot help but see the similarity between the daubing of the horns of the altar and the daubing of the extremities of Aaron and his sons. If some sort of conceptual explanation is provided for either gesture, we may seek to explain the one by the other. In Exodus 29, no such conceptual explanation is provided. We are left with a sequence of unexplained ritual actions. In Leviticus 8, however, the daubing of blood on the altar is explained: the act purifies the altar (Lev 8:15). If we move further and inquire about the significance of this purification, we may understand that impurity offends the deity and provokes him to strike out at his people and vacate his dwelling place. If, then, we attempt to reason by analogy (within the world of the text), we may propose to understand the daubing of blood on the extremities of Aaron and his sons as achieving the same effect: the blood purifies Aaron and his sons, making contact with Yahweh and his sancta possible. I must emphasize, at this juncture, that this interpretation of the "meaning" of the ritual should be understood as "private." It is the individual observer who is left to draw the conclusion, since the text provides no hint of a public explanation of the ritual activity. Indeed, even if there were such a public explanation, articulated presumably by ritual specialists, this would not prevent individuals from forming their own opinions about the meaning of the rituals. Furthermore, it would not mean that the "public" or "official" meaning was the one I have suggested that the observer had constructed.

I have noted how the blood daubing serves to index a relationship between Aaron and his sons and the altar, especially as the altar is the recipient of the analogous blood manipulation in the case of the *ḥaṭṭā't*. We may also observe that Aaron is prioritized in the enactment of the ritual, just as he has been in the enactment of all other rituals. His special status is constantly being indexed and enacted by the priority he is given. In the representation of the text, he is daubed first. At the same time, however, a basic relationship is indexed between Aaron and his sons, in that they all receive the same treatment. The proper conclusion seems to be that Aaron is "first among equals."

The daubing also serves to index a sharp distinction between Aaron and his sons and all other Israelites, including Moses and other members of the tribe of Levi. This blood manipulation serves to further the "setting apart" of Aaron and his sons, already enacted by their ritualized transfer into sacred space, the ritualized bathing, their being clothed in special garments, and Aaron's anointing with oil. This fact is evident, even apart from the specific articulation that the rituals are directed at making Aaron and his sons "holy." We may conclude, therefore, that the blood daubing, apart from any specific "meaning" or "effect" attributed to it, plays a role in achieving the overall goal of the complex: the consecration—the setting apart—of Aaron and his sons as cultic specialists.

Furthermore, we may observe that this goal is related to the holy character of the altar. The blood daubing serves to enact the special proprietary status of the Aaronids in relation to the altar, a role we have seen indexed by other ritual acts, particularly those involving blood. This special relationship between the Aaronids and the altar is further emphasized by the ritual act that follows the blood daubing: the remainder of the blood is dashed on the altar. This action produces the situation that Aaron, his sons, and the altar share the blood of the single animal. The manipulation is, of course, not identical, but the indexing power of the action is still evident. One can fruitfully compare the indexing quality of the blood manipulations, in this context, with that of the blood manipulations in the covenant ceremony represented in Exod 24:3–8. In both cases, blood is applied to people and to an altar, indexing a relationship between the people and the altar.[43] However, whereas the altar in the covenant ceremony is apparently abandoned after serving its purpose, the altar in the ordination ceremony is the altar at which Aaron and his sons will serve in perpetuity. The relationship between them and this altar, first indexed by blood manipulation, will continually be reemphasized by their blood manipulation activity.

As if the two manipulations were not enough to indicate the special relationship between the Aaronids and the altar, a third blood manipulation is performed in connection with the ordination ram. Blood is taken from the altar, combined with holy anointing oil, and sprinkled (*hiphil* of *nzh*) onto Aaron and his sons and onto their garments (Exod 29:21; Lev 8:30). In this instance, both Exodus 29 and Leviticus 8 provide an explicit interpretation of the action. Its effect is to consecrate (make holy) Aaron and his sons and their garments. The oil is inherently holy, and, according to Priestly theory, what is holy can communicate holiness to an object or person through physical contact. Is the blood also represented as holy in this context? Since the effect attributed to its sprinkling along with the oil is that the Aaronids are made holy, it appears that it is. Milgrom suggests that the blood is made holy by its contact with the altar. It differs, therefore, in quality from the blood that was daubed on the Aaronids earlier.

Apart from the explicit interpretation of the action, we may again note its indexing effect. Again, the priority of Aaron over his sons is indicated. At the same time, because they all received the same gesture, their common status is also indexed. Again, we find Aaron identified as "first among equals." Furthermore, the distinction between the Aaronids and all other Israelites receives further emphasis. They, and no other Israelites, receive this ritual treatment. In this instance, its effect is stated explicitly. They become holy. According to P, only the priests are holy.[44] This fundamental distinction between the priests and all other Israelites (including other members of the tribe of Levi) is indexed by the ritual act represented in Exod 29:21 and Lev 8:30. Even were the action not interpreted for us in the text, we would be able to conclude, on the basis of the indexical effect of the ritual action, that the Aaronids were uniquely distinguished from all other Israelites.

Since the ordination blood manipulations both establish an existential relationship between the Aaronids and the altar and distinguish the Aaronids from all other Israelites, it comes as little surprise to find that only Aaronids have access to the altar. Moreover, their access is constantly reaffirmed by their primary cultic act, the manipulation of blood. Because the priests are holy, they have access to the altar. When we observe them acting within the world of the text, we know that they enjoy such access—and therefore are holy—because they apply blood to the altar. Thus, blood manipulation actions create special status, indicate the existence of such status, and reinforce it.

The Reparation Offering (*'āšām*)

Prescriptions for the reparation offering follow on the instructions for the "graduated *ḥaṭṭā't*" (Lev 5:14–26). These prescriptions simply indicate that the priest is to "effect removal" (*kipper*) with the offering animal on behalf of the one who has transgressed against sancta, with the result that the offerer will be forgiven (Lev 5:16, 18, 26). In this pericope we are not told what the priest does with the animal to effect removal. In the supplementary prescriptions that follow in Leviticus 6–7, however, we find instructions for the blood manipulation, the burning of an altar offering, and the treatment of the carcass (Lev 7:1–7). According to these instructions, the reparation offering animal is to be slaughtered where the burnt offering is slaughtered, and the blood is to be tossed onto the altar round about (Lev 7:2). The blood manipulation for the reparation offering is identical to that for the burnt offering and the sacrifice of well-being. Thus, we may speak of ritual acts that index a strong connection between the three types of offerings. Moreover, while the altar offering distinguishes the reparation from the burnt offering, in that only fat portions are burned in the altar fire, the reparation offering cannot be distinguished from the well-being sacrifice in this regard. It is only when the flesh is dealt with that the two offerings can be distinguished. Whereas the offerer takes the bulk of the flesh of the sacrifice of well-being for his own use, the priests receive the whole of the reparation offering as a prebend (Lev 7:6–7). Specifically, the flesh goes to the priest "who effects removal with it" (*'ăšer yĕkapper-bô*) (Lev 7:7).

From the scant information that is provided about the reparation offering, we can conclude that the blood manipulation has something to do with attaining "removal," which is a precondition for forgiveness. There is no reason, however, to identify the blood manipulation alone as the means of attaining this goal. Rather, because the formulations that refer to the priest effecting removal for the offerer seem to summarize the whole ritual complex, we may conclude that "removal" is achieved by that whole process.

Although Lev 7:2 prescribes that the blood of the reparation offering is to be tossed onto the altar, the prescriptions for the cleansing of someone who has been healed of a skin disease require a special application of blood from a reparation offering animal. According to Lev 14:12–14, 24–25, the person being cleansed is to bring a lamb as a reparation offering. It is taken along with an offering of oil and elevated by the priest as an elevation offering (vv. 12, 24). The lamb is then slaughtered and the priest takes some of the animal's blood (vv. 14a, 25ab) and places it on the right earlobe, the right thumb, and the right big toe of the one being purified (vv. 14b, 25b). Afterward, the priest takes some of the oil in the palm of his left hand, sprinkles it seven times "before Yahweh," and then daubs some over the blood on the earlobe, thumb, and big toe of the person being purified. Finally, he applies what remains in his hand to the head of the person being purified (vv. 15–18a, 26–29a). The effect of the whole ritual complex is that the priest effects removal for the one being purified "before Yahweh" (vv. 18b, 29b). In neither of the representations of the ritual complex is there any reference to the application of blood to the altar. The reader who knows the prescription that appears in Lev 7:2 may supply this manipulation in Leviticus 14. However, it is not clear if we should envisage the priest tossing the blood on the altar before he applies it to the person being healed, or if we should imagine him tossing the blood following the represented manipulation.

Apart from the declaration that the complete complex effects removal for the person being purified, there is no information provided about the specific effect of the blood manipulation. Whereas the rites that precede the actions at the shrine complex are said to result in the purification of the individual being purified, there is no mention of purification in the unit on the reparation offering complex. Only at the end of the representation of the complete sequence of sacrificial rites in the shrine complex are we told again that the individual has been made pure (v. 20).

Clearly, the blood manipulation represented in Lev 14:14, 25 is formally the same one represented in Exod 29:21 and Lev 8:30 in the context of the priestly ordination. I noted that scholars disagree about how to relate the two executions of this manipulation. Should the same effect be attributed to both? It is possible, of course, to argue that identity of form indicates identity of function. However, I have noted that this is not a necessary conclusion. Different symbolic meanings or instrumental effects can be attributed to identical actions. It should also be noted that the two executions of the manipulation take place in very different liturgical contexts and that different individuals are recipients of the blood. Still, if we seek a conceptual meaning for the application of blood to the body of the person healed of a skin disease, in my view, Milgrom has made a convincing case for identifying the blood manipulation as effecting purification.[45]

Yet, we can do more than identify a conceptual meaning. If we give attention again to the indexical nature of the blood manipulation, we can gain some important insights about this ritualized action. First, although the immediate textual context does not refer explicitly to the application of blood to the altar, we may refer to the larger context and note that the person healed of a skin disease receives an application of blood in the locus where blood is normally applied to sancta. Thus, the fact that he belongs in this locus is indexed. Furthermore, since he is the recipient of the same blood manipulation that the priests received when they were inducted into the priesthood, an existential relationship is established between the person healed of the skin disease and the priests. He certainly does not become a priest, but his bond with the priests, as those who mediate between him and Yahweh, is emphasized. Thus, he is marked as one who is permitted to seek priestly mediation in the cult place.

Conclusions

The blood manipulation in the case of the well-being sacrifice is the same as that which is prescribed for the burnt offering. The blood is tossed (*zrq*) onto the altar. As is the case with that action in the burnt offering complex, we find no unambiguous explanation of the tossing of the blood of the sacrifice of well-being. This identity of rites suggests the legitimacy of attributing the same significance to the manipulation in the case of both offerings. Further support for this approach comes from noting the basic unity of the two offerings in terms of the altar-burning rite: what is burned on the altar is termed a "food gift" and the burning produces a "soothing odor" for Yahweh. It follows that whatever insight we may gain about the significance of the blood manipulation from the study of one rite may be applied to understanding the blood manipulation in the other.

On the basis of the prescriptions in Leviticus 3, we cannot identify the blood as an offering, at least as an offering given by the lay offerer. The blood is clearly to be distinguished from the *'iššeh* burned in the altar fire. Thus, we must also reject suggestions that the blood functions as a part of the offering in the case of the burnt offering. Apart from this negative observation, however, it is difficult to determine how we can identify a Priestly explanation of the tossing of blood. For many interpreters, Lev 17:11 is a key for unlocking the "meaning" of the act. Yet, these interpreters differ about what Lev 17:11 itself means and, hence, about how it serves to explain the blood manipulation in the well-being sacrifice. The P texts themselves are silent about how the action is to be explained.

In my view, it is far more productive to focus on the represented activity and to reflect on how blood manipulation actions function indexically in the world of the text. In P's representation, the priests stake a special claim on the blood, removing it from the purview of the offerer as soon as the animal is slaughtered. In contrast, the offerer is responsible for the handling of the fat portions that go to the altar. This distinction indicates that the priests have special proprietary control over the blood. A similar distinction can be identified in the case of the burnt offering. The manipulation of blood is the priests' primary ritual action, and it establishes their right of access to the altar, indexing their special status, and distinguishing them from the lay offerers, as well as from the Levites. The burning of the fat portions by the priests takes place in the context established by their prior blood manipulation activity. Their access to the altar to burn the altar offering follows from and depends on their access to manipulate blood.

Furthermore, in Leviticus 9, where the act of conveying the blood to the altar is distinguished from the act of tossing it, the reservation of the latter act to Aaron serves to indicate his higher status relative to his sons. He performs the altar rite, whereas they simply make the blood available to him. Aaron's special status is also indexed in the ordination rituals, where he receives the applications of the blood of the ordination ram ahead of his sons. At the same time, since his sons receive the same applications, they are identified as sharing something of their father's status. Aaron is indexed as "first among equals." In addition, the application of blood to Aaron and his sons, especially when that blood is taken from the altar, indexes their special relationship with that appurtenance of sacred space. Thus, it comes as little surprise to find the priests enjoying exclusive access to the altar and to see this exclusive access being indexed by blood manipulation. Status created through blood manipulation is reinforced by subsequent blood manipulation activity.

Blood manipulation serves to distinguish priests from nonpriests and to mark status distinctions within the priesthood. It also creates a link between the offerer and the altar, since the blood comes from an offering brought by the offerer and upon which the offerer has pressed his hand, indicating his relationship to the animal. This relationship between the offerer and the altar is mediated by the priests. Such mediation indicates their essential role in maintaining contact between Yahweh and his people. In the sacrificial complex of the well-being offering, as in the burnt offering, blood manipulation, as the first priestly act, is the fundamental means of maintaining this contact.

Clearly, then, attention to the represented ritual actions, and to their indexing functions, leads to important insights about the workings of blood manipulation activity. In addition to, or even apart from, identifying and elucidating the Priestly writers' textual interpretations of blood manipulation, we can identify ways in which that mode of ritualized action creates, indicates, and reinforces fundamental distinctions between cultic actors. In the world of the Priestly texts, the manipulation of blood is socially potent activity.

CHAPTER FIVE

The *Ḥaṭṭā't* Blood Manipulations in P

Whereas the burnt offering, the sacrifice of well-being, the ram of ordination, and the reparation offering have in common the tossing of blood onto the altar of burnt offering, this mode of blood manipulation is not practiced in the case of the *ḥaṭṭā't* as represented in P. Instead, we find other types of manipulation—daubing (*nātan*), sprinkling (*hizzâ*), and pouring (*šāpak* or *yāṣaq*)—in a variety of combinations. Furthermore, P devotes considerably more attention to the *ḥaṭṭā't* blood manipulations than to those of the other sacrificial offerings.

I present my treatment of the *ḥaṭṭā't* blood manipulations in two parts: first, I deal with textual representations of the *ḥaṭṭā't* blood manipulations as they appear in the context of complete ritual complexes, clarifying what is represented and identifying the ways in which these manipulations function, as ritualized actions, to index status and sociocultic relationships and to construct sacred space; second, I deal with "native" textual interpretations of the *ḥaṭṭā't* blood manipulations. In both parts, I reflect on how readers read the texts and attempt to make sense of what is represented and of what the P tradents write about the purposes of the represented activity. Throughout the chapter, I pay close attention to the reading-interpretation activity of scholars, noting especially how Priestly texts on the *ḥaṭṭāʾt* are coordinated to provide the basis for synthetic explanations and the role that acts of "gap-filling" play in this process.

Representation of *Ḥaṭṭāʾt* Blood Manipulation

The Ḥaṭṭāʾt *in Lev 4:1–5:13*

This block of material provides information about *ḥaṭṭāʾt* offerings brought for violations of Yahweh's commandments, indicating what sort of offering is required and how the sacrificial complex is carried out. Other prescriptions for the offering of *ḥaṭṭāʾt* do not indicate what ritual complex is to be enacted and seem to assume the instructions given in this unit for the performance of the ritual complexes.[1] One must gap-fill the procedure from the instructions supplied in Lev 4:1–5:13. The H tradents also assume the Priestly instructions in Lev 4:1–5:13, since H texts provide no additional representations of the performance of *ḥaṭṭāʾt* ritual complexes.[2]

Leviticus 4:1–5:13 can be divided into two sections. The first, consisting of Lev 4:1–35, deals in sequence with the *ḥaṭṭāʾt* brought for inadvertent sins[3] committed by "the anointed priest" (*hakkōhēn hammāšîaḥ*) (vv. 3–12), "the whole congregation of Israel" (*kol-ʿădat yiśrāʾēl*) (vv. 13–21), a "chieftain" (*nāśîʾ*) (vv. 22–26), and an individual Israelite (*nepeš ʾaḥat*) (vv. 27–35). The second section, Lev 5:1–13, lists several specific wrongs (vv. 1–4) and prescribes that the guilty party must confess the offense (5:5) and bring the standard offering for an individual Israelite (a female flock animal) (5:6; cf. 4:28, 32). The text then indicates that reductions in the size and composition of the sacrifice are granted to those who are too poor to bring the offering normally required of an individual Israelite: poor individuals may substitute birds or even a cereal offering for the flock animal (5:7–13). There has been considerable scholarly disagreement about the significance of Lev 5:1–13 and its relationship to Leviticus 4.[4] According to some interpreters, Lev 5:1–13 identifies some specific examples of sins dealt with by the *ḥaṭṭāʾt* for the lay individual, and provides a supplementary set of prescriptions for the poor.[5] This would mean that the reductions permitted for the poor apply to the *ḥaṭṭāʾt* as described in Lev 4:27–35. Others understand Lev 5:1–13 to deal with a distinct subtype of *ḥaṭṭāʾt*, the "graduated" *ḥaṭṭāʾt*, in which the size of the offering is reduced according to the economic condition of the offerer: the poorer she or he is, the smaller the offering.[6] In this case, the reductions would apply only to the specific situations listed and would not be granted for the *ḥaṭṭā't* of the ordinary Israelite prescribed in Leviticus 4. Because of the uncertainty in this matter I have opted for caution and follow the approach of distinguishing between the two sections.

Leviticus 4: The Ḥaṭṭā't for Inadvertent Sins

Leviticus 4 sets out procedures for four types of *ḥaṭṭā't* sacrifices, with the fourth type subdivided according to the choice of animal. The animal to be offered and the ritual procedures to be followed are determined by the identity of the one whose sin requires the sacrifice.[7] The primary distinction between the types is whether blood from the animal is taken into the shrine building, a distinction highlighted by P texts (Lev 6:23; 10:17–18; 16:27). Many interpreters assume that the severity of the sin determines what is done with the blood.[8] Yet, the text does not focus on the specific quality of the transgression. Rather, the focus is on "the cultic status of the sinner."[9] The question is, Who has sinned? When it is the anointed priest or the whole congregation, blood is taken into the shrine building. When it is a "chieftain" or an ordinary Israelite, blood is not conveyed into the shrine building.

The procedure for each type of offering is the same at the beginning: the animal is brought to the shrine; the hand-pressing act is performed by the offerer;[10] the animal is slaughtered. The types of *ḥaṭṭā't* offering do not differ from one another in these details of execution or from the burnt offering and the well-being sacrifice.[11] There is nothing in the practices represented in the text that automatically allows us to distinguish one offering from another.

In P's "sanctuary of silence,"[12] where, in the representation of the text, rituals are executed without any verbal declarations,[13] the blood manipulation sets off the *ḥaṭṭā't* offering from the other sacrifices. As we observe the ritual complex unfold within the world of the text, we become aware that a distinctive ritual is unfolding only when the blood manipulation begins. The blood manipulation signals that the *ḥaṭṭā't* is a different offering from the burnt offering and the well-being sacrifice. Furthermore, when we observe the different blood manipulations executed in the case of different *ḥaṭṭā't* offerings, we become aware of distinctions within the *ḥaṭṭā't* category itself.

At the point of the blood manipulation the priest's formal activity begins. By now, this fact about P's representation of sacrificial activity is familiar. It has been true so far of every offering we have considered. Again, blood manipulation indexes the priest's distinction from the lay offerer. Furthermore, as we shall see, the blood manipulations also mark distinctions *within* the priesthood. In view of these preliminary observations, I turn now to a focused analysis of the blood manipulations that are part of the ritual complex for each type of *ḥaṭṭāʾt*, giving attention to their place within the total complex.

The Ḥaṭṭāʾt *for the "Anointed Priest" and the Congregation*

The first type of *ḥaṭṭāʾt* treated in Leviticus 4 is offered if "the anointed priest" sins "so that the people incur guilt" (Lev 4:3a).[14] The second type is offered if the whole people sins (Lev 4:13). In both cases, a bull is offered and the same ritual process is executed (Lev 4:3–12; 13–21).

In the prescriptions for the offering for the anointed priest, the instructions for the ritual acts preceding the blood manipulation do not identify the subject of the actions (vv. 3b–4). Since the *ḥaṭṭāʾt* is offered for the anointed priest because of his sin, it is reasonable to identify him as the subject of the prescribed actions, especially the hand-pressing,[15] but this identification is not explicit in the text. It is at the point where the blood manipulation begins that "the anointed priest" is specified as the subject (v. 5). This is consistent with what I have previously noted about the significance of the blood manipulation as the dividing line between lay and priestly action. Until he handles the blood, the priest has been performing ritual actions that could also be performed by the laity. When he takes the blood, he performs the first specifically priestly act.[16] Thus, this is another instance of the priest acting as both offerer and officiating priest.[17] As we observe the world of the text, we see the anointed priest bring the animal, press his hand on its head, slaughter it, and then take the blood. There is no disjunction or transition between participants in this ritual complex. One person acts throughout. Thus, again, but in a new and dramatic way, we find an affirmation of the distinctive status of the priesthood in relation to the laity indexed by the manipulation of blood. At the point in the ritual where a lay person would be excluded from ritual activity, the anointed priest continues to function as the ritual subject. He takes the blood of his own offering. He does not stand by passively while the ritual is performed for him. He acts for himself and the people who have become guilty because of his mistake (v. 3a). This fact indicates that the anointed priest requires no mediation. He can act on his own behalf.

In the case of the offering for the congregation, the cultic distinction between the laity and the priesthood is fully enacted in the typical manner. The assembly brings the animal (4:14), and "the elders of the congregation" press their hands on its head (4:15a). The animal is slaughtered (4:15b). Then, "the anointed priest" takes over as ritual actor, and is identified explicitly as such (v. 16).

In both types of *ḥaṭṭāʾt* the blood ritual is identical (Lev 4:5–7, 16–18). The anointed priest conveys some of the blood of the bull (*middam happār*) into the shrine building (vv. 5, 16). We must assume that there was a collection of the blood and that the priest conveys the blood in a vessel of some sort.[18] Although this is not indicated in the text, readers will typically engage in gap-filling in an effort to construct a full and meaningful picture of what is happening in the world of the text. Taking the vessel containing the blood, the anointed priest proceeds from the place of slaughter and enters into the shrine building. The text does not specify that the priest enters alone, nor is there any stated prohibition of his being accompanied by other priests. Still, even if we envisage the anointed priest being accompanied upon his entry to the shrine, he is *functionally* alone: he is the lone ritual actor. Accompanying priests would be ritually insignificant. In my reading of the text, I envisage the anointed priest entering the shrine alone. At this juncture, his activity is lost to the inhabitants of the world of the text but is seen by the reader, who is granted access to the shrine building with the anointed priest. The reader sees what the narrator represents in the text. In this instance, the Priestly narrator is quoting Yahweh's prescriptions about what the anointed priest is to do. Thus, it is Yahweh's speech that grants us access to activities not observed by inhabitants of the world of the text. Inside the shrine, we observe the anointed priest move from the entrance to a point immediately in front of the curtain that separates the main room of Yahweh's residence from his "private apartment," the adytum.

Verses 6, 7, and 17 explicitly identify the subject of the activity inside the shrine as "the priest."[19] This further identification of the subject of the blood manipulation emphasizes that blood manipulation is a priestly prerogative. Rolf Rendtorff claims that the references to "the priest" in verses 6, 7, and 17 rather than to "the anointed priest" indicate a change of subject: while the anointed priest conveys the blood into the shrine, another priest performs the specified manipulations.[20] However, the mere designation of the subject of the shrine manipulation as "the priest" is insufficient reason to identify a change of subject. In verses 5 and 16, the anointed priest has been identified as such. He can simply be called "the priest" thereafter, without the need for added specification. There is, moreover, a serious conceptual problem with Rendtorff's interpretation. He claims that the anointed priest brings his offering as a sinner, not as a priest, and that he conveys the blood as a representative of the people. However, if the anointed priest is represented throughout as conveying blood into the shrine, he is represented as performing a *priestly* activity. He is not acting as the offerer, since the offerer never handles blood. Because, as I noted, the anointed priest functions as a priest from the moment he takes the blood, he would not need to hand over responsibility to another priest inside the shrine. To do so would index a striking reversal of normal status distinctions. If such a reversal were to be understood, we might expect more than the simple omission of the adjective "anointed." I conclude, therefore, that the anointed priest is the actor and that "the priest" is mentioned for emphasis, making it clear that only a priest manipulates blood.[21]

Standing before the curtain, the priest dips a finger into the blood in the vessel he carries. We are not told which finger he dips. Later readers maintained that it was the right index finger.[22] Again, the reader must fill out the information provided by the text to create a complete picture. The priest sprinkles the blood. In line with the meaning of the *hiphil* of *nzh,* we should picture here a gesture by which small drops of blood are scattered before the priest. He performs the gesture seven times.[23] The Hebrew text indicates the direction of the sprinkling with the formulation *'et pĕnê.* Most interpreters seem to understand this phrase to indicate that blood was sprinkled "toward," "before," or "in the direction of" the curtain, without making contact with it.[24] A few, however, suggest that the blood made contact.[25] Grammatically, either understanding seems possible. With the majority of interpreters I understand the phrase to indicate that the priest sprinkles in the direction of the curtain, without the blood necessarily making contact with it. What must be noted here is that the phrase seems to emphasize the direction of the sprinkling. It is not merely "before" (*lipnê*) but "faceward," directly toward the curtain.[26] The sprinkling is directed at "the curtain of the holy place" (*pārōket haqqōdeš*) (v. 6).[27] In Leviticus 4, as Milgrom notes, "holy place" must indicate the outer room.[28] Thus, the curtain is characterized as marking off the outer room from the inner room, rather than the inner room from the outer room. It is an appurtenance of the outer shrine room rather than of the adytum. According to Milgrom, therefore, the formulation "the curtain of the holy place" (i.e., "the curtain of the outer shrine room") indicates that the shrine room is the focus of the action.[29] In contrast, Kiuchi maintains that a sprinkling directed at the curtain is focused on the adytum behind it: "[I]t is undeniable that the phrase refers to the direction where the adytum is located."[30]

In support of Kiuchi's interpretation, we may begin with the basic fact that the priest's action is directed at the curtain. This is its purely physical direction. There is, however, a relational and "theological" direction to the act. It is "before Yahweh" (vv. 6, 17). While the curtain is identified in its relation to the outer room, the gesture directed at it is defined in relation to Yahweh's manifest presence in the inner room. Thus, I would question Milgrom's claim that the blood gesture is performed in relation to the shrine room and not the adytum. Furthermore, because the curtain itself is decorated with an image of what lies behind it,[31] we seem bound to see the gesture directed at the curtain and described as "before Yahweh" as directed at the adytum. It seems insufficient and misleading to base an argument primarily on the fact that the curtain is characterized as an appurtenance of the outer room. As an appurtenance of the outer room, it functions as the boundary that marks the limit of that locus in relation to the adytum. Therefore, I affirm Kiuchi's claim that the blood sprinkling has the adytum as its focus.

Why does the priest not actually enter the adytum? The reason is that Leviticus 4 assumes the rules set forth in Leviticus 16.[32] Direct access to the adytum requires careful preparation, and seems to take place only rarely. Leviticus 16:2 decrees that Aaron may not enter the adytum "at every time" (*běkol-ʿēt*), and 16:3ff. describes what must be done to allow such access. For the ritual described here only partial access is possible. The blood is sprinkled in the direction of the adytum but not in the adytum. Thus, it points to—indexes—the adytum, and anticipates the blood manipulations in the adytum represented in Leviticus 16.

After the blood sprinkling, the priest steps back from the curtain and turns his attention to one of the appurtenances in the shrine room, the altar of spice incense. He daubs blood on the horns of this altar (vv. 7a, 18a). According to the text, the physical location of the altar of spice incense is "in the Tent of Meeting." Relationally, this locus is "before Yahweh." Thus, the daubing of blood on the altar takes place "before Yahweh," just as the prior sprinkling gesture did.

The priest then exits the shrine building and pours out (*špk*) the blood "to the base of the altar of burnt offering" (*ʾel-yěsôd mizbaḥ hā ʿōlâ*) (vv. 7b, 18b). The text says "all the blood." Translations and commentaries typically render this "the rest of the blood."[33] It seems that we should picture the anointed priest dealing in this manner with what remains of the blood he took into the Tent, as well as the blood he left outside. Since nothing is said about the blood not taken into the shrine, it seems reasonable to conclude that the pouring out of the blood is to be envisaged as involving all the blood from the animal. The expression "all the blood" also points to this understanding, since it most naturally would indicate both the blood taken into the shrine building and the blood left outside: "all the blood" rather than a part of the blood. This last observation speaks against Ziony Zevit's assertion that only the blood taken inside the shrine building was poured out at the base.[34]

From this discussion, what can be said about the spatial, relational, and in-dexical characteristics of the blood manipulation gestures? We can note that the act of sprinkling is located twice, first theologically and then physically. Its physical focus is the curtain of the holy place (Lev 4:6, 17). Its theological-relational focus is Yahweh. That is, the physical place, "the curtain of the holy place" is defined as "before Yahweh." Likewise, the application of blood to the horns of the altar of spice incense is "before Yahweh" (Lev 4:7a, 18a). Significantly, this is the first instance in this block of material (Lev 1–7) where a blood manipulation is explicitly characterized as being performed "before Yahweh."[35] Other acts have been designated as taking place "before Yahweh,"[36] thus making explicit their relational-indexing quality as ritual actions that point from the human actors to Yahweh and indicate a connection between the parties. Here, acts of blood manipulation join the list of explicitly identified relational-indexing acts.

Given the information that P provides about the conceptualization of the divine presence in the shrine, the expression "before Yahweh" must be taken seriously as expressing Yahweh's physical relationship to the acts performed. They are in his presence. Since his "glory" (*kābôd*) abides in the Most Holy Place behind the curtain,[37] when the anointed priest sprinkles blood toward this curtain he stands in close proximity to the manifest Deity and points to him—"indexes" him—with the gesture. The sprinkling of blood toward the abode of Yahweh's presence indexes a relationship between the anointed priest and Yahweh, as well as between Yahweh and the community that the anointed priest represents inside the shrine.

Within the world of the text, we observe that when the anointed priest commits an inadvertent transgression of a prohibitive command so that the people become liable to punishment, or when the whole congregation sins inadvertently, the anointed priest must journey from the outer sphere of holiness, the external portion of that locus which is characterized as "before Yahweh," and enter the inner sphere of holiness, the realm that is directly "before

Yahweh." He does so bringing blood from the animal offered in response to the transgression. He acts within the holy sphere in reverse order to his entry. He first sprinkles blood toward the curtain that separates the "reception room" of the divine abode from the "private apartment" in which the actual divine presence resides. He next steps back and daubs blood onto the horns of the incense altar, which is still "before Yahweh," yet not as close to the manifest presence as the curtain. He then exits the shrine building and pours out what remains of the blood at the base of the altar in the external sphere. This altar is "at the entrance of the Tent of Meeting" (Lev 4:7, 18), an area we know to be "before Yahweh" (Lev 4:4).

Ingress and egress are both associated with the handling of blood. The process of ingress begins with the anointed priest taking the blood, a simple and practical "manipulation." Indeed, conveying the blood into the shrine building is the sole purpose of the priest's entry. Inside the Tent of Meeting, he performs no other ritual actions besides blood manipulations. The first manipulation in the shrine building—the sevenfold sprinkling—takes place at the inner limit of the priest's access. The second manipulation—the daubing of blood on the horns of the incense altar—takes place as the priest moves out of the shrine building. The end of the process of egress is marked by another simple blood manipulation, the pouring out of the blood.

Blood, therefore, is used to mark access to the divine presence, to mark an encounter with the manifest Deity. The taking and conveying of blood into the Tent of Meeting provide the basis for the encounter. A blood manipulation marks the inner limit of access. A subsequent blood manipulation marks withdrawal from the encounter. A final manipulation marks the end of the encounter. This much can be said with certainty, apart from any identification of the symbolic or instrumental character of the individual blood manipulations in the different locations.

The Ḥaṭṭā't *for a Chieftain and for Individual Israelites*

The other two types of *ḥaṭṭā't* offerings prescribed in Leviticus 4 do not involve conveying blood into the shrine building. Instead, the blood is manipulated at the altar of burnt offering in the shrine courtyard. The preliminary actions for these *ḥaṭṭā't* sacrifices are the same as those prescribed for the *ḥaṭṭā't* for the anointed priest or the congregation. The individual who has sinned conveys his offering (*qorbānô*) (4:23, 28, 32) to the shrine complex. In the case of the "chieftain," the animal is to be a male goat (v. 23), while the ordinary layperson is to bring either a female goat (v. 28) or a ewe (v. 32). This offering of different animals indexes a distinction between the "chieftain" and all other lay offerers. In each case, the offer carries out the hand-pressing rite; then the animal is slaughtered (4:24, 29, 33).

The blood manipulation follows (vv. 25, 30, 34). The priest takes "some of the blood of the *ḥaṭṭā't* with his finger" (*middam haḥaṭṭā't bě'eṣbā'ô*) (vv. 25, 34; v. 30 reads "some of its blood" [*middāmāh*]), and puts (*ntn*) it on the horns of the altar of burnt offering. Then, he pours out (*špk*) "all of its blood" (*'et-kol-dāmāh*) (vv. 30, 34), or "its blood" (*'et-dāmô*) (v. 25)[38] "to the base" (*'el-yěsôd*) of the altar. With the blood manipulation a clear distinction can be recognized between the *ḥaṭṭā't* offered for the anointed priest or the congregation and the type offered for a layperson. Instead of carrying blood into the shrine building, the officiating priest takes it to the altar in the courtyard and manipulates it there. The manipulation is the same as that performed inside the shrine on the altar of spice incense. After this manipulation, the blood is poured out at the base of the altar, just as it is poured out following the manipulations inside the shrine in the first two types of *ḥaṭṭā't*. Thus, blood manipulation serves not only to distinguish the *ḥaṭṭā't* from other sacrifices but also to index distinctions between types of *ḥaṭṭā't*. At the same time, the types of *ḥaṭṭā't* are drawn together again at the conclusion of the manipulations. The distinct manipulations index distinctions. The common final act indexes unity.

Another important distinction that should be noted is that the officiant who manipulates the blood in the latter types of *ḥaṭṭā't* is identified simply as "the priest" (vv. 25, 30, 34), presumably indicating that an ordinary priest officiates, while the prescriptions for the first two types identify the officiant as "the anointed priest" (vv. 5, 16). When we observe the rituals unfold in the world of the text, we note that the anointed priest is the one who takes blood into the shrine building, whereas ordinary priests perform the blood manipulation on the altar of burnt offering. This distinction indexes a status distinction. The anointed priest bears the responsibility for taking blood into the presence of Yahweh inside his abode, whereas ordinary priests act only in the external sphere. Given what we know about the character of the inner sphere, we cannot help but conclude that the special access of the anointed priest is a function of his special status. Putting this another way, we may note how the special access of the anointed priest enacts his special status. In this context, with its representation of the regularly functioning cult, we may say that the blood manipulations performed by the "anointed priest" serve to *reinforce* or *recreate* a status that was *created* by other ritual acts (those represented in Exod 29, Lev 8–9). As we observe the rituals unfold, we become aware of who holds high status by noting who enters the Tent of Meeting. Access to the shrine building, as well as access to the lesser locus (the altar of burnt offering), is marked by blood manipulation. As with other sacrifices, the blood manipulation in the *ḥaṭṭāʾt* is a priestly prerogative. At the moment of the blood manipulation the priest steps in and is explicitly identified by the text as ritual actor, which serves to enact and index the distinction between priests and laity in their access to sancta. Furthermore, within the priesthood, a distinction is drawn between "the anointed priest" and ordinary priests, again in terms of access to sancta. Access in every case is marked by blood manipulation. We know to which sancta a priest has access because he applies blood to them. In contrast, lay Israelites have no access to sancta, because they do not manipulate blood, or, to put it another way, they do not manipulate blood because they do not have access to sancta. In either case, the fact that lay Israelites do not manipulate blood indexes their lack of access to sancta.[39]

The Offering of a Bird as a Ḥaṭṭāʾt

In the unit on the "graduated *ḥaṭṭāʾt*," the first prescribed offering is a female flock animal (Lev 5:6), the same *ḥaṭṭāʾt* as is prescribed for an individual Israelite in Lev 4:27–35. Following this prescription, the text continues by indicating that an individual who is too poor to provide a flock animal is permitted to bring two birds (5:7a). One bird is to be offered as a *ḥaṭṭāʾt,* the other as a burnt offering (v. 7b). The offerer is to present them to the priest (v. 8). As with the burnt offering of a bird, the layperson's activity seems to cease when he hands over the birds, since all of the ritual acts are performed at the altar, which is an exclusive preserve of the priesthood. The bird for the *ḥaṭṭāʾt* is offered first (v. 8). The priest is to wring the neck at the nape but not divide the head from the body (v. 8b).[40]

The text then prescribes the blood manipulation: "Then he shall sprinkle some of the blood of the *ḥaṭṭāʾt* upon the side of the altar and what remains of the blood shall be squeezed out to the base of the altar. It is a *ḥaṭṭāʾt*" (v. 9). Although the bird is offered as a *ḥaṭṭāʾt* for a layperson, the blood is not applied to the horns of the altar. Rather, it is sprinkled on the side of the altar.[41] This is the same locus where the blood of a burnt offering bird is to be squeezed out. Only some of the blood is sprinkled. It is not clear how we are to envisage this sprinkling being accomplished. The text does not specify that the priest uses his finger.[42] We might envisage the priest shaking the slaughtered bird in order to spatter some of its blood onto the side of the altar as it flows from the incision he made on the neck. After the sprinkling act, the rest of the blood is "squeezed out" to the base of the altar. The verb *mṣh* is the same one employed in connection with the manipulation of the blood of the burnt offering bird. It seems to indicate that the blood was pressed out of the body. The same twofold pattern of manipulation is prescribed here as for the offering of a herd or flock animal as a *ḥaṭṭā't*: a small amount of blood is to be applied to a sanctum in a specified way, and the rest is to be disposed of at the base of the altar. This procedure seems to be explained as a defining characteristic of the *ḥaṭṭā't*, since the prescription is followed directly by the formula *ḥaṭṭā't hû'* (5:9).[43] Although the manipulation of the bird's blood differs from the manipulation of the blood of a herd animal, the locus of manipulation and the final treatment of the blood index a relationship between the bird *ḥaṭṭā't* and the herd animal *ḥaṭṭā't*. At the same time, the character of the blood manipulation (along with the mode of slaughter) indexes a distinction between the offering of a bird as a burnt offering and the offering as a *ḥaṭṭā't*. Again, we find ritual action indicating conceptual distinctions. When we observe the rituals unfold in the world of the text, we recognize that two distinct offerings are being made because we observe differences in the mode of execution. We also recognize connections between offerings on the basis of important common elements in the complexes.

Bloodless Ḥaṭṭā't

Quite striking is the provision for the poorest of the poor to bring a bloodless "graduated *ḥaṭṭā't*" in the form of an offering of wheat meal (5:11). In this case, the priest takes a handful as a "memorial portion" (*'azkārâ*), which he burns on the altar. This constitutes the *ḥaṭṭā't* (Lev 5:12 states, *ḥaṭṭā't hû'*).

The Ḥaṭṭā't in the Priestly Ordination Ceremony

In the ritual complex for the ordination of Aaron and his sons as priests, a bull is offered as a *ḥaṭṭā't*. Aaron and his sons press their hands on the head of the bull (Exod 29:10; Lev 8:14), and it is slaughtered by Moses (Exod 29:11; Lev 8:15).[44] Why Aaron and his sons do not slaughter their own sacrifice is an interesting question, but it cannot be pursued at this juncture. I simply note that the emphasis in both texts on Aaron and his sons as the passive recipients of the ritual activity of Moses probably extended to taking from them the obligation to slaughter their sacrifice and giving it to Moses, who is the responsible actor throughout the whole ritual complex.

Following the slaughter, Moses takes "some of the blood of the bull" (*middam happar*) (Exod 29:12)[45] and puts (*ntn*) it on the horns of the altar with his finger. Here, Lev 8:15 has an additional specification that the blood was applied "round about" (*sābîb*).[46] Except for Lev 16:18, this is the only instance where "round about" is used in connection with the manipulation of the *ḥaṭṭā't* blood on the altar. Following the application to the horns, Moses pours out the remainder to the base of the altar.[47] Although the bull is offered for Aaron and his sons, as is indicated by the fact that they press their hands on its head, the blood manipulation is what is prescribed in Leviticus 4 for a *ḥaṭṭā't* offered for an individual. Blood is not conveyed into the shrine building.

It is a striking fact that Moses is the ritual actor in this blood manipulation complex, especially if we reflect on this textual representation in the light of the representations we find elsewhere in P. In P, only priests apply blood to the altar. Thus, we should conclude that Moses is functioning as a priest on this occasion. This blood manipulation complex is the first one carried out in the ordination ceremonial complex. Although it is not Moses' first ritual action, it is the first action that is clearly a priestly prerogative and thus the first explicit index to Moses' priestly role in the ceremonial complex. In the subsequent sacrificial complexes, Moses reinforces his priestly status by continuing to manipulate blood.

The Ḥaṭṭā't *Offerings at the Inauguration of the Cult*

According to the account in Leviticus 9, when Aaron and his sons presided as priests for the first time at the Tent of Meeting, two animals were presented as *ḥaṭṭā't* offerings, one for Aaron, a "calf of the herd" (9:2), and another for the people, a he-goat (9:3). After the animals had been produced and the assembly had gathered, Moses instructed Aaron to begin his liturgical duties (9:7). Aaron began by offering his *ḥaṭṭā't* : "Then Aaron drew near to the altar, and he slaughtered the *ḥaṭṭā't* calf which was for him. Aaron's sons presented the blood to him, he dipped his finger into the blood and put [*ntn*] [it] on the horns of the altar, and the rest of the blood he poured out [*yṣq*] to the base of the altar" (9:8–9).

If we compare the description of the blood manipulation for Aaron's *ḥaṭṭā't* with the subsequent account of the manipulation of the blood of his burnt offering, we find a striking correspondence between the two (an observation that also holds true for the manipulation of the blood of the people's well-being sacrifices [v. 18]). In both accounts, Aaron's sons convey the blood to Aaron, and Aaron performs the blood rite at the altar. Thus, there is a division of labor represented in the handling of the blood. Aaron performs the rites directly at the altar, while his sons deal with getting the blood from the spot where the slaughter takes place to where Aaron performs the manipulation. This division of labor functions as a status index. Aaron is clearly superior to his sons, since he performs the actual blood manipulation, applying blood to the altar, whereas his sons perform a subordinate action that simply facilitates Aaron's ritual action.

The blood ritual performed by Aaron is not the one prescribed in Lev 4:5–7 for the *ḥaṭṭāʾt* of the anointed priest. Rather, it is what is prescribed for the *ḥaṭṭāʾt* offered for a chieftain or a common person (Lev 4:22–35). It is also what is prescribed in Exod 29:12 and described in Lev 8:15. Blood is not conveyed into the Tent of Meeting.

The account of the offering of the people's *ḥaṭṭāʾt* is quite brief, amounting simply to a notice that the ritual was performed (Lev 9:15): "Then he brought forward the offering of the people, and took the *ḥaṭṭāʾt* he-goat which was for the people and slaughtered it and offered it as a *ḥaṭṭāʾt* like the first." Here the complex of ritual acts performed following the slaughter is indicated with a single verb, the *piel* construction of the root *ḥṭʾ*. The verb in this context almost certainly refers to the whole ritual, the blood manipulation and the burning of an altar offering.[48] Another point to note is that the slaughter is distinguished from whatever acts are designated by the *piel* form of *ḥṭʾ* ("offered as a *ḥaṭṭāʾt*"). Slaughter is a necessary prerequisite for the performance of the ritual actions that constitute a *ḥaṭṭāʾt*, but is not itself represented as one of those rites.

The Ḥaṭṭāʾt Offerings of the "Day of Removal"

In the P stratum of the account of the "Day of Removal" in Leviticus 16,[49] two animals are brought as *ḥaṭṭāʾt* offerings, a bull for Aaron and the priestly family and a goat for the people. The detailed prescriptions for the rituals with Aaron's bull and the people's goat, in which the blood manipulations constitute the key element, begin at verse 11. First, Aaron is to bring forward his bull. The animal is to be slaughtered. As is typical, the slaughter is indicated with an abstract third-person, masculine singular verb, apparently signifying that the subject of the slaughter is insignificant. The reader must gap-fill here, assuming the collection of the blood in some kind of vessel.[50] Aaron must then take coals from the altar fire and incense into the adytum, "inside the curtain," and place the incense on the fire "before Yahweh" so that a cloud of incense will shroud the *kappōret* (cover).[51] This act ensures that Aaron will not die (vv. 12–13), apparently from seeing Yahweh's manifest presence above the cover (v. 2).

Having produced the apotropaic cloud of incense, Aaron turns to the performance of the blood manipulations: "Then he shall take some of the blood of the bull, and shall sprinkle with his finger on the eastern[52] surface of the cover, and before the cover he shall sprinkle seven times from the blood with his finger" (16:14). As in other texts, the representation provided here requires interpretation and supplementation on the part of the reader. We may ask, for example, whether Aaron is to be understood to take the fire, incense, and blood into the shrine building all at once, or to take in the fire and incense first, proceed back out to get the blood, and then enter again. The Mishnah (*Yoma* 4:3; 5:1–3) opts for the latter, and apparently most logical, understanding. (It is difficult to envisage how Aaron could simultaneously carry a fire pan, a container of incense, and a vessel holding blood.)[53]

When Aaron completes this activity, the text indicates that he is to turn his attention to the people's *ḥaṭṭāʾt* goat (v. 15): "Then he shall slaughter the *ḥaṭṭāʾt* goat which is for the people and shall convey its blood[54] to the area inside the curtain and shall manipulate its blood just as he manipulated the blood of the bull:[55] he shall sprinkle it on the cover and before the cover." The text seems to represent the slaughter of the goat as following upon the complete execution of the manipulation of the bull's blood. That is, having performed the manipulations with the blood of the bull, Aaron emerges from the Tent, the goat is slaughtered, Aaron collects the blood, and reenters the Tent.[56]

Aaron is to perform the same manipulations with the blood of the people's goat as he performed with the blood of his bull. Both verses represent a two-part manipulation complex. According to verse 14, the first manipulation is directed at the east-facing surface of the cover. Verse 15 simply says that the blood is to be sprinkled "on the cover." According to both verses, in the second manipulation, blood is sprinkled "before" (*lipnê*) the cover. Elliger suggests that it is not quite certain that the first manipulation involves only a single sprinkling gesture while the second consists of seven sprinklings; possibly "seven times" could apply to both manipulations.[57] Milgrom responds to this interpretation by emphasizing that the prescription seems to be constructed in such a way that "seven times" can refer only to the second manipulation. If "seven times" applied to both manipulations, the second occurrence of "sprinkle" (*hiphil* of *nzh*) would be superfluous.[58] To this observation, I would add that the appearance of "from the blood" in connection with the second manipulation parallels "from the blood of the bull" in the first part of the verse, and that "with his finger" is also repeated. These repetitions suggest that each prescription is self-contained and complete. Thus, "seven times" applies only to the second manipulation. The first manipulation involves only a single sprinkling.[59]

How are we to envisage the first manipulation, the single sprinkling, being performed? Does *'al-pĕnê* (lit., "upon the face") indicate the application of blood to the surface of the cover or merely "before" it?[60] Both interpretations are supported by lexical evidence.[61] However, the subsequent use of *lipnê* (before) suggests that *'al-pĕnê* means something other than "before" the cover. This deduction finds confirming evidence in verse 15, where *'al* takes the place of *'al-pĕnê* while *lipnê* is retained.[62] Milgrom notes these facts and affirms that *'al-pĕnê* is properly interpreted in this context as "on the surface of."[63] He adds, however, that the rabbis interpreted it as meaning "over against," in the direction of the cover but not onto it.[64] While not an impossible interpretation, the use of *'al* in verse 15 renders it less likely.

Leviticus 16:14–15 represents two executions of a two-part blood manipulation complex—first, a single sprinkling of blood onto the east-facing surface of the cover, and, second, seven sprinklings in front of the cover. These sprinklings would fall on the floor of the adytum.[65] Both manipulations are oriented to the cover. Thus, even though the second manipulation applies blood to the floor of the adytum, the sprinklings themselves are located in relation to the cover.

These blood manipulations function as relational indexes. Blood is sprinkled on and before the cover where the divine presence is manifest, hidden behind the cloud of incense smoke. As Vriezen emphasizes, the blood falls at Yahweh's feet.[66] The act takes place in the context of a moment of close encounter. For Aaron, the encounter is almost direct. Through his mediation, the people also enter into a connection with the Deity. The encounter is marked by the blood manipulation. As I have indicated repeatedly, every blood manipulation in the cult, whatever else it may be said to do, indexes a relationship between Yahweh, the priestly mediator, and the lay individual or the community of Israel. There is an identity between the two *ḥaṭṭāʾt* offerings reflected in the identity of the ritual performances. Given that the blood of Aaron's bull and the blood of the people's goat receive the same treatment in the adytum, it seems reasonable to conclude that the people's relationship with Yahweh is as significant as is Aaron's, although the precedence of Aaron's relationship is reflected in the fact that blood from his offering is manipulated first. Furthermore, while Aaron acts directly for himself, the people require Aaron to act for them. Thus, there is a tension between the ways in which the ritual acts index equality of status and the ways in which they index hierarchy and privilege.

Leviticus 16:16b apparently indicates that Aaron is to manipulate the blood of the bull and the goat in the outer room of the shrine building: "Then he shall do likewise to the Tent of Meeting, which is dwelling with them in the midst of their impurities." While seemingly indicating that additional blood manipulations are to be executed in the outer room of the shrine,[67] the text does not tell us what the manipulations are. Readers must fill in the gap, and there is, not surprisingly, a variety of opinions about what is intended here. The simplest approach is to supply the known ceremony prescribed for the shrine room in Lev 4:5–7, 16–18. In this case, we would envisage Aaron sprinkling blood seven times in the direction of the curtain, and then applying blood to the four horns of the altar of incense.[68] According to Milgrom, *wĕkēn* (and so) indicates that the outer room is to be purged of impurity in the same manner as the adytum.[69] The single sprinkling upon the face of the ark corresponds to the daubing on the horns of the altar, and the sevenfold sprinkling before the ark corresponds to the sevenfold sprinkling against the curtain.

The rabbis, who understood Lev 16:18–19 to deal with blood manipulations on the incense altar (*m. Yoma* 5:5; *Sipra Aḥare* 4:8), interpreted *wĕkēn* to indicate that just as blood was sprinkled once on the cover and seven times before it, so in the outer room blood was sprinkled once upward and seven times downward in the direction of the curtain before the adytum (*m. Yoma* 5:4). This became the commonly accepted traditional Jewish interpretation.[70] Noordtzij offers a variation on this interpretation, asserting that the blood "was sprinkled seven times on the ground before the curtain."[71]

In the absence of an explicit textual representation of what Aaron is to do in the outer room, it is clearly impossible to arrive at a firm conclusion about what is indicated by Lev 16:16b, except to affirm that it prescribes additional blood manipulation acts in the outer room of the shrine building. Nevertheless, as in Lev 4:3–21, blood manipulation marks ingress and egress, and Aaron manipulates blood in reverse order to his ingress. The blood manipulations we envisage being performed in the outer room of the shrine building function to mark Aaron's egress. With the manipulation of blood in the adytum, he had a direct encounter with the manifest divine presence. With the manipulation of blood in the outer room, he marks his withdrawal from that encounter.

Leviticus 16:18–19 prescribe another complex of blood manipulations, which have "the altar which is before Yahweh" as their object: "Then he shall proceed out to the altar which is before Yahweh and shall effect removal upon it. He shall take some of the blood of the bull and some of the blood of the goat and daub (it) round about on the horns of the altar. Then he shall sprinkle some of the blood upon it with his finger seven times, and shall cleanse it and consecrate it because of the impurities of the children of Israel."

These verses indicate that the next act in the ritual process is a two-step blood manipulation at the altar. This is clearly the altar of burnt offering, despite ancient rabbinic identification of it as the incense altar.[72] The altar is located theologically as "before Yahweh." Thus, by extension, the ritual acts are located theologically "before Yahweh." The first of the two acts is the daubing of blood on the horns of the altar. This is the same gesture as is prescribed for the *ḥaṭṭāʾt* for lay individuals in Leviticus 4, as well as what is prescribed in Exodus 29 and represented as being enacted in Leviticus 8 and 9. We should note the appearance here of the word *sābîb* ("round about"), which occurs in connection with this blood manipulation only here and at Lev 8:15. Blood from both the bull and the goat is daubed. Then there is a sevenfold sprinkling gesture, prescribed with the same language as the sprinkling gestures enacted inside the shrine. In this instance, the altar is uniquely the object of the gesture. Again, blood from both animals is sprinkled.

This act is unique to the rites of Leviticus 16. No other text prescribes the sprinkling of blood from a *ḥaṭṭāʾt* animal on the altar of burnt offering.[73] The sevenfold sprinkling with the finger is the same gesture as is prescribed to take place before the curtain and inside the adytum. What we see here is an obvious elaboration of the blood manipulation rites in Leviticus 16 as compared with those prescribed in other texts. As we observe the ritual unfold in the world of the text, we see a more complex ritual on this special occasion. The elaboration indexes the special character of the ritual complex. Using Bell's terminology, we may speak of a privileging ritualization. The elaboration of the altar blood manipulation with the seven sprinklings serves to distinguish this ritual complex from other manipulations of *ḥaṭṭāʾt* blood on the altar.

The sevenfold sprinkling on the altar is the last of the *ḥaṭṭāʾt* blood manipulations. There is no mention of the pouring out of the blood at the base of the altar, which we find in other representations of the *ḥaṭṭāʾt* ritual.[74] According to verse 20, Aaron is to proceed from the *ḥaṭṭā't* blood manipulations immediately to the rite with the live goat.

The Ritual Acts Following the Blood Manipulations

In the Priestly representations, when a herd or flock animal is offered as a *ḥaṭṭā't,* following the blood manipulations, fat pieces and internal organs are extracted and burned on the altar by the presiding priest (see Lev 4:8–10, 19, 26, 31, 35; 8:16; 9:10;16:25; Exod 29:13). These are the same portions offered from the well-being sacrifice, a fact noted explicitly four times in Leviticus 4 (vv. 10, 26, 31, 35). In the case of a bird offered as a *ḥaṭṭā't* (Lev 5:8–9), the textual prescriptions do not refer to the burning of any part of the bird in the altar fire. Since the body of a *ḥaṭṭā't* is never burned in the altar fire, all that could be offered from the bird would be a tiny bit of internal fat, which would not be an adequate altar offering. Thus, the *ḥaṭṭā't* bird is accompanied by a burnt offering bird, which provides the altar offering.[75] Finally, when a cereal offering is brought by the poorest of the poor as a *ḥaṭṭā't,* the priest is to take a handful of the flour, which is called "its memorial" (*'azkārātāh*), and burn this in the altar fire, "with the food gifts of Yahweh." This constitutes the *ḥaṭṭā't,* as Lev 5:12 indicates with the final declaration, "it is a *ḥaṭṭā't*" (*ḥaṭṭā't hû'*).

If we compare all of the representations of the ritual complex for the *ḥaṭṭā't,* the single common element we find is the burning of an offering on the altar. Blood manipulation may be omitted when a grain offering takes the place of an animal offering, but the altar-burning element is never absent. We also find the altar-burning element emphasized by the provision of a burnt offering bird to accompany a bird offered as a *ḥaṭṭā't* .

Blood Manipulation and the Disposal of the Carcass

According to Lev 4:11–12, 21, all that remains of the carcasses of the bulls offered for the anointed priest or the congregation is to be conveyed outside the camp to "a clean place" (v. 12). The same procedure is followed with the bull offered at the ordination of Aaron and his sons (Exod 29:14; Lev 8:17), the *ḥaṭṭā't* bull provided by Aaron at the inauguration of the cult (Lev 9:11), and the bull and the goat offered on the Day of Atonement (Lev 16:27). However, we are not told in Leviticus 4 what is to be done with the carcasses of the animals offered for a chieftain or an individual Israelite, nor are we told why the carcasses of the bulls offered for the anointed priest and the congregation are to be treated as prescribed.

The additional instructions on the *ḥaṭṭā't* that appear in Lev 6:17–23 (EV 6:24–30) fill in this information, verses 19 and 22 (EV 6:26, 29) answering our question about what happens to the carcasses of the chieftain's and individual's *ḥaṭṭā't* animals. According to verse 19, the priest who offers the *ḥaṭṭā't* (*hakkōhēn haměḥaṭṭē' 'ōtāh*)[76] is the one who will enjoy use of the flesh ("he shall eat it"). It is to be consumed "in a holy place in the court of the Tent of Meeting." Verse 22 adds that, "Every male in the priestly family may eat it. It is most holy."[77]

Leviticus 6:23 indicates that there is an exception to the provisions for the consumption of the *ḥaṭṭā't* flesh and explains why the bulls offered for the anointed priest and the congregation are taken out and burned: "Now every *ḥaṭṭā't* from which blood is conveyed into the Tent of Meeting to effect removal in the holy place may not be consumed. It shall be burned with fire." According to verse 23, the act of taking blood into the Tent of Meeting determines that the flesh cannot be eaten. It must be burned. Thus, the verse provides information not supplied in Leviticus 4. The same principle is indicated as the reason why the carcasses of the bull and the goat offered on the Day of Removal are to be burned : "Now the *ḥaṭṭā't* bull and the *ḥaṭṭā't* goat, whose blood was conveyed to effect removal in the holy place, he shall convey outside of the camp, and they shall burn their hides, their flesh, and their dung with fire" (Lev 16:27).

Following the deaths of Aaron's sons Nadab and Abihu, when Moses discovers that the *ḥaṭṭā't* offered for the people at the inauguration of the cult had been burned rather than eaten by Aaron and his remaining sons, Moses insists that they should have eaten it and adduces the reason (Lev 10:18): "Indeed, its blood was not conveyed inside the holy place. You should certainly have eaten it in the sacred precinct just as I commanded."

According to these texts, there are two basic types of *ḥaṭṭā't* offerings. The first involves conveying blood into the Tent of Meeting. The carcass of the animal is to be burned outside the camp. According to the texts, the reason why the carcass is handled this way is that blood was taken into the Tent of Meeting. The other type of *ḥaṭṭā't* is one whose blood is not conveyed into the shrine building. The flesh belongs to the priest who performs the rituals and may be consumed by any male of the priestly family. The flesh may be eaten because blood was not taken into the Tent of Meeting. This seems to be the necessary inference to be made from the prescription in Lev 6:23.

Interpretations of the *Ḥaṭṭā't* Blood Manipulations

Having examined how the texts represent the manipulation of the blood of *ḥaṭṭā't* offerings, and with my reflections on the indexical functions of these ritual actions in view, some consideration may now be given to the explicit interpretations of *ḥaṭṭā't* blood manipulations given in the texts.

In Lev 8:15 we find an interpretation of the daubing of blood onto the horns of the altar: "Moses took the blood and put (it) on the horns of altar round about with his finger, and purified [*wayĕḥaṭṭē'*] the altar." Whereas in Lev 6:19 and 9:15 the *ḥaṭṭā't* is the direct object of the *piel* construction of *ḥṭ'*, here the altar is the direct object of the verb, which means "purify." The text indicates rather clearly that the blood manipulation effects the purification of the altar. However, it does not tell us what impurity is eliminated, or how the blood manipulation accomplishes this effect.

How does the application of blood to the altar effect its purification? Jacob Milgrom identifies the blood as the "ritual detergent" and explains that it absorbs impurity and, *pars pro toto,* transmits that impurity to the carcass of the animal.[78] According to this interpretation, the removal of impurity from sancta is accomplished by the blood manipulation, while the final elimination of the impurity is accomplished either by the burning of the carcass outside the camp or by priests eating the flesh. This explanation is based, in part, on comparing the Priestly blood manipulations with Mesopotamian and Hittite purification rites, in which various substances and objects are applied to the person or thing needing to be cleansed, and then disposed of. The Hittite examples are closest to the Priestly model. The ritual of Ulippi, for example, involves the smearing of blood onto a new cult image, the walls of its shrine, and its cult utensils. The result is that the cult image and its shrine become pure.[79] In response to this use of comparative evidence, three observations are in order. First, as David Wright cautions, interpretive comparison, which involves interpreting a phenomenon in one society by referring to a similar phenomenon in another, is fraught with methodological hazards, since there is no way of knowing whether similarity of form indicates similarity of meaning or attributed effect.[80] Anthropologists have long understood that phenomena in different cultures that appear similar should be compared with great caution.[81] As Wright concludes, "Interpretive comparison, because it is based on unsound anthropological theory, should, theoretically, not be pursued at all."[82] Second, the Mesopotamian rituals, from which Milgrom derives the conception of purification agents absorbing impurity, do not involve the application of substances that are left on an object or person. Mesopotamian purification agents are wiped across persons and objects, functioning essentially as "sponges," which draw impurity into themselves. These agents of purification, laden with impurity, are then disposed of.[83] In the Priestly rites, in contrast, blood is left on the sancta to which it is applied. Thus, the phenomena are significantly different. Third, in the case of the very similar Hittite rituals, there is no indication that purification is achieved by the blood absorbing impurity. The Hittite texts are as silent as the Priestly writings on the actual mechanism by which blood purifies.

Given the fact that the blood remains on the sancta to which it is applied, and a purifying effect is attributed to this application, it seems better to extend Milgrom's characterization of blood as a "detergent" and to refer to it as a "disinfectant" that destroys impurity.[84] If, however, we affirm that the carcass absorbs the impurity, we must then think of the blood as driving the impurity from sancta, setting it free to be absorbed into the animal's flesh. Noam Zohar objects to this latter explanation of how blood purifies sancta by asking, "how does the contamination ever come to reside in the *flesh* of the sacrificial animal," and "just how and why would the impurity leap from the inner shrine to the carcass, which lies outside?"[85] Zohar seems to believe that raising such questions renders Milgrom's basic thesis invalid. However, the lack of detailed explanation means only that the Priestly tradents failed to provide the kind of information we desire. As we have seen, this is not atypical. Priestly texts very rarely provide any explanation of how ritual acts achieve their effect, let alone the kind of precise explanation Zohar demands. Although Milgrom addresses Zohar's questions by appealing to the principle of *pars pro toto* and arguing that the carcass absorbs impurity because part of the animal, its blood, has absorbed impurity,[86] a simpler answer can be provided. If the texts do in fact indicate that the carcass becomes infected with impurity following the blood manipulation, we may simply affirm that the Priestly tradents believed that impurity driven from sancta found its way inevitably to the carcass of the animal. To claim, as Zohar does, that the lack of a precise explanation of the mechanism of impurity transfer renders such a conception impossible is to place ourselves in the position of objecting to the logic of Priestly ritual.

Leviticus 16:19b interprets the two blood manipulations Aaron is to perform at the altar of burnt offering on the Day of Removal: "And he shall cleanse it and consecrate it because of the impurities of the children of Israel."

The two blood manipulation acts—daubing blood on the horns of the altar and sprinkling blood seven times on the altar—achieve two effects, cleansing and consecration. These effects are required because of the impurities of the Israelites, which have apparently attached themselves to the altar, rendering it impure and threatening its holiness.

Are the two effects achieved through both types of manipulation, or is each effect tied to a specific manipulation? Milgrom argues persuasively that the daubing manipulation effects the purification while the sprinkling consecrates.[87] He notes that the daubing gesture is *exactly* identical to the one described in Lev 8:15, which is explicitly identified as purifying the altar. In the same connection, Milgrom notes that the sprinkling of blood that has been in contact with a sanctum effects consecration.[88] The blood has been inside the adytum and shrine room, where it has evidently absorbed contagious holiness, just as the blood dashed on the altar during the priestly ordination rites apparently absorbed holiness through its contact with the altar and was then capable of transmitting that holiness when sprinkled on Aaron and his sons. This interpretation seems to make good sense of the activity described here and the effects attributed to it. Thus, with Milgrom, I conclude that the daubing cleanses the altar and the sprinkling (re)consecrates it.

The blood manipulations directed at the altar reestablish both its purity and its holiness. Purity is a precondition for holiness but is distinct from holiness, in that ritual purity does not itself constitute holiness; a person or thing may be pure without being holy. Holiness is added to purity through rites of consecration that establish a new identity for the person or object being consecrated. The blood manipulations on the altar of burnt offering may be understood to constitute a rite of passage. The two blood manipulations mark stages in the transition of the altar from a condition of impurity, which is inherently incompatible with its holiness,[89] to a condition of purity, which is the basic precondition for its reconsecration, to a state of renewed holiness. At the outer boundary of sacred space, the structure of holiness is reestablished.[90]

The Priestly tradent who composed Lev 16:19b attributes an instrumental effect to blood manipulation actions. The daubing of blood onto the horns of the altar achieves the instrumental effect of eliminating impurity. The act cleanses (*wĕṭihărô*) the altar. The sprinkling of blood is the medium for communicating holiness to the altar (*wĕqiddĕšô*). Similarly, Lev 8:15 indicates that the daubing of blood purifies the altar (see also Exod 29:36). Is it possible to apply these explanations of the effects of blood manipulation actions beyond their immediate contexts to other representations of the same or similar blood manipulation actions? Can these interpretive comments be applied where explanations are lacking?

If the sevenfold sprinkling on the altar serves to (re)consecrate it, might the same consecratory effect be attributed to the sevenfold sprinkling in the adytum before the cover (Lev 16:14–15)? Frank Gorman answers this question affirmatively, asserting that, just as the sevenfold sprinkling on the altar reestablishes the outer boundary of the holy realm, so the sevenfold sprinkling in the adytum reestablishes the inner boundary: "Thus, the logic of the rite of (re)consecration relates to spatial categories—the act of reconsecration, of refounding, takes place at the boundaries of the holy complex of the tabernacle. This is in line with the idea that the purpose of reconsecration is precisely to reestablish the boundaries of the holy realm—the bounds of the holy are reestablished at the boundaries."[91]

This interpretation makes a certain amount of sense and can be supported by further evidence. First, the beginning of Lev 16:18 identifies the manipulation acts performed on the altar as directed at effecting "removal," while 16:19b indicates that they purified and consecrated the altar "because of the impurities of the children of Israel." Thus, purification and consecration seem both to be related to "removal" (*kipper*). It follows that the effecting of removal inside the adytum (16:16a) could also include both purification and consecration. Also, because the act performed at the altar takes the same basic form as the rite in the adytum, we might attribute the same effect to both, drawing on the explicit interpretation in verse 19b to supply information not given in verse 16a. As I have emphasized, this kind of gap-filling is all but demanded by the fragmentary nature of the interpretive material in the texts.

Nevertheless, while I am sympathetic to Gorman's interpretation, it contains some potential difficulties. First, Milgrom has emphasized that the use of the blood to reconsecrate the altar makes sense because the blood has been in the adytum, where it has been exposed to the holiness of that realm, which it can communicate to the altar. However, there is no holier place than the adytum. From whence comes the holiness that is allegedly communicated to the adytum by the sevenfold sprinkling? If we refer only to the "symbolic meaning" of the act, we might not need to be troubled by this question, since the blood would require no real potency to merely "symbolize" consecration. However, since the Priestly tradents attribute an instrumental effect to their ritual acts and regard ritual materials as possessing or obtaining real power, we cannot settle for this solution. Another difficulty with Gorman's interpretation is that the blood is sprinkled *on* the altar of burnt offerings but *before* the cover. Gorman asserts that blood does not need to be placed on an object it (re)consecrates but never adduces evidence to support this claim. Additionally, the blood manipulations in the adytum, on and before the cover, are said to have their effect "upon the holy place." Thus, while the cover is the object of the first sprinkling act and orients the second manipulation, the whole adytum is identified as the locus of the removal effect. Yet, if the first manipulation purifies and the second consecrates, we have the unusual situation of an object being purified while the place where it is located is consecrated. One might argue that the purification of the cover effects the purification of the whole adytum. However, if this is the case, why would the sevenfold sprinkling not also be applied to the cover? Gorman's claim that blood that consecrates need not make contact with its object fails to deal with this problem both because Gorman fails to adduce evidence to support the claim, and because he fails to explain why the blood was not, in fact, applied directly to the cover just as blood was applied directly to the altar. Finally, we must note that the sevenfold sprinkling represented in Lev 4:6, 17 is not preceded by any other blood manipulation act. Gorman appears to understand this act simply as effecting purgation.[92] However, since this sevenfold sprinkling act is essentially identical to the sevenfold sprinkling in the adytum, differing only in its locus, we may wonder why it must be assigned a different effect. From all of these observations, we can recognize how difficult it is to apply an interpretive comment directed at one ritual blood manipulation to other, similar blood manipulations.

Nevertheless, there is some virtue in Gorman's recognition of a pattern in the execution of manipulations. In the adytum, an act of blood manipulation results in the application of blood to a sacred object. This manipulation is followed by a sevenfold sprinkling manipulation that is oriented toward the sacred object. In the shrine courtyard, an act of blood manipulation (the daubing on the horns) results in the application of blood directly to another sacred object. This application is followed by a sevenfold sprinkling manipulation oriented toward the object. Thus, in a basic form, the rites enacted in the adytum are repeated in the shrine courtyard. According to N. Kiuchi's interpretation of Lev 16:16b, the same pattern is also enacted in the outer room of the shrine building, with a single sprinkling onto the altar of incense and seven sprinklings before it.[93] In contrast, Milgrom's identification of the manipulations in the outer room reverses the sequence so that blood is first sprinkled seven times and then applied to the horns of the altar of incense. This, according to Milgrom, "is no random aberration but, on the contrary, creates a classical symmetrical introversion."[94] Whatever the case, it is clear that we have to do here with ritual actions that are represented as being carried out in a carefully regulated manner, according to a pattern. Our difficulties as interpreters emerge when we attempt to determine whether there is some "meaning" to this pattern beyond the enacting of order and structure.

Perhaps this difficulty should give us pause to consider again whether the quest for a symbolic or instrumental "meaning" should be our primary concern. Is it not significant to find that the careful orchestration of ritual itself produces an ordered world? That is, whatever else might be said about the meaning or instrumental effect of the discrete manipulations, we should note that the complete enactment maps an ordered world in which the same patterns are repeated in each of its parts. Impurity and sin, the forces that threaten the sacral order, are confronted by ordered activity. As Jonathan Z. Smith suggests, at least one of the functional characteristics of ritual is that it *"represents the creation of a controlled environment* where the variables (i.e., the accidents) of ordinary life may be displaced *precisely* because they are felt to be so overwhelmingly present and powerful."[95] Sin and impurity are fundamental characteristics of life. The creation of the Priestly system of expiatory sacrifices affirms that there is an ongoing need to confront these threats to sacral order, admitting that their permanent elimination is not possible. Bodily impurity typically is beyond human control, or a necessary outcome of otherwise positive activities that cannot be avoided (e.g., menstruation, sexual activity, and childbirth). Sin happens by accident (*bišĕgāgâ*); or where it is deliberate, it is not possible for the community to control or prevent every act of open defiance against Yahweh's commands.

As Lev 16:16b asserts, the Tent of Meeting is present in the midst of the impurities of the Israelites. This is its normal setting. In the *ḥaṭṭāʾt* blood rites represented in P, an ordered pattern of ritualized actions in sacred space stands in explicit tension with these forces of chaos and disruption that threaten the divine presence. As Smith further asserts, "Ritual is a means of performing the way things ought to be in conscious tension to the way things are in such a way that this ritualized perfection is recollected in the ordinary, uncontrolled course of things."[96] The force of the rites executed in the shrine complex, as represented for us in the text, may lie, therefore, in our reflection on them as "perfect" activities. In contrast to conditions that cause physical impurity, accidental sin, and the deliberate sins of individuals who flout communal norms, the blood manipulation acts in the shrine complex are controlled acts that enact an ordered pattern in sacred space, which stands in contrast to the chaos outside that realm. The contrast, therefore, is established between the order of sacred space and the chaos of common space. As the chaos of common space is experienced by the reader, it is possible to reflect on the order of sacred space. Thus, the ritual acts in the shrine complex, by creating an ordered space through mapping ordered patterns onto this space, establishes a hierarchical opposition between sacred space and common space, an opposition that is maintained by keeping the characteristics of common space from invading sacred space and negating its quality as sacred space.

Blood Manipulation and Removal (Kipper)

I understand the basic meaning of the verb *kipper* to be "effect removal" (see the appendix to chapter 1). This interpretation provides a very broad semantic range for the verb. Most of the occurrences of this verb in P are in connection with the *ḥaṭṭāʾt,* and some of these are linked with blood manipulation. Interpreters of the Priestly corpus continue to debate the precise meaning of *kipper* when used in connection with the *ḥaṭṭāʾt* and its blood manipulations. Many scholars affirm that it often has a general sense such as "atone" or "expiate."[97] Jacob Milgrom insists, however, that *kipper* always means "purge" when it appears in connection with the *ḥaṭṭāʾt* and that it indicates the effect of blood manipulation activity. I argue here, however, that in P *kipper* should be understood to have a broader and less concrete meaning than "purge," especially when used in connection with the *ḥaṭṭāʾt* and its blood manipulations. In addition to my treatment of the term in P, I also note the ways in which a number of interpreters have attempted to use Lev 17:11 to explain how the *ḥaṭṭāʾt* blood manipulations effect "removal" (*kipper*).

I begin my discussion with texts where *kipper* specifically identifies the effect of *ḥaṭṭāʾt* blood manipulation activity. Leviticus 6:23 speaks of blood being conveyed into the Tent of Meeting "to effect removal [*lĕkappēr*] in the holy place." This seems to indicate that the blood manipulation is especially implicated in achieving the "removal" effect. Must we conclude from this that "removal" in the case of the *ḥaṭṭāʾt* is only an effect of blood manipulation, or is blood manipulation but one of the means of attaining the goal? Of the various ritual acts performed in the *ḥaṭṭāʾt,* the only one carried out inside the shrine is blood manipulation. For this reason, it bears a special quality in relation to "removal" in the case of the *ḥaṭṭāʾt* offerings of the anointed priest and the congregation. While I conclude that Lev 6:23 tells us that blood manipulation plays a role in effecting "removal," the verse need not be interpreted to limit the means of achieving "removal" to blood manipulation.

Pushing the limits of our knowledge, I would observe that "removal" appears to be achieved in the shrine building by two actions, the sevenfold sprinkling of blood toward the curtain and the daubing onto the horns of the incense altar. In the case of the sprinkling toward the curtain, the text specifies that the sprinkling is "before Yahweh." It appears, as well, that the daubing on the altar horns is also "before Yahweh." May we not conclude, then, that Yahweh is directly implicated in the achievement of the action-effect? Indeed, as much as physical sancta are the objects of the blood manipulation, it seems that Yahweh is the true focus. For the anointed priest to stand before the curtain and to sprinkle blood toward it, especially since this action is said to occur "before Yahweh," is surely for him to engage in a relational enactment. That is, whatever the exact quality of the action-effect, and whatever the actual mechanism by which it is achieved, it seems likely that Yahweh is directly implicated in its realization. It is not the mere act of blood manipulation that is related to the action-effect *kipper*; it is blood manipulation "before Yahweh." This point may seem obvious, but given our real lack of information and explanation, its relative certainty as an interpretive "fact" means that it should be emphasized.

Leviticus 16:16a refers back to, and summarizes, the blood manipulations Aaron performs in the adytum with the blood of his bull and the people's goat: "Thus[98] he shall effect removal for the Holy Place because of the impurities of the children of Israel, and because of their acts of rebellion,[99] including all their sins."[100] Again, blood manipulation is identified as a means of achieving "removal." The effecting of "removal" is directed at the impurities, acts of rebellion and all the sins of the people. There seems to be a strong scholarly consensus that *kipper* in Lev 16:16a refers to an act that purifies the adytum, or to the effect of such an act.[101] The basis for this strong consensus seems to be the fact that "removal" seems to be directed primarily at "impurities."[102] It must be emphasized, however, that the use of *kipper* here to refer to purification through blood manipulation does not require us to limit its meaning to "purify" or "purge" in other contexts. In a number of contexts *kipper* seems to indicate the effect of the total sacrificial complex, rather than simply the blood manipulations. Here, however, it clearly refers to the acts of blood manipulation, the effect of which seems to be the "removal" of impurity and various types of sin from the adytum.

As I noted, Lev 16:18a appears to indicate that the two acts of blood manipulation performed at the altar of burnt offering are directed at achieving "removal." Lev 16:19b then indicates that the two manipulations purify and (re)consecrate the altar. I concluded that this indicates that "removal" includes both purifying and consecratory actions. In other words, *kipper* refers to the "removal" of both impurity *and* the state of being common (*ḥōl*). As Kiuchi puts it, the verb *kipper* serves as a "hypernym" for the other two verbs. Thus, if the verb *kipper* includes "consecration," Milgrom's insistence on rendering it as "purge" may be questioned. "Purge" seems to be an overly narrow translation, reflecting the position that the verb refers only to the elimination of impurity.

On this basis, when *kipper* refers to *ḥaṭṭāʾt* blood manipulations, I conclude that it includes all of the specific effects that can be attributed to those ritual actions. It is the general term, the "hypernym," while verbs such as *ḥiṭṭēʾ* (purify), *ṭihar* (cleanse) and *qiddēš* (consecrate) are more specific.

In some instances, however, *kipper* in my view, does not refer to the effect of blood manipulation activity. In Leviticus 4, it is after the descriptions of the altar offering that declarations about achieving "removal" are introduced. Similar formulas appear in verses 20, 26, 31, and 35. The common elements in each formula are: the priest is the subject of the verb *kipper;* this verb is followed by the preposition *ʿal* with a pronominal suffix indicating the human indirect object of *kipper;* and the granting of forgiveness seems to be marked as the final effect and is contingent on what is indicated by *kipper*. In two instances the reason why *kipper* is required is indicated: the priest "shall effect removal for him because of his sin" (vv. 26 and 35).[103] In other words, whatever action or effect is indicated by *kipper* is required by the sin (*ḥaṭṭāʾt*) committed by the person(s) who brought the offering.

Due to the location of this notice *after* the description of the ritual complex, it seems reasonable to conclude that *kipper* refers back to the whole ritual process in its several parts.[104] Furthermore, it is directed at the sin itself. Finally, forgiveness is dependent on achieving "removal."

Leviticus 5:6 prescribes that the individual who has committed one of the offenses listed in verses 1–5 must bring the standard *ḥaṭṭāʾt* offering for an ordinary individual: a female sheep or goat (cf. 4:27–28, 32). No description is given of the ritual procedure, presumably because the instructions have already been provided in Lev 4:27–35. We are told simply that "the priest shall effect removal on his behalf because of his sin." As in Leviticus 4, this formula seems to indicate the effect of the whole ritual process through to the burning of the altar offering. In this context, it serves as a shorthand summary of the ritual complex.[105] This usage provides further support for understanding *kipper* as indicating more than just the blood manipulation.

In the pericope on the offering of a bird *ḥaṭṭā't* (Lev 5:7– 10), following the notice of the offering of the burnt offering bird (v. 10a), the text concludes by telling us that "the priest shall effect removal on his behalf because of his sin which he sinned, and forgiveness shall be granted to him" (v. 10b). Even more so than in Leviticus 4, the location of this formula in the text suggests that it serves to characterize the overall effect of the ritual process. It is the offering of the *ḥaṭṭā't* and burnt offering together that effects "removal" and provides the basis for the granting of forgiveness.[106]

After the ritual for the cereal *ḥaṭṭā't* has been described (Lev 5:12), the text tells us that "the priest shall effect removal on his behalf because of his sin which he sinned with regard to one of these things [i.e., the various offenses treated in 5:1–4], and forgiveness shall be granted to him" (v. 13a). Again, the formula should be understood to indicate the final effect of the total ritual. In this case we may assert, without any fear of contradiction, that whatever action or effect is indicated by the verb *kipper* does not require blood manipulation. The burning of a grain offering on the altar achieves the same effect.[107]

Finally, I would emphasize the observation I made earlier, that the burning of an offering on the altar seems to be an essential component of the *ḥaṭṭā't* complex. It is never omitted. Therefore, the burning of an offering on the altar plays a central role in achieving the goal of the sacrifice. Also, *kipper* need not refer exclusively to the activity or effect of blood manipulation. It must be conceptually broad enough to comprehend the activity or effect of offering a *ḥaṭṭā't* along with a burnt offering, as well as of presenting a grain offering as a *ḥaṭṭā't*. "Effect removal," in my opinion, is still an acceptable basic translation, if we understand that more than impurity or sin, as concrete pollutants of sancta, is removed. In addition, it appears that the sin, as an offense against Yahweh, as well as Yahweh's decision to punish violations of his commandments, are removed by the ritual complex. As Lev 4:20, 26, 31, and 35 indicate, forgiveness follows on "removal." Thus, the verb *kipper* can be used to refer to the "removal" of anything that disrupts the proper workings of the divine-human relationship.

To conclude this discussion, some attention must be given to the possible relevance of Lev 17:11 for understanding the *ḥaṭṭā't* blood manipulations and the use of the verb *kipper* to identify their effect. Jacob Milgrom insists that Lev 17:11 should not be invoked in an attempt to identify the meaning of *kipper* when used in connection with the *ḥaṭṭā't*. Many scholars, however, adopt a very different attitude toward that text, identifying it as a key to understanding the workings of the *ḥaṭṭā't* blood manipulations. Here, I deal with but one example of this approach.[108] As I noted in chapters 3 and 4, Bernd Janowski, developing a thesis advanced by his teacher, Hartmut Gese, maintains that Lev 17:11 explains cultic blood manipulation as a symbolic devotion of the life of the offerer to God in the medium of the sacrificial animal's blood. "Atonement" (*Sühne*), then, involves the offerer's self-devotion to God and not primarily the removal of impurity from sancta.[109] Clearly, Gese and Janowski understand the blood-life identification as essential to the "meaning" of the *ḥaṭṭā't* blood manipulation. In my treatment of Lev 17:11 in the next chapter, I give further attention to this interpretation.

Finally, I note that although Milgrom maintains that Lev 17:11 is not to be used to explain the *ḥaṭṭā't* blood manipulations, nevertheless, he affirms that the conceptual identification of blood with life lies behind its use in the *ḥaṭṭā't* ritual complexes. Thus, he writes that blood, as life, "symbolically purges the sanctuary by symbolically absorbing its impurities" and this represents a "victory of life over death."[110] Although this explanation makes a great deal of sense, it must be emphasized that the Priestly tradents themselves never refer to the blood-life connection to explain blood manipulation. The identification of the blood-life relationship as the conceptual basis of the *ḥaṭṭā't* blood manipulations requires conceptual gap-filling.

Conclusions

In the *ḥaṭṭā't*, as in other sacrificial complexes, P reserves blood manipulation activity to members of the Aaronid priesthood. Thus, blood manipulation in a sacrificial complex functions, in the world of the text, to index the distinction between priests and thc laity as ritual actors and also to define the spatial dimensions of the priests' activity: only priests have access to the altar in the shrine complex courtyard and to the shrine building, and this access is both created and signaled by blood manipulation activity.

Within the priesthood itself, status distinctions are indexed by the identification of the different loci in which blood is manipulated. Any priest may manipulate blood on the altar of burnt offering. However, only the head priest (identified generically as "the anointed priest" or specifically as Aaron) manipulates blood inside the shrine building.[111] The head priest's ingress to this sacred area with blood functions dialectically, both to define this space as special, since a status-marked priest (Aaron, the father of the priestly house, or his uniquely "anointed" successor) is the only one who enters it to perform crucial ritual acts, as well as to index the special status of this priest, since he alone is granted access to a space defined by its heightened degree of holiness.[112] Aaron's ingress to the adytum on the Day of Removal is the supreme case of this dialectical indexing. Only Aaron may enter the adytum. Thus, his high cultic status is indexed, and, correspondingly, the supreme holiness of the adytum is indexed by the restriction of access only to Aaron. Furthermore, the fact that blood manipulation is the only act that legitimates access to the adytum[113] indexes blood as a singularly important cultic material, and its manipulation as a singularly important cultic act.

The sprinkling of blood toward or in the abode of Yahweh's presence is a relational-indexing act, indicating a relationship between the head priest and Yahweh, as well as between Yahweh and the community, which the priest represents inside the shrine. His blood manipulation activity indexes the priest as a mediator between the people and Yahweh. The priest points to Yahweh when he sprinkles blood toward the curtain, and especially when he manipulates blood in the adytum, and the blood manipulation establishes an existential link between Yahweh and the individual or group who makes an offering, mediated by the priest. The offerer indexes a relationship with the animal in the hand-pressing; the priest takes the blood of this animal and brings it into relationship with sancta, in Yahweh's presence, or points directly to Yahweh and, thus, establishes the relationship between offerer and Yahweh

In the absence of either explicit textual interpretation or scholarly attempts to reconstruct "native" interpretations, much can still be said about the *ḥaṭṭa't* blood manipulations. In my view, the results of an analysis that focuses on the indexical functions of blood manipulation actions represent a definite advance in constructive knowledge. We are able to see that, as ritual actors perform blood manipulation acts—however they may explain them—they are establishing and reinforcing important sociocultic distinctions and hierarchical relationships. In short, blood manipulation is effective in creating and reestablishing the identities of a variety of ritual actors. It is socially potent, and not merely symbolic, in the weak sense of communicating abstract concepts, or simply "spiritually" effective.

We find a small handful of interpretive comments scattered through the Priestly texts on the *ḥaṭṭāʾt*. Twice, a purifying function is attributed to the daubing of blood onto the horns of the altar of burnt offering (Lev 8:15; 16:18–19). It is likely, as Jacob Milgrom argues, that the Priestly tradents understood this manipulation to eliminate any impurity clinging to that sanctum. However, Milgrom's attempt to extend this interpretation to the act of sprinkling blood lacks textual support, since P never attributes a purifying effect to the sprinkling of blood. The only interpretive comment associated with the sprinkling of *ḥaṭṭāʾt* blood identifies the effect of the manipulation as the (re)consecration of the sanctum that is sprinkled (Lev 16:19).

However we may understand and seek to apply the Priestly textual interpretations, a key theoretical point must be emphasized: even if we identify an explicit official or public interpretation of a ritual act, and even if we assume that it is legitimate to apply this interpretation in contexts where it is not expressly stated, we should not assume that this explanation exhausts what can be said about the ritual gesture. Even for "native" cultic specialists, as well as for "lay" participants in ritual performances, ritual acts are characteristically multivalent, and there is diversity of interpretation even within unified cultic communities. Moreover, the outside interpreter is also in a position to move beyond the explicit interpretations offered by ritual participants to investigate the latent social functions and effects of ritual actions. As I noted, P's *ḥaṭṭāʾt* blood manipulations function regularly, in the world represented in the texts, to establish and reinforce distinctions between priests and nonpriests, as well as within the priestly family. Access to sacred space, and the status such access both reflects and reinforces, is marked repeatedly by the act of manipulating blood. Especially in the case of the *ḥaṭṭāʾt*, blood manipulation functions to signal and enact the high cultic status of the head priest, who is alone permitted access to the adytum of the shrine complex, and who gains access to this sacred locus by taking in blood and manipulating it there. Finally, blood manipulation activity functions, as ordered ritual activity, to map the contours of sacred space as ordered space. In other words, sacred space is ordered space because ordered activity is enacted within its bounds. The primary ordered action represented in the Priestly texts about the *ḥaṭṭāʾt* is blood manipulation. Thus, it is blood manipulation, above all, that reinforces and maintains the structure of sacred space. As Bell puts it, ritualized action is not merely a response to the sacred; in fact, it creates the sacred.

CHAPTER SIX

Blood Manipulation in Ezekiel and 2 Chronicles

Ezekiel and 2 Chronicles have evident affinities with the priestly sources (P and H) of the Pentateuch. Given those affinities, I reserved treatment of these texts until I had delved into the extensive body of P texts that refer to cultic blood manipulation. My treatment of blood manipulation in P, therefore, represents the background against which I examine the references to blood manipulation in Ezekiel and 2 Chronicles. When I have completed the examination of the relevant texts in Ezekiel and 2 Chronicles, in the next chapter I can attend to Lev 17:11, the one biblical text that is cited by numerous scholars as a key to understanding blood manipulation as it appears in the rest of the Bible, including in the works treated in this chapter.

As in the preceding chapters, my goal here is to elucidate what the texts tell us about blood manipulation by giving attention to what is represented and to how the represented activity is interpreted within the texts themselves and by reader-interpreters of the texts. I also reflect on how blood manipulation activity in these textual representations functions as ritualized activity and on its indexical significance, that is, on the ways in which it points to and defines relationships and status within the cultic sphere.

Ezekiel

The book attributed to the prophet Ezekiel contains date notices indicating that major parts of the work were composed during the early years of the exile, both before and after the destruction of Jerusalem by the Babylonians. Scholars disagree, however, about whether to accept these notices as reliable indicators of the date of the work as a whole and about whether it underwent a process of redaction that involved the addition of substantial amounts of material at later times.[1]

These questions about dating the parts and the whole are directly connected with questions about Ezekiel's relationship to the P and H pentateuchal materials. Ezekiel has obvious affinities with P and H but nevertheless is clearly independent of those sources.[2] In dealing with blood manipulation in Ezekiel, questions about the historical relationship between the book and P and H cannot be ignored. If we assume that the material in Ezekiel on blood manipulation antedates P and H, we may assess it on its own terms, and then consider how it may be reflected in the later works.[3] If, on the other hand, one holds that P and H antedate Ezekiel, it is possible to argue that Ezekiel draws on and interprets P and H teachings.[4] If it is affirmed that the relationship between Ezekiel and P and H is more complicated than either of the previous options, involving layers of compilation, matters necessarily become more complicated.[5] In this study I do not attempt to settle these questions about relative dating. My primary focus is on analyzing and evaluating the relevant materials in Ezekiel on their own terms. Nevertheless, I do consider how different assumptions about the relative dating of Ezekiel and P and H lead to different ways of evaluating the textual data.

All references to cultic blood manipulation in Ezekiel are concentrated in the so-called Temple Vision (Ezek 40–48),[6] a not surprising locus for such material, given the concern of this part of the work with the Temple and its cult. Nevertheless, there is one relevant text outside of the Temple Vision, with which I begin.

Exposed Blood as a Provocation

Ezekiel 24 begins with a parabolic quotation of a poem about stewing meat in a caldron (vv. 3b–5).[7] This is followed by what appears to be the interpretation of the poem (vv. 6ff.).[8] Jerusalem is addressed as "the city of blood(guilt)" (*ʿîr haddāmîm*) (v. 6a; see also, v. 9)[9] and identified with the caldron, which is marred with *ḥel'â* (dirty residue or soiling).[10] Apparently, the "soiling" on or in the caldron stands for Jerusalem's bloodguilt.[11] Verses 7–8 elaborates on this point: "For the blood she shed[12] remains in her midst. She has placed it on a bare rock; she has not poured it out on the earth in order to cover it over with dirt. To provoke wrath, to exact vengeance, I have placed the blood she shed on a bare rock without it being covered."

The basic sense of the verses is fairly clear. According to verse 7, sinful Jerusalem has made no effort to hide her bloodguilt. Indeed, it seems that the city is represented as advertising it.[13] The shed blood is placed on the surface of a rock in full view, rather than being poured on the ground and covered with dirt to hide it. Verse 8 adds a striking twist on the message of the previous verse by indicating that Yahweh is responsible for the exposure of the blood. He is the one who has placed it on the bare rock in order to provoke wrath and execute vengeance.[14]

When explaining Ezek 24:7–8, a number of interpreters refer to Job 16:18, in which Job cries out, "O earth, do not cover my blood" (*'ereṣ 'al-tĕkassî dāmî*).[15] This verse reflects the assumption that shed blood will provoke vengeance against the one who shed it if it remains in view. Covering blood would prevent vengeance. Ezekiel 24:7–8 appears to reflect the same idea. It is the fact that the blood is in full view—on a bare rock and not covered—that will provoke wrath and allow the execution of vengeance, as verse 8 makes clear. Ezekiel 24:7–8 is concerned with innocent human blood.

What of animal blood? Does the same principle apply? Leviticus 17:13 clearly shares terminology with Ezek 24:7–8, as I noted in my treatment of the former text (see chapter 1). However, Lev 17:13–14 does not tell us why the blood of game animals is to be poured out and covered, except by identifying it with life and placing a ban on consuming it. Ezekiel 24:7–8 indicates that exposed blood provokes vengeance, and some interpreters have used that text to explain Lev 17:13, claiming that spilled animal blood also cries out for vengeance. Not every interpreter of that verse, however, has arrived at this conclusion. As I emphasized in chapter 1, Ezek 24:7–8 deals with human blood whereas Lev 17:13 deals with animal blood. We cannot simply assume, on the basis of Ezek 24:7–8, that the covering of animal blood serves the same function as the covering of illegitimately shed human blood. Again, we confront the problems raised by attempts to make sense of an uninterpreted ritual action. While it may be legitimate to draw on evidence from another textual context, it cannot be assumed that the action in question had but one meaning or significance for ritual actors. It is certainly possible that some ancient Israelites understood the covering of animal blood to prevent it provoking vengeance, as later Jewish interpreters apparently did.[16] Others, however, may have understood the covering of blood simply to eliminate the danger that it might be consumed. It should be noted, at this juncture, that the book of Deuteronomy seems to reject the notion that shed animal blood is dangerous. The commandment to "pour it out like water" suggests that the blood, if left exposed, poses no threat to the one who shed it. Deuteronomy does not require that the blood be covered.[17]

Blood Manipulation and the Altar

In the Temple Vision, following instructions for the construction of an altar for the temple courtyard (Ezek 43:13–17),[18] we find prescriptions for the dedication of the new altar:

> Then he said to me, "Human one! Thus says the Lord Yahweh, 'These are the statutes of the altar. On the day it is made for offering up a burnt offering upon it and for tossing blood upon it, you shall give to the Levitical priests, who are of the lineage of Zadok, who draw near to me—oracle of the Lord Yahweh—to serve me, a bull of the herd as a *ḥaṭṭāʾt*. You shall take some of its blood and shall put [it] onto its four horns, and onto the four corners of the platform, and onto the rim round about,[19] and shall purify it and effect removal to it. Then you shall take the *ḥaṭṭāʾt* bull, and someone shall burn it at the appointed place of the House, outside the sanctuary. On the following day[20] you shall present a flawless male goat as a *ḥaṭṭāʾt,* and they shall purify the altar just as they purified with the bull. When you have finished purifying, you shall present a flawless bull of the herd and a flawless ram of the flock, and shall present them before Yahweh, and the priests shall cast salt upon them and shall offer them up as a burnt offering to Yahweh. For seven days you shall offer daily a *ḥaṭṭāʾt* goat; also they shall offer a flawless bull of the herd and a flawless ram of the flock. For seven days they shall effect removal to the altar and purify it and ordain it. Then, when the days are completed, on the eighth day and afterward the priests shall offer upon the altar your burnt offerings and your well-being offerings, and I will accept you favorably—oracle of the Lord Yahweh.'" (Ezek 43:18–27)

According to verse 18, the altar is made for two purposes, the offering up of burnt offerings upon it—that is, the burning of the animal's carcass in the altar fire—and the tossing of blood upon it. While the reference to the burning of

the altar offering refers explicitly to the burnt offering, the reference to the tossing of blood does not indicate which offering is the source of the blood that is
manipulated in this fashion. According to P, the blood of herd or flock animals
offered as burnt offerings, sacrifices of well-being, and reparation offerings is to
be tossed on the altar. Thus, it is reasonable to conclude that all such blood is
included here. According to Rolf Rendtorff and Jacob Milgrom, however, the
tossing of blood mentioned in this verse refers specifically to the sacrifice of
well-being.[21] They both refer to the final verse of the unit (v. 27), which tells us
what the priests will do on the altar after it has been consecrated: they will
"make" (*ya'ăśû*) burnt offerings and well-being offerings. Rendtorff and Milgrom maintain that verse 27 refers back to verse 18 and that it identifies the
mention of the tossing of blood in verse 18 as a shorthand way of referring to
the well-being sacrifice. Clearly, we have to do with the same problem I addressed in my treatment of 2 Kgs 16:13–15 in chapter 2 and in my discussion of
the well-being sacrifice in P in chapter 4. Is the blood manipulation of the well-
being sacrifice singled out for special emphasis? If so, why is this? In chapter 4,
I concluded that the blood manipulation is emphasized because it is the primary index that identifies the animal with the altar. The animal's relationship
with the altar is emphasized in this way, because most of the flesh is taken away
for consumption by the lay offerer. This flesh is identified as coming from an
animal offered as a sacrifice at the altar, as a gift given to the offerer from
Yahweh's well-being sacrifice. I would suggest that the same principle is at work
here. The tossing of the blood of the well-being sacrifice is emphasized as the
primary index of Yahweh's claim to the offering. In contrast, it is the burning of
the whole carcass of the burnt offering in the altar fire that indexes Yahweh's
claim to that offering. Thus, the blood manipulation of the well-being sacrifice
is significant, but not for the reason adduced by Milgrom.

Verses 19–26 prescribes rites of consecration over which Yahweh commands
the prophet to preside. If we compare these rites with the consecration rites in
P (Exod 29; Lev 8), we may note that Ezekiel performs a similar role to that of
Moses as he presides over the establishment of the cult.[22] The consecration
rites begin with the presentation of a bull for a *ḥaṭṭā't*. Ezekiel is to give the
bull to the Levitical priests (v. 19), presumably so that they can slaughter it.[23]
Then, according to the Massoretic Text, Ezekiel is to perform the blood manipulations.[24] Ezekiel is to take some of the blood and apply it to three places
on the altar, descending from top to bottom. All of the applications are governed by the verb *nātan* (put, daub). Thus, we may envisage Ezekiel smearing

blood onto the altar, probably with his finger. Ezekiel performs the primary altar rite. Again, if we read the text in the light of P, we see Ezekiel indexed to a special priestly status. He is the first priest to manipulate blood at the altar. We may also compare the division of labor represented here with what is represented in Exod 24:3–8, where the young men of Israel prepare the sacrifices, while Moses is assigned the task of manipulating the blood, the crucial rite of the complex. Like Moses, Ezekiel is indexed as the central actor in the complex. Moreover, his is the first priestly activity performed on the altar, and it makes subsequent priestly activity possible (vv. 18, 27).

Ezekiel first smears blood onto the four horns of the altar. This manipulation of *ḥaṭṭā't* blood is familiar to us from P. In P's ordination ceremony, Moses daubs blood onto the horns of the altar as the first blood manipulation of the ritual complex. The following two applications of blood to the altar are unique to Ezekiel in the Hebrew Bible, and we find nothing like them in P. Ezekiel daubs blood "onto the four corners of the platform"[25] and then applies blood to the rim "round about" (*sābîb*). A reader who is familiar with P may recall the threefold applications of blood to the earlobes, thumbs, and toes of Aaron and his sons at the time of their ordination, or the identical application of blood to the person healed of a skin disease. The three parts of the altar daubed with blood correspond closely to the three parts of the body to which blood is applied. As I noted in chapter 3, Milgrom refers to Ezekiel's representation, and the subsequent interpretation of the manipulation complex, in an attempt to recover a priestly interpretation of the threefold application of blood to the body in P.

At the end of verse 20, we are apparently provided with an explanation of the effect of the blood manipulations. Ezekiel purifies the altar (*wĕḥiṭṭē'tā 'ôtô*). This is the same effect attributed to the application of blood to the horns of the altar in Lev 8:15. We are also told that Ezekiel effects removal (*wĕkippartā hû*). In this case, the altar is the direct object of the verb. This construction of *kipper* with a sanctum as direct object appears also in Lev 16:20 (P) and Lev 16:33 (H). Clearly, the altar is the object of the action or effect. To what action or effect does the verb refer? Many interpreters understand *kipper* to refer specifically to an effect of the blood manipulation, just as *ḥiṭṭē'* does. It is possible, however, to gap-fill on the basis of P's usage of the verb and to interpret it as a summary statement of the full *ḥaṭṭā't* rite. Note that there is no mention of the burning of an altar offering. Verse 21 moves immediately to the burning of the carcass outside the sanctuary. Thus, I would suggest that the burning of the altar offering is assumed in the use of *kipper,* which can refer to this action, as I have indicated in my analysis of the Priestly usage. Given Ezekiel's obvious affinities to that tradition, it is reasonable to conclude that he conceived of the *ḥaṭṭā't* as including an altar offering, and that it is referred to in the verb *kipper.* The alternative interpretation, that *kipper* interprets the blood manipulations, would make the verb redundant, since we have already been told that the blood manipulations purify the altar. This is especially true for Milgrom's rendering, which would have Ezekiel "purify" and "purge" the altar. Such unnecessary repetition is out of character with the concise, even elliptical, style of Ezekiel's cultic prescriptions.

The text next prescribes that Ezekiel is to offer a male goat on the following day (v. 22a). In this case, the MT then prescribes that "they shall purify the altar just as they purified with the bull" (*wĕḥiṭṭĕ'û 'et-hammizbēaḥ ka'ăšer ḥiṭṭĕ'û bappār*) (v. 22b). The use of third-person, masculine plural verbs suggests that the priests as a group perform the blood manipulation. The present form of the text suggests a picture of a ritual complex in which Ezekiel takes the lead role, establishes the basic purity and fitness of the altar, and then hands over cultic responsibility to the other priests. By acting on the second day, the priests index the fact that they are fit to serve at the newly built altar. The prescription indicates that the same manipulations are performed with the blood of the goat as with the blood of the bull. It is striking that, here, the verb that indicates the effect of the blood manipulations is used to summarize the whole blood manipulation procedure. Furthermore, although it is the blood that is used, the text refers to the animal itself as the agent by which purification is achieved. According to verses 23–24, once the purification rites have been completed, animals are presented as burnt offerings. The making of burnt offerings indexes the fitness of the altar for cultic usage, for making offerings.

These rites are to be carried out for seven days (v. 25), and they effect removal for the altar (*yĕkappĕrû 'et-hammizbēaḥ*), cleanse it (*wĕṭihărû 'ōtô*), and ordain it (*ûmil'û yādāyw*) (v. 26). Again, we should distinguish between *kipper* (effect removal) and *ṭihar* (cleanse). Since "ordination" (*millē' yād*) is a different effect than cleansing, so presumably is "removal." I would suggest that the verb is used here as a hypernym, as in Lev 16:18, referring in a preliminary and comprehensive fashion to the two subsequently listed effects: cleansing (removal of impurity) and ordination (removal of common status). Thus, we have another instance of *kipper* with a broader meaning than "purge."

Blood Manipulation and Sancta Purification

Ezekiel 45:18–20 prescribes a ritual complex for the annual purification of the whole sanctuary: "Thus says the Lord Yahweh, "On the first day of the first month you shall take a flawless bull of the herd and you shall purify the sanctuary. The priest shall take some of the blood of the *ḥaṭṭā't* and shall daub (it) onto the doorposts of the House, and onto the four corners of the platform of the altar, and onto the doorposts of the inner courtyard. You shall do the same on the seventh day of the month because of the man who sinned by mistake or from ignorance, and you shall effect removal for the House."

Verse 18 indicates the purpose of the blood manipulations prescribed in verse 19. The three acts of daubing blood purify the sanctuary (*wĕḥiṭṭē'tā 'et-hammiqdāš*). In this context, the term *miqdāš* seems to refer to the whole sacred complex. Although Ezekiel seems to be addressed directly in verse 18, being told to take a bull and purify the sanctuary, verse 19 refers to "the priest" in the third person, and the verbs are third-person, masculine singular. It appears that Ezekiel is marked as the one who is to preside over the rite but that the actual blood manipulation is not assigned specifically to him. In any case, verse 19 indicates that blood manipulation is a priestly duty. As in P, it indexes priestly access to sancta. In this case, the priest who performs the blood manipulations indexes his access to the entrance of the temple building and the altar as well as to the gate leading out of the sacred enclosure.

The blood manipulations mark egress from the entrance of the shrine building, via the altar, to the gate leading into the courtyard before the temple. Whereas in Ezek 43:20 the altar receives three applications of blood, here it receives only one, directed at the corners of the platform. As in Ezek 43:20, however, that application is the second of three, and this three-application complex can be related to what is prescribed in Ezek 43:20. Just as the altar receives three applications of blood, marking its top, center, and base, the sacred enclosure receives three applications, marking its inner and outer boundaries and its center. This latter blood manipulation complex can be fruitfully compared with what we find represented in P, where manipulation complexes also move from the inner sphere of holiness to an outer boundary.[26] As in P, the blood manipulation complex prescribed here maps an ordered pattern onto sacred space, constructing it as sacred through this mapping. Specifically, the first and the last blood manipulations mark entrance points, thereby specifically indexing the boundaries of sacred space. As I noted, the blood manipulations also index the priest's access to sancta. I would add that the mapping of order onto sacred space also defines the total area of the priest's service. It is noteworthy that Ezekiel does not prescribe blood manipulations inside the shrine building. According to the instructions in Ezek 45:18–19, the three-part complex of applications from the entrance of the building to the gate of the courtyard is sufficient to purify the whole sanctuary complex.

Verse 20 apparently too prescribes a repetition of the same three-part complex on the seventh day of the first month, specifying that the rituals are observed for those who have sinned by mistake or from ignorance. Why should this second rite be required? Why did the ritual complex of the first day of the month not suffice? Also perplexing is the statement that the goal of the rite is to effect removal for the House. Since "the House" seems specifically to indicate the shrine building, we may wonder whether the focus of the blood manipulations is different in this case. Or, in this instance, does "the House" mean the same thing as "the sanctuary," and indicate the whole sacred complex? In any case, here the verb *kipper* seems to refer to the same effect as the *piel* of the verb *ḥṭ'*. As I noted in chapter 5, there are cases in P where *kipper* refers specifically to the effect of blood manipulation activity. We seem to have the same phenomenon here. As I argued in chapter 5, however, we should not conclude from this that *kipper,* in connection with the *ḥaṭṭā't,* refers only to the effect of blood manipulation. In the earlier discussions I have noted instances where *kipper* appears to be used to refer more generally to the effects of ritual activity.

Blood Manipulation and Cultic Status

Ezekiel 44:4–5 introduces instructions concerning access to the sanctuary. The prophet is instructed on who may be admitted to the sanctuary and on who is to be excluded, and is told to rebuke the rebellious house of Israel (v. 6) for bringing foreigners (*běnê-nēkār*), "uncircumcised in heart and uncircumcised in flesh," into the sanctuary so as to profane it (*lěhallělô*) "when you present my food, fat and blood" (*běhaqrîběkem 'et-laḥmî ḥēleb wādām*) (v. 7).

The word "food" (*leḥem*)[27] here is explained by the words "fat and blood," which stand in apposition.[28] "Fat and blood" are identified as Yahweh's "food." Both substances are offered by the Israelites. Here we encounter a significant difference between P and Ezekiel. According to Ezekiel, blood is "food" offered to Yahweh. P, in contrast, never characterizes blood as food and generally avoids even the suggestion that it is an offering, except when priests are the subjects of the verb *hiqrîb.*

Ezekiel 44:9 emphatically bans any foreigner from the sanctuary. The pericope then turns its attention from banning the access of foreigners to defining the duties of cultic functionaries, of those who may have access.[29] Verse 10 declares that the Levites are to be punished for their former faithlessness. They are assigned service tasks in the sanctuary—watching over the gates, attending to the needs of the lay offerers, and slaughtering the burnt offering and eaten sacrifice for them. Because of their previous cultic misdeeds (v. 12), they are prohibited from serving as priests, and they are not to draw near to Yahweh or to his holy things (v. 13). Note here the emphasis on access to the divine presence and to sacred things.[30]

Whereas P leaves the task of slaughtering sacrificial animals to the lay offerer and does not mention the Levites in the sacrificial manual or in connection with other cultic instructions in Exodus and Leviticus, Ezekiel assigns the task of slaughtering to the Levites. In the cult as represented by Ezekiel, the lay offerers have far less to do.[31] They are removed one step back from the manipulation of blood. The control of slaughter by the Levites places them between the priests and the laity. Thus, we should expect that blood manipulation will function primarily as an index that distinguishes priests from Levites. This is, in fact, the case.

At verse 15, the pericope turns its attention to "the Levitical priests, the descendants of Zadok" (*hakkōhănîm halĕwîyim bĕnê ṣādôq*), who are rewarded for their faithfulness.[32] Yahweh permits them to draw near to him and serve him and to stand before him, unlike the Levites, who stand before the people and serve them (compare v. 11 with v. 15). Specifically, the Zadokites are to offer Yahweh fat and blood (*lĕhaqrîb lî ḥēleb wādām*) (v. 15b). As in verse 7, the verb *hiqrîb* governs both objects. Both fat and blood are presented to Yahweh. As in P, the offering of fat and blood is marked as a priestly prerogative. Ezekiel emphasizes this quite strongly: only priests of the line of Zadok may offer fat and blood. As in P, the special status of the priests is indexed by their exclusive access to the altar, which access is itself indexed by the offering of fat and blood.[33] It is noteworthy that here, as in verse 7, fat is listed before blood. In P, as I have noted, the priests are represented as applying blood to the altar before they burn the fat portions. Does Ezekiel's construction suggest a different procedure, or is it simply a matter of emphasis? In my opinion, the latter explanation is to be preferred. Fat seems to be listed first to mark it as the primary food offering. This interpretation is supported by reference to H texts that deal with fat and blood. In Lev 17:6, H follows P's prescriptions: the priest manipulates the blood and then offers the fat (see chapter 7 for further discussion of this text). In other contexts, however, H presents laws governing the uses and treatment of fat before dealing with blood, adding blood almost as an afterthought (see Lev 3:16b–17; 7:23–27, and the discussion of these passages in chapter 1). Thus, although the manipulation of blood is the primary priestly duty, Ezekiel does not identify the blood itself as the primary food offering.

2 Chronicles

The two books commonly referred to as 1 and 2 Chronicles are a single narrative of the history of Israel from creation to the beginning of the restoration under Cyrus.[34] The work is clearly a product of the Second Temple period, almost certainly of the Persian era. The work draws on and reworks the Deuteronomistic History, especially 1–2 Samuel and 1–2 Kings, but has its own distinct ideological agenda. This agenda is reflected in the ways in which the material drawn from the Deuteronomistic History is reworked. Of special relevance to this study is the evident interest of the work's author(s) in cultic matters. The author adds details of ritual practice when retelling narratives of cultic events drawn from 1–2 Kings. For example, 2 Chron 35:1–19 is evidently based on the account of Josiah's Passover in 2 Kgs 23:21–23. However, the account in 2 Chronicles refers explicitly to the slaughter of the Passover animals and the manipulation of their blood, details absent from the 2 Kings account.[35] Although there are references to cultic activity throughout 1–2 Chronicles, there is a special concentration of cultic material at the end of 2 Chronicles, and it is in this context that we find all of the references to blood manipulation activity.

In 2 Chron 29:3ff., we find an account of the cleansing and restoration of the Temple carried out under Hezekiah. Following the rites of cleansing, sacrificial rites are carried out in the cleansed cult place:

> Then Hezekiah the king arose early and gathered together the city officials and went up to Yahweh's house. They conveyed seven bulls, seven rams, and seven lambs [for a burnt offering],[36] and seven male goats for a *ḥaṭṭā't* for the royal household, and for the sanctuary, and for Judah. He instructed the sons of Aaron the priests to offer up (burnt offerings) upon Yahweh's altar. So they slaughtered the herd animals, and the priests received the blood and tossed (it) onto the altar. They slaughtered the rams and they tossed the blood onto the

altar. Then they slaughtered the lambs and they tossed the blood onto the altar. Then they brought forward the *ḥaṭṭā't* goats before the king and the assembly, and they pressed their hands upon them. The priests slaughtered them and performed the *ḥaṭṭā't* manipulations with their blood at the altar in order to effect removal for all Israel. For the king had instructed that the burnt offering and the *ḥaṭṭā't* were for all Israel. (2 Chron 29:20–24)

It is not clear who the subjects are of "they slaughtered" (*wayyišḥāṭû*) in verse 22.[37] The priests are specified as the subjects of the next verb to appear in the verse, "they received" (*wayĕqabbĕlû*). This construction may be understood to indicate that the priests are not the subjects of the previous verb.[38] That is, the specification of priests as subjects in the case of "they received" may be understood to indicate a change of subject from the previous verb. Clearly, the priests perform the blood manipulations. First, they receive (*wayĕqabbĕlû*) the blood. This verb does not appear in P. It is not entirely clear whether it indicates that the priests collected the blood at the slaughter, or that they received it from others who had collected it. Some clarification may be provided by representations of blood manipulation activity elsewhere in 2 Chronicles. Whatever the case, it is clear that the priests take responsibility for the blood and apply it to the altar. Handling blood is explicitly marked here as a priestly prerogative, just as it is in P and Ezekiel. All verbs that have "blood" as the object have priests as the subjects. In the world of the text, we observe the priests applying blood to the altar, and as in P, this action functions as the primary index of the priests' access to that locus.

Verses 23–24 contains the only mention of the *ḥaṭṭā't* offering in 1–2 Chronicles. As in P, the slaughter of the victims is preceded by the hand-pressing rite. In this case, the king and representatives of the assembly perform the act. Here, as elsewhere, this act is uninterpreted. Nevertheless, the gesture establishes a relationship between the king, the assembly, and the animals, indicating that the animals are offered as a communal *ḥaṭṭā't* for the whole nation. According to verse 24, the priests slaughter the animals. In this case, there is no ambiguity.[39] It is possible to appeal to this verse in support of the claim that the priests also should be identified as the ones who slaughtered the burnt offering animals. However, one could also argue that the specificity in this case indicates that the procedure with the *ḥaṭṭā't* animals is different. In any event, lay participation in the ritual complex represented in the text ends with the hand-pressing. Unlike in P, the first priestly act is the slaughter, not the blood manipulation. Thus, the lay community is removed one step further from the altar.[40]

In verse 24, the verb *wayěhattě'û* (*piel* of *ht'*) has "their blood" (*'et-dāmām*) as its direct object. This is a unique construction. Some precedent for the construction is provided, however, by the usage we have seen in P where the verb has the *hattā't* animal as its direct object. As my translation indicates, we must understand the formulation here to indicate that the blood was manipulated according to the procedure for the *hattā't*. The text seems to reflect the assumption that readers would know what this manipulation activity involved. Second Chronicles 29:24a indicates clearly that the altar is the locus of the blood manipulation. A reader familiar with P's representations will "gap-fill" the acts of daubing the blood onto the horns of the altar and pouring out of the rest to the base.

The end of verse 24 identifies the purpose of the blood manipulation activity. It is "in order to effect removal for all Israel" (*lěkappēr 'al-kol-yiśrā'ēl*). The verse then explains that the king had instructed that the burnt offerings and *hattā't* offerings were for all Israel. As in P, it is not clear what effect is indicated by *kipper*. If the verb *hittē'* may be understood to indicate not merely the mode of blood manipulation but also its effect ("purify"), we might assert that "removal" involved the elimination of impurity from sancta. Any conclusion we reach about these questions will depend on the use we make of the relevant P material and, therefore, on our interpretation of that material. As I argued in chapter 5, the verb *kipper* can refer to any act that eliminates whatever disrupts the positive relationship between Yahweh and his devotees. In this context, the verb could certainly refer to the removal of impurity from the altar. However, we need not assume that this effect is the only one that could be attributed to the manipulation of *hattā't* blood.

A striking difference between what is represented in P and what we find here is in the order of the offerings. While P's prescriptive manual of sacrifice begins with the burnt offering, other texts make clear that the *hattā't* offering is to precede the burnt offering when the two are offered on the same occasion. Here, however, it appears that the burnt offering rites are carried out before the *hattā't* rites. Only the argument that the text is not presenting a sequential narrative would allow the harmonization of this text with P's representations.[41] Matters are somewhat complicated by the fact that verse 22 describes only the blood manipulations. Verses 27–29 may pick up where verse 22 leaves off with an account of the burning rites.[42] Does this indicate that the blood rites of the burnt offering were separated from the burning of the altar offering by the *ḥaṭṭā't* blood rites, or must we advance another argument that the text does not provide a sequential narrative? Again, answers to these questions will depend on assumptions about the relationship of Chronicles with P. If one assumes that Chronicles must correspond to P in its ritual prescriptions, one will likely judge the narrative to be nonsequential and reorganize the details to construct an image of ritual activity that corresponds to what one understands P to represent. If, however, one affirms Chronicles' independence from P, one may argue that the ritual process represented here differs from what we find in P. It is certainly possible that 2 Chronicles does represent the offering of the burnt offering as taking place before that of the *ḥaṭṭā't.*

If we take 2 Chron 29:20–29 as presenting a sequential narrative, we may draw the following conclusions about the text's approach to blood manipulation. According to the text, the first application of blood to the newly purified altar was accomplished with the tossing of the blood of burnt offerings. We are not told anything about the purpose of this blood manipulation. Verse 24, however, indicates that the burnt offerings were sacrificed for all Israel. Therefore, we may conclude that whatever benefit followed from the blood manipulation went to the whole people. Likewise, the manipulation of the blood of the *ḥaṭṭā't* animals benefited the whole people. Although the altar is the locus of the blood application, the benefit of this manipulation is experienced by the people. Given these facts, it is possible to conclude that the sequence of sacrifices and blood manipulations did not matter to the author of this text. Although only the *ḥaṭṭā't* blood manipulation is said to effect removal, the author of 2 Chron 29:20–24 does not seem to have believed that the effecting of removal with *ḥaṭṭā't* blood was a prerequisite for the offering of burnt offerings. Rather, one could maintain that he understood the offering of burnt offerings, and particularly the manipulation of their blood, to be a prerequisite for offering *ḥaṭṭā't* sacrifices and the manipulation of their blood. Nevertheless, the evidence provided by the text is so ambiguous that no certainty is possible. As I have emphasized, almost all of our conclusions depend on how we relate this passage to texts from P.

The other two references to blood manipulation in 2 Chronicles both concern the blood of Passover offerings. Second Chronicles 30 describes the Passover celebrated under Hezekiah following the purification of the Temple. Second Chronicles 30:15 seems to indicate that the lay offerers slaughtered their own lambs at the Temple. Verse 16 tells us that the priests and Levites stood in their assigned places, "the priests tossing the blood from the hand of the Levites" (*hakkōhănîm zōrĕqîm 'et-haddām miyyad halĕwîyim*). Verse 17 then explains that many members of the assembly had not purified (or "sanctified") themselves (*lō'-hitqaddāšû*). Therefore, the Levites slaughtered the Passover animals for all who were not clean (*lō' ṭāhôr*) so that the offering would be holy for Yahweh (*lĕhaqdîš lyhwh*). This indicates rather clearly that the normal procedure envisaged by the author of the text is that the lay offerer slaughtered his animal.[43] Since verse 17 explains verse 16, it is reasonable to conclude that normally the priests received the blood from the offerers. The Levites' role in the ritual process is unusual, determined by the unusual circumstance that many of the offerers were not pure.[44] Thus, it appears that the author of this text held a different position on the role of the Levites in the cult than the author of Ezekiel 44. While Ezekiel 44 prescribes that the Levites always slaughter the offerings of the laity, this text indicates that the Levites perform this task only when the lay offerers are unable to do so.

Second Chronicles 35:6 and 11, however, complicate the picture, since they indicate that the Levites also slaughtered the offerings for the lay offerers at the time of Josiah's renewed Passover. In fact, verse 6 has Josiah instruct the Levites to slaughter the Passover offering. In this case, the text does not indicate a reason for this procedure. I would suggest, however, that the author assumes the procedures followed in Hezekiah's time and represents Josiah's renewed Passover as being observed with the same strictness.[45] That is, we may assume the same basic problem, the danger that an impure layperson would slaughter the Passover offering. As in Hezekiah's day, the Levites were interposed between the priests and the laity. This means that we cannot take 2 Chron 35:6 and 11 as representing standard practice and establishing the Levites as cultic slaughterers. It must be conceded, however, that this interpretation requires gap-filling from the account of Hezekiah's Passover. Such gap-filling can be justified by the assumption that a common viewpoint informs the two passages within the same document. Still, it must be affirmed as gap-filling.

The two verses fail to indicate where the blood is tossed. It seems rather obvious that the altar is the locus. Nevertheless, it is necessary to recognize that the reader must fill the gap. As elsewhere in 2 Chronicles, and in agreement with P and Ezekiel, blood manipulation is reserved to the priests, and indexes their special cultic status. In this specific instance, the Levites' intermediary status is indexed by the fact that they make the blood available to the priests. Clearly, they may handle it, but they do not perform the cultic manipulations. Thus, their intermediate cultic status—above lay Israelites but below the priests—is indexed.

Conclusions

In both Ezekiel and 2 Chronicles we find representations of blood manipulation that are similar to what we have seen in P texts. Both works refer to the tossing of blood onto the altar, and Ezekiel mentions the daubing of blood onto the horns of the altar. Ezekiel also represents distinctive manipulations, the daubing of blood onto the "platform" and the "rim" of the altar. Second Chronicles refers to the manipulation of the blood of the *ḥaṭṭā't* using the *piel* of the verb *ḥṭ'* but does not clearly represent the blood manipulation actions.

Ezekiel attributes a purifying effect to the application of the blood of the *ḥaṭṭā't* to sancta. The book also refers to the effect of these manipulations using the verb *kipper*. As in P, it can refer quite generally to the "removal" of whatever disrupts the divine-human relationship or, more specifically, to a purifying effect. The same conclusion may be made about *kipper* as it is used once in 2 Chronicles to refer to the effect of blood manipulation activity.

Considerably more can be said about blood manipulation as represented in Ezekiel and 2 Chronicles if we refer to the indexing function of ritualized activity. In Ezekiel and 2 Chronicles, as in P, blood manipulation is a priestly duty. When we observe the performance of ritual actions in the textually constructed worlds of Ezekiel and 2 Chronicles, we see that only priests apply blood to the altar. Thus, blood manipulation activity indexes the special status of the priests and distinguishes them from nonpriests (both lay Israelites and Levites). In Ezekiel, Levites are explicitly banned from dealing with fat and blood, the two substances that are assigned to the altar as Yahweh's "food" (Ezek 44:7). Their lower status is indexed by this lack of access. In 2 Chronicles, on the other hand, the Levites are permitted to perform the subordinate act of passing the blood of the Passover offerings to the priests, who toss it onto the altar. In this representation, the Levites are marked as cultic intermediaries who stand between priests and lay Israelites.

We may also note that the *ḥaṭṭā't* blood manipulations represented in Ezekiel function, as precise and ordered activity, to map order onto space and thereby to construct and reinforce the existence of *sacred* space. The care exercised in applying blood to sancta establishes a privileged opposition between the locus where such care is exercised and those loci where such careful activity is not enacted. Thus, ritualized activity creates ritualized space by marking it off from nonritualized space.

CHAPTER SEVEN

Leviticus 17:11 and the Power of Blood

In the preceding chapters, I noted the important role Lev 17:11 plays in a number of attempts to identify the meaning or purpose of cultic blood manipulations. In this chapter, I focus on Lev 17:11 in its immediate context and in the context of the work of the H tradents as a whole, with a twofold goal in view: to clarify what the verse says about blood manipulation, and to consider how this might be applied to manipulation activity represented in other contexts, both in the H corpus and in other parts of the Hebrew Bible. In these latter reflections, I give special attention to the implications that follow from identifying Lev 17:11 as a secondary and interpretive composition in relation to the P stratum of the Pentateuch.

Interpreting Leviticus 17:11: A Brief *Status Questionis*

Many interpreters understand Lev 17:11 to refer to any application of blood to the altar and, thus, to provide a conceptual explanation for blood manipulation in all sacrifices.[1] Others go further and affirm that the text explains all uses of sacrificial blood, even when it is not applied to the altar.[2] Although many interpreters affirm that Lev 17:11 explains most, if not all, blood manipulations, there is no consensus on what the verse, in fact, says about blood manipulation.

For David Hoffmann, Lev 17:10–12 serves as the basis for his interpretation of every sacrificial blood manipulation as a symbolic self-giving of the offerer to God, and of "atonement" as involving God's acceptance of this self-giving.[3] Notker Füglister notes the association of sin and impurity with death and understands Lev 17:11 to interpret blood manipulation as effecting the restoration or intensification of the life-force that characterizes sancta.[4]

According to Ibn Ezra, the verb *kipper* means "serve as a ransom,"[5] and Lev 17:11 indicates that the life in the blood ransoms the life of the offerer ("life in place of life" [*npš tḥt npš*]) (Ibn Ezra on Lev 17:11). As I noted in previous chapters, Ibn Ezra applies this understanding of blood as a ransom payment (*kōper*) to the explanation of a variety of blood manipulations, including the tossing of the blood of the burnt offering, the daubing of blood onto Aaron and his sons at their ordination to the priesthood, the manipulation of the blood of the Passover sacrifice as represented in Leviticus 12, and even Zipporah's action when she circumcised her son and touched the bloody foreskin to Moses' feet![6] Note, in addition, Ibn Ezra's explanation of the statement "he shall effect removal upon the holy place" in Lev 16:16 (ad loc.): "The blood functions as a ransom payment [*kōper*] so that he will not be destroyed [*šl'yšḥt*] because of the impurity of the impure."

Other interpreters limit the scope of the verse's application. Schmid maintains that the verse refers only to the blood of those sacrifices that are explicitly identified as expiatory, primarily the *ḥaṭṭā't* and the reparation offering. Thus, he asserts, the verse does not apply to the blood of the well-being sacrifice.[7] Janowski understands Lev 17:11 to apply primarily to the *ḥaṭṭā't*.[8] Baruch Levine maintains that the verse applies only to "the blood libation," the tossing (*zrq*) of blood onto the altar, which figures in the burnt offering, the sacrifice of well-being, and the reparation offering. It does not, however, explain the blood manipulations of the *ḥaṭṭā't* sacrifice.[9] Jacob Milgrom and Herbert C. Brichto argue that the verse refers only to the blood manipulation in the sacrifice of well-being.[10]

Related to these differences over the application of Lev 17:11 are different views over the meaning of the verb *kipper* in the verse. Most interpreters seem to hold that it has the same basic meaning as elsewhere in the Priestly texts and must be understood in relation to its usage in those other texts. Thus, for example, Füglister and Sabourin note the association of *kipper* with purification in the case of the *ḥaṭṭāʾt* and seek to explain how blood, as life, functions to remove impurity or to deal with its effects.[11] Both claim that "atonement" involves the restoration or intensification of life-force. Janowski, in contrast, minimizes the importance of those texts that attribute a purifying effect to blood manipulation and argues that *kipper* indicates primarily the symbolic devotion of life to Yahweh.[12] Schenker begins with the assumption that *kipper* (*sühnen*) refers to forgiveness of sins and interprets Lev 17:11 as an explanation of how blood manipulation activity is related to God's gracious act of forgiveness.[13]

Levine, Brichto, and Milgrom, on the other hand, assert that *kipper* in Lev 17:11 means "ransom."[14] The placing of the animal's blood on the altar saves the life of the offerer. However, Levine differs with Milgrom and Brichto over the reason why the offerer's life is in danger. According to Levine, offerers face the threat of death every time they enter Yahweh's presence, because of their basic sinfulness and impurity, which may provoke an outburst of divine wrath. Milgrom and Brichto, on the other hand, maintain that the offerer's life is endangered because Yahweh regards the killing of an animal for food as murder and will exact vengeance against the one who slaughters it.

Despite the wide variety of conflicting interpretations of the verse, most interpreters affirm that the teaching set forth in the verse—whatever this might be—may be applied beyond its immediate context, either to the explanation of all blood manipulation activity, or to specific types of manipulation activity. Leviticus 17:11 is treated as providing an explanation for blood manipulation activity that is not interpreted in other texts. Thus, it is necessary, first, to clarify what the verse says about blood manipulation and, then, to consider how this teaching might be applied to the blood manipulation actions represented in other texts. I begin my exploration of these questions with a discussion of the immediate context in which Lev 17:11 appears.

Leviticus 17:11 in Context

Leviticus 17 begins with an introductory statement, indicating that Yahweh spoke to Moses and told him to transmit commandments to Aaron and his sons and to all the children of Israel (17:1–2). The commandment material that follows the introductory statement (vv. 3–16) can be divided into five units (vv. 3–7, 8–9, 10–12, 13–14, and 15–16).[15] Baruch Schwartz, in his analysis of the structure of the chapter,[16] identifies the third unit, consisting of verses 10–12, as "a Janus-faced passage, looking forward and backward at once,"[17] and as "the axis upon which the chapter revolves."[18] From this analysis of the structure of the chapter, and the place of verses 10–12 within it, Schwartz concludes that the proper treatment of the blood of animals that may be eaten is the thematic thread that binds the chapter together.[19] Schwartz makes a very persuasive case for his structural and thematic analysis of the chapter, and this analysis serves as the basis for my own treatment here.

The first unit of the chapter (vv. 3–7) establishes its key themes. In the normal sequential reading process, this unit is what the reader first encounters, and it shapes his or her expectations about what will follow. In order to clarify what it communicates, I offer here a close reading of the unit, divided into smaller subsections. I begin with Lev 17:3–4: "As for any man from the house of Israel who slaughters an ox, a sheep, or a goat in the Camp or who slaughters outside the Camp, and does not convey it to the entrance of the Tent of Meeting to present an offering to Yahweh before Yahweh's Tabernacle, bloodguilt will be reckoned to that man; he has shed blood, and that man will be severed from the midst of his people."

Verses 3–4a refers to a proscribed act, the slaughter of a domestic animal without first conveying it to the Tent of Meeting in order to make an offering to Yahweh. The act of slaughter is emphasized by the repetition of the verb *šḥṭ* (slaughter). However, missing from the verse is any indication of the reason for slaughtering the animal. Although one might assume that the primary reason for slaughtering an animal is to consume its flesh,[20] this reason is not made explicit. The act of slaughter is not itself problematic, nor is its motivation. Slaughtering a domestic animal becomes problematic, in the circumstances indicated in verse 4a, when a specified praxis is not followed.[21] Failure to convey the animal to the Tent of Meeting so as to make an offering to Yahweh renders the act of slaughter illegitimate.

Verse 4b indicates that slaughtering a domestic animal without conveying it to the Tent of Meeting to present an offering to Yahweh is a negative act that carries a negative consequence. First, the text tells us how the act will be regarded: "Bloodguilt will be reckoned to that man; he has shed blood." To speak of bloodguilt and the shedding of blood evidently draws attention to the act of slaughter itself, by which the animal's blood is caused to pour out. As well, as I noted earlier, the act is emphasized by the repetition of the verb *šḥṭ* in verse 3. According to this text, if the act of slaughter is carried out "in the camp . . . or outside the camp," and is not associated with an offering rite at the Tent of

Meeting focused relationally on Yahweh, it will be treated as murder. The formulations here are unambiguous. "They are," as Milgrom emphasizes, "precise legal terms which define and categorize the guilt."[22] Having indicated the nature of the guilt that follows from the negative act, the text then identifies the penalty. Classed as a murderer, the man who is guilty of this offense is subject to the penalty of "severing" (*krt*): "and that man shall be severed [*wěnikrat hā'îš hahû'*] from the midst of his people." However, as I noted, the act of slaughtering an animal is not itself treated as problematic. What is at issue is whether the act of slaughter plays a role in the process of making an offering to Yahweh. I emphasize this point in response to Milgrom's assertion that slaughtering an animal for food is itself always a "crime."[23]

The threat form of the text implies a prohibitive command directed against slaughtering a domestic animal except in order to make an offering to Yahweh.[24] The prohibitive command may be rephrased as a positive command: domestic animals may only be slaughtered if they are brought to the shrine in order to make an offering to Yahweh. From the command stated this way, we may deduce a solution to the threat enunciated in verses 3–4. If one wishes to avoid the "severing" penalty, one will slaughter animals only in connection with making an offering to Yahweh. Verses 5–6 sets forth this proper praxis and elaborates on the proscribed alternative: "This is in order that the children of Israel will convey their eaten sacrifices, which they are wont to slaughter in sacrifice[25] upon the surface of the field, and will convey them to Yahweh to the entrance of the Tent of Meeting to the priest, and will slaughter them in sacrifice as sacrifices of well-being to Yahweh. Then the priest will toss the blood on Yahweh's altar at the entrance of the Tent of Meeting and will turn the fat into smoke for a soothing odor for Yahweh."

The first words of verse 5 indicate that the "severing" threat in verse 4 is made "in order that" (*lěma'an*) the children of Israel will follow the approved praxis represented in verses 5–6.[26] The alternative to this prescribed sacrificial activity is sacrificial slaughter carried out "upon the surface of the field." Verse 5 clearly establishes an opposition between the approved locus for sacrifice and an illegitimate locus. Whereas verses 3–4 is ambiguous, verse 5 indicates that slaughter must take place at the Tent of Meeting for it to be a legitimate act. Moreover, the verse indicates that slaughter outside the Tent of Meeting involves the offering of a sacrifice. Whereas verse 3 refers simply to slaughtering (*šḥt*) an animal, verse 5 says that the Israelites are in the habit of making sacrifices ("their eaten sacrifices which they are wont to slaughter in sacrifice"), explicitly characterizing the act of slaughter as a cultic act. Slaughter at the Tent of Meeting makes "their eaten sacrifices" (*zibḥêhem*) into "sacrifices of well-being" (*zibḥê šĕlāmîm*). The text also emphasizes that sacrifices performed at the Tent of Meeting are "for Yahweh," the formula *lyhwh* being repeated twice in verse 5. Note, as well, that verse 6 specifies that the blood is applied to "*Yahweh's* altar" and that the burning of the fat portions on the altar produces a soothing odor "for *Yahweh.*" This emphasis on the theological-relation focus of the conveying of the animals and of their subsequent slaughter suggests that the sacrifices made "upon the surface of the field" are *not* offered to Yahweh. Thus, in my view, the text reflects concern with the cultic motivations of those who slaughter and not with their desire to consume meat.

Verse 5 indicates that conveying an animal to the Tent of Meeting involves conveying it to a priest. Verse 6 describes the priest's activity. He performs the same two key priestly duties emphasized in P: he manipulates the blood and he burns an altar offering. The specific form of the acts conforms to what is required by P for a sacrifice of well-being. The priest dashes the blood on the altar,[27] and he turns the fat into smoke "for a soothing odor for Yahweh." As in P, the blood manipulation is the first official priestly act and is mentioned first. The burning of the altar offering is the culmination of the altar ritual and is, therefore, mentioned last. Thus, the representation of the priest's activity in verse 6 amounts to an *inclusio* for all priestly acts. The blood manipulation is not singled out for special emphasis. It is certainly important, but it is not mentioned first because it has a unique significance. Rather, this text is affirming what I have already established through an analysis of the P texts on sacrifice: blood manipulation is the act that marks the beginning of the priestly activity in a sacrificial complex. Likewise, the burning of the altar offering marks the end of this activity. It should also be noted that, as in P's account of the sacrifice of well-being, the purpose of the fat-burning is identified while there is no explanation of the blood manipulation.[28]

Nevertheless, the characterization of slaughter outside the shrine as murder in verse 4 *does* emphasize the blood. It is difficult to account for this characterization apart from the recognition of a special focus on the flow of blood that follows the cutting of the animal's throat. According to verse 4, if the blood of a domestic animal is shed otherwise than in connection with making an offering to Yahweh, this shedding of blood will be regarded as equivalent to the illegitimate shedding of human blood. The significance of this characterization can be understood by examining an H text that we may treat as part of the informational repertoire of a competent reader of Lev 17: Num 35:30–34.

Israel Knohl makes a persuasive case for regarding all of Numbers 35 as a composition of the H tradents.[29] We may certainly identify the material of direct relevance to this discussion as a product of H, given the special concern with the purity of the land, which we also find in the core of H.[30] Numbers 35:30–34 reads:

> As for anyone who strikes down a person—the slayer shall be slain according to the testimony of witnesses; but a single witness against a person shall not be sufficient for him to be put to death. You shall not accept a ransom payment [*kōper*] for the life of one who has slain, who is indeed subject to the death penalty, for he must definitely be put to death. Furthermore, you shall not accept a ransom payment for one who has fled[31] to his city of refuge, for him to return to live in the land before the death of the (high) priest. You shall not pollute the land in which you are; for the blood indeed pollutes the land, and for the land there is no effecting of removal for the blood which is shed in it except with the blood of the one who shed it. You shall not render impure the land in which you dwell, in the midst of which I reside; for I Yahweh reside in the midst of the children of Israel

A "ransom payment" (*kōper*) is given to save an individual from death or serious harm.[32] This text indicates that such payment may not be made for a deliberate murderer, who must be put to death, or for the person who has accidentally killed someone, who is safe from being killed by the "avenger of blood" only while resident in a city of refuge (Num 35:25–27), and who is finally freed from the threat of death only after the high priest dies (Num 35:28, 32).

According to verse 33, shed blood pollutes the land, and this situation of pollution can only be remedied with the blood of the one who shed the blood. The fact that the verb *kipper* indicates the solution to the problem of the land's pollution with blood suggests to me that the verb is used here to indicate some kind of purification, rather than a legal transaction.[33] Milgrom, however, treats *kipper* in verse 33 as indicating the effect of paying a *kōper*,[34] a problematic interpretation. A *kōper* is paid by or for the person who is in danger of death. This is assumed by the text here, which rejects the idea that any payment could be made to free a murderer from the death penalty or to allow the accidental killer to return from the city of refuge before the death of the high priest. The impurity of the killer is not at issue. Legal guilt and the killer's liability to being executed are the matters of concern with which the *kōper* might deal. In contrast, the earth *has* been polluted, and its ability to sustain the divine presence has been called into question. It is not guilty and certainly is not in danger of death. Thus, a *kōper* would not be paid for it. Rather, it needs to be purified. This text seems to assume the Priestly practice of using blood to remove impurity and indicates the action-effect using the standard verb *kipper*, which has the general meaning "effecting removal" of whatever causes a disruption in the proper workings of the divine-human relationship. In this instance, the execution of the killer removes that which endangers the continued residence of the deity in the land. What verse 33 declares, then, is that the pollution caused by shed blood, which "pollutes" the land, cannot be removed by any blood other than the blood of the one who shed the blood. Execution of the murderer, with the pouring out of his blood, is likened to a sacrificial rite.

Another point to note, which may be deduced from this verse, and from the overall teaching of the chapter about the execution of murderers, is that there is legitimate shedding of blood as well as illegitimate. Killing an innocent person produces shed blood that pollutes the land and disrupts the order that sustains the divine presence in Israel. In contrast, when the properly designated executioner ("the redeemer of blood") strikes down a murderer or one who has accidentally taken a human life, his act is legitimate. As the text specifies, the "redeemer of blood" is not liable to bloodguilt (v. 27: *'ên lô dām*).

Because Lev 17:4 characterizes the slaughter of a domestic animal away from the shrine as murder ("bloodguilt will be reckoned to that man"), a reader familiar with the teaching presented in Num 35:30–34 could legitimately draw the conclusion that there is no possibility that a *kōper* could be paid to escape the penalty for this act. Once an illegitimate killing has taken place, the murderer's condition cannot be changed. The reader also knows that it is possible for a killing to be fully legitimate and for the one who sheds blood to be free of any guilt. If the slaughter of an animal outside of the shrine is illegitimate killing—and, therefore, murder—whereas slaughter of the animal as a sacrifice of well-being at the shrine is legitimate, and not murder, it follows that the offerer is guilty of no offense. He is like the "avenger of blood." His act of killing has been legitimized by being authorized by Yahweh. Within the shrine there is no crime to be confronted, while for the crime of "murdering" an animal outside the shrine, no *kōper* can be offered.[35] Thus, I affirm again that the act of slaughter itself is not at issue in Lev 17:3ff. It becomes an issue only when the slaughter takes place outside of the shrine and is not associated with making an offering to Yahweh. In this case, the slaughter is an illegitimate killing and is classed as murder. Moreover, in verse 5 the act is characterized as cultic slaughter.

Why this illegitimate cultic slaughter of an animal can be classed as murder is explicated by the final verse of the unit (v. 7): "Thus, they will no longer slaughter their eaten sacrifices in sacrifice to satyrs after which they are wont to go like loose women.[36] This shall be a perpetual statute for them for their generations." According to verse 7, when the Israelites bring their domestic animals to the shrine, slaughter them there, and have the priest perform the requisite rites, this prevents them from sacrificing to "satyrs" (*śĕʿîrim*; literally, "goats"), probably to be identified as spirits—demons—appearing in the form of goats, which were believed to inhabit the wilderness.[37] Thus, at issue is not simply the slaughter of a domestic animal "in the camp or outside the camp," or "upon the surface of the field"; rather, it is the object of this activity as identified by the text. According to the author of this text, there can be no "common" or noncultic slaughter, not merely because slaughter must be sacrifice to Yahweh, but because slaughter that is not constituted as sacrifice to Yahweh is actually sacrifice to some other being. Slaughter away from the shrine, according to the author of this unit, is not illegitimate simply because it is not at the shrine, but because it is an act of disloyalty to Yahweh, amounting to the worship of other gods! It is hardly surprising, therefore, that the shedding of blood can, in this context, be likened to murder. It is supremely illegitimate. The animal has died, and its blood has spilled on the ground, in service of some other being, a "satyr."[38] On this reading of the text, what is at issue is not the life of the animal per se but the context in which that life is terminated. The text says nothing about the subsequent eating of the flesh. The tradent does not appear interested in the desire to eat meat as a motivation for slaughtering an animal. To acknowledge this would simply confuse the emphasis on the locus and cultic focus of slaughter. Without the mention of the motive for slaughter, our focus remains on whether the animal has died in Yahweh's shrine and as an offering to him. This is what is at issue. We may, of course, speculate about whether the reason offered by the text for opposition to slaughter away from the shrine is the "real" one, and whether there really was a problem with sacrifice to "satyrs." However, we must begin with what the text represents. In this case, traditionalist readings that embrace the rhetoric of the text are more successful in making sense of the import of the text for an ancient reader than those readings that are suspicious of the veracity of the claims the text makes.

Concern with cultic legitimacy is further emphasized by the next, very short unit, verses 8–9. Whereas verses 3–7 concentrated on the well-being offering, verses 8–9 includes the burnt offering: "And you shall say to them: 'As for any man from the house of Israel or any resident alien who dwells in their midst who offers up [*ya'ăleh*] a burnt offering or eaten sacrifice, and does not convey it to the entrance of the Tent of Meeting to offer it to Yahweh, that man shall be severed from his people.'"

Whereas the first unit focused attention on the act of slaughter, the killing of the animal, this unit deals with the altar offering. The verb "offer up" (*ya'ăleh*) governs both the "burnt offering" (*'ōlâ*) and the "eaten sacrifice" (*zebaḥ*), and indicates the altar rite, the burning either of the whole carcass or of the fat portions in the altar fire. There is no explicit reference to blood in the text. Given this fact, how does this unit fit into the chapter if, as Schwartz and others have suggested, the whole of Leviticus 17 is about the proper treatment of blood? Schwartz does make an effective case for regarding Lev 17:10–12 as the core or "hub" of the chapter. His overall reading is compelling, but it does depend on Lev 17:10–12. Without these core verses, it is by no means necessary to see a focus on proper treatment of blood in Lev 17:8–9, or even in verses 3–7. To find teaching about blood in verses 8–9 requires a retrospective reading in the light of verses 10–12.

Like verse 3, verse 8 refers to a legitimate act—the offering of a burnt offering or eaten sacrifice—that becomes illegitimate if specific prescriptions are not observed. If an Israelite or a resident alien offers up a burnt offering or an eaten sacrifice and fails to convey it to the Tent of Meeting to offer it to Yahweh, that man will be severed. From the threat construction we may deduce a prohibitive command: no one, whether Israelite or resident alien, may offer up a burnt offering or eaten sacrifice away from the Tent of Meeting. Like the first unit, this unit reflects concern about the locus of sacrifice (where it is performed) and its relational focus (to whom it is offered).[39]

From the foregoing discussion some key conclusions may be drawn. First, the concern with blood in the first unit has to do with the locus where it is shed and the cultic significance of the act of slaughter. The killing of the animal is not itself at issue. There is no mention of the desire to eat meat as a reason for slaughtering the animal. Rather, the texts evidence a strong concern with the cultic significance of an act of slaughter. The designation of the act of slaughter outside of the shrine complex as murder is connected with its cultic illegitimacy. Thus, I conclude that the thesis advanced by Milgrom and Brichto, that the slaughter of an animal for food is itself murder, should be rejected.

Finally, if, as Schwartz maintains, Lev 17:10–12 functions as the thematic core of the chapter, its emphasis on the proper treatment of blood must be brought to verses 3–9 secondarily. The first unit of the chapter does refer to the proper treatment of blood, but this is hardly its central focus. The second unit does not mention blood at all. It might be better to maintain that the references to blood in verses 3–7, and the emphasis on proper sacrificial practice in verses 8–9, provide the basis for the focused treatment of blood and its use in the cult that follows in verses 10–14.

Leviticus 17:11 in the Context of Leviticus 17:10–12

Because I introduced Lev 17:10–12 in chapter 1, I add here only a few contextual points against the background of the earlier discussion. First, whereas the first unit of the chapter (vv. 3–7) is concerned with the legitimate cultic purpose and context for the shedding of animal blood, and the second unit (vv. 8–9) deals with the purpose and context of making an altar offering, the third unit of the chapter (vv. 10–12) deals with the possibility that blood might be consumed when meat is eaten. This focus is evident from the verses that open and close the unit, both of which refer to the ban on consuming blood. Thus, for the first time, the text expresses concern with the eating of animal flesh rather than with the act of slaughter that makes the meat available.

In verse 10, as in verses 3–4 and 8–9, the identification of a negative act is followed by the declaration of the negative divine response, the threat of severing.[40] The negative declaration amounts to a prohibition against eating blood. The solution to the threat of divine extirpation is to refrain from consuming blood. The rule against the consumption of "any blood" (*kol-dām*) applies to both Israelites and resident aliens, and amounts to a general declaration against the consumption of any and all blood, regardless of its source. In further support of this claim, I note that the previous unit (vv. 8–9) has already broadened the focus of the text beyond the sacrifice of well-being by referring inclusively to all sacrifices. It is in the light of the fact that verses 10 and 12 refer to all blood that one should read Lev 17:11, which is bracketed and emphasized by the two prohibitive declarations in verses 10 and 12.

Virtually every word in Lev 17:11 has been the focus of scholarly disagreement. My analysis of the verse begins with its overall structure. I then deal sequentially with its individual elements. The verse can be divided into three clauses: Lev 17:11a ("For the life of the flesh is in the blood" [*kî nepeš habbāśār baddām hî'*]); Lev 17:11b ("and I myself have assigned it for you upon the altar to effect removal for your lives" [*wa'ănî nĕtattîw lākem 'al-hammizbēaḥ lĕkappēr 'al-napšōtêkem*]); Lev 17:11c ("for the blood itself effects removal by the life" [*kî-haddām hû' bannepeš yĕkappēr*]).[41]

The first word of Lev 17:11a, *kî*, indicates that what follows is an explanation of the prohibition of consuming blood that appears in verse 10.[42] If the clause were complete in itself, it would indicate that eating blood is prohibited because it is the seat of life. However, as Schwartz indicates, the first clause does not present an independent reason for the prohibition of consuming blood. Rather, it establishes a basis for the rest of the explanation, which follows in the second clause (v. 11b).[43]

As I noted in chapter 1, *nepeš habbāśār baddām hî'* may be rendered "the life of the flesh *is in* the blood" or "the life of the flesh *is* the blood," depending on whether the *bet* preposition is construed as *bet* locative or as *bet essentiae*. Whichever interpretation of the preposition we adopt, it is evident that the clause affirms an intimate connection between animal blood and animal life. As in other texts, blood is associated with the animation of the flesh.

Leviticus 17:11b, the second clause of the verse, is linked to the previous clause with a conjunctive *waw* and by the third-person, masculine singular pronominal suffix on *nĕtattîw* ("I have assigned *it*"), which must refer back to "blood" (*dām*) in the first clause. The clause continues the explanation of the rationale for the prohibition of consuming blood.[44] Consuming blood is not prohibited simply because it is identified with life. In this clause, Yahweh indicates that he has done something with the life-identified blood. The first half of the clause has Yahweh declare, "I have assigned it [the blood] for you upon the altar." The use of the personal pronoun with the verb is emphatic.[45] It emphasizes that Yahweh is the one who has acted. According to the text, it is Yahweh's decree that blood be placed upon the altar. Clearly, Yahweh is not claiming that he himself has placed blood on the altar. Rather, the deity claims to be the source of the practice of priests applying blood to the altar. As Jacob Milgrom indicates, the verb *ntn*, with Yahweh as subject, means "assign" or "designate."[46] Here it does not mean "put" in a physical sense because the verb *ntn* never refers in a general way to all modes of blood manipulation; rather, it indicates the specific act of daubing blood.[47] It is noteworthy that the verb has two indirect objects. The blood is assigned "for you upon the altar." In this clause, Yahweh claims that he has instituted the application of blood to the altar for the benefit of the Israelites. It is his gift to them.[48]

The verse has not indicated, at this juncture, the significance of the identification of blood with "life," or the connection of this identification with the application of blood to the altar. The present clause simply says that Yahweh has assigned the blood to the altar. Nevertheless, the prior identification of blood with "life" permits the deduction that the placing of animal blood on the altar amounts to the placing of animal life on the altar.

The next part of the clause indicates the purpose for which Yahweh has assigned the blood to the altar. It is "to effect removal for your lives" (*lĕkappēr ʿal-napšōtêkem*). The placing of animal blood on the altar is directed at achieving a positive goal for human lives. The construction *ʿal-napšōtêkem* means "for your lives" and not simply "for you."[49] The positive goal is indicated with the verb *kipper*. Human lives ("your lives") are the indirect objects of the verb, marked with the preposition *ʿal*, which is regularly employed in P with objects of *kipper*. Because the placing of blood on the altar may be identified as the placing of animal life on the altar, we may conclude that this placing of animal life on the altar achieves the positive goal for human lives. There is some kind of relationship between animal life and human lives in the ritual act of blood manipulation, and the action-effect indicated with the verb *kipper* has something to do with this relationship.

The verb *kipper* is employed in P with the basic meaning "effect removal," with different nuances determined according to context. Most interpreters assume that *lĕkappēr* here has the same basic meaning as it does elsewhere in P. Commonly, it is rendered "to make atonement" or some close variant.[50] At the same time, however, the interpretation of the verb in Lev 17:11 plays an important role in defining its meaning elsewhere. As I have noted, not a few scholars appeal to Lev 17:11 to explain the meaning and significance of *kipper* in other contexts.

Levine and Milgrom, followed by Schwartz, have emphasized that we do not simply have the verb *kipper* in 17:11.[51] Rather, we have it combined with the distinctive formula "for your lives" (*ʿal-napšōtêkem*). The combination of *kipper* with *ʿal-napšōtêkem* appears in only two other passages in the Hebrew Bible (Exod 30:11–16 and Num 31:48–54). Levine, Milgrom, and Schwartz rightly insist that these other occurrences should be taken into consideration when attempting to determine the meaning of the idiom in Lev 17:11. They assume a reader who knows the idiomatic usage from other contexts and reads Lev 17:11 in the light of that usage. In treating the texts, it is necessary to examine the other occurrences of the idiom and to consider the source to which they belong. As I demonstrate here, the idiom appears *only* in H material, a fact that has obvious implications for our understanding of Lev 17:11.

Both Exod 30:11–16 and Num 31:48–54 refer to an offering of precious metal given to Yahweh following a head count.[52] In the following discussion, I focus on Exod 30:11–16, since this pericope is the more detailed of the two, offers less ambiguous explanatory comments, and seems to be assumed by Num 31:48–54. Exodus 30:11–16 provides a general rule about what to do whenever a head count is made of the men over the age of twenty years. Each man who is counted is to pay "the ransom price of his life [*kōper napšô*] to Yahweh." Payment of the head tax, half a sheqel of silver, is intended to prevent any plague from falling upon the people (v. 12). The "donation of Yahweh" (*tĕrûmat yhwh*)[53] is "to effect removal for your lives" (v. 15).[54] It is called "silver of removal" (*kesep hakkippûrîm*), is assigned to the service of the Tent of Meeting, and "will be for the children of Israel for a memorial before Yahweh to effect removal for your lives" (v. 16).[55]

In this pericope we find the noun *kōper* (ransom price) employed in connection with the verb *kipper*. The fact that the construction *kōper napšô* is employed alongside the idiom *lĕkappēr ʿal-napšôtêkem* (to effect removal for your lives) strongly suggests that the verbal idiom indicates the act of paying the "ransom price" or the effect of such an act. In other words, *kipper* here is employed as a denominative of the noun *kōper*.[56] Thus, if we are to grasp the significance of the usage of the verb *kipper* here, we must inquire after the meaning of *kōper*. From its usage in various contexts, we can determine that *kōper* designates a payment that removes the danger of death or some serious harm from the one who pays it, or on whose behalf it is paid.[57] The English term "ransom" may be used if we do not allow this usage to import the concept of a payment made to free a captive into the semantic range of *kōper*, since this concept is not present in the term as it is employed throughout the Hebrew Bible. A better rendering might be "appeasement payment."[58] The payment of a *kōper* gains "peace" for the one who pays it or on whose behalf it is paid. That is, it obtains security from a serious threat to life and well-being. In legal contexts, and in cases of interpersonal conflicts, the *kōper* is apparently paid to the injured party or to that person's near kin.

In Exod 30:11–16, the threat met by the payment of a *kōper* is a plague. Why would a plague threaten the people as a result of census taking? As Levine notes, interpreters offer a variety of answers to this question.[59] The most common view is that the counting of the men of the army somehow impinges on

Yahweh's prerogatives or authority.[60] The point that must be noted is that the plague threatens all who have been counted. Moreover, it is directed at those who have been counted, not at those doing the counting.[61] Can we speak in this instance of a "crime" for which the men are liable to "the death penalty"?[62] This question must be answered in the negative. If we compare the situation envisaged in Exod 21:29–30 with that described in Exod 30:11–16, we can see that they are fundamentally different. According to Exod 21:29, if the owner of an ox was warned that the animal was dangerous, and he failed to take the necessary precautions, he is liable to be executed if it gores someone. He is culpable for a death caused by his own negligence. However, Exod 21:30 declares that such an individual can save his life by paying a *kōper,* which is the price to ransom his life (v. 30). In Exod 30:11–16, however, the men who are counted have not acted willfully or even negligently; they are being counted by their leaders, who are the ones who made the decision to carry out a census. It hardly seems likely that a man over twenty could refuse to be counted. Clearly, in Exod 30:11–16, we are not dealing with culpability in a legal sense. Rather, we have to do with the threat of what seems like a capricious outburst of divine wrath falling randomly on anyone who has been registered. This conclusion allows us to identify the danger met by the payment of what is clearly a *kōper* in Num 31:48–54. The men of the returning army have been counted. This amounts to a census. Therefore, the law set forth in Exod 30:11–16 applies. It is evident that Num 31:48–54 depends in some fashion on Exod 30:11–16. It not only presupposes the rule set forth in that pericope but reproduces its language. There is, of course, the use of the idiom *lĕkappēr ʿal-napšōt.* Note, in addition, the characterization of the gold as a *zikārôn* (memorial) that is "before Yahweh" and the use of the idiom *nśʾ rʾš* (lift a head) to indicate the act of counting the men.[63]

Numbers 31:48–54 is an H text. To what source is Exod 30:11–16 to be assigned? In my view, the pericope is also an H composition. According to Martin Noth, Exod 30:11–16 is a secondary addition in its context.[64] Furthermore, it expresses concern about the danger of census taking that is not attested elsewhere in P.[65] U. Cassuto and N. Sarna note the connection between Exod 30:10 and 30:11–16 in the use of the root *kpr.*[66] The verb appears twice in 30:10 and twice in 30:11–16. The abstract plural noun *kippurîm* appears once in 30:10 and once in 30:11–16. In both cases, it is preceded by a noun in the construct state that it modifies. These connections suggest that one unit depends on the other. Since Exod 30:10 is most likely an addition of the H editors,[67] we may wonder how what follows in Exod 30:11–16 is related to the work of the H school. If Exod 30:10 is an H addition, and Exod 30:11–16 is secondary in relation to Exod 30:1–9, it is likely that Exod 30:11–16 was composed and added with Exod 30:10. Thus, it would be a product of the H school.

Further evidence in support of this conclusion can be supplied by noting the terminology and language of the pericope. The construction *tĕrûmat yhwh,* with the offering in a construct relationship to Yahweh, is characteristic of H.[68] P, in contrast, avoids establishing direct possessive relationships between Yahweh and offerings or sancta. Although not decisive, it is also worth noting that the noun *kippurîm* appears primarily in H texts. Most important, the second-person plural address to Israel (*napšōtêkem*) is typical of H and not of P. In this context it is odd, because Israel is not otherwise addressed directly. It seems to be a stereotyped formula.

This combination of evidence strongly suggests either that Exod 30:11–16 as a whole is an H composition or that it is a late P text worked over by H tradents, who added the contextually awkward formula *lĕkappēr ʿal-napšōtêkem.*[69] In either case, this formula reflects H's terminology. In my view, the weight of the evidence leads to the conclusion that Exod 30:11–16 as a whole is an H composition. Thus, I conclude that the construction "to effect removal for your lives" (*lĕkappēr ʿal-napšōtêkem*) appears only in H texts.

If we identify *lĕkappēr ʿal-napšōtêkem* as a unique H formulation, we are faced with a new problem of interpretation. How is the use of this formula in Lev 17:11, where it refers to the effect of applying animal blood to the altar, related to the usage in Exod 30:11–16 and Num 31:48–54, where it refers to the effect of making a payment of precious metal? In my opinion, the usage in Lev 17:11 is secondary to that in Num 31:48–54 and Exod 30:11–16. The idiom fits the context of census taking and tax collecting far better than a sacrificial context once its relationship to the noun *kōper* is fully appreciated. Lev 17:11 must represent an attempt to import the concept of "ransom payment" into the sacrificial context by playing on the uses of the verb *kipper* to refer to blood manipulation.[70] As Schwartz explains: "The passage is reflective and interpretive: it puts forth a new and unique theory of what sacrificial 'atonement' is and how it works. . . . It is a case of inner-biblical exegesis, almost midrashic in nature."[71]

I conclude that Lev 17:11 is not only secondary to all P material on blood manipulation, as Milgrom and Knohl have established, but also that the application of the ransom concept to blood manipulation is secondary even in H. It results from an act of creative exegesis of Priestly cultic terminology. This conclusion has important implications for decisions about how Lev 17:11 may be applied beyond its immediate context. This would be true even if one were to embrace Milgrom's interpretation of the verse. It would be a striking explanation of blood manipulation, but serious questions would have to be raised about its applicability beyond the immediate context of Leviticus 17. Although Milgrom affirms that H is secondary to P, he continues to argue for the general applicability of Lev 17:11 as if it represented an old tradition that exercised a decisive influence over the thinking of the P tradents.[72] However, what we have here is the expression of the exegetical work of a particular school, perhaps even of one tradent. The same observation applies even more strongly to every other attempt to employ Lev 17:11 as a general explanation of blood manipulation. Lev 17:11 does not provide the conceptual basis for the blood manipulation activity represented in P and elsewhere but is a late and unique interpretation. Before continuing this discussion, however, I must deal with the final clause of Lev 17:11. Having established that the idiom *lĕkappēr 'al-napšôtêkem* should be rendered "to act as a ransom for your lives," I now consider how the final clause of Lev 17:11 develops the interpretation of blood manipulation advanced in the preceding two clauses.

Leviticus 17:11c says, "for the blood itself effects removal by the life" (*kî-haddām hû' bannepeš yĕkappēr*). As Baruch Schwartz demonstrates, this clause brings together the first two clauses, indicating the connection between the facts that blood is identified with life and the fact that it is applied to the altar to ransom human life.[73] The "life" of this clause is the animal's, and *bannepeš* means "by the life (of the animal, which is in the blood)."[74] In other words, the blood is able to serve as a *kōper* for human life through its identification with the animal's life. Animal life is used to save human life.

Baruch Levine affirms that Lev 17:11 identifies animal blood as a *kōper* given to save human life. However, he maintains that the *bet* is *bet pretii* (of price),[75] and that the *nepeš* is the "life" of the offerer.[76] According to this rendering, the blood achieves the effect indicated by *kipper* in exchange for, or as the functional equivalent to, the life of the offerer. The primary problem with Levine's interpretation was identified long ago by Ibn Ezra (ad loc.), who responded to those commentators who argued that *bannepeš* means "for the life (of the offerer)." As Ibn Ezra notes, this rendering makes the final clause of Lev 17:11 redundant, since the previous clause has already indicated that the blood effects a ransom for the lives of the Israelites. It should also be noted that the nouns *nepeš* (life) and *dām* (blood) in the first and the final clauses of Lev 17:11 form a chiasm, and since in the first clause *nepeš* is the "life" of the animal, so it should be the "life" of the animal in the final clause.[77] Although I am not persuaded by Levine's interpretation of *bannepeš*, his basic thesis still holds: animal blood, animal life, is given as a ransom payment for human life. The fact that I am able to reject Levine's translation of *bannepeš* and yet retain his basic thesis about the message of Lev 17:11 indicates quite clearly that the thesis does not depend on any particular rendering of the expression. What is crucial is that the idiom *lĕkappēr 'al-napšōtêkem* is understood as "to effect a ransom for your lives."

Because I have affirmed that Lev 17:11 teaches that animal life is given as a *kōper* to save human life, it is appropriate, at this juncture, to give some attention to the concept of "substitution." In his most recent treatment of the Hebrew root *kipper* and its relation to the Akkadian cognate *kuppuru*, Milgrom suggests that the Mesopotamian practice of eliminating the elements used to purge impurity "leads to the phenomenon of the 'substitute' or 'ransom,' the substance to which the evil is transferred and thereupon eliminated."[78] Milgrom then speaks of a "ransom principle" being operative in such cases as the payment of a census tax or tribute (Exod 30:11–16; Num 31:48–54) and the H laws on homicide (Num 35:30–33). What is problematic in Milgrom's analysis is the confusion of "substitute" and "ransom."[79]

A "ransom" should not be equated with a "substitute." A ransom frees a person from some sort of danger. A substitute takes the person's place. This act of substitution *may* free a person from danger, as does the payment of a ransom, but the mechanism is different. A half sheqel of silver may save a person from the danger of being struck down in a plague, but the silver is not that person's substitute. The silver is not struck down in his place.[80] Conversely, while the scapegoat substitutes for Israel, in that it is laden with their sins, it is not called a *kōper* and is not given the way a *kōper* would be given.

Although the concept of substitution is not inherent in the verb *kipper* and the associated noun *kōper*, this does not mean that the concept of substitution is lacking in Lev 17:11. One must simply identify its actual textual source. This, I suggest, is provided by the juxtaposition of animal life with human life in tandem with the use of *kipper* with the meaning "ransom." If animal life ransoms human life, it is obvious that we are dealing with substitution.[81] However, we can only see substitution at work because of the possibility of identifying a basic equivalency of animal life and human life. On its own, *kipper* does not refer to substitution because there is no necessity of actual equivalency for a ransom to work. That is, a payment in precious metal is not the equivalent of a human life. Rather, it is the price set to save a human life from some serious threat. In contrast, since human life and animal life are both designated as *nepeš*, it is possible to identify animal life as equivalent to human life, at least for the purpose of having the former act as a ransom price for the latter. Therefore, it is the association of animal life and human life in connection with the concept of ransom that allows for the identification of a substitutionary interpretation of blood manipulation in Lev 17:11.

In the light of these facts we can see what a striking departure is represented by Lev 17:11. It is not the fact that H declares that blood effects removal, or even that it declares that it is the blood, by means of life, that effects removal. Both of these claims are compatible with what is found elsewhere in the P tradition. What is truly striking is the fact that H links this "removal" explicitly with the security of the lives of the Israelites, attaching the meaning "ransom" to the verb *kipper* when used to refer to the effect of blood manipulation. It is doubtful that *kipper* is employed in P in connection with blood manipulation with the meaning "ransom." Thus, I conclude that Lev 17:11 should not be employed as a key for explaining blood manipulation in P or elsewhere in the Hebrew Bible, at least if one's goal is the historical elucidation of the texts. The Priestly tradents would not have known this unique H interpretation.[82] What, however, of other H representations of blood manipulation? I turn, now, to a test example of an attempt to apply Lev 17:11 outside of its immediate context.

Leviticus 17:11 and Exodus 30:10: An Experiment in Interpretation

Exodus 30:10, which Jacob Milgrom and Israel Knohl both identify as an H composition,[83] prescribes the once annual application of blood to the altar of spice incense in the Tent of Meeting: "Aaron shall effect removal upon its horns once in the year; with some of the blood of the *ḥaṭṭā't* of removal once in the year he shall effect removal upon it for your generations. It is most holy to Yahweh." This verse is unique in identifying the horns of the altar as the objects of the verb *kipper.* However, the second half of the verse indicates that the act of effecting "removal" on the horns of the altar amounts to the effecting of removal on the whole altar.[84] The second half of the verse also makes clear that *kipper* refers to blood manipulation activity. A reader familiar with P can gap-fill from Leviticus 4 and envisage this blood manipulation as the daubing of blood onto the horns of the altar. Thus, according to Exod 30:10, the act of daubing blood on the horns of the altar effects "removal" upon the altar.

If we continue to draw on information provided by P, we may recall that Lev 8:15, Lev 16:19, and Exod 29:36 attribute a purifying effect to the application of *ḥaṭṭā't* blood to the horns of the altar of burnt offering. Furthermore, I have suggested that *kipper* includes the idea of purification within its range of meaning. Thus, it is possible to interpret Exod 30:10 as referring to the purification of the incense altar with blood. H would be understood as building on P's representation of the rites of the Day of Removal by specifying that the incense altar received an application of blood on its horns.

Can Lev 17:11 be employed to further elucidate the meaning or effect of the blood manipulation? Or must we privilege Lev 17:11 and argue that Exod 30:10 has nothing to do with purification with blood? In attempting to answer these questions, attention should be given to the occurrence of the abstract noun *kippurîm* in the following pericope on the census tax (Exod 30:11–16). In verse 16, the silver paid by the men counted in the census is referred to as *kesep kippurîm* (removal money or ransom money). The use of this noun in a context where *kipper* seems to mean "ransom," as well as where the verb seems to have the broader meaning "remove," raises a question about the claim that there are two distinct usages of *kipper* or even two distinct homographs. Is it possible that we have not only a verb, but also an abstract noun, with two distinct meanings? In my view, it is more reasonable to affirm that the meaning "ransom" is part of the semantic range of the root *kpr* (remove).

Furthermore, as I have suggested, it is likely that Exod 30:11–16 is an H composition, or a P composition that has received H editing. In either case, and even if the pericope is a purely P composition, the relationship between P and H, which I assume in this study, requires us to affirm that the H tradents placed Exod 30:10 immediately before Exod 30:11–16. As Sarna and Cassuto suggest, the terminological relationship between the two texts hardly seems accidental. It seems, therefore, that the play on the different nuances of the verb *kipper,* which we find in Lev 17:11, is reproduced in Exod 30:10–16. First, we have a prescription for the application of blood to the altar of incense. This application effects "removal." Drawing on P, we might explain this effect more precisely as the removal of impurity from sancta. However, when we read verses 11–16 and encounter *kipper* with the meaning "ransom" (i.e., "remove the danger of death"), and the abstract noun *kippurîm* with the meaning "ransom" (i.e., "the removal of the danger of death"), we may wish to reconsider our reading of verse 10. This is especially true if we are aware of Lev 17:11. A reading practice that takes all of the H materials together and attempts to synthesize them will need to take the verse into account. According to Lev 17:11, the application of blood to the altar has the same effect as the payment of the census silver. The close relationship between verse 10 and verses 11–16 suggests that we may also interpret the blood manipulation prescribed in verse 10 in this manner.

I would emphasize, however, that the application of Lev 17:11 to Exod 30:10 need not limit the possibilities for understanding the blood manipulation prescribed in the verse. We need not assume that a ritual act is univalent, or that the act of offering a public or official interpretation requires acceptance only of that interpretation. An interpreter may not intend his interpretation to exclude others. Instead, the interpreter may simply intend to add another nuance to the meaning of a ritual act. A multivalent ritual act can be identified in Exod 30:10 if the reader brings to bear the full range of interpretive information derived from the corpus of P and H texts. My own proposal is to understand Exod 30:10 to indicate that the purification of sancta through the application of blood also ransoms the lives of those on whose behalf the blood manipulations are performed. Indeed, H treats impurity as posing a serious threat to the lives of Yahweh's people.[85] Whenever impurity is eliminated from Yahweh's presence, that danger is deflected. Thus, there is no reason to maintain that *kipper* as "remove" (i.e., "purify") excludes *kipper* as "ransom."

Conclusions

In the few instances where the H tradents provide representations of blood manipulation activity, these correspond quite closely to what we find in P. According to H texts, the blood of animals offered as sacrifices of well-being is tossed onto the altar, and in this sacrificial complex the blood manipulation is represented as the primary duty of the priests. As in P, blood manipulation marks the priests' access to the altar and defines their sphere of responsibility for the whole sacrificial complex.

Like P, H has little in the way of interpretation of blood manipulation. Exodus 30:10 apparently indicates that the application of blood to the horns of the altar of incense effects the altar's purification. However, Lev 17:11 introduces a conception of the workings of blood manipulation not anticipated in P. According to this text, animal blood is identified with animal life, and the application of animal life to the altar has a positive impact on the life of the offerer: the animal's life, in the animal's blood, functions as a ransom for the life of the offerer. The association of the life of the animal and the life of the offerer is unique to this text.

My adoption of Knohl's and Milgrom's thesis that the H stratum of the Pentateuch is secondary to the P stratum, and represents editorial intervention in P, has shaped the way in which I have reflected on the relationship of H's representations and interpretations of blood manipulation activity to what we find in P. While the older approach to the H materials treated them as background to P, and as providing a key for interpreting P, this evaluation of the relationship between the two traditions problematizes attempts to explain P by reference to H. Moreover, my analysis of the secondary and exegetical character of Lev 17:11, which draws on Schwartz's important work on the text, reinforces the conclusion that Lev 17:11 should not be used as a key for identifying the "meaning" of blood manipulation in P. In P texts we find no explicit indication that the identification of blood with life played a role in the understanding of blood manipulation. Clearly, there is not even a hint in the P corpus that blood was understood to ransom the lives of those upon whose behalf it was applied to the altar. Thus, attempts to identify P's interpretation of the blood manipulation by drawing on Lev 17:11 must be questioned. It is evident that many such interpretive ventures were based on the assumption that H was an older source incorporated by P.[86] Given this assumption, scholars could argue that Lev 17:11—as they interpreted it—articulates the P tradents' working understanding of the blood manipulation. However, if H is secondary and interpretive, as Milgrom and Knohl have argued, it is not possible to affirm that the P tradents accepted the interpretation of blood manipulation in Lev 17:11. All of this must be affirmed even before we consider the validity of any specific interpretation of the verse. That is, whatever it is that Lev 17:11 says about blood manipulation, we need not embrace the position that the P tradents accepted this interpretation. However, if we adopt the standpoint of the H tradents, who apparently expected that their interpretation of the P stratum would be accepted by readers of the edited whole, we must consider how Lev 17:11 might be applied to P. As I have indicated in the discussion of Exod 30:10, it is quite possible to apply Lev 17:11 to texts that represent blood manipulation activity, and which could be explained without reference to that verse.

This chapter has highlighted the importance of our assumptions about the relationship between layers of biblical tradition to the process of interpretation. It has also indicated that greater attention needs to be given to the problems connected with applying interpretive comments to represented ritual activity or to the elucidation of other interpretive comments. Although Lev 17:11 clearly presents an interpretation of blood manipulation, this interpretive verse is itself in need of careful interpretation so that we may determine both what it says about blood manipulation and the scope of application its author intended it to have. Even if we judge the verse to offer an interpretation of all blood manipulation activity, however, we may ask whether this interpretation must be accepted and applied to the represented activity throughout the extant textual corpus, and whether other interpretive comments should be set aside or subordinated. Thus, in looking at Exod 30:10, I affirmed that we should not seek to identify a single effect for the represented blood manipulation actions.

Finally, while it is important that we recognize that ritual actions are characteristically multivalent for native participants, there is yet another element in the multivalency of ritual activity, the latent meaning or function, which is not obvious to the ritual actors. In a recent critique of scholarly interpretations of Lev 17:11, Stanley K. Stowers draws on Catherine Bell's insights and correctly insists that the critical interpreter must move beyond what the textual tradents say about ritual activity to reflection on how cultic acts function as "ritualized" activity to create privileged oppositions and structures.[87] Throughout this study, I have followed that urging, and I have highlighted what can be said about the power of blood when we look at how blood manipulation rites function indexically to create, define, and reinforce relationships, cultic status, and identity, and to map ordered patterns onto space, thereby creating the sacred—even if we are unable to confidently determine how Lev 17:11 explains blood manipulation and its power.

Conclusions

In an influential work on social scientific theory, R. K. Merton emphasizes that every social action has both a *manifest* and a *latent* function.[1] The manifest function is that which social actors consciously attribute to their own activities. For example, the manifest purpose of the sacrificial slaughter of an animal and the communal consumption of its flesh may be to celebrate some positive event in the life of an individual or community. The latent function of a social act is generally not recognized by social actors unless they step back and reflect critically on how their actions contribute to larger social processes. Various latent functions can be attributed to the sacrificial feast. For example, the provision of the animal by a patron may serve to index his or her wealth and status, while the inclusion of individuals in the feast, or their exclusion therefrom, may indicate their social place, and their membership, or lack thereof, in a specified group.

Generally, it is outside observers, scholarly interpreters who are concerned with developing a comprehensive picture of the workings of a cultural system, who identify latent functions. As Stanley K. Stowers observes, "the way that societies and practices work is largely invisible to the participants who have a practical knowledge of their culture."[2] Ritual activity, as social activity, has both manifest and latent functions or meanings. In this study, I have explored both manifest and latent functions of cultic blood manipulation activity represented in the literature of the Hebrew Bible, but I have given special attention to elucidating latent functions, as this has been a neglected area of inquiry.

Manifest Functions

According to several biblical texts, blood may not be consumed because it is identified with the animation of the flesh, with the "life" (*nepeš*) of the animal. The manifest function of abstaining from consuming blood, according to these texts, is to avoid ingesting an animal's "life" with its flesh. Is there a relationship between these conceptual statements about the nature of blood and the uses made of animal blood in the cult? In addressing this question, I have emphasized the striking fact that only one biblical text, Lev 17:11, explicitly links the identification of blood with "life" with the use of blood in the cult. Thus, although the D, P, and H strata of the Pentateuch do evidence a conviction that blood embodies the force that animates the body, it is problematic to assume that all ancient Israelites understood blood manipulation activity to be based on this conceptual identification. There is very little textual support for such an assumption.

There are relatively few instances of explicit interpretation or explanation of blood manipulation in the biblical texts. Of the explanatory statements that do appear, some are rather ambiguous. In Exod 24:8, for example, Moses refers to the blood tossed onto the people as "the blood of the covenant" (*dam-habbĕrît*), but the significance of this designation is far from obvious. Other interpretive statements amount to little more than simple identifications of the instrumental effects of specific manipulation acts. Leviticus 8:15 tells us that daubing blood onto the horns of the sacrificial altar purifies it. According to Lev 16:18–19, a complex of blood manipulations involving daubing blood onto the altar's horns and then sprinkling the altar with blood results in the cleansing and consecration of that altar. Exodus 29:21 and Lev 8:30 indicate that the act of sprinkling blood mixed with oil onto Aaron, his sons, and their liturgical vestments effects their transition to a state of holiness.

In some cases, the interpretations provided by Israelite tradents appear clear enough, but readers of the texts have been unwilling to take these explanations seriously. For example, in the account of the first Passover in Exodus 12, we are told that, when Yahweh sees the blood of the Passover sacrifices marking the houses of the Israelites, he will spare the occupants of those houses (Exod 12:13, 23). On a basic level, this explanation is easy to understand: the blood's apotropaic function depends on Yahweh seeing it and responding as promised. However, some modern interpreters have set aside the textual interpretation of the blood manipulation in favor of their own reconstruction of what they understand to be its *real* or *original* significance and have, unfortunately, failed to distinguish between their interpretive reconstructions and what the text itself declares. In responding to these readers, I would emphasize the methodological necessity of taking seriously what ancient Israelite tradents tell us. Once these textual explanations have been clarified, it is possible to explore alternative ways of understanding the represented activity. However, care must be exercised not to confuse these alternative interpretations with the interpretations provided in the texts.

Matters become more complicated when we encounter blood manipulation rites that lack textual explanations. I noted, in chapters 3 and 4, that P provides no explicit interpretation of the act of tossing (*zrq*) blood onto the altar. In response to this situation, many scholars have attempted to fill the interpretive gap by making the identification of blood with life the conceptual basis for the act. More specifically, a number of interpreters have identified Lev 17:11 as the key for understanding this blood manipulation. However, there is no consensus on what specific interpretation of blood tossing follows from the blood-life identification or from what Lev 17:11 says about blood manipulation. Another example of blood manipulation activity lacking a textual interpretation is the rite of daubing the blood of the ordination ram onto the right earlobes, right thumbs, and right big toes of Aaron and his sons (Exod 29:20; Lev 8:23–24). The same explanatory gap is encountered when we find the same manipulation performed with the blood of a reparation offering for an individual healed of a skin disease (Lev 14:14, 25). As in the case of the gesture of tossing blood, readers have filled this gap in a variety of ways, not infrequently by drawing on the blood-life identification.

Another way of filling gaps is to apply an interpretive statement beyond its immediate context to the interpretation of the same or similar blood manipulations represented elsewhere. For example, it is possible to affirm that the P tradents understood the daubing of blood onto the horns of the altar always to effect its purification on the basis of the explicit statement, in Lev 8:15, that the altar was purified by this blood rite. However, we need not assume that a ritual gesture must inevitably be accorded the same explanation in every context, and we should take care to distinguish the few explicit textual interpretations available to us from scholarly reconstructions of ancient interpretations. It should also be noted, in this connection, that the biblical tradents seemed far more interested in describing and prescribing ritual *praxis* than in providing comprehensive and coherent conceptual explanations of this activity. Scholarly questions about the meaning or purpose of blood manipulation are directed at texts that do not appear to have been composed to address such questions.

In Priestly texts, the verb *kipper* (effect removal) appears frequently to indicate the effect of blood manipulations, most often in connection with the *ḥaṭṭā't* sacrifice. In some instances, it appears that *kipper* indicates the elimination of impurity (Lev 16:16, 17, 18). However, in many other cases it seems to have a broader, more abstract meaning and to indicate the effect of the complete sacrificial complex and not simply the blood manipulation acts (Lev 4:20, 26, 31, 35; 5:6, 10, 13). We also find the verb *kipper* employed in Ezekiel in connection with blood manipulation activity, but it is not clear whether it refers specifically to the blood manipulation or designates the effect of a complete sacrificial complex. In 2 Chron 29:24, the verb *kipper* clearly indicates the effect of the *ḥaṭṭā't* blood manipulation. However, again, it is far from clear what the verb means in this context. Thus, although *kipper* clearly indicates an effect of blood manipulation rites, the precise identification of that effect remains problematic.

Throughout this study, I emphasized the significant lack of explicit textual interpretations of blood manipulation activity, and I noted that readers have responded to this lack by looking to the conceptual identification of blood with life as the basis for a comprehensive interpretation of blood manipulation activity. In particular, many interpreters have identified Lev 17:11 as the key to understanding blood manipulation activity, since it is the one text in the Hebrew Bible that links the blood-life identification with the cultic manipulation of blood. In chapter 7, I focused my attention on this text, clarifying what it says about blood manipulation and reflecting on the legitimacy of using it as an interpretive key. Leviticus 17:11 employs the verb *kipper* with a distinctive meaning, derived from its use, in other contexts, to indicate the effect of paying a *kōper* (ransom payment). Here it means "effect ransom." The author of this text claims that the application of the blood of a sacrificial animal to the altar ransoms the lives of the offerers. Because the blood is identified with the life of the animal, Lev 17:11 is correctly understood to advance a substitutionary explanation of "atonement." The application of the life of the animal to the altar, in the form of its blood, saves—ransoms—the lives of the Israelites. Life saves life. At the same time, I would emphasize that Lev 17:11 refers to the *life* of the animal, not to its death, and that the substitutionary offering of its blood must be understood against the background of the practice of paying a *kōper* to Yahweh described in other texts. I can see no evidence of a *penal* theory of substitution lying behind the textual formulation. Like the "ransom payment" given when a census is taken, the blood of an animal applied to the altar deals with any threat to the lives of the Israelites coming from Yahweh rather than with a specific offense for which the worshiper is liable to a "death penalty." Furthermore, it is the *life* of the animal that Yahweh accepts in place of human life. The death of the animal is not integral to the process of substitution. It simply makes the blood—the life—available to be offered as a "ransom payment."

As I noted, however, the common practice of using Lev 17:11 to explain all blood manipulation represented in P, and elsewhere in the Hebrew Bible, is problematic. There are two reasons for this. First, Lev 17:11 is a product of the H tradents and is almost certainly late relative to most of P. Because it is both secondary and clearly interpretive, caution should be exercised in using it to explain blood manipulation as represented in the earlier P stratum. If we should be cautious about assuming that the P tradents knew the interpretation of blood manipulation presented in Lev 17:11, we must exercise even stronger caution when we come to non-P texts. Second, the way in which the tradent who composed Lev 17:11 seems to have played with the alternative meanings of *kipper* suggests that this explanation does not reflect a dominant consensus. Rather, Lev 17:11 is the product of creative, exegetical exploration of the possibilities following from understanding *kipper* to mean "act as a ransom" rather than "effect removal" or "expiate." Only in Lev 17:11 is blood declared to function as a "ransom payment," and this identification is an innovation. In P, and even elsewhere in H, *kipper* appears to be used with the meaning "effect removal."

Leviticus 17:11 is the only biblical text that specifically interprets blood manipulation by referring to the identification of blood with life. However, drawing on this verse and on other texts that identify blood with the animation of the flesh (Gen 9:4; Deut 12:23), many interpreters have argued that ancient

Israelites based the practice of cultic blood manipulation on this conceptual identification: it is blood, as life or as the locus of "life," that accomplishes the effects attributed to it. Certainly, Lev 17:11 indicates that some ancient Israelites interpreted blood manipulation in the light of the blood-life identification. However, I have emphasized that other sources, notably P and the book of Deuteronomy, do not exploit the blood-life identification to explain blood manipulation. Thus, I would argue against an overhasty conclusion that the identification of blood with life provides the conceptual key for understanding Israelite blood manipulation activity. There may have been other public and official explanations of why blood did what was attributed to it, not to mention a host of private interpretations. However, none of these has survived.

Whereas many modern interpreters of the Hebrew Bible seek to identify a symbolic "meaning" for each blood manipulation, I have found that the biblical tradents interpreted blood manipulation instrumentally. The texts refer simply to the effect of a blood manipulation action: it purifies, it cleanses, it makes holy, it produces a mark that Yahweh sees, and to which he responds by restraining the destroyer or withholding a plague. There is very little evidence to support the view that the ancient tradents themselves understood blood manipulation acts to be symbolic-communicative. Thus, modern interpreters should avoid attributing such an interpretive approach to ancient Israelites. Rather, we should seek to understand their interpretive statements in their own terms. It is possible, nevertheless, that an approach to ritual as symbolic-communicative activity could identify communicative dimensions of the ritual activity represented in the Bible. However, I believe that we begin then to identify latent functions, rather than the manifest functions articulated by the social actors themselves.

Latent Functions

As I emphasized at the beginning of this study, it is insufficient and misleading to limit our understanding of ritual activity to what "native" informants tell us, as important as this information is.[3] We must also seek to understand what social actions accomplish apart from the conscious intentions or explicit interpretations of social actors. This would be necessary even if we had available to us an abundance of explicit "native" interpretations. Since we are faced with a definite lack of such interpretive statements, however, it is especially necessary to explore the latent functions of blood manipulation activity. In my view, given the methodological problems I have identified with attempts to reconstruct ancient Israelite interpretations, a change of focus to latent functions opens up possibilities for deeper and surer understanding of the workings of Israelite ritual activity.

The starting point for the elucidation of the latent functions of blood manipulation activity is the close reading of the available textual representations in order to clarify what is represented. The goal is to develop as complete a picture as possible of living practice within the textual world, with special attention to identifying those who perform blood manipulation activity. We are fortunate to find a relative abundance of representational material in the Hebrew Bible. Indeed, as I have several times noted, the biblical authors give considerably greater attention to representing ritual activity than to explaining its meaning or purpose. This suggests that the primary concern of the biblical tradents was with the practical execution of ritual actions rather than with the conceptual explanation of those actions. Nevertheless, there are gaps in every representation, and a careful reader must reflect on how he or she fills those gaps in the process of constructing a picture of living practice. Following on the construction of an image of ritual activity, one may explore ways of bringing out the latent meanings or functions of blood manipulation actions, giving special attention to the ways in which these ritual actions establish and define social-cultic relationships, status, and identity, as well as serve in the construction and maintenance of sacral space and of its boundaries with nonsacral space.

In Exod 24:3–8, Moses tosses the blood of the sacrifices onto the altar and onto the people. These ritual actions are indexed, therefore, as the prerogative of the ritual specialist who presides over the ritual complex. Blood manipulation is marked as elite activity. At the same time, since the manipulation of blood is clearly the central element of the ritual complex, the fact that it is assigned to Moses serves to index his status. By manipulating "the blood of the covenant" Moses signals his identity as the one who mediates between Yahweh and his people. Thus, Moses' status is ritually inscribed. Similarly, in the J stratum of Exodus 12, the elders of Israel are assigned the task of applying the blood to the lintels and doorposts of the houses of the Israelites (Exod 12:21–22). Again, the assignment of this blood manipulation activity to status-marked individuals indexes it as high-status activity, and reciprocally, the assignment of the central ritual act to the elders functions to index their status.

Furthermore, if we read Exod 12:21–22 in the light of P's representations of priestly blood manipulation activity, we may understand the elders' blood manipulation activity to index a quasi-priestly status.[4] In 2 Kgs 16:13, Ahaz inaugurates a new altar with a ritual complex that includes the tossing of blood onto the altar. Because, in 2 Kgs 16:15, Ahaz assigns the responsibility for making regular offerings and manipulating blood to his chief priest, the king's ritual actions at the inauguration of the altar are easily identified as indexes to his special cultic status. In the representation of 2 Kgs 16:13, he functions as a priest and makes possible the future use of the altar.

In P, many examples of the status-indexing function of blood manipulation activity may be identified. In P's prescriptive and descriptive representations of the ordination of Aaron and his sons to the priesthood (Exod 29; Lev 8), Moses performs all of the altar rituals, including blood manipulations, which are reserved to the priesthood in P's general prescriptions for the practices of the cult. Thus, we are able to draw the conclusion that Moses is indexed as a priestly figure here in P. If we next turn to the priestly stratum of Exodus 12, we may note that the manipulation of blood is not assigned to priests. Indeed, it could not be assigned to the priests, since P's narrative indicates that the establishment of the priesthood took place after the Passover and the exodus from Egypt. Thus, in this context, nonpriests manipulate the blood. This representation can be read within the larger framework of P's representation of the cult, and it is possible to see a unique occasion here, when all Israel acts in a priestly capacity,[5] because the represented rites take place in the absence of the shrine complex and the priesthood.

The representation of blood manipulation activity in the priestly stratum of Exodus 12 stands in sharp contrast to its representation elsewhere in P and in H. In both of the priestly sources, blood manipulation activity is represented as a priestly responsibility. Whereas the lay offerer presses his hand on the head of the animal and may slaughter it, the priests, the Aaronids, are explicitly identified as those who handle the blood. Because the blood is conveyed to the altar, the locus where offerings are transferred to Yahweh, the exclusive control of blood by the priesthood grants them access to this locus, and indexes their special cultic status. Priests are permitted access to the altar, whereas lay Israelites are not.[6] Blood manipulation is the first priestly duty in a sacrificial complex. Thus, it functions to indicate the parameters of priestly access. The priests' subsequent burning of the flesh or selected internal organs of the animal in the altar fire reinforces their status, but it is the blood manipulation that first enacts it in each sacrificial complex. Thus, we may speak of blood manipulation as having a special importance as the rite that functions as the primary index of priestly prerogatives and status. In other words, since blood manipulation indexes priestly access to the altar, their activity at the altar subsequent to the manipulation of blood comes as no surprise to one who observes their activity in the world of the text. Furthermore, since blood manipulation is the primary priestly duty, it is not surprising that the application of blood to the bodies of Aaron and his sons plays a role in their transition to a consecrated state that allows them access to the divine presence. In the ordination rites, the application of blood to Aaron and his sons, after blood has been applied to the altar, places the new priests in an existential relationship with the altar and with other appurtenances of sacred space to which blood may be applied. This is especially the case with the sprinkling of blood onto Aaron and his sons, since this blood is taken directly from the surface of the altar.[7]

In addition to distinguishing Aaronids from non-Aaronids, blood manipulation in P indexes the status of Aaron, or of his successor in the office of head priest, relative to all other priests. According to Lev 4:3–21, it is the "anointed priest" who conveys blood into the shrine building and manipulates it there, while ordinary priests are assigned the task of manipulating blood when it is applied only to the altar of burnt offering. Access to the inner realm of holiness is reserved to the anointed priest and is marked by blood manipulation. In Leviticus 16, Aaron is assigned all blood manipulation activity, including the responsibility for conveying blood directly into the divine presence in the adytum of the shrine complex. Aaron's special status in relation to his sons is signaled and established in the inaugural rites of the cult as represented in Leviticus 9, when Aaron's sons convey blood to him at the altar where he manipulates it. In this representation, Aaron is indexed as the one who bears primary responsibility for applying blood to the altar, while his sons are indexed as those who make Aaron's activity possible. Their subordination to their father is obvious and is ritually inscribed.

In Ezekiel we find the same insistence that blood manipulation is a priestly prerogative. Indeed, Ezekiel asserts that only the Zadokites may offer fat and blood to Yahweh, explicitly excluding the Levites from doing so (Ezek 44:10–15).[8] The prophet Ezekiel, himself a priest, seems to be assigned the responsibility for manipulating blood when the new altar is dedicated (Ezek 43:20). If this representation is read in the light of P's representation of Moses' cultic activity, it is possible to identify Ezekiel as a new Moses, reestablishing the functioning of the cult. Even in the absence of P's representations, we could still affirm that Ezekiel's privileged access to the altar, and his responsibility for preparing it for use, indicate his special status. As in P, Ezekiel's access to the altar is marked with blood manipulation.

In 2 Chronicles we find P's representation of sacrificial activity reproduced with some interesting variations. As in P, only Aaronids apply blood to the altar (2 Chron 29:22, 24). However, in the descriptions of the Passover festivals celebrated by Hezekiah and Josiah, we are told that the Levites play a subordinate role in the blood manipulation complex, handing the blood over to the priests (2 Chron 30:16; 35:11). By slaughtering the Passover victims for the lay offerers (2 Chron 30:17), and conveying the blood to the priests, the Levites index their intermediate cultic status. Since they are able to handle blood, passing it on to the priests, it is evident that they stand closer to the altar than do the lay offerers. At the same time, it is the priests who take the blood and toss it. Thus, in the representation of 2 Chronicles, the Levites stand between the priests and the laity.[9] Furthermore, the exclusion of the laity from the altar is reinforced by this representation.

Blood manipulation activity, as represented in the texts treated in this study, also functions to establish boundaries around a realm of order standing in opposition to chaos. The regulated, patterned quality of blood manipulation maps order onto sacred space. This is especially true for the elaborate complex of blood manipulation actions prescribed in Leviticus 16 for the "Day of Atonement." On this occasion, the careful execution of patterned rites confronts and neutralizes the chaos represented by the impurities and sins of the people of Israel. Although there are texts that explicitly identify blood manipulation as effecting the consecration of persons and objects, I understand the construction of the boundaries of sacred space to be a latent function of blood manipulation, since no text explicitly draws attention to the significance of the regulated and ordered patterns mapped by a blood manipulation complex.

The identification of latent functions of blood manipulation activity, in my view, makes these ritual performances more comprehensible. We are able to see that they fulfill important social functions, establishing and reinforcing status and identity, even as they fulfill the functions social actors attribute to them. Blood has both manifest and latent power. Given the relative paucity of textual interpretations of blood manipulation activity, our ability to move beyond problematic attempts to identify symbolic meanings and a conceptual basis for cultic blood manipulation represents a definite scholarly advance. When we carry through a program of asking about the latent functions of blood manipulation—when we ask how blood manipulation actions function as indexes and how they serve to create order and structure—we gain new knowledge and acquire a deeper, more sophisticated understanding of this mode of ritual activity.

Notes

Introduction

Epigraph: *The Mennonite Hymnal* (Scottdale, Penn.: Herald Press, 1969), 555.

1. Catherine Bell, *Ritual Theory, Ritual Practice* (New York: Oxford University Press, 1992); Bell, *Ritual: Perspectives and Dimensions* (New York: Oxford University Press, 1997); Nancy Jay, *Throughout Your Generations Forever: Sacrifice, Religion, and Paternity* (Chicago: University of Chicago Press, 1992); Jonathan Z. Smith, "The Bare Facts of Ritual," in *Imagining Religion: From Babylon to Jonestown* (Chicago: University of Chicago Press, 1982), 53–65.

2. For a critical review of approaches to defining and identifying ritual, see Bell, *Ritual Theory, Ritual Practice,* 69–74.

3. Mary Douglas, *Natural Symbols: Explorations in Cosmology* (New York: Random House, 1970), 20. See also, Roy A. Rappaport, *Ritual and Religion in the Making of Humanity* (Cambridge Studies in Social and Cultural Anthropology 110; Cambridge: Cambridge University Press, 1999), 46–58, 69–106; Edmund Leach, *The Political Systems of Highland Burma: A Study of Kachin Social Structure* (2d ed.; London: Athlone Press, 1964), xiv, 13–14; Leach, "Ritual," in *The International Encyclopedia of the Social Sciences* (vol. 13; ed. David L. Sills; New York: Macmillan, 1968), 523–25.

4. According to Leach, *Political Systems,* 13, "ritual . . . is a symbolic statement which 'says' something about the individuals involved in the action." See also David I. Kertzer, *Ritual, Politics, and Power* (New Haven: Yale University Press, 1988), 9, 11; Raymond Firth, *Symbols: Public and Private* (Symbol, Myth, and Ritual Series; ed. Victor Turner; Ithaca, N.Y.: Cornell University Press, 1973), 54–91; Victor Turner, "Symbols in African Ritual," in *Magic, Witchcraft, and Religion: An Anthropological Study of the Supernatural* (2d ed.; ed. Arthur C. Lehmann and James E. Myers; Mountain View, Calif.: Mayfield Publishing, 1989), 55–63; repr. from *Science* 179 (1973): 1100–1105.

5. For this approach to ritual as communicative activity that affects status and identity, see, e.g., Rappaport, *Ritual and Religion,* 107–38; Leach, "Ritual," 525.

6. Saul M. Olyan, *Rites and Rank: Hierarchy in Biblical Representations of Cult* (Princeton, N.J.: Princeton University Press, 2000), 4. Olyan identifies several scholars who understand ritual this way (125 n. 8). See also Bell, *Ritual: Perspectives and Dimensions,* 82.

7. Note, in particular, Ronald S. Hendel, "Sacrifice as a Cultural System: The Ritual Symbolism of Exodus 24, 3–8," *ZAW* 101 (1989): 366–90; Frank H. Gorman, *The Ideology of Ritual: Space, Time and Status in the Priestly Theology* (JSOTSup 91; Sheffield: JSOT Press, 1990); Jacob Milgrom, *Leviticus 1–16* (AB 3; New York: Doubleday, 1991), 566–69, 719–28, 1000–1003; Saul M. Olyan, "Honor, Shame, and Covenant Relations in Ancient Israel and Its Environment," *JBL* 115 (1996): 201–18; Olyan, "What Do Shaving

Rites Accomplish and What Do They Signal in Biblical Ritual Contexts?" *JBL* 117 (1998): 611–22; Olyan, *Rites and Rank.*

8. See Turner, "Symbols in African Ritual," 57: "Ritual symbols are multivocal— that is, each symbol expresses not one theme but many themes simultaneously by the same perceptible object or activity (symbol vehicle)." See also Firth, *Symbols,* 81–82; Rappaport, *Ritual and Religion,* 50–54; Kertzer, *Ritual, Politics, and Power,* 11. For reflections on levels and types of meaning in the context of a study of biblical representations of ritual practice, see David P. Wright, *The Disposal of Impurity* (SBLDS 101; Atlanta: Scholars Press, 1987), 3; Olyan, "What Do Shaving Rites Accomplish?" 621–22.

9. Milgrom, *Leviticus 1–16,* 46.

10. Ibid., 566–69 (drawing on A. Van Gennep's classic work on "rites of passage" to help explain P's representations of priestly ordination), 719–28 (discussing Mary Douglas's theories on dietary rules about clean and unclean animals, and A. S. Meigs's response to Douglas), 1000–1003 (comparing Mary Douglas's and A. S. Meigs's views on impurity constructions).

11. In his commentary on Leviticus, Milgrom does offer a brief discussion of theories of sacrifice, in which he affirms its multivalent character (*Leviticus 1–16,* 440–43). However, his exploration of this issue is not well developed and is not applied elsewhere to specific instances of biblical sacrifice.

12. Dennis J. McCarthy, "The Symbolism of Blood and Sacrifice," *JBL* 88 (1969): 166–76; McCarthy, "Further Notes on the Symbolism of Blood and Sacrifice," *JBL* 92 (1973): 205–10.

13. For trenchant criticism of McCarthy's claims about the significance of blood in Greek culture, as well as general reflections on the problems associated with seeking a *unique* meaning for blood manipulation in ancient Israel, see Stanley K. Stowers, "On the Comparison of Blood in Greek and Israelite Ritual," in *Hesed ve-Emet: Studies in Honor of Ernest S. Frerichs* (ed. Jodi Magness and Seymour Gitin; BJS 320; Atlanta: Scholars Press, 1998), 179–88.

14. Kertzer, *Ritual, Politics, and Power,* 11.

15. Ibid.

16. See also Olyan, "What Do Shaving Rites Accomplish?"

17. Bell, *Ritual Theory, Ritual Practice,* 72. See also Nancy Jay's critique of attempts to distinguish " 'instrumental action,' which *does* things, which causally affects the material world," from " 'expressive action,' which *says* things or communicates meanings" (*Throughout Your Generations Forever,* 4; emphasis in original).

18. N. Kiuchi, *The Purification Offering in the Priestly Literature: Its Meaning and Function* (JSOTSup 56; Sheffield: JSOT Press, 1987), 13. See also Adrian Schenker, "Das Zeichen des Blutes und die Gewißheit der Vergebung im Alten Testament: Die sühnende Funktion des Blutes auf dem Altar nach Lev 17.10–12," *MTZ* 34 (1983): 195.

19. Milgrom, *Leviticus 1–16,* 711–12.

20. Bell, *Ritual Theory, Ritual Practice,* 183. A classic study that notes diversity of participant explanation and interpretation is James W. Fernandez, "Symbolic Consensus in a Fang Reformative Cult," *American Anthropologist* 67 (1965): 902–29.

21. On the categories of "public," "official," and "private" interpretations of ritual actions, see Lawrence A. Hoffman, *Covenant of Blood: Circumcision and Gender in Rabbinic Judaism* (Chicago: University of Chicago Press, 1996), 17–22.

22. Bell, *Ritual Theory, Ritual Practice,* 3–66.

23. Ibid., 67–168.

24. Smith, "Bare Facts of Ritual," 63 (emphasis deleted).

25. Bell, *Ritual Theory, Ritual Practice,* 91.

26. Jay, *Throughout Your Generations Forever,* 6–7.

27. For a helpful examination of Peirce's distinctions between different types of signs (symbol, index, and icon), see Rappaport, *Ritual and Religion,* 54–68.

28. As Peirce puts it, "Anything which focuses the attention is an index" (quoted in Justus Buchler, *The Philosophical Writings of Peirce* [New York: Dover, 1955], 108).

29. Jay, *Throughout Your Generations Forever,* 6–7 (emphasis in original).

30. Rappaport, *Ritual and Religion,* 37.

31. Gorman, *Ideology of Ritual,* 7 n. 1.

32. Recently, Gorman has revised his position on the importance of giving attention to the textuality of biblical representations of ritual. See his review of Gerald A. Klingbeil, *A Comparative Study of the Ritual of Ordination as Found in Leviticus 8 and Emar 369, JBL* 118 (1999): 535.

33. See Stanley Fish, *Is There a Text in This Class? The Authority of Interpretive Communities* (Cambridge, Mass.: Harvard University Press, 1980), esp. 303–71.

34. See Wolfgang Iser, "The Reading Process: A Phenomenological Approach," in *Reader-Response Criticism from Formalism to Post-Structuralism* (ed. Jane P. Tompkins; Baltimore: Johns Hopkins University Press, 1980), 50–69.

35. While it is quite likely that living practice corresponded in significant ways to what is represented in the texts, the focus of this study is on the first-level enterprise of elucidating the textual picture—the representation—of ritual activity. However, I believe that the major conclusions of this study provide a sound basis for second-level reflections on the relationship of textual representation to living practice. On the problems associated with relating textual representation to living practice, see Olyan, *Rites and Rank,* 13–14; Gorman, review of Klingbeil, 535.

C H A P T E R 1: The Identification of Blood with "Life"

1. Milgrom, *Leviticus 1–16,* 711–12; cf. John E. Hartley, *Leviticus* (WBC 4; Dallas, Tex.: Word Books, 1992), 21 (on the blood manipulation of the burnt offering, Lev. 1:5): "The blood rite signifies that the animal's life is poured out to Yahweh."

2. On the book of Deuteronomy, see Moshe Weinfeld, *Deuteronomy and the Deuteronomic School* (Oxford: Clarendon Press, 1972); Weinfeld, "Deuteronomy, Book of," *ABD* 2:168–83.

3. The classic and influential treatment of the pentateuchal sources, including P, is Martin Noth, *A History of Pentateuchal Traditions* (trans. Bernard W. Anderson; Englewood Cliffs, N.J.: Prentice-Hall, 1972; originally, *Überlieferungsgeschichte des Pentateuch* [Stuttgart: W. Kohlhammer Verlag, 1948]). Noth elaborated and modified his identification and analysis of the sources in his commentaries on Exodus, Leviticus, and Numbers. See Martin Noth, *Exodus: A Commentary* (trans. J. S. Bowden; OTL; Philadelphia: Westminster Press, 1962; originally *Das zweite Buch Mose, Exodus* [ATD 5; Göttingen: Vandenhoeck & Ruprecht, 1959]); Noth, *Leviticus: A Commentary* (trans. J. E. Anderson; OTL; London: SCM Press, 1965; originally *Das dritte Buch Mose, Leviticus* [ATD 6; Göttingen: Vandenhoeck & Ruprecht, 1962]); Noth, *Numbers: A Commen-*

tary (trans. J. D. Martin; OTL; London: SCM Press, 1962; originally *Das vierte Buch Mose, Numeri* [ATD 7; Göttingen: Vandenhoeck & Ruprecht, 1966]). For a useful presentation and analysis of the results of Noth's work, see Anthony F. Campbell and Mark A. O'Brien, *Sources of the Pentateuch: Texts, Introductions, Annotations* (Minneapolis: Fortress Press, 1993). See also Richard Elliott Friedman, "Torah (Pentateuch)," *ABD* 6:605–22; Douglas A. Knight, "The Pentateuch," in *The Hebrew Bible and Its Modern Interpreters* (ed. Douglas A. Knight and Gene M. Tucker; Philadelphia: Fortress Press, 1985), 263–96.

4. For a brief but useful survey of scholarship on H, see Israel Knohl, *The Sanctuary of Silence: The Priestly Torah and the Holiness School* (Minneapolis: Fortress Press, 1995), 1–7.

5. Ibid.

6. For Knohl's account of his interaction with Milgrom, see ibid., 226. Milgrom's views on the relationship between P and H are set forth in *Leviticus 1–16*, 13–28. He notes both his basic agreement with Knohl (pp. 13–16) and areas where he evaluates the evidence differently (pp. 16–28). For Knohl's response to some of Milgrom's criticisms, see *Sanctuary*, 225–30.

7. Scholars hold conflicting positions on the dating of P and H relative to the other source strata of the Pentateuch. The following are useful introductions to P and the debates about its time of composition: Baruch A. Levine, "The Priestly Writers," *IDBSup*, 683–87; Douglas A. Knight, foreword to *Prolegomena to the History of Israel*, by Julius Wellhausen (Scholars Press Reprints and Translations Series; Atlanta: Scholars Press, 1994); repr. of *Prolegomena to the History of Israel* (trans. J. Sutherland Black and Allan Menzies, with preface by W. Roberston Smith; Edinburgh: Adam & Charles Black, 1885).

8. I hope to engage questions about the historical relationship between the Deuteronomic, Priestly, and Holiness sacrificial traditions in another study. At present, I continue to find myself in agreement with those scholars who argue for the relative priority of the Deuteronomic materials in relation to P and H. See, e.g., Frank Moore Cross, *Canaanite Myth and Hebrew Epic: Essays in the History of the Religion of Israel* (Cambridge, Mass.: Harvard University Press, 1973), 293–325 (esp. pp. 322–25); Erhard S. Gerstenberger, *Leviticus: A Commentary* (trans. Douglas W. Stott; OTL; Louisville, Ky.: Westminster John Knox Press, 1996), 3–14; Baruch A. Levine, "Late Language in the Priestly Source: Some Literary and Historical Observations," in *Proceedings of the Eighth World Congress of Jewish Studies: Panel Sessions: Bible Studies and Hebrew Language* (Jerusalem: World Union of Jewish Studies, 1983), 69–82; Levine, *Numbers 1–20* (AB 4; New York: Doubleday, 1993), 102–8; S. David Sperling, "Pants, Persians, and the Priestly Source," in *Ki Baruch Hu: Ancient Near Eastern, Biblical, and Judaic Studies in Honor of Baruch A. Levine* (ed. Robert Chazan, William W. Hallo, and Lawrence H. Schiffman; Winona Lake, Ind.: Eisenbrauns, 1999), 373–85. For the contrary view that P—in whole or in substantial part—is both preexilic and pre-Deuteronomic, see, e.g., Menahem Haran, *Temples and Temple Service in Ancient Israel* (Oxford: Clarendon Press, 1978; repr., Winona Lake, Ind.: Eisenbrauns, 1985); Haran, "The Character of the Priestly Source: Utopian and Exclusive Features," in *Proceedings of the Eighth World Congress of Jewish Studies* (Jerusalem: World Union of Jewish Studies, 1983), 131–38; Moshe Weinfeld, "Social and Cultic Institutions in the Priestly Source against Their Ancient Near Eastern Background," in *Proceedings*, 95–129; Knohl, *Sanctuary*, 199–224; Milgrom; *Leviticus 1–16*, 3–13, 29–34; Avi Hurvitz, *A Linguistic Study of the Relationship*

between the Priestly Source and the Book of Ezekiel (CahRB 20; Paris: J. Gabalda, 1982; Hurvitz, "The Language of the Priestly Source and Its Historical Setting—The Case for an Early Date," in *Proceedings*, 83–94.

9. In addition to works already cited, the following commentaries and monographs on Deuteronomy are cited in this section: Pierre Buis and Jacques Le Clercq, *Le Deutéronome* (SB; Paris: Librairie Lecoffre, 1963); Peter C. Craigie, *The Book of Deuteronomy* (NICOT; Grand Rapids, Mich.: Eerdmans, 1976); S. R. Driver, *A Critical and Exegetical Commentary on Deuteronomy* (3d ed.; ICC; Edinburgh: T & T Clarke, 1901); C. J. Labuschagne, *Deuteronomium* (vol. 2; De Prediking van het Oude Testament; Nijkerk: Uitgeverij G. F. Callenbach, 1990); A. D. H. Mayes, *Deuteronomy* (NCB; Grand Rapids, Mich.: Eerdmans, 1979); Anthony Phillips, *Deuteronomy* (CBC; Cambridge: Cambridge University Press, 1973); Gerhard von Rad, *Deuteronomy: A Commentary* (trans. Dorothea Barton, OTL; Philadelphia: Westminster Press, 1966); J. Ridderbos, *Deuteronomy* (trans. Ed M. van der Maas; BSC; Grand Rapids, Mich.: Zondervan, 1984); Jeffrey H. Tigay, *Deuteronomy* (JPS Torah Commentary; Philadelphia: Jewish Publication Society, 1996); Moshe Weinfeld, *Deuteronomy 1–11: A New Translation with Introduction and Commentary* (AB 5; New York: Doubleday, 1991).

10. On the context as a whole, and the structure of the chapter, see von Rad, *Deuteronomy*, 87–94.

11. Introduced with the particle *raq* (only); see GKC §153 on the use of *raq* "to introduce restrictive clauses," which place a limitation on something previously stated.

12. Noted, e.g., by von Rad (*Deuteronomy*, 93); Tigay (*Deuteronomy*, 124).

13. On the thesis that all slaughter was sacrificial before centralization, see J. Bergman, H. Ringgren, and B. Lang, "*zābaḥ*," *TDOT* 4:21 and n. 107; William Roberston Smith, *Lectures on the Religion of the Semites: The Fundamental Institutions* (3d ed.; 1927; repr., Hoboken, N.J.: Ktav, 1969), 234, 241, 307; S. R. Driver, *Deuteronomy*, 145–46; Mayes, *Deuteronomy*, 225; Weinfeld, *Deuteronomy and the Deuteronomic School*, 213; Tigay, *Deuteronomy*, 118, 122–23.

14. Treatment of blood in the cult is referred to in Deut 12:27. See chapter 2 for my discussion of this verse.

15. Von Rad, *Deuteronomy*, 93.

16. Phillips, *Deuteronomy*, 90–91; cf. Ridderbos, *Deuteronomy*, 161; Mayes, *Deuteronomy*, 228; Buis and Le Clercq, *Deutéronome*, 108.

17. Noordtzij, *Leviticus* (trans. Raymond Togtman; BSC; Grand Rapids, Mich.: Zondervan, 1982), 203.

18. See, e.g., Anna S. Meigs, *Food, Sex, and Pollution: A New Guinean Religion* (New Brunswick, N.J.: Rutgers University Press, 1984). According to Meigs, the Hua people of New Guinea attribute positive effects to the consumption of human blood by certain individuals. Thus, a male who consumes the blood of his father, or of a man who is among his "classificatory fathers," partakes of his strength and vitality (57, 61, 110, 127). The Hua also formerly practiced cultic cannibalism, in which individuals consumed the bodies of certain dead relatives on the assumption that such eating would "increase the growth and vitality of certain eaters." For example, one who consumed the body of his or her same-sex parent obtained an "inheritance of vitality" (110). In Hua ideology, flesh and blood contain *nu,* "vital essence" (99, 115), and their consumption transfers this positive force to the one who partakes of them. The conceptual similarity between *nu* and *nepeš* is striking.

19. The blood prohibitions that appear within the P portion of Leviticus were added by H tradents, as Milgrom and Knohl indicate. On Lev 3:17, see Milgrom, *Leviticus 1–16*, 63, 214–16; Knohl, *Sanctuary*, 49–51. On Lev 7:26–27, see Milgrom, *Leviticus 1–16*, 63, 426; Knohl, *Sanctuary*, 49–51. See later in this chapter for further discussion of these texts.

20. For the identification of the permission to consume animal flesh as an innovation, see Herman Gunkel, *Genesis* (trans. Mark E. Biddle; Macon, Ga.: Mercer University Press, 1997), 148; S. R. Driver, *The Book of Genesis* (5th ed.; WC; London: Methuen, 1906), 95; John Skinner, *A Critical and Exegetical Commentary on Genesis* (ICC; New York: Charles Scribner's Sons, 1910), 169; G. von Rad, *Genesis: A Commentary* (trans. John H. Marks; OTL; Philadelphia: Westminster Press, 1961), 127; U. Cassuto, *A Commentary on the Book of Genesis,* (vol. 2; trans. Israel Abrahams; Jerusalem: Magnes Press, 1964), 126; Milgrom, *Leviticus 1–16*, 417, 705–06.

21. On the use here of *'ak* with a restrictive meaning, see GKC §153; BDB, 36b. The rendering of *bĕnapšô* as *"with* its life" is widely accepted. See S. R. Driver, *Genesis,* 96; Cassuto, *Genesis,* 2:126; RSV; NRSV. The *bet* indicates association (*beth comitatus*). See GKC §119n (where *bĕnapšô* is cited as an example); Claus Westermann, *Genesis 1–11: A Commentary* (trans. John J. Scullion; Minneapolis: Augsburg Publishing House, 1984), 459, 460 n. 4a; Victor P. Hamilton, *The Book of Genesis, Chapters 1–17* (NICOT; Grand Rapids, Mich.: Eerdmans, 1990), 311 n. 2.

22. This explanation is affirmed by M. Vervenne, "'The Blood Is the Life and the Life Is the Blood': Blood as Symbol of Life and Death in Biblical Tradition (Gen. 9,4)," in *Ritual and Sacrifice in the Ancient Near East* (ed. J. Quaegebeur; Orientalia Lovaniensia Analecta 55; Leuven: Uitgeverij Peeters en Departement Oriëntalistiek, 1993), 465–69 (esp. 469). RSV and NRSV capture the sense well: "with its life, that is, its blood." See also S. R. Driver, *Genesis,* 96.

23. See, e.g., Hamilton, *Genesis 1–17,* 311; E. A. Speiser, *Genesis* (AB 1; Garden City, N.Y.: Doubleday, 1964), 57; NIV; NJPS. The translation is at least as old as the LXX, which renders Gen 9:4 as *plēn kreas en haimati psychēs ou phagesthe* (But flesh with the blood of soul you shall not eat).

24. Westermann, *Genesis 1–11,* 465 (citing Jacob).

25. See S. R. Driver, *Genesis,* 96; Vervenne, "'The Blood Is the Life and the Life Is the Blood,'" 452.

26. Vervenne, "'The Blood Is the Life and the Life Is the Blood,'" 453.

27. Nahum M. Sarna, *Genesis* (JPS Torah Commentary; Philadelphia: Jewish Publication Society, 1989), 61; Milgrom, *Leviticus 1–16,* 417.

28. Bruce Vawter, *On Genesis: A New Reading* (Garden City, N.Y.: Doubleday, 1977), 133; Skinner, *Genesis,* 170.

29. Contra Skinner, *Genesis,* 170; Milgrom, *Leviticus 1–16,* 417.

30. Note, as well, that neither Deuteronomy nor Gen 9:4 prescribes that blood must be disposed of in a clean or holy place (Saul M. Olyan, personal communication).

31. Cassuto, *Genesis,* 2:126.

32. Following most commentators and translations, I take the *lamed* preposition with *napšōtêkem* as a possessive marker; cf. RSV; NRSV.

33. I translate the difficult text with the RSV. The NRSV renders it, "from human beings, each one for the blood of another."

34. In his commentary on Gen 9:4–6, von Rad must look to Ezek 18:14 for such a declaration ("Know that all lives are mine") (*Genesis,* 128).

35. Von Rad, *Genesis,* 128.

36. Knohl and Milgrom agree in identifying Lev 3:16b–17 as an H text. See Knohl, *Sanctuary,* 49–51, 68; Milgrom, *Leviticus 1–16,* 63, 214–16. Both Knohl and Milgrom suggest that the P version of 3:16b originally ended with *leḥem ʾiššeh lĕrêaḥ nîḥōaḥ lyhwh* (food, a food gift for a soothing odor for Yahweh) (compare vv. 5b, 11b). The H tradents inserted the words *kol-ḥēleb* before *lyhwh,* creating the new declaration, "all fat is Yahweh's" (*kol-ḥēleb lyhwh*), and then added the text of v. 17.

37. This prohibition is specifically directed against consuming the fat of a domestic animal, that is, fat that could be offered to Yahweh as a "food gift" (*ʾiššeh*) (note 7:25).

38. Knohl and Milgrom agree in identifying Lev 7:22–27 as a creation of the H tradents. See Knohl, *Sanctuary,* 49–50, 68; Milgrom, *Leviticus 1–16,* 63, 426.

39. This observation speaks against Jacob Milgrom's claim that Lev 17:10–12 deals only with the blood of the well-being sacrifice ("A Prolegomenon to Leviticus 17:11," *JBL* 90 [1971]: 149–56; repr. in *SCTT,* 96–103). I elaborate on this point in the discussion of Lev 17:10–12 below.

40. Milgrom offers persuasive arguments for understanding Lev 7:23–25 to prohibit only consumption of the fat of domestic animals and thus to permit implicitly the eating of the fat of game animals (*Leviticus 1–16,* 428–29). In contrast, Lev 7:26–27 prohibits the consumption of *all* blood.

41. See chapter 7 for a fuller discussion of the structure of Lev 17.

42. Schenker, "Zeichen," 196–97; Baruch J. Schwartz, "The Prohibitions Concerning the 'Eating' of Blood in Leviticus 17," in *Priesthood and Cult in Ancient Israel* (ed. Gary A. Anderson and Saul M. Olyan; JSOTSup 125; Sheffield: Sheffield Academic Press, 1991), 43–46. Note Schwartz's explanation of how this structural pattern functions to emphasize the motive statement given in v. 11: "This is a concentric structure, in which the law is stated twice, both before and after the motive clause, which is thus placed in the center, and its purpose is to emphasize. It is not the law, however, which receives the emphasis (even though it is repeated), but the motive, which is surrounded on both sides by the law it explains" ("Prohibitions," 45).

43. "Severing" (*krt*) is a penalty carried out by Yahweh, divine extirpation, involving the untimely death of the sinner and the termination of his lineage. See Schwartz, "Prohibitions," 38 n. 3; Schwartz, *The Holiness Legislation: Studies in the Priestly Code* (Jerusalem: Magnes Press, 1999), 52–57 (esp. 52 n. 1, and the literature cited there); D. J. Wold, "The Meaning of the Biblical Penalty of KARETH" (Ph.D. diss., University of California at Berkeley, 1978); Wold, "The KARETH Penalty in P: Rationale and Cases," *SBL Seminar Papers, 1979* (vol. 1; SBLSP 16; Chico, Calif.: Scholars Press, 1979), 1–45.

44. As noted by Rashi (ad loc.).

45. See David Hoffmann, *Das Buch Leviticus: Übersetzt und Erklärt* (vol. 1; Berlin: M. Poppelauer, 1905), 474; Karl Elliger, *Leviticus* (HAT 4; Tübingen: J. C. B. Mohr [Paul Siebeck], 1966), 218; Léopold Sabourin, "Nefesh, sang, et expiation (*Lv* 17, 11.14)," *Sciences ecclésiastiques* 18 (1966): 25; Notker Füglister, "Sühne durch Blut: Zur Bedeutung von Leviticus 17, 11," in *Studien zum Pentateuch: Walter Kornfeld zum 60. Geburtstag* (ed. Georg Braulik; Vienna: Herder, 1977), 143; Gordon Wenham, *The Book of Leviticus*

(NICOT; Grand Rapids, Mich.: Eerdmans, 1979), 239, 244; Schwartz, "Prohibitions," 49; Milgrom, *Leviticus 1–16,* 706; Hartley, *Leviticus,* 261; NRSV; NJPS; NIV. See also *Targum Onqelos; Targum Pseudo-Jonathan.*

46. Note Saadiah's explanation (ad loc.) that the life has its dwelling in the blood. Ibn Ezra (final comment on Lev 17:7) affirms that the *nepeš* that animates a person is located in the blood of the heart.

47. On *beth essentiae,* see Williams, *Hebrew Syntax* §249 (p. 45); GKC §119i. Translations reflecting this interpretation include LXX; NEB. Jacob Milgrom originally affirmed this translation; see "Prolegomenon," *SCTT,* 96.

48. The words *dāmô běnapšô* are difficult to render in this context, and may be a gloss. I have rendered the *bet* preposition as the *beth essentiae* and interpreted *hû'* to refer back to the blood. The words seem to explain that the life is identified with blood to the extent that blood is in fact what animates the flesh. For a brief but useful discussion of approaches to the problem, see Hartley, *Leviticus,* 263 n. 14a.

49. As Schwartz notes ("Prohibitions," 38–39), this unit differs from Lev 17:10–12 in that it does not present a negative act followed by a negative divine response. Rather, we are told about a neutral act which requires a specific action to avoid becoming a negative act.

50. Schwartz, "Prohibitions," 61. According to Schwartz, tossing dirt over the blood removes it from view and makes its consumption all but impossible. See also Noth, *Leviticus,* 132.

51. Schwartz's argument that the pouring out and covering do not constitute a "ritual" ("Prohibitions," 61–62) reflects a narrow understanding of "ritual" as cultic activity. However, in my view, Schwartz is right to question explanations of the treatment of the blood that identify it as a means of returning the blood to God or fulfilling some other cultic purpose (see "Prohibitions," 61 n. 3).

52. Milgrom, "Prolegomenon," *SCTT,* 99; Milgrom, *Leviticus 1–16,* 712. See also Hartley, *Leviticus,* 277 (citing Gen 4:10).

53. If an Israelite slaughters a domestic animal without having conveyed it to the Tent of Meeting in order to make an offering to Yahweh, he is identified as a murderer (Lev 17:3–4). For further discussion, see chapter 7.

54. For the following, I have drawn on two articles: G. André, "*zāraq,*" *TDOT* 4:162–65 (= *TWAT* 2:686–89); Norman H. Snaith, "The Sprinkling of Blood," *ExpTim* 82 (1970–71): 23–24.

55. "Sprinkle" appears in AV; NIV. "Sprinkle" in the AV seems to be derived from William Tyndale's use of "sprinckell" to render *zrq* in his 1530 English translation of the Pentateuch. Martin Luther consistently rendered *zrq* with *sprengen* (sprinkle). Most German translators have followed his lead and continue to identify *sprengen* as an appropriate translation, on the basis of rather weak evidence. See KBL3, s.v. *zrq,* which offers *streuen* (toss, strew) for the verb when dry substances are in view, but insists upon *sprengen* for blood manipulations. See also Rolf Rendtorff, *Leviticus* (BKAT 3.1–3; Neukirchener-Vluyn: Neukirchener Verlag, 1985–92). Snaith ("Sprinkling") argues persuasively against the translation "sprinkle." See also S. R. Driver, *The Book of Exodus* (Cambridge Bible for Schools and Colleges; Cambridge: Cambridge University Press, 1911; repr. 1918), 318: "'Sprinkle' not only conveys an incorrect idea of the action meant, but also confuses it with an entirely different action, correctly represented by 'sprinkle.'"

56. See RSV ("throw," except at Num 18:17 where, inexplicably, "sprinkle" appears); NRSV ("dash"); NJPS ("dash"); S. R. Driver, *Exodus,* 318 ("toss"); Milgrom, *Leviticus 1–16* ("dash"); Hartley, *Leviticus* ("dash"); Wenham, *Leviticus* ("splash"). BDB, 284b translates the verb with "to toss or throw (in a volume), scatter abundantly" and affirms that it is distinct from sprinkling. The only difficulty faced by this conclusion is that Num 19:13, 20 have the *qal* passive form of the root in a context where the verb *nzh* in the *hiphil* (sprinkle) is otherwise used to describe the handling of the water used to purify those who have been in contact with a corpse (cf. Ezek 36:25, which probably refers figuratively to the corpse-impurity ritual and uses the *qal* of *zrq*). This usage suggests that the verb refers to the same gesture as is indicated by the *hiphil* of *nzh*. However, the two verses come from H (Knohl, *Sanctuary,* 92–93), not the original P layer of the text, and it appears that H is indicating that a different manipulation of the water was to be employed than that indicated by P, or rather, that H regards "sprinkling" as a subtype of "tossing" (compare the Ezekiel text cited above) (see Knohl, *Sanctuary,* 93 n. 114).

57. See, e.g., John Gray, *I & II Kings: A Commentary* (2d ed.; OTL; London: SCM Press, 1970), 634, 636; Gwilym H. Jones, *1 and 2 Kings* (2 vols.; NCB; Grand Rapids, Mich.: Eerdmans, 1984), 2:539.

58. For further discussion of 2 Kgs 16:12–15, see chapter 2. On blood sprinkling and consecration in P, see chapters 4 and 5.

59. For the source identification, see Knohl, *Sanctuary,* 53–54, 105, 116.

60. The following is a helpful treatment of the verb and the blood manipulation it indicates: Jacob Milgrom and David P. Wright, "*nāzāh,*" *TWAT* 5:322–25. See also Th. C. Vriezen, "The Term *hizza:* Lustration and Consecration," *OTS* 7 (1950): 201–12.

61. See BDB, 678a–81b, for the range of possible meanings.

62. For detailed discussion of these texts, including the identification of the loci of the blood applications, see chapter 6.

63. Priestly ordination: Exod 29:20; Lev 8:23–24; purification after the healing of a skin disease: Lev 14:14, 25. The latter ritual complex also involves the application (*ntn*) of oil to the right earlobe, right thumb, and right big toe over the blood (Lev 14:17, 28).

64. The J text (Exod 12:22) prescribes that a bundle of hyssop is to be dipped into the blood and "touched" (the *hiphil* of *ngʿ*) to the lintel and doorposts. For further discussion of the Passover blood manipulations, see chapter 2.

65. Ziony Zevit asserts that the two verbs refer to slightly different gestures, but adduces rather weak evidence to support making such a distinction ("Philology, Archaeology, and a Terminus a Quo for P's *ḥaṭṭā't* Legislation," in *Pomegranates and Golden Bells: Studies in Biblical, Jewish, and Near Eastern Ritual, Law, and Literature in Honor of Jacob Milgrom* [ed. David P. Wright, David Noel Freedman, and Avi Hurvitz; Winona Lake, Ind.: Eisenbrauns, 1995], 30 n. 4).

66. The most detailed recent study of the verb *kipper* and related forms is Bernd Janowski, *Sühne als Heilsgeschehen* (WMANT 55; Neukirchen-Vluyn: Neukirchener Verlag, 1982). Janowski's study rests on the work of his teacher, Hartmut Gese (see "The Atonement," in *Essays on Biblical Theology* [trans. Keith Crim; Minneapolis: Augsburg Publishing House, 1981; 2d ed., 2000], 93–116). The following are also worthy of note: Milgrom, *Leviticus 1–16,* 255–26, 1079– 10; Baruch A. Levine, *In the Presence of the Lord: A Study of Cult and Some Cultic Terms in Ancient Israel* (SJLA 5; Leiden: E. J. Brill, 1974), 56–77; Kiuchi, *Purification Offering,* 87–109.

67. See, e.g., Hoffmann, *Leviticus*, 1:123.

68. For examples, see *CAD* K, *kapāru* A, 178–80; *AHw, kapāru(m)* I, 442–43.

69. Milgrom, *Leviticus 1–16*, 1080–82. See also Wright, *Disposal of Impurity,* 291–99.

70. Milgrom, *Leviticus 1–16*, 1080–82. However, according to Wright, "The meaning of *kuppuru* and the nouns [*takpertu* and *kupīrātu*] should . . . never be abstracted to mean simply 'purify' and 'purification rite'" (*Disposal of Impurity,* 298).

71. Levine, *Presence,* 61–62; in a recent personal communication, Levine indicates that he continues to regard the noun *kōper* (ransom payment) as deriving from the root *kpr* with the meaning "wipe away."

72. Schwartz, "Prohibitions," 52, 54.

73. See BDB, 306b; KBL3, 292–93.

74. For *ḥṭ'* with the meaning "sin," see Exod 9:34; 20:20; Lev 4:3, 22, 27, 28; 5:1, 6, 7, 10, 11, 17, 21, 23; Num 16:22; Josh 7:11. For other examples, see BDB, 306b–307a.

75. GKC §52h (p. 141); Joüon, *GHB* §52d.

76. GKC §52h (p. 141).

77. Ibid., 142.

78. For the translation "unsin," see George Buchanan Gray, *A Critical and Exegetical Commentary on Numbers* (ICC; Edinburgh: T & T Clark, 1903), 81; cf. German, "entsündigen"; see KBL3, 293.

79. James Barr, "Etymology and the Old Testament," in *Language and Meaning: Studies in Hebrew Language and Biblical Exegesis* (*Oudtestamentische Studiën* 19; Leiden: E. J. Brill, 1974), 1. See also Barr, *The Semantics of Biblical Language* (London: Oxford University Press, 1961), 107–60.

80. Barr, *Semantics,* 107.

81. A fifteenth occurrence may be *'ăḥaṭṭennâ* in Gen 31:39. However, the meaning of the verb here is obscure, and is probably not actually an example of the *piel* of the root *ḥṭ'*. See S. E. Loewenstamm, "*'anōkî 'ăḥaṭṭennâ*" [in Hebrew], *Leshonenu* 29 (1965): 69–70 (ET in *Comparative Studies in Biblical and Ancient Oriental Literatures* [AOAT 24; Neukirchen-Vluyn: Neukirchener Verlag, 1980], 225–27). Since the verbal form that appears in Gen 31:39 probably has nothing to do with the verb *hiṭṭē',* Noam Zohar's recent attempt to argue, on the basis of this example, that *hiṭṭē'* means "displace," or "transfer," must be rejected. See Zohar, "Repentance and Purification: The Significance and Semantics of *ḥaṭṭā't* in the Pentateuch," *JBL* 107 (1988): 615–617; and Jacob Milgrom's response to Zohar's thesis, "The *Modus Operandi* of the *ḥaṭṭā't*: A Rejoinder," *JBL* 109 (1990): 112 (Milgrom refers to Loewenstamm's study).

82. See BDB, 307b (specifically rejecting the translation "cleanse the altar"); RSV; NRSV ("Also you shall offer a sin offering for the altar"); Brevard S. Childs, *The Book of Exodus* (OTL; Philadelphia: Westminster Press, 1974), 520; Kiuchi, *Purification Offering,* 95–96.

83. In basic agreement with Milgrom, *Leviticus 1–16*, 524, 583; see also KBL3, 293 (*hiṭṭē'* means "als Sündopfer darbringen" *only* in Lev 6:19; 9:15; 2 Chron 29:24]).

84. Milgrom, "Sin-Offering or Purification-Offering?" *VT* 21 (1971): 237; Milgrom, *Leviticus 1–16*, 253.

85. There is a large body of scholarship on the *ḥaṭṭā't*. In addition to his commentary on Leviticus, special note should be made of the following articles by Jacob Milgrom, "Sin-Offering or Purification-Offering?" *SCTT*, 67–69; Milgrom, "Function of the *ḥaṭṭā't* Sacrifice" [in Hebrew], *Tarbiz* 40 (1970–71): 1–8; Milgrom, "Two Kinds of

ḥaṭṭā't," *VT* 26 (1976): 333–37 (repr. in *SCTT,* 70–74); Milgrom, "Israel's Sanctuary: The Priestly 'Picture of Dorian Gray,'" *RB* 83 (1976): 390–99 (repr. in *SCTT,* 75–84); Milgrom, "Sacrifices and Offerings, OT," *Interpreter's Dictionary of the Bible: Supplementary Volume,* 766–68; Milgrom, "The Paradox of the Red Cow (Num. xix)," *VT* 31 (1981): 62–72 (repr. in *SCTT,* 85–95). See also Gary A. Anderson, "Sacrifice and Sacrificial Offerings. Old Testament," *ABD* 5:879–80; Herbert Chanan Brichto, "On Slaughter and Sacrifice, Blood and Atonement," *Hebrew Union College Annual* 47 (1976): 19–55; Gorman, *Ideology of Ritual;* Janowski, *Sühne;* Kiuchi, *Purification Offering;* Levine, *Presence,* 101–14; Rolf Rendtorff, *Studien zur Geschichte des Opfers im Alten Israel* (WMAT 24; Neukirchen-Vluyn: Neukirchener Verlag, 1967), 53, 62–63, 199–234, 239–41; Wright, *Disposal,* 16–21, 95–96, 129–59; Angel M. Rodriguez, *Substitution in the Hebrew Cultus* (Andrews University Seminary Doctoral Dissertation Series 3; Berrien Springs, Mich.: Andrews University Press, 1979), 76–149; Zevit, "Philology," 29–38; Zohar, "Repentance and Purification," 609–18.

86. Milgrom, "Sin-Offering or Purification-Offering?" 237; Milgrom, *Leviticus 1–16,* 253. See also James Barr, "Sacrifice and Offering," *Dictionary of the Bible,* 874; Levine, *Presence,* 101–2; Hartley, *Leviticus,* 55.

87. LXX renders *ḥaṭṭā't* as *peri tēs hamartias* in some instances (see, e.g., Lev 4:3, 14; 5:6; 12:6, 8), and simply as *hamartia* in others (see, e.g., Lev 4:21, 24).

88. Levine, *Presence,* 102.

89. "Sin-Offering or Purification-Offering?"; *Leviticus 1–16,* 253–54. For examples of contrary views, see Rodriguez, *Substitution,* 80–83; Kiuchi, *Purification Offering,* 21–66, 161.

90. Baruch J. Schwartz, "The Bearing of Sin in the Priestly Literature," in *Pomegranates and Golden Bells: Studies in Biblical, Jewish, and Near Eastern Ritual, Law, and Literature in Honor of Jacob Milgrom* (ed. David P. Wright, David Noel Freedman, and Avi Hurvitz; Winona Lake, Ind.: Eisenbrauns, 1995), 3–21.

91. As Milgrom ably demonstrates; see *Leviticus 1–16,* 257–58.

92. Note, especially, Lev 4:3, where *ḥaṭṭā't* [sin], and the *qal* construction of *ḥt'* are closely juxtaposed with the name of the sacrifice: "If the anointed priest should sin [*yeḥĕṭā'*] so that the people become liable, he shall present for his sin which he sinned ['*al ḥaṭṭā'tô 'ăšer ḥāṭā'*] a flawless bull of the herd to Yahweh as a *ḥaṭṭā't* offering [*lĕḥaṭṭā't*]."

93. I offered some preliminary development of the approach to the *ḥaṭṭā't* suggested here in a paper read at the 2003 international meeting of the Society of Biblical Literature, Cambridge, England, 25 July 2003: "*Ḥaṭṭā't* as 'Sin Offering': A Reconsideration." I anticipate developing this paper for publication in the near future.

CHAPTER 2: Cultic Blood Manipulation

1. Throughout this study, I use the designation "priestly" (with a lower-case p) to refer to P and H together, while "Priestly" will refer exclusively to P, in distinction from H.

2. There is a great deal of scholarship on the "Book of the Covenant." Note, in particular, Yuichi Osumi, *Die Kompositionsgeschichte des Bundesbuches Exodus 20, 22b–33* (OBO 105; Göttingen: Vandenhoeck & Ruprecht, 1991).

3. Classic source criticism attributed this legal collection (Exod 34:17–26) to the J tradent(s). Other scholars have argued that it is based on an old legal collection uti-

lized by the author(s) of J as well as the tradent(s) who composed the Book of the Covenant. For a survey of scholarship to the late 1960s, see Franz-Elmar Wilms, *Das Jahwistische Bundesbuch in Exodus 34* (SANT 32; Munich: Kösel-Verlag, 1973), 15–135. More recently, some scholars have argued that the legal collection is "a post-Deutero-nomic redactional composition," which had the Book of the Covenant as one of its sources; see Bernard M. Levinson, *Deuteronomy and the Hermeneutics of Legal Inno-vation* (New York: Oxford University Press, 1997), 69–70, and the works cited there.

4. On the verb *zbḥ*, see J. Bergman, H. Ringgren, and B. Lang, "*zābaḥ*," *TDOT* 4:8–29; BDB, 256b–257a; Milgrom, *Leviticus 1–16*, 713–15.

5. On the "eaten sacrifice" (*zebaḥ*), see William Barron Stevenson, "Hebrew 'Olah and Zebach Sacrifices," in *Festschrift Alfred Bertholet zum 80. Geburtstag* (ed. Walter Baumgartner, Otto Eissfeldt, Karl Elliger, and Leonhard Rost; Tübingen: J. C. B. Mohr [Paul Siebeck], 1950), 488–97; Norman H. Snaith, "Sacrifices in the Old Testament," *VT* 7 (1957): 308–17; J. Licht, "*zebaḥ*" [in Hebrew], *EM* 2:901–2; Rendtorff, *Studien*, 133–49; Bergman, Ringgren, and Lang, *TDOT* 4:8–29. Milgrom (*Leviticus 1–16*, 218) offers the more elaborate rendering "slain offering whose meat is eaten by the worshiper."

6. See, for example, Saadiah (ad loc.), who bluntly comments that blood cannot be slaughtered; S. R. Driver, *Exodus*, 245 (Driver describes this combination of the verb *zābaḥ* with the noun *dām* as "peculiar"); Haran, *Temples*, 329.

7. U. Cassuto, *A Commentary on the Book of Exodus* [in Hebrew] (1942; repr., Jerusalem: Magnes Press, the Hebrew University, 1987), 212. Menahem Haran accepts Cassuto's interpretation; see *Temples*, 329 and n. 27.

8. In GKC's note on this construction (§128r) all of the "substantives used to con-vey an attributive idea in the construct state before a partitive genitive" are abstract nouns.

9. See NRSV and NIV ("its tallest cedars"); NJPS ("its loftiest cedars").

10. Noth, *Exodus*, 264–65.

11. AV; RSV; NRSV; NIV; NJPS; Childs, *Exodus*, 485; G. Henton Davies, *Exodus: In-troduction and Commentary* (TBC; London: SCM Press, 1967), 189. John I. Durham paraphrases, even more freely, "You are not to combine with anything leavened the blood of my sacrifice" (*Exodus* [WBC 3; Waco, Tex.: Word Books, 1987], 310).

12. See, e.g., Childs, *Exodus*, 485; G. Henton Davies, *Exodus*, 189; W. H. Gispen, *Ex-odus* (trans. Ed van der Maas; BSC; Grand Rapids, Mich.: Eerdmans, 1982), 232; Durham, *Exodus*, 333–34; Cassuto, *Exodus*, 304. A number of commentators note that Lev 2:11 (P) explicitly prohibits the burning of a leavened cereal offering on the altar.

13. Noth, *Exodus*, 265.

14. *Mekilta* (*Mishpatim* 20); *Targum Pseudo-Jonathan*; Rashi; Ibn Ezra; Ramban; Rashbam (on Exod 23:18a). The vast majority of modern critical scholars interpret Exod 23:18a and Exod 34:25a to refer to all sacrifices (see Childs, *Exodus*, 485). For mod-ern arguments in favor of the traditional rabbinic interpretation, see Haran, *Temples*, 327–32; Nahum Sarna, *Exodus* (JPS Torah Commentary; Philadelphia: Jewish Publica-tion Society, 1991), 146; Benno Jacob, *The Second Book of the Bible: Exodus* (trans. Wal-ter Jacob; Hoboken, N.J.: Ktav, 1992), 725–26. Note also the recent suggestion by C. J. Labuschagne that Exod 23:18–19 is an appendix to the festival calendar of Exod 23:14–17, and that the laws of Exod 23:18 apply to the previously mentioned festival of unleavened bread (Exod 23:15): "'You Shall Not Boil a Kid in Its Mother's Milk': A New Proposal for the Origin of the Prohibition," in *The Scriptures and the Scrolls: Studies*

in Honour of A. S. van der Woude on the Occasion of his 65th Birthday (ed. F. García Martínez, A. Hilhorst, and C.J. Labuschagne; VTSup 49; Leiden: E. J. Brill, 1992), 13.

15. Noth, *Exodus*, 192.

16. G. Henton Davies, *Exodus*, 189. See also Durham, *Exodus*, 334.

17. Durham, *Exodus*, 333–34.

18. As Martin Noth notes, "The question of the larger literary context to which this narrative version of the covenant belongs is not easy to answer" (*Exodus*, 198). For a survey and discussion of opinions on the source identification of Exod 24:1–2, 9–11, see Childs, *Exodus*, 499– 501. For the purposes of this study, it suffices to note that there is a scholarly consensus to assign the text to the nonpriestly stratum of the Pentateuch.

19. In this construction, *šĕlāmîm* stands in apposition to *zĕbāḥîm* and identifies the specific type of *zebaḥ*. See Hendel, "Sacrifice as a Cultural System," 381 n. 63, on this "apposition of genus and species." See also GKC §131b on appositional constructions. Some interpreters assert that one or the other member of the pair should be eliminated as secondary. See Bergman, Ringgren, and Lang, *TDOT* 4:12; Rendtorff, *Studien*, 150–51. The arguments advanced in support of this position do not seem decisive.

20. E. W. Nicholson, "The Covenant Ritual in Exodus XXIV 3–8," *VT* 32 (1982): 81.

21. This relationship between cultic activity and cultic status is noted by Nicholson, who affirms that the assignment of blood manipulation activity to Moses, "whose implied role is . . . that of priest proper," emphasizes that activity (ibid., 81). For general reflections on status and cultic activity, see Olyan, *Rites and Rank*, 11–12.

22. See, e.g., Josef Scharbert, "Blood," *EBT* 1:78. The medieval Jewish commentator Ḥizquni (ad loc.) is an early witness to this interpretation. Ibn Ezra characterizes this explanation as midrashic as opposed to the plain sense of the text (Short Commentary, on Exod 24:8).

23. Leon Morris offers a similar explanation, also citing Lev 8:30 (*The Apostolic Preaching of the Cross* [Grand Rapids, Mich.: Eerdmans, 1956], 71). R. J. Thompson (*Penitence and Sacrifice in Early Israel Outside the Levitical Law* [Leiden: E. J. Brill, 1963], 71) affirms Morris' explanation.

24. Sforno (on Exod 24:6) is an early witness to this interpretation. For modern scholars, see S. R. Driver, *Exodus*, 253; Noth, *Exodus*, 198; Cassuto, *Exodus*, 312; Sarna, *Exodus*, 152; Jacob, *Exodus*, 741–744; Ronald E. Clements, *Exodus* (CBC; Cambridge: Cambridge University Press, 1972), 159; J. Philip Hyatt, *Exodus* (rev. ed.; NCB; Grand Rapids, Mich.: Eerdmans, 1980), 256. Nicholson identifies this as the dominant explanation ("Covenant Ritual," 76).

25. G. Henton Davies, *Exodus*, 194.

26. Bell, *Ritual Theory*, 74.

27. Ibid., 91.

28. Ibid., 98.

29. Ibid., 98–100.

30. Ibid., 98.

31. Sarna, *Exodus*, 152.

32. Clements, *Exodus*, 159. Recall, also, G. Henton Davies's reference to "a space of time and experience bounded at each end by sacrificial blood and life" (*Exodus*, 194).

33. Gispen (*Exodus*, 238) and Hendel ("Sacrifice as a Cultural System," 388), e.g., reject the identification of the altar with Yahweh.

34. Cassuto, *Exodus*, 312.

35. Noth, *Exodus*, 198. Cf. Sarna, *Exodus*, 152; G. Henton Davies, *Exodus*, 194.

36. Hyatt, *Exodus*, 257.

37. Bell, *Ritual Theory*, 99–100 (emphasis is Bell's). See also Roy A. Rappaport, *Ecology, Meaning and Religion* (Richmond, Calif.: North Atlantic Books, 1979), 200; Jay, *Throughout Your Generations Forever*, 6.

38. Many scholars identify P, J, and Deuteronomic (or "proto-Deuteronomic") materials. See Childs, *Exodus*, 184–85; Hyatt, *Exodus*, 131–41.

39. Noth, *Exodus*, 97; Childs, *Exodus*, 184; Hyatt, *Exodus*, 131, 136–37.

40. Knohl, *Sanctuary*, 19–21, 52, 64 nn. 11 and 14, 88 n. 89, 104.

41. Ibid., 19

42. See BDB, 706.

43. Levinson, *Deuteronomy*, 58–59. Levinson cites A. M. Honeyman, "Hebrew *sap* 'Basin, Goblet,'" *JTS* 37 (1936): 56–59, and notes that the LXX and Vulgate render *sap* as "threshold," while the Targums (*Onqelos, Pseudo-Jonathan,* and *Neofiti*) identify it as a vessel. Ibn Ezra (Longer Commentary, ad loc.) records both interpretations without deciding for one or the other.

44. Levinson, *Deuteronomy*, 60.

45. Ibid., 58.

46. Ibid., 59.

47. Levine, *Presence*, 74–75.

48. Ibid., 74.

49. Ibid., 75.

50. See for example, J. H. Kurtz's argument that the blood manipulation "is to be regarded as an act of atonement" (*Sacrificial Worship of the Old Testament* [trans. James Martin; 1863; repr., Minneapolis: Klock and Klock, 1980], 367), in connection with his lengthy argument for understanding sacrificial blood manipulation and atonement in terms of *satisfactio vicaria* (101–49). See also Gispen's explanation (*Exodus*, 117): "*The blood has atoning power* and points to the blood of the Lamb that will take away the sin of the world (John 1:29, 36). . . . The blood was . . . a visible sign and seal. Israel's first-born ones were spared by the blood of an animal, *which thus had substitutionary significance.* The Passover was a reminder that this being spared was not a matter of course" (emphasis added).

51. Ibn Ezra, Long and Short Commentaries (on Exod 12:7).

52. For further examples of Ibn Ezra's identification of sacrificial blood as *kōper,* see chapters 3–5. See chapter 7 for a review of Ibn Ezra's understanding of blood manipulation, and discussion of the significance of Lev 17:11 for that understanding.

53. The identification of "elders" as status-marked is based on understanding "elder" as an honorific designation. On "elders" in ancient Israel, see Hanoch Reviv, *The Elders in Ancient Israel: A Study of a Biblical Institution* (trans. Lucy Pitmann; Jerusalem: Magnes Press, 1989); Timothy M. Willis, "Elders in Pre-Exilic Israelite Society" (Ph.D. diss., Harvard University, 1990).

54. Olyan, *Rites and Rank*, 11.

55. All such texts are part of the P and H strata of the Pentateuch.

56. The formulation "the assembly of the congregation of Israel" in v. 6 is also not characteristic of P, and appears again only in Num 14:5. Knohl identifies it as an H formulation (*Sanctuary*, 92 n. 109).

57. For further discussion of this gap-filling move, see chapter 3.

58. According to *Mekilta de-Rabbi Ishmael,* which presents a holistic reading of Exod 12, these differing prescriptions indicate that the order of application has no impact on the validity of the rites.

59. Exod 24:6 (discussed earlier); 2 Kgs 16:12, 15 (discussed later); P (see chapter 4); Ezekiel (see chapter 6); H (see chapter 7). See, also, the discussion of *zrq* in the appendix to chapter 1.

60. Cf. David Hoffmann, *Das Buch Deuteronomium* (vol. 1; Berlin: M. Poppelauer, 1913), 173.

61. So Buis and Le Clercq, *Deutéronome,* 108; Phillips, *Deuteronomy,* 90–91.

62. Ridderbos, *Deuteronomy,* 161.

63. In addition to those previously cited, the following commentaries and studies on 2 Kings are cited in this section: Mordechai Cogan and Hayim Tadmor, *II Kings* (AB 11; New York: Doubleday, 1988); T. R. Hobbs, *2 Kings* (WBC 13; Waco, Tex.: Word Books, 1985); Burke O. Long, *2 Kings* (FOTL 10; Grand Rapids, Mich.: Eerdmans, 1991); Ernst Würthwein, *Die Bücher der Könige: 1. Kön. 17–2. Kön. 25* (ATD 11.2; Göttingen: Vandenhoeck & Ruprecht, 1984).

64. For a brief but helpful survey of scholarly views, see Long, *2 Kings,* 174–75. See Rendtorff, *Studien,* 46–50, for an attempt to distinguish layers of sources within 2 Kgs 16:10–18. Most significant for this study is Rendtorff's claim that vv. 12 and 15 belong to different editorial layers. See also Würthwein, *Könige,* 389. However, as Long emphasizes, "The evidence for identifying such literary breaks is equivocal and heavily dependent on a priori theories of composition that rule out alternatives" (*2 Kings,* 175). Given these observations, caution should be exercised in drawing a sharp distinction between vv. 13 and 15 in 2 Kgs 16:10–18.

65. As Long notes, "all commentators notice the priestly language and technical interest in cultic affairs" (*2 Kings,* 175).

66. Cogan and Tadmor, *II Kings,* 189.

67. Rendtorff, *Studien,* 46.

68. Cogan and Tadmor, *II Kings,* 189. Cf. 2 Sam 6:17–18 (David); 1 Kgs 8:63 (Solomon); 1 Kgs 12:32 (Jeroboam I).

69. Rendtorff, *Studien,* 46.

70. John Gray, *I & II Kings,* 634, 636; Jones, *1 and 2 Kings,* 2:539; Hobbs, *2 Kings,* 216.

71. See chapter 5.

72. Each of the commentators cited in note 70 refers to the "sprinkling" of the blood. Strikingly, Hobbs does so even though he employs "toss" in the translation of the pericope that precedes the commentary.

73. The following commentaries and studies on 1 Samuel are cited in this section: Walter Brueggemann, *First and Second Samuel* (Interpretation; Louisville, Ky.: John Knox Press, 1990); Karl Budde, *Die Bücher Samuel* (KHC 8; Tübingen: J. C. B. Mohr [Paul Siebeck], 1902); Paul Dhorme, *Les Livres de Samuel* (EBib; Paris: Librairie Victor Lecoffre/J. Gabalda, 1910); S. R. Driver, *Notes on the Hebrew Text and the Topography of the Books of Samuel* (2d ed.; Oxford: Clarendon Press, 1913); Hans Wilhelm Hertzberg, *I & II Samuel* (trans. J. S. Bowden; OTL; Philadelphia: Westminster Press, 1964); C. F. Keil and F. Delitzsch, *Biblical Commentary on the Books of Samuel* (trans. James Martin; Clark's Foreign Theological Library, Fourth Series, vol. 9; Edinburgh: T & T Clark, 1880); Ralph W. Klein, *1 Samuel* (WBC 10; Waco, Tex.: Word Books, 1983); P. Kyle McCarter, *I Samuel* (AB 8; Garden City, N.Y.: Doubleday, 1980).

74. Reading with the LXX instead of the MT. See *BHS* note ad loc.

75. David Qimḥi (on 1 Sam 14:32); Keil and Delitzsch, *Books of Samuel*, 144; S. R. Driver, *Books of Samuel*, 115; Budde, *Bücher Samuel*, 99; Dhorme, *Livres de Samuel*, 122; Brueggemann, *First and Second Samuel*, 105; McCarter, *I Samuel*, 249; Klein, *1 Samuel*, 139; J. G. McConville, *Law and Theology in Deuteronomy* (JSOTSup 33; Sheffield: JSOT Press, 1984), 47.

76. Dhorme, *Livres de Samuel*, 122; S. R. Driver, *Books of Samuel*, 116; Budde, *Bücher Samuel*, 99; Brueggemann, *First and Second Samuel*, 105; Klein, *1 Samuel*, 139. Rashi (on 1 Sam 14:33) asserts that the large stone was employed as a "high place" upon which the blood was tossed and fat portions were burned.

77. See, e.g., Budde, *Bücher Samuel.*, 99; S. R. Driver, *Books of Samuel*, 116; Klein, *1 Samuel*, 139.

78. Hertzberg, *I & II Samuel*, 116.

79. McCarter, *I Samuel*, 243; Klein, *1 Samuel*, 130; NIV.

80. Budde, *Bücher Samuel*, 99.

81. Hertzberg, *I & II Samuel*, 116. Although McCarter affirms that the people's offense was the eating of blood, he adds that the blood "was supposed to be reserved for Yahweh" (*I Samuel*, 249). Likewise, Klein states, "It was on the altar that the blood belonged" (*1 Samuel*, 139).

82. Cf. Rashi (on 1 Sam 14:32–33); Weinfeld, *Deuteronomy 1–11*, 27 (following Rashi).

83. He understands v. 35 to explicitly identify the stone as an altar. See also Klein, *1 Samuel*, 139. For other examples of large stones used as altars, see 1 Sam 6:14, 15; Judges 13:19, 20.

84. Rashbam; Nachmanides; Sforno; Ḥizquni (all on Lev 19:26); Maimonides, *Guide to the Perplexed* III.46. It should be noted that Qimḥi (on 1 Sam 14:32) quotes and affirms Rashbam's interpretation of Lev 19:26, but rejects its relevance for understanding 1 Sam 14:32–35.

85. Grintz, "'Do Not Eat on the Blood': Reconsiderations in Setting and Dating of the Priestly Code," *Annual of the Swedish Theological Institute* 8 (1970–71): 78–105.

86. Zevit, "The Earthen Altar Laws of Exodus 20:24–26 and Related Sacrificial Restrictions in Their Cultural Context," in *Texts, Temples, and Tradition: A Tribute to Menahem Haran* (ed. Michael V. Fox et al.; Winona Lake, Ind.: Eisenbrauns, 1996), 57–61. Like Grintz, Zevit draws on Maimonides, who refers to the alleged Sabean practice of eating blood in order to commune with demons.

87. Ibid., 58–62.

CHAPTER 3: The Blood of the Burnt Offering

1. On the burnt offering in P, see Milgrom, *Leviticus 1–16*, 172–77.

2. In addition to those previously cited, the following commentaries and monographs on Leviticus are cited in this chapter: A. Bertholet, *Leviticus* (KHC 3; Tübingen: J. C. B. Mohr [Paul Siebeck], 1901); August Dillmann, *Die Bücher Exodus und Leviticus* (2d ed.; Kurtzgefasstes exegetisches Handbuch zum Alten Testament 12; Leipzig: S. Hirzel, 1880); Gerstenberger, *Leviticus*; Rolf P. Knierim, *Text and Concept in Leviticus 1:1–9* (FAT 2; Tübingen: J. C. B. Mohr [Paul Siebeck], 1992).

3. The third section is perhaps an appendix to the other two sections, added secondarily by an editor. For this position, see Bertholet, *Leviticus*, 6; Elliger, *Leviticus*, 26, 33; Milgrom, *Leviticus 1–16*, 63, 166–67.

4. According to Martin Noth, "the second person plural address in v. 2 belongs to secondary additions" (*Leviticus,* 19); see also Elliger, *Leviticus,* 26.

5. For identification of the subject of *wĕśāḥaṭ* as the offerer, see Ḥizquni, ad loc.; Ramban (on Lev 1:6); Hoffmann, *Leviticus,* 1:123–24; Carl F. Keil and Franz Delitzsch, *The Pentateuch* (vol. 2 of *Biblical Commentary on the Old Testament;* trans. James Martin; Edinburgh: T & T Clark, 1891), 286; Bertholet, *Leviticus,* 5; Elliger, *Leviticus,* 35; Rendtorff, *Leviticus,* 49; Milgrom, *Leviticus 1–16,* 154; Hartley, *Leviticus,* 21; Gerstenberger, *Leviticus,* 29.

6. Rendtorff, *Leviticus,* 17 n. 5a.

7. Elliger, *Leviticus,* 35; Hartley, *Leviticus,* 13 n. 5a.

8. Rabbinic texts claim that anyone could slaughter a sacrificial animal, even slaves and women (*m. Zebaḥ.* 3:1; *Sipra, Nedaba* par. 4:2). See also Rashi (on Lev 1:5); Hoffmann, *Leviticus,* 1:124. Interestingly, Ibn Ezra (on Lev 1:5) rejects the standard rabbinic position and identifies the subject of the verb as a priest. The reasons I have adduced for identifying the offer as the subject speak against Ibn Ezra's interpretation. For a critique of Ibn Ezra's position, see Hoffmann, *Leviticus,* 1:123–24.

9. Ramban, ad loc.; Hoffmann, *Leviticus,* 1:131–32; Keil and Delitzsch, *Pentateuch,* 287; Elliger, *Leviticus,* 35; Noth, *Leviticus,* 23; Rendtorff, *Leviticus,* 55; Milgrom, *Leviticus 1–16,* 156, 157; Hartley, *Leviticus,* 21; Gerstenberger, *Leviticus,* 29.

10. Bertholet, *Leviticus,* 5; Rendtorff, *Leviticus,* 51; Hartley, *Leviticus,* 13 n. 6a.

11. Rendtorff, *Leviticus,* 51.

12. A few MT manuscripts have *hakkōhănîm* (pl.), and the Samaritan version, LXX, Syriac, and some Targum mss assume this reading.

13. Elliger, *Leviticus,* 26; Rendtorff, *Leviticus,* 15, 55; Milgrom, *Leviticus 1–16,* 133, 157.

14. For discussion of this formulation and several different reconstructions of an original reading, see Elliger, *Leviticus,* 27 n. 7a, 31, 33; Noth, *Leviticus,* 23; Rendtorff, *Leviticus,* 57; Milgrom, *Leviticus 1–16,* 157; Hartley, *Leviticus,* 13 n. 7b. See also S. Talmon, "Conflate Readings (OT)," *IDBSup,* 170–73.

15. Rendtorff, *Studien,* 100. Note that Rendtorff has changed his mind on this matter and now understands the changes of subject to reflect a definite principle: wherever priests are not explicitly identified as the subjects of an action, the subject is the offerer (see *Leviticus,* 51).

16. Elliger (*Leviticus,* 31) and Rendtorff (*Leviticus,* 51) both emphasize the duties that may be performed by the offerer.

17. Noth, *Leviticus,* 23; Milgrom, *Leviticus 1–16,* 155. Most other interpreters seem simply to assume this.

18. Bertholet, *Leviticus,* 5; Hoffmann, *Leviticus,* 1:125.

19. Noth, *Leviticus,* 22; Wenham, *Leviticus,* 53. According to *Sipra* (*Nedaba* par. 4:4), the expression "they shall present" naturally assumes the collection of the blood in vessels.

20. Rendtorff, *Leviticus,* 52; Bertholet, *Leviticus,* 5.

21. Hartley, *Leviticus,* 21; see also Norman H. Snaith, *Leviticus and Numbers* (Century Bible; London: Thomas Nelson and Sons, 1967), 30.

22. Milgrom, *Leviticus 1–16,* 155. See also Philip J. Budd (*Leviticus,* NCB [Grand Rapids, Mich.: Eerdmans, 1996], 48), who suggests that the presentation of the blood "probably implies some ritual gesture or action which brings the blood near to Yahweh."

23. Wenham, *Leviticus,* 54.

24. See also Lev 7:3 (presentation of the fat of the reparation offering), although the subject of the verb here is ambiguous; 7:33 (presentation of the blood and fat of the well-being sacrifice), where the priest is clearly the subject.

25. Budd, *Leviticus*, 51.

26. Bertholet, *Leviticus*, 5; Keil and Delitzsch, *Pentateuch*, 287; Dillmann, *Exodus und Leviticus*, 434; Hoffmann, *Leviticus*, 1:126; Rendtorff, *Leviticus*, 52; Noth, *Leviticus*, 22; Elliger, *Leviticus*, 35; Wenham, *Leviticus*, 54; Milgrom, *Leviticus 1–16*, 156. See also Rashi, ad loc.

27. This seems to be what Elliger (*Leviticus*, 35) envisages. See also Noth, *Leviticus*, 22; Noordtzij, *Leviticus*, 36. The modern interpreters were anticipated by Philo, who asserted that the priest sprinkled blood as he went about the altar "in a circle" (*en kyklō*) (*Spec.* I.199); see also *Spec.* I.205. *Sipra* (*Nedaba* par. 4:9) considers, but rejects, the possibility that the blood could be applied to the altar so that it runs around it in an unbroken band.

28. Hoffmann, *Leviticus*, 1:125–26. See also *Sipra* (*Nedaba* par. 4:9), which asserts that the use of the verb *zāraq* precludes the application of blood in a single strip around the altar.

29. Hoffmann, *Leviticus*, 1:126.

30. Milgrom (*Leviticus 1–16*, 156) also notes the Tannaitic representation. See *m. Zebaḥ.* 5:4; *Sipra, Nedaba* par. 4:9.

31. *Sipra* (*Nedaba* par. 4:10) attributes to R. Ishmael an argument for envisaging four separate applications of blood.

32. On Moses' priestly status, see Milgrom, *Leviticus 1–16*, 555–58. See also Cross, "The Priestly Houses of Early Israel," in *Canaanite Myth and Hebrew Epic*, 195–215.

33. Keil and Delitzsch, *Pentateuch*, 2:346; Hartley, *Leviticus*, 118 n. 12a.

34. Rashi (ad loc.); Ibn Ezra (ad loc.); Hoffmann, *Leviticus*, 1:287; Milgrom, *Leviticus 1–16*, 581.

35. Milgrom, *Leviticus 1–16*, 133–34, 171; Rendtorff, *Leviticus*, 75; Gerstenberger, *Leviticus*, 28; Hartley, *Leviticus*, 23.

36. Noth, *Leviticus*, 25.

37. Milgrom, *Leviticus 1–16*, 169. Milgrom cites *t. Zebaḥ.* 7:4 for the rabbinic understanding of the procedure. He also notes the personal experience of one of his students, "an experienced taxidermist," who describes how the head can be removed from a bird without using a knife! See also Noth, *Leviticus*, 25.

38. So Keil and Delitzsch, *Pentateuch*, 290; Noth, *Leviticus*, 25; Elliger, *Leviticus*, 37–38; Rendtorff, *Leviticus*, 75–76.

39. So Hoffmann, *Leviticus*, 1:138–39. See also Rashi, ad loc.

40. The blood itself is the subject of the *Niphal* construction from the root *mṣh* (drain, drain out; BDB, 594b).

41. Milgrom, *Leviticus 1–16*, 169.

42. Ḥizquni (ad loc., citing Bekhor Shor); Keil and Delitzsch, *Pentateuch*, 290; Bertholet, *Leviticus*, 6; Noth, *Leviticus*, 25; Rendtorff, *Leviticus*, 76; Milgrom, *Leviticus 1–16*, 169.

43. The Samaritan text has *'el* rather than *'al*. LXX reads *pros*.

44. See also Noth, *Leviticus*, 25; Hartley, *Leviticus*, 23.

45. Elliger, *Leviticus*, 38; Rendtorff, *Leviticus*, 76.

46. Bertholet (*Leviticus*, 6) argues that the reference to the burning of the head should be identified as a badly placed gloss and deleted.

47. My thanks to Stanley K. Stowers for suggesting this interpretation (personal communication).

48. Elliger speaks of the "schwerlich noch verstandene Sitte des Rundumgießens" (*Leviticus,* 35), while Rendtorff notes that "die Bedeutung des Blutsprengens wird nirgends expliziert" (*Leviticus,* 52).

49. Noth, *Leviticus,* 22–23; see also Dillmann, *Exodus und Leviticus,* 422, 434.

50. Knierim, *Text and Concept,* 56.

51. Rendtorff, *Leviticus,* 53.

52. Elliger, *Leviticus,* 35.

53. Knierim, *Text and Concept,* 56–57.

54. Ibid., 57.

55. For the identification as an H text, see the discussion in chapter 1.

56. Noordtzij, *Leviticus,* 35; Budd, *Leviticus,* 48.

57. For discussion, see Knierim, *Text and Concept,* 34–45, 77–82; Rendtorff, *Leviticus,* 35–38; Milgrom, *Leviticus 1–16,* 153.

58. Cf. Hartley (*Leviticus,* 21), who identifies the blood as "the means of atonement" and cites Lev 17:11.

59. On the translation "ransom payment" for the noun *kōper,* see chapter 6.

60. Hoffmann, *Leviticus,* 1:123.

61. See, e.g., *t. Menaḥot* 10:12; *b. Yoma* 36a; cited by Hoffmann (*Leviticus,* 1:120).

62. Hoffmann, *Leviticus,* 1:127.

63. One can fruitfully compare Hoffmann's symbolic interpretation of the blood rite and atonement with Samson Raphael Hirsch's symbolic explanation of ritual activity in Judaism, presented in such works as *Horeb, The Nineteen Letters,* and his Torah commentary.

64. Hoffmann, *Leviticus,* 1:475; see also pp. 89, 173.

65. Ibid., 173.

66. In line with older views, Hoffmann understands *kipper* as signifying "covering" (*Leviticus,* 1:123). It is evident that, for Hoffmann, the "covering" of sin is effected by the symbolic devotion of human life to God.

67. Hoffmann, *Leviticus,* 1:121–22.

68. For categorization and discussion of the various explanations and interpretations of the gesture, see Rendtorff, *Leviticus,* 40–45; Rodriguez, *Substitution,* 201–8; Hartley, *Leviticus,* 19–21, Milgrom, *Leviticus 1–16,* 151–52.

69. This explanation of the hand-leaning gesture and its relationship to expiation has most recently been defended by Janowski (*Sühne,* 215–21).

70. For a recent defense of the theory, see Rodriguez, *Substitution,* 214–32. For a detailed discussion and vigorous critique of the theory, see Janowski, *Sühne,* 205–15.

71. Noordtzij, *Leviticus,* 33.

72. Ibid., 35.

73. Cf. Hartley's comment on the death of the animal: "The offerer certainly recognizes that the animal's death is necessary, because the penalty for sin is death" (*Leviticus,* 21).

74. Milgrom, *Leviticus 1–16,* 151–53. Milgrom lists others who share this interpretation on p. 151. See also Rendtorff, *Leviticus,* 43–44. Milgrom's student, David P. Wright, makes an important contribution to the discussion in his article, "The Gesture of Hand Placement in the Hebrew Bible and in Hittite Literature," *JAOS* 106 (1986):

433–46. He provides much of the cross-cultural evidence with which Milgrom supports his explanation of the hand-pressing gesture.

75. Von Rad, *Old Testament Theology* (vol. 1; trans. D. M. G. Stalker; New York: Harper and Row, 1962), 256; quoted in Rodriguez, *Substitution*, 201.

76. Kiuchi, *Purification Offering*, 112–13.

77. Knierim, *Text and Concept*, 38.

78. I agree with those scholars who reject claims that Lev 16:21 functions as a key for the understanding of hand-pressing. The major reason for rejecting the relevance of the text is that the scapegoat is not a sacrifice. It is not slaughtered and there are no altar rituals. Although it is linked to an animal offered as a "sin offering," the hand-leaning follows the sacrificial rites rather than precedes them. For a helpful discussion of Lev 16:21, see Janowski, *Sühne*, 206–15.

79. Hoffmann, *Leviticus*, 1:475.

80. Janowski, *Sühne*, 360. See also pp. 221, 241–42, 359.

81. Levine, *Presence*, 67.

82. Ibid.; Levine, prolegomenon to *Sacrifice in the Old Testament: Its Theory and Practice,* by George Buchanan Gray (1925; repr., New York: Ktav, 1971), xxvii.

83. Both texts deal with payment of a head tax during a census. For further discussion of these texts, see chapter 7.

84. Levine, "Prolegomenon," xxvii–xxviii.

85. Levine, *Presence*, 68–73; see also Levine, *Leviticus* (JPS Torah Commentary; Philadelphia: Jewish Publication Society, 1989), 6–7.

86. Levine, *Presence*, 73 n. 51.

87. Levine, *Leviticus*, 6–7. Levine cites Ibn Ezra (ad loc.) in support of his interpretation. However, Levine's reference to Ibn Ezra is somewhat misleading. Ibn Ezra does refer to Exod 30:11–16 in his comment on Lev 1:1, but he does not identify *kipper 'al* as an abbreviation of *kipper 'al-napšōt*. Furthermore, although Ibn Ezra interprets *kipper* in Lev 1:4 as "serve as a ransom," a review of all of his interpretive comments on blood manipulation and the verb *kipper* indicates that his explanation of the meaning of the verb applies beyond Lev 1:4. Unlike Levine, Ibn Ezra applies Lev 17:11 to all sacrifices and to all occurrences of *kipper.*

88. Milgrom, *Leviticus 1–16,* 156.

89. Jay, *Throughout Your Generations Forever,* 6–7.

90. Ibid., 6.

CHAPTER 4: Blood Manipulation in the Sacrifice of Well-Being, the Ordination Offering, and the Reparation Offering

1. On the "sacrifice of well-being," see Milgrom, *Leviticus 1–16,* 220–21. I have adopted Milgrom's translation. For other renderings, see, e.g., Rendtorff, *Studien,* 132–33; Levine, *Presence,* 3–52, 120–22; Rudolf Schmid, *Das Bundesopfer in Israel: Wesen, Ursprung und Bedeutung der alttestamentlichen Schelamim* (SANT 9; Munich: Kösel-Verlag, 1964), 13–44, 101–27.

2. Jacob Milgrom has made significant contributions to our understanding of the "reparation offering." Note, in particular, *Cult and Conscience: The* asham *and the Priestly Doctrine of Repentance* (SJLA 18; Leiden: E. J. Brill, 1976); see also Milgrom, *Leviticus 1–16,* 339–78; Milgrom, "Sacrifices," 768–69; Levine, *Presence,* 91–101; Ander-

son, "Sacrifice," 5:880–81; Rendtorff, *Studien*, 207–11, 227–28, 229–30. In this study, I have adopted Milgrom's rendering of the name of the sacrifice: "reparation offering."

3. On the relationship between the ordination ram and the well-being sacrifice, see Milgrom, *Leviticus 1–16*, 527; Wenham, *Leviticus*, 142.

4. See Milgrom, *Leviticus 1–16*, 213; Noth, *Leviticus*, 31.

5. See, e.g., Kurtz, *Sacrificial Worship*, 74.

6. As Saul M. Olyan demonstrates in his study of biblical shaving rites ("What Do Shaving Rites Accomplish?"), the same basic act can accomplish or signal different things depending on the context in which it is carried out.

7. Noted by Rendtorff, *Leviticus*, 130; Wenham, *Leviticus*, 75, 80.

8. On the identification of the fat portions, internal organs, and the "broad tail," see Milgrom, *Leviticus 1–16*, 205–8, 210–13; Levine, *Leviticus*, 16–17.

9. According to Lev 7:29b–30, the offerer is, in fact, *required* to present the fat (along with the breast): "The one who offers his well-being sacrifice to Yahweh shall convey his offering to Yahweh from his well-being sacrifice. His hands shall convey the food gifts of Yahweh; he shall convey the fat with the breast, the breast to be elevated as an elevation offering before Yahweh." According to Milgrom, these verses belong to P, and, therefore, directly supplement Lev 3 (*Leviticus 1–16*, 63, 426, 429). Knohl argues, however, that vv. 29b–30 is part of an extended addition by H tradents (*Sanctuary*, 51). Whatever the case, the prescriptions in these verses make explicit what is strongly implied in Lev 3.

10. For the translation "food gift," or simply "gift" (rather than the traditional "offering by fire" [AV; RSV; NIV; NRSV]), see Milgrom, *Leviticus*, 161–62; Wenham, *Leviticus*, 56 n. 8; Rendtorff, *Leviticus*, 63–66.

11. Schmid, *Bundesopfer*, 30–33. See also Noordtzij, *Leviticus*, 49.

12. Levine, "Prolegomenon," xxv. See "Prolegomenon," xxiii–xxv, for Levine's review of Robertson Smith's interpretation.

13. Ibid., xxvi.

14. Kurtz, *Sacrificial Worship*, 74.

15. Cf. Wenham, *Leviticus*, 80.

16. Hoffmann, *Leviticus*, 1:163.

17. Milgrom, "Prolegomenon" 149–56 (repr. in *SCTT*, 96–103); Levine, *Leviticus 1–16*, 222, 416–17, 704–13.

18. Milgrom, *Leviticus 1–16*, 222, 223.

19. For a full discussion of this formulation and the translation, see chapter 5.

20. Milgrom, *Leviticus 1–16*, 416.

21. Ibid., 219.

22. Knohl identifies Lev 7:33 as part of an H addition to the P text (*Sanctuary of Silence*, 51). Due to its role in Milgrom's overall explanation of the well-being sacrifice, and because Milgrom does not agree with Knohl on this identification (see *Leviticus 1–16*, 63), I treat it here.

23. Milgrom, *Leviticus 1–16*, 416.

24. Ibid., 222. Milgrom also completely ignores the references to blood and fat in his comment on the verse (432), where one would expect some discussion of the mention of both blood and fat together.

25. In Lev 7:33, the *qrb* in the *hiphil* construction indicates the act of offering on the altar. See Milgrom, *Leviticus 1–16*, 432; Wenham, *Leviticus*, 115.

26. I follow the MT reading here, in which the first verb of v. 20 pl. (with Aaron's sons the implicit subjects) and the second sg. (with Aaron as the implicit subject). LXX, Samaritan version, and Syriac have the first verb sg.; the LXX has the second verb pl.

27. The identification of the subjects, except in the case of the elevation offering, depends on the validity of my evaluation of the MT version of the text. To some extent, decisions about who is to be identified as the subject of which action reflect the initial indexing of distinctions in the blood manipulation complex. This observation points to the important role that attention to the indexing function of ritual activity can play in making sense of a textual representation of ritual activity.

28. For arguments in support of this position, see Milgrom, *Leviticus 1–16*, 545–49; Gerstenberger, *Leviticus*, 99–100. For the opposite perspective, that Exod 29 depends on Lev 8, see Elliger, *Leviticus*, 104–20.

29. Milgrom (*Leviticus 1–16*, 513–15) provides good evidence that Lev 8 does not come from the same tradent(s) who produced Exod 29.

30. On the name of the sacrifice, and on "ordination" as "filling (of the hands)," see Milgrom, *Leviticus 1–16*, 526–27, 538–39.

31. Milgrom's comment, "The meaning of the rite is much debated" (*Leviticus 1–16*, 528), indicates his mode of approach. Likewise, Wenham declares, "There are several levels of meaning in this ritual" (*Leviticus*, 142).

32. See, e.g., Philo, *De vita Mosis* II.150; M. M. Kalisch, *Exodus* (vol. 2 of *A Historical and Critical Commentary on the Old Testament, with a New Translation;* London: Longman, Brown, Green and Longmans, 1855), 674; Hartley, *Leviticus*, 113.

33. Cornelis Houtman, *Exodus* (vol. 3; trans. Johan Rebel and Sierd Woudstra; Historical Commentary on the Old Testament; Leuven: Peeters, 2000), 541; see also René Péter-Contesse, *Lévitique 1–16* (CAT 3a; Geneva: Éditions Labor et Fides, 1993), 144.

34. Cf. Péter-Contesse's denial that the two rites must have the same significance (*Lévitique 1–16*, 144).

35. See Ibn Ezra on Lev 1:1 and Lev 1:4 for his explanation that the verb *kipper* means "serve as/effect a ransom," and my examination of this interpretation in chapters 3 and 7.

36. Milgrom, *Leviticus 1–16*, 528; for the texts cited by Milgrom, see *ANET*[3], 338; Wright, *Disposal*, 34–36.

37. Milgrom, *Leviticus 1–16*, 528.

38. Ibid., 529.

39. Ibid.

40. Milgrom, "Paradox," 66 (repr. in *SCTT*, 89).

41. Bell, *Ritual Theory, Ritual Practice;* see also Jay, *Throughout Your Generations Forever*, 1–16 (Jay refers to Robertson Smith's statements on the priority of ritual action to mythic interpretation).

42. While not employing the theoretical model I have followed here Martin Noth (*Leviticus*, 72) nevertheless identifies the relational effect of the blood manipulation ritual. See also Houtman, *Exodus*, 3:541.

43. Noted by Wenham (*Leviticus*, 143), although without explicit use of the concept of "indexing."

44. On P's doctrine of the exclusive holiness of the Aaronids, see Olyan, *Rites and Rank*, 28–29.

45. Milgrom, *Leviticus 1–16*, 528–29, 853.

C H A P T E R 5: The *Ḥaṭṭā't* Blood Manipulations in P

1. See Lev 12:7–8; 14:10, 19, 22–23, 30–31; 15:14–15, 29–30; Num 6:9–12, 14, 16; 28:15.

2. See, e.g., Num 15:22–29. For the identification of this text as a composition of the H school, see Knohl, *Sanctuary*, 53, 171–72.

3. Hebrew *bišĕgāgâ* (Lev 4:2, 22, 27). The exact significance of the expression is debated. For discussions and debates, see Jacob Milgrom, "The Cultic Š͏ᵉgāgāh and its Influence in Psalms and Job," *JQR* 58 (1967): 115–25 (repr. in *SCTT*, 122–32); Milgrom, *Leviticus 1–16*, 228–29; Rodriguez, *Substitution*, 83–85; Rolf Knierim, "*šgg*," *THAT* 2:869–72 (ET: *TLOT* 3:1302–4); Kiuchi, *Purification Offering*, 25–31; Gerstenberger, *Leviticus*, 62–65; Hartley, *Leviticus*, 58–59. I am persuaded by Knierim, and others, who argue, against Milgrom, that *bišĕgāgâ* "describes the objective result of a deed as an undeliberate, unintended error, without reference to the subjective state of the actor" (Knierim, *TLOT* 3.1303).

4. On the problems involved in interpreting the text, and for various solutions to those problems, see Jacob Milgrom, "The Graduated *Ḥaṭṭā't* of Lev 5:1–13," *JAOS* 103 (1983): 249–54; Milgrom, *Leviticus 1–16*, 292–318; Hartley, *Leviticus*, 67–70; Noth, *Leviticus*, 43–46; Kiuchi, *Purification Offering*, 21–38; Rodriguez, *Substitution*, 89–100; Rendtorff, *Leviticus*, 145–46, 188–99.

5. Roland de Vaux, *Studies in Old Testament Sacrifice* (Cardiff: University of Wales Press, 1964), 92; Wenham, *Leviticus*, 100–101; Péter-Contesse, *Lévitique 1–16*, 85–86.

6. Milgrom, "Graduated *Ḥaṭṭā't*," 249–54; Milgrom, *Leviticus 1–16*, 292–318. See also Levine, *Leviticus*, 25, 28–29. The label "graduated" is based on the rabbinic designation, *qrbn 'wlh wywrd* (ascending and descending offering); see *m. Šebu'ot* 1:2; 3:10; *m. Horayot* 2:7; *m. Keritot* 2:3–4.

7. The sins included are defined as violations of negative ("you shall not") commandments (4:2, 13, 22, 27). The term "commandments" almost certainly includes *both* cultic *and* "ethical" rules; see Milgrom, *Leviticus 1–16*, 229–31.

8. As noted by Kiuchi (*Purification Offering*, 124). See, e.g., Levine, *Leviticus*, 18; Wright, *Disposal*, 20.

9. Kiuchi, *Purification Offering*, 124.

10. In the case of the *ḥaṭṭā't* for the congregation, the "elders of the congregation" perform the hand-pressing (Lev 4:15), acting as the representatives of the whole people. See Ibn Ezra, ad loc.; Milgrom, *Leviticus 1–16*, 244; Hartley, *Leviticus*, 62; Levine, *Leviticus*, 23; Rodriguez, *Substitution*, 85.

11. That the preliminary rites of the *ḥaṭṭā't* and burnt offering are identical is noted by Bertholet, *Leviticus*, 12.

12. The characterization of the Priestly shrine as a "sanctuary of silence" was coined by Yehezkel Kaufmann (*History of Israelite Religion from Early Times to the End of the Second Temple Era* [in Hebrew] [vol. 2.2 (= vol. 5); Tel Aviv: Mosad Bialik,1937], 476–78; abridged ET, *The Religion of Israel: From Its Beginning to the Babylonian Exile* [trans. Moshe Greenberg; Chicago: University of Chicago Press, 1960], 303–5). See also Knohl, *Sanctuary*, 148–49.

13. The *one* exception is the confession uttered by the priest when he presses his hands on the scapegoat during the ritual complex represented in Lev 16 (v. 21).

14. The designation "anointed priest" indicates the chief priest, who was established in his special status through anointing with oil (Lev 6:13, 15). See Milgrom, *Leviticus 1–16*, 231.

15. So Rendtorff, *Leviticus*, 155.

16. Rendtorff (*Leviticus*, 155) notes the parallel between the explicit reference to the "anointed priest" here and the explicit introduction of "the sons of Aaron, the priest" in Lev 1:5.

17. Cf. Lev 9:12 on the burnt offering provided by Aaron and his sons at the inauguration of the cult, discussed in chapter 3.

18. Wenham, *Leviticus*, 90; Hartley, *Leviticus*, 60; Rendtorff, *Leviticus*, 155; Milgrom, *Leviticus 1–16*, 234.

19. This specification is absent from the MT v. 18; however, the Samaritan text includes *hkhn* in this verse and LXX reflects this reading.

20. Rendtorff, *Leviticus*, 155–56.

21. Note Ibn Ezra's concise comment on "the priest" (on Lev 4:6): "This is the anointed (priest) himself"; see also Milgrom, *Leviticus 1–16*, 233.

22. Milgrom, *Leviticus 1–16*, 233, citing *Sipra Ḥobah* par. 3:8; *b. Zebaḥim* 53a. Almost certainly contributing to this ancient interpretation is the explicit notice in Lev 14:16, 27 that oil is to be sprinkled with a finger of the right hand as part of the rituals for the purification of an individual healed of a skin disease. Cf. Noordtzij, *Leviticus*, 57, who cites Lev 14:16 in this connection.

23. According to rabbinic interpreters, *min-haddām* (from the blood) "implies that the high priest dips his finger into the vessel containing the blood for each sprinkling" (Milgrom, *Leviticus 1–16*, 234, citing *Sipra Ḥobah* par. 3:8; *Sipre Zuta* on Num 19:4). Practical considerations support this interpretation. It seems that we should envisage the priest wetting his finger for each sprinkle.

24. LXX (4:6: *kata*; 4:17: *katenōpion*); Vulgate (*contra*; but the translation is ambiguous); Targum Onqelos (*qdm*); *b. Yoma* 57a (baraita); *y. Yoma* 5:4; Rashi, on Lev 4:6 (*kngd*); Hoffmann, *Leviticus*, 1:179, 185 ("gegen" with the sense "toward); Bertholet, *Leviticus*, 12 ("vor dem Vorhang"); Elliger, *Leviticus*, 53, 54 ("vor den Vorhang"); Hartley, *Leviticus*, 44, 60 ("before the curtain"); Milgrom, *Leviticus 1–16*, 234 ("against," with the sense "toward"; Milgrom cites the Talmudic texts listed above); RSV; NRSV; NIV; NJPS (all, "in front of").

25. Snaith, *Leviticus and Numbers*, 42; Péter-Contesse, *Lévitique 1–16*, 71, 78 and n. 22; Wenham, *Leviticus*, 84. Kiuchi (*Purification Offering*, 125) considers that the phrase may indicate that blood made contact with the curtain, but does not take a firm position in favor of this interpretation.

26. Hoffmann, *Leviticus*, 1:179.

27. Reference simply to "the curtain" in the parallel account in v. 17 is likely merely a reflection of the abbreviated quality of the secondary and dependent account. LXX reflects the presence of *haqqōdeš* in v. 17. This translation probably resulted from a desire to harmonize v. 17 with v. 6.

28. Milgrom, *Leviticus 1–16*, 234. Kiuchi (*Purification Offering*, 124–25), in contrast, argues that it designates the adytum; see also Hoffmann, *Leviticus*, 1:179. As Milgrom correctly notes, *haqqōdeš* refers to the adytum only in Lev 16, which employs terminology differently than other units of the Priestly document. That *haqqōdeš* indicates the outer room is confirmed by its use in Lev 6:23.

29. Milgrom, "Israel's Sanctuary," *SCTT*, 78; Milgrom, *Leviticus 1–16*, 234.

30. Kiuchi, *Purification Offering*, 125; cf. Budd, *Leviticus*, 82; Kurtz, *Sacrificial Worship*, 216.

31. This point is emphasized by Haran, *Temples,* 161.

32. Effectively argued by Kiuchi (*Purification Offering,* 125–26); see also Janowski, *Sühne,* 235; Klaus Koch, *Die Priesterschrift von Exodus 25 bis Leviticus 16: Eine über-lieferungsgeschichtliche und literarkritische Untersuchung* (FRLANT n.s. 53; Göttingen: Vandenhoeck & Ruprecht, 1959), 56. Note that Lev 4 is dependent on Lev 16 both from the point of view of literary history and in terms of the text's present form. According to the scholars cited above, Lev 4 reflects Lev 16; the tradent who composed Lev 4 knew Lev 16, and the rituals represented in Lev 4 were constructed in the light of those in Lev 16. In the present form of the text, the elaborate rites of Lev 16 provide a context and background for understanding the rites in Lev 4.

33. Saadiah, ad loc.; Rashi, ad loc.; Bertholet, *Leviticus,* 12; Wenham, *Leviticus,* 84; Milgrom, *Leviticus 1–16,* 238; NRSV; NJPS; NIV.

34. Zevit, "Philology, Archaeology, and a Terminus a Quo," 33–34 n. 14.

35. The prescriptions for the burnt offering and the sacrifice of well-being indicate only the physical direction of the blood manipulation ("onto the altar") without reference to its theological locus (see Lev 1:5, 11, 15; 3:2, 8, 13).

36. The anointed priest is to convey his *ḥaṭṭā't* bull "to the entrance of the Tent of Meeting *before Yahweh*" (Lev 4:4a). The elders of the congregation press their hands on the head of their *ḥaṭṭā't* bull "before Yahweh" (Lev 4:15b). The animal is slaughtered "before Yahweh" (Lev 4:4b, 15b).

37. On the *kābôd,* "the refulgent and radiant aureole which surrounds the deity in his manifestations or theophanies," see Cross, *Canaanite Myth and Hebrew Epic,* 153 n. 30, 165–67, 245 n. 113, 322.

38. A few manuscripts of MT include "all," as in the other two verses, and LXX reflects this reading. In v. 25, the masculine pronominal suffix refers to the *male* animal, while in the other two verses the feminine pronominal suffix indicates the *female* animal.

39. Although non-Aaronid members of the tribe of Levi are not referred to explicitly in Lev 1–7, we may identify this very absence as an indication that, like lay Israelites, they are not permitted to manipulate blood, and thus indexed as excluded from access to sancta. Their exclusion is spelled out explicitly in the book of Numbers (3:6–10; 4:15, 19–20; 16:1–17:5 [ET 16:1–40]; 18:1–7). On the distinction between Aaronids and Levites, and the source identification of the Numbers texts, see Olyan, *Rites and Rank,* 27–30.

40. The subject of the verbs is not given in MT, but must be the priest, since the text has referred explicitly to the offerer surrendering the birds to the priest. The Samaritan text and LXX both explicitly identify the priest as subject. For an explanation of the procedure represented here, see Milgrom, *Leviticus 1–16,* 169, 305; Levine, *Leviticus,* 8.

41. As Vriezen notes ("Hizza," 206), "This act seems to be a reduced form of those mentioned [in] iv 25, 30, 34, caused by the simple fact that the bird had not blood enough for the whole blood manipulation." See also Milgrom, *Leviticus 1–16,* 305; *Sipra Ḥoba* 18:8.

42. Compare Lev 4:6, 17.

43. Milgrom (*Leviticus 1–16,* 305) comments that "this nominal sentence is an explanatory note, giving the reason that there are two discrete blood manipulations: such is the requirement of the purification offering."

44. Exod 29:11 clearly prescribes that Moses slaughter the bull, while Lev 8:15 simply says, "he slaughtered." The use of a third-person, masculine singular verb in Lev 8:15 could indicate that no specific slaughterer is in view. However, on the basis of Exod

29:11 one could identify Moses as the subject of the verb. Since I assume that Lev 8 is based on Exod 29, I supply Moses as the subject in the latter text. See also Gerstenberger, *Leviticus*, 97; Hoffmann, *Leviticus*, 1:278; Péter- Contesse, *Lévitique 1–16*, 137, 138 n. 15a; RSV; NIV. Levine (*Leviticus*, 52) follows the NJPS rendering, "and it was slaughtered," commenting that "third person verbs can be translated as passive when no subject is specified." He makes no reference to Exod 29:11. Milgrom also translates, "and it was slaughtered" (*Leviticus 1–16*, 493), noting that the slaughter could be performed by anyone, asserting that the verb should be rendered in the passive and, like Levine, ignoring the formulation in Exod 29:11 (520–21). NRSV translates the verb as a passive ("and it was slaughtered"). Hartley (*Leviticus*, 113) takes Aaron as the subject of the third-person, masculine singular verb in Lev 8:15, also ignoring Exod 29:11.

45. MT of Lev 8:15 has simply "the blood" (*'et-haddām*). LXX has *apo tou haimatos* (cf. Syriac), probably reflecting an attempt to harmonize the language of Lev 8:15 with that in Exod 29:12. As Hartley notes, this Greek rendering may reflect a Hebrew *Vorlage* with *min* instead of *'et* (*Leviticus*, 107 n.15b). Milgrom declares the reading in Exod 29:12 "preferable" without directly challenging the originality of the reading in Lev 8:15 (*Leviticus 1–16*, 521).

46. According to Elliger, *sābîb* was dropped by the tradents who composed Exod 29 on the basis of Lev 8, in conformity with its absence in normal P usage (*Leviticus*, 107). However, as I affirmed in chapter 4, it seems that Lev 8 is based on Exod 29. Thus, we may speak of Exod 29 as a more basic text, while Lev 8 is more elaborate. The addition of *sābîb* is simply part of this elaboration.

47. Exod 29:12: "and all the blood he poured out [*špk*] to the base of the altar." Lev 8:15: "and the blood he poured out [*ysq*] to the base of the altar." The verb *ysq* is used only in Lev 8:15 and in Lev. 9:9 to indicate the gesture of pouring out the blood. The use of *špk* in Exod 29:12 corresponds with what we find elsewhere in P. Elliger takes the usage in Lev 8:15 as evidence that it is the earlier and independent text, with the use of *špk* in Exod 29 reflecting secondary harmonization with the standard vocabulary of P (*Leviticus*, 107). However, the use of *ysq* in Lev 8 and 9 may simply reflect a tradent's stylistic decisions. The two occurrences of *ysq* appear as the last two references in P to the disposal of blood at the base of the altar. As well, they constitute the middle elements in a chiastic 3/2/3 pattern that extends across the division between P and H (Wilfried Warning, *Literary Artistry in Leviticus* [BIS 35; Leiden: E. J. Brill, 1999], 136–37). This suggests that the appearance of *ysq* in Lev 8:15 and 9:9 rests ultimately on the stylistic decision of an H tradent. Further scholarly attention to the evidence for the coherence and artistic creativity of the H redaction of Leviticus is a desideratum.

48. Milgrom, however, renders it as "and performed the purification rite with it" (*Leviticus 1–16*, 570) and asserts that the verb refers only to the blood manipulation (583). See also Wenham, *Leviticus*, 146, 149 n. 5. However, the object of the verb is not the blood but the animal itself. The third-person, masculine singular pronominal suffix must refer back either to the noun *qorbān* (offering) or to the male animal. Thus, I conclude that the *piel* of *ht'* here means "and he offered it as *hattā't*." Cf. Rashi; Hoffmann, *Leviticus*, 1:287–88 (citing Rashi); Hartley, *Leviticus*, 117, 118 n. 15c; Elliger, *Leviticus*, 121; NRSV; NIV; NJPS; NEB. See my treatment of Lev 6:19 below in this chapter for further discussion of this verb and its meaning.

49. In its present form, Lev 16 presents a complex of rituals to be observed annually on the tenth day of the seventh month (16:29; cf. Lev 23:27; 25:9). This annual obser-

vance receives the designation "Day of Removal" (*yôm hakkippurîm*) elsewhere in Leviticus (23:27, 28; 25:9). It appears, however, that the identification of the date of this ceremonial and the designation of the day are secondary developments. The section of Lev 16 (vv. 29–34a) in which the date notice appears has been widely identified as a secondary addition (see Noth, *Leviticus,* 117, 126; Elliger, *Leviticus,* 207; de Vaux, *Studies in Old Testament Sacrifice,* 95–96; J. R. Porter, *Leviticus* (CBC; Cambridge: Cambridge University Press, 1976), 124; Snaith, *Leviticus and Numbers,* 109; Vriezen, "Hizza," 224–25; Hartley, *Leviticus,* 230). Milgrom and Knohl agree in identifying it as a composition of the H editors who worked over the P texts (Milgrom, *Leviticus 1–16,* 63, 1062, 1064–65; Knohl, *Sanctuary,* 27– 28; see also Elliger [*Leviticus,* 207], who notes the similarities with H texts). Moreover, according to Knohl (*Sanctuary,* 32–33, 122), the introduction of the name "Day of Removal" is a contribution of the H editors. It appears, as Milgrom and Knohl note (Milgrom, *Leviticus,* 1061–63; Knohl, *Sanctuary,* 28 and n. 59), that the original P composition did not identify the day on which the ceremonial was to be carried out. Rather, P's prescriptions in vv. 1–28, 34b concern an emergency ritual, conducted whenever the chief priest ("Aaron") deemed it necessary. Both Milgrom and Knohl refer to the opinion of Elijah, the Gaon of Vilna, that originally the date was not specified. See also *Lev. Rab.* 21:7; *Exod. Rab.* 38:8. Since vv. 29–34a is a secondary addition, and likely the work of H editors, I do not treat this passage here. My attention will focus on Lev 16:1–28, 34b, the original P composition. This block of material appears to be the end product of a complex compositional process, and there is considerable disagreement among interpreters about the identification of sources and editorial additions. In many instances, these disagreements center on considerations about the development of the Priestly group's understanding of the significance of the rituals performed in the shrine complex, specifically the meaning and significance of the blood manipulations. While the focus of my analysis is Lev 16:1–28, 34b in its received form, I note such historical speculations where I deem them relevant to the elucidation of what is indisputably a complex text. As examples of attempts to distinguish compositional layers, note Max Löhr, *Das Ritual von Lev. 16* (Schriften der Königsberger Gelehrten Gesellschaft 2.1; Berlin: Deutsche Verlagsgesellschaft für Politik und Geschichte, 1925); Gerhard von Rad, *Die Priesterschrift im Hexateuch: Literarisch Untersucht und Theologisch Gewertet* (BWANT 4.13; Stuttgart: Verlag W. Kohlhammer, 1934), 85–87; Elliger, *Leviticus,* 200–210; Noth, *Leviticus,* 117–26.

50. See, e.g., *m. Yoma* 4:3; Milgrom, *Leviticus 1–16,* 1024.

51. The translation "cover," which I employ, following NJPS, is speculative and based primarily on the actual function of the *kappōret*: it is the lid of the *'ărōn hā'ēdut* ("Ark of the Pact"; so NJPS) (Exod 25:10–22; 37:1–9) that is located in the adytum. On this "untranslatable, so far" term, see Milgrom, *Leviticus 1–16,* 1014.

52. The term *qēdmâ* can indicate either "eastward" directionally, or the "east side" of something. For Aaron to sprinkle blood "eastward" would require that he stand behind the Ark with his back to the rear wall of the adytum and sprinkle outward. The text is so understood by Loewenstamm (*EM* 3:596). This seems most unlikely. Rather, as Milgrom argues (*Leviticus 1–16,* 1032), we should envisage Aaron sprinkling the front (i.e., the "eastern side") of the cover. See also Kurtz, *Sacrificial Worship,* 391; Dillmann, *Exodus und Leviticus,* 579; Vriezen, "Hizza," 232; Porter, *Leviticus,* 130; RSV; NRSV; NIV.

53. See also S. E. Loewenstamm, "*yôm hakkippurîm,*" *EM* 3:596; Milgrom, *Leviticus 1–16,* 1031.

54. LXX reads "some of its blood" (assuming the same formula as appears in v. 14). Milgrom (*Leviticus 1–16*, 1033) argues, however, that "its blood" is the original and correct reading, and that, in fact, all the blood was conveyed into the shrine building. I am persuaded by Milgrom's reasoning and see no reason to favor the LXX reading over that of MT.

55. Lit., "and shall do with its blood just as he did to the blood of the bull." Here we have a fine example of stylistic variation. The author has avoided repetition by using first *'et* (to be identified either as the preposition meaning "with" [Bertholet, *Leviticus,* 55; cf. Ezek 20:44] or as the direct object marker [Milgrom, *Leviticus 1–16*, 1033]), and then the *lamed* preposition. Both formulations use of *'śh* here mean "manipulate."

56. For this interpretation, see Ibn Ezra (ad loc.); Kurtz, *Sacrificial Worship,* 391–92; Keil and Delitzsch, *Pentateuch,* 2:399; Hartley, *Leviticus,* 239–40.

57. Elliger, *Leviticus,* 213. Milgrom notes that Karaite interpreters understood both manipulations to involve seven sprinkling acts, and that Josephus (*Ant.* 3.243) seems to have anticipated this interpretation (*Leviticus 1–16*, 1032).

58. Milgrom, *Leviticus 1–16*, 1032. Milgrom also notes in this connection the rabbinic interpretation that the first manipulation involved only one sprinkling (see *m. Yoma* 5:3, 4).

59. Cf. Bertholet, *Leviticus,* 55; Hoffmann, *Leviticus,* 1:447; Keil and Delitzsch, *Pentateuch,* 2:399; Vriezen, "Hizza," 226; Noth, *Leviticus,* 123; Rendtorff, *Studien,* 219; Wright, *Disposal,* 16; Gorman, *Ideology of Ritual,* 83–84.

60. For the latter view, see Keil and Delitzsch, *Pentateuch,* 2:399; Noth, *Leviticus,* 98, 105 (German); Loewenstamm, *EM* 3:596.

61. See BDB, 818b–819a; GKC §119aa–dd.

62. As Dillmann notes (*Exodus und Leviticus,* 579), *'al* in v. 15 clarifies the meaning of *'al-pĕnê* in v. 14.

63. Milgrom, *Leviticus 1–16*, 1031–32. See also Dillmann, *Exodus und Leviticus,* 579; Kurtz, *Sacrificial Worship,* 391; Wenham, *Leviticus,* 226; Hartley, *Leviticus,* 220, 239; Gorman, *Ideology of Ritual,* 83.

64. Milgrom, *Leviticus 1–16*, 1031; Milgrom cites *b. Yoma* 55a (baraita).

65. Interpreters are generally agreed that the second sprinkling applied blood to the floor of the adytum. See, e.g., Kurtz, *Sacrificial Worship,* 391; Hoffmann, *Leviticus,* 1:447; Keil and Delitzsch, *Pentateuch,* 2:399; Wright, *Disposal,* 16; Gorman, *Ideology of Ritual,* 83 and n. 1; Elliger, *Leviticus,* 214.

66. Vriezen, "Hizza," 232–33; see also Kurtz, *Sacrificial Worship,* 391.

67. That "Tent of Meeting" indicates the outer room, is especially evident from v. 20, which places "Tent of Meeting" after "the Holy Place" (*haqqōdeš*), which is the adytum. For the identification of "the Tent of Meeting" as the outer shrine room, see Ibn Ezra, ad loc.; Hoffmann, *Leviticus,* 1:448–49; Noth, *Leviticus,* 124; Milgrom, *Leviticus 1–16*, 1035; Budd, *Leviticus,* 230; Noordtzij, *Leviticus,* 166.

68. Wright, *Disposal,* 16; Milgrom, *Leviticus 1–16*, 1034–35, 1038. See also Ibn Ezra, ad loc.

69. Milgrom, *Leviticus 1–16*, 1034.

70. Rashi, ad loc.; Hoffmann, *Leviticus,* 1:449; Levine, *Leviticus,* 105. Ibn Ezra (ad loc.) was the sole premodern Jewish commentator to question the rabbinic interpretation.

71. Noordtzij, *Leviticus,* 166.

72. See Hoffmann, *Leviticus,* 1:450–55, for a lengthy discussion and defense of the rabbinic interpretation against the lone dissenting position of Ibn Ezra and Well-

hausen's thesis that the incense altar is unknown in Lev 16. Levine (*Leviticus,* 105) accepts the rabbinic interpretation, asserting that "context" requires that we understand "that altar that is before Yahweh" as the altar of incense. Levine is almost certainly following Hoffmann, who begins his treatment of the question with a sophisticated argument about context (*Leviticus,* 1:450). In contrast, Milgrom sides with the majority of non-Jewish scholars in identifying the altar as the altar of burnt offering (*Leviticus 1–16,* 1034–35, 1036).

73. It is true that the blood of a *ḥaṭṭā't* bird is sprinkled on the altar, but this sprinkling of a small amount of blood is clearly a substitute for daubing on the horns of the altar. In Lev 16, sprinkling comes in addition to prior daubing.

74. Rabbinic tradition fills this gap. See *m. Yoma* 5:6, which indicates that the remainder of the blood was poured out to the base of the altar of burnt offering. According to the rabbinic representation, this was the only application of blood to this altar on the Day of Removal.

75. For this explanation, see Ibn Ezra, ad loc.; Milgrom, *Leviticus 1–16,* 304; Levine, *Leviticus,* 304 (both citing Ibn Ezra); Hartley, *Leviticus,* 69–70; Noordtzij, *Leviticus,* 67–68.

76. As in Lev 9:15, the *piel* construction of *ḥṭ'* here means "offer as a *ḥaṭṭā't,*" and indicates both the blood manipulation and the burning of the altar offering. The object of the verb is the *ḥaṭṭā't* itself. The third-person, feminine singular direct object pronoun must refer to the noun *ḥaṭṭā't.* For this understanding of the verb, see Wenham, *Leviticus,* 114; Elliger, *Leviticus,* 80; Levine, *Leviticus,* 40; Hartley, *Leviticus,* 87; RSV; NRSV; NIV; NJPS; NEB. Hoffmann translates the verb as "der es also Sündopfer darbringt" (*Leviticus,* 1:236), identifying the *piel* of *ḥṭ'* as a denominative of *ḥaṭṭā't,* but adds, "Hier ist aber vorzüglich an die Blutspengung zu denken" (237). Again, Milgrom argues that the verb refers only to the blood manipulation (*Leviticus 1–16,* 402), citing *Targum Onqelos.* See also *Targum Pseudo-Jonathan;* Ibn Ezra (ad loc.).

77. This declaration seems to clarify the intent of v. 19. The priest who performs the ritual gains possession of the flesh, but any male of the priestly family may be invited to consume the flesh. See Milgrom, *Leviticus 1–16,* 402, 407. Consumption of the flesh of the *ḥaṭṭā't* is an index of priestly status. For further details, see Olyan, *Rites and Rank,* 30–32.

78. Milgrom, "*Modus Operandi,*" 112. See also Wright, *Disposal,* 129–31; Gorman, *Ideology of Ritual,* 81, 87.

79. Ulippi 4.38–40, cited by Wright, *Disposal,* 36 n. 67. See also Milgrom, *Leviticus 1–16,* 254–55.

80. Wright, *Disposal,* 5–8.

81. Ibid., 6, and the anthropological literature cited there in n. 9.

82. Ibid., 7.

83. See Wright, *Disposal,* 60–64. See also *CAD* K, 178–79, *s.v. kapāru* A. On the fifth day of the Babylonian *akitu* festival, for example, a ram is decapitated and its carcass is used to wipe the cella of the god Nabu. The carcass is then thrown into a river (see Wright, *Disposal,* 64, for a translation; see also *ANET* [3], 333, ll. 353–54; for the Akkadian text, see F. Thureau-Dangin, *Rituels accadiens* [Paris: E. Leroux, 1921], 127–48). Milgrom ("*Modus Operandi,*" 113) asserts that it was the blood of the ram that was wiped onto the cella, obviously assimilating the Babylonian rite to what is represented in P. "It would be ridiculous," Milgrom asserts, "to imagine that the priest carried the car-

cass bodily through the temple and wiped it on the temple walls. Most likely, a portion of the carcass (possibly the blood) was applied to a portion of the temple. . . in keeping with the *pars pro toto* principle." However, the text says that the cella was wiped with the carcass itself. There is no reference to the blood. That the room was wiped with the carcass itself is affirmed by Wright (*Disposal*, 64), and Milgrom originally interpreted the text in this fashion (see "Israel's Sanctuary," *SCTT*, 81). The basic problem with Milgrom's interpretation of this Mesopotamian text is that he cites it as evidence that the principle of *pars pro toto* was operative in Mesopotamian ritual but then must assume the principle in order to interpret the text.

84. Schwartz seems to understand the effect of the blood manipulations in this way. He suggests that "the blood of the [*ḥaṭṭā't*] not only removes them [i.e. impurities] from sancta, it *eradicates* them" ("Bearing of Sin," 17–18). He adds, "In using the term *eradicate*, I allow for the possibility that the impurity, or its residue, is retro-absorbed by the carcass of the slain animal and eradicated by its eventual disposal" (17 n. 55).

85. Zohar, "Repentance and Purification," 612.

86. Milgrom, "*Modus Operandi*," 112–13.

87. Milgrom, *Leviticus 1–16*, 1037–39.

88. Recall that the blood sprinkled on Aaron and his sons during their ordination to the priesthood is taken from the altar (Exod 29:21; Lev 8:30) (see chapter 4).

89. I note, in this connection, Milgrom's thesis that, according to Priestly thinking, "impurity displaces an equal amount of sanctuary holiness" (*Leviticus 1–16*, 981). This is a helpful way of thinking about the matter, as it allows us to understand how an object defined as holy might also be identified as impure.

90. Gorman, *Ideology of Ritual*, 88.

91. Ibid.

92. Ibid., 85. Compare, however, Gorman's comment that "this sprinkling rite is best understood as an act of presentation of the blood to Yahweh" (83). Gorman states that he will discuss this point, but fails to do so, offering only the general conclusion that the sevenfold sprinkling at the curtain "is intended to effect purgation" (85).

93. Kiuchi, *Purification Offering*, 128.

94. Milgrom, *Leviticus 1–16*, 1038.

95. Smith, "Bare Facts," 63 (emphasis in original).

96. Ibid.

97. German scholars commonly employ the verb *sühnen* and the noun *Sühne*. See, e.g. Janowski, *Sühne*; Schenker, "Zeichen."

98. With Milgrom (*Leviticus 1–16*, 1033), I understand this verse to identify the purpose of the previously represented ritual activity. The initial *waw* should, therefore, be rendered "thus" or "so." Compare the summary statements in Lev 4 (vv. 20, 26, 31, 35), discussed later, which also follow on the descriptions of ritual activity.

99. For this translation of *piš'êhem*, see Milgrom, *Leviticus 1–16*, 1034; Gorman, *Ideology of Ritual*, 82, and the literature cited there in nn. 1 and 2; Schwartz, "Bearing of Sin," 18.

100. My translation here follows Milgrom (*Leviticus 1–16*, 1034).

101. See, e.g., Milgrom, *Leviticus 1–16*, 1010; Vriezen, "Hizza," 226; Budd, *Leviticus*, 230, 240; Noth, *Leviticus*, 124; Elliger, *Leviticus*, 214; Wenham, *Leviticus*, 28, 232–33; Levine, *Leviticus*, 103–4.

102. See Milgrom, *Leviticus 1–16*, 1033: "Of the three Israelite malfeasances listed in this verse, the focus is clearly on the term 'pollution.'"

103. Verse 26: *mēhaṭṭā'tô*; v. 35: *'al-ḥaṭṭā'tô*. The prepositions *min* and *'al* before *ḥaṭṭā'tô* both mean "because of" or "for." They mark "sin" as the reason for *kipper*. See Janowski, *Sühne*, 187 and nn. 12 and 16; GKC §119z (causative *min*); GKC §119aa (causative *'al*); Ibn Ezra (on Lev 4:3); Kiuchi, *Purification Offering*, 88; Milgrom, *Leviticus 1–16*, 251; Elliger, *Leviticus*, 54, 55; Péter-Contesse, *Lévitique*, 72, 73; Wenham, *Leviticus*, 85; Hartley, *Leviticus*, 44, 45, 47 n. 26a; NJPS; NRSV; NIV.

104. See Dillmann, *Exodus und Leviticus*, 465; Rendtorff, *Leviticus*, 176; Brichto, "Slaughter and Sacrifice," 31. In contrast to this approach, Milgrom renders *kipper* as "effect purgation" (*Leviticus 1–16*, 227–28), and specifies that the blood manipulation achieves the effect (254–61). Thus, he interprets the formula as referring only to the blood manipulation.

105. As in Lev 4, Milgrom renders *kipper* in 5:1–13 as "effect purgation" (*Leviticus 1–16*, 293).

106. Milgrom translates *kipper* here, as elsewhere in the pericope, as "effect purgation" (*Leviticus 1–16*, 293). Given that Milgrom denies a purgating function to the burnt offering blood manipulation (ibid., 156), and renders *kipper* as "expiate" in connection with the burnt offering (ibid., 133, 153), it is clear that he understands the formula in Lev 5:10 to refer only to the *ḥaṭṭā't* and its blood manipulation. The location of the formula, however, speaks against this interpretation. Here, *kipper* should be rendered in such a way that it can refer to the effect of offering the *ḥaṭṭā't* and the burnt offering together, and to the ritual complex in its entirety. See Brichto, "Slaughter and Sacrifice," 31–32, for a similar argument.

107. Milgrom (*Leviticus 1–16*, 306) renders *kipper* in v. 13 as "effect purgation," as he does elsewhere in Lev 4:1–5:13, but recognizes that this translation is problematic in the context, given his position on the workings of the *ḥaṭṭā't*. "How," Milgrom asks, "can semolina effect purgation when it contains no blood, the ritual detergent of the purification offering?" (ibid.). Milgrom offers two answers to this question, neither of which is very convincing. First, he draws an analogy between the use of flour in Mesopotamian purification rites and its use in Lev 5:12 (ibid., 306–7). This strikes me as a very strained analogy, given that the flour in Mesopotamian rites is wiped on the person or thing being purified and disposed of by burning (evidently because it has absorbed impurity) (note the example cited by Milgrom [ibid., 306]), while in Lev 5:12, a handful of flour is burned in the altar fire like a regular cereal offering (but with the conspicuous omission of frankincense). If the flour did absorb impurity, it should have been wiped on the altar and disposed of elsewhere than in the holy altar fire, where offerings were transferred to Yahweh in the form of smoke. Note that Lev 5:12 says that the priest "shall turn [the handful] into smoke on the altar with the food gifts of Yahweh." The verb *hiqṭîr* (turn into smoke) is not used for disposal by burning (*śrp* is; see Lev 4:12, 21). It is used for the burning of an offering. Milgrom's second answer is based on asserting that the "graduated" *ḥaṭṭā't* is a "borderline case" (ibid., 307). On this basis, Milgrom argues (ibid., 315–16) that there was doubt in the minds of the Priestly tradents about whether the altar was in fact in need of purification and suggests that "it may be the anomalous nature of the impurity and its potency that have . . . been responsible for creating the cultic fiction that semolina can purge the sanctuary" (ibid., 316). The primary problem with this argument is that Milgrom simply assumes that the text attributes a purgative function to the offering of a cereal *ḥaṭṭā't*. Yet, this is precisely what is in question. See also Kiuchi, *Purification Offering*, 100, who makes this basic point, but fails to note how crucial the burning rite is.

108. For other examples, see Zohar, "Repentance and Purification"; Rodriguez, *Substitution.*

109. Cf. David Hoffmann's explanation of cultic blood manipulation and *kipper,* treated in chapters 3 and 4. Interestingly, neither Gese ("Atonement") nor Janowski (*Sühne*)cite the nineteenth-century Jewish scholar's *German*-language commentary.

110. Milgrom, *Leviticus 1–16,* 46.

111. Note, as well, that Aaron's superior status in relation to his sons is enacted in their first service as consecrated priests when Aaron's sons perform the subordinate role of bringing the blood of the bull to Aaron at the altar, while Aaron is the one who applies it to the altar (Lev 9:9).

112. Given what we know about the character of the inner sphere, we cannot help but conclude that the special access of the anointed priest is a function of his special status.

113. The burning of incense before Aaron enters with the blood is simply a *preparatory* act, which makes possible the key ritual acts, ingress with blood and its manipulation inside the adytum.

CHAPTER 6: Blood Manipulation in Ezekiel and 2 Chronicles

1. The following commentaries provide useful introductions to the book of Ezekiel and to the debates about its composition: Walter Zimmerli, *Ezekiel 1: A Commentary on the Book of the Prophet Ezekiel, Chapters 1–24* (trans. Ronald E. Clements; Hermeneia; Philadelphia: Fortress, 1979); Zimmerli, *Ezekiel 2: A Commentary on the Book of the Prophet Ezekiel, Chapters 25–48* (trans. James D. Martin; Hermeneia; Philadelphia: Fortress, 1983); John W. Wevers, *Ezekiel* (NCB; London: Thomas Nelson and Sons, 1969); Moshe Greenberg, *Ezekiel 1–20* (AB 22; New York: Doubleday, 1983); Daniel I. Block, *The Book of Ezekiel, Chapters 1–24* (NICOT; Grand Rapids, Mich.: Eerdmans, 1997).

2. On differences between Ezekiel's cultic legislation and what we find in P and H, see Milgrom, *Leviticus 1–16,* 283–284.

3. This is the approach of scholars who identify P and H as postexilic works. See, e.g., Janowski, *Sühne,* 175–276.

4. Scholars who date P and H to the preexilic era generally assume that Ezekiel's affinities with P and H reflect appropriation and interpretation of those source traditions. See, e.g., Greenberg, *Ezekiel 1–20;* Greenberg, *Ezekiel 21–37* (AB 22A; New York: Doubleday, 1997); Milgrom, *Leviticus 1–16,* 281–84. See also Hurvitz, *Linguistic Study,* for arguments in support of the position that P is linguistically prior to Ezekiel.

5. For example, although Knohl maintains that the terminus a quo of H is the time of Hezekiah (late eighth century B.C.E.), he affirms a terminus ad quem in the early Persian period (*Sanctuary,* 204–20, 226). If Knohl's dating of H is correct, it follows that some parts of H antedate Ezekiel while others postdate the composition of the prophetic book. Milgrom, for his part, affirms Knohl's terminus a quo, but argues for an earlier terminus ad quem during the exile (*Leviticus 1–16,* 27–28). Thus, the composition of some components of H would be contemporary with the formation of the book of Ezekiel. Both Knohl and Milgrom affirm that all (or almost all) of P antedates H, and consequently also antedates the composition of Ezekiel.

6. For a useful survey of scholarship on the composition of Ezek 40–48, see Steven S. Tuell, *The Law of the Temple in Ezekiel 40–48* (HSM 49; Atlanta: Scholars Press, 1992), 1–17. Note, also, the important study of Hartmut Gese: *Der Verfassungsentwurf des*

Ezechiel (Kap. 40– 48): Traditionsgeschichtlich Untersucht (BHT 25; Tübingen: J. C. B. Mohr [Paul Siebeck], 1957).

7. The poem seems to be in the form of a work song accompanying the preparation of a feast. See Zimmerli, *Ezekiel 1,* 33, 496–97, 499; Block, *Ezekiel, Chapters 1–24,* 770, 775–76.

8. The first word of v. 6, *lākēn* (therefore), can indicate the beginning of the interpretation of a prophetic sign or parabolic statement. See A. B. Davidson, *The Book of the Prophet Ezekiel,* (Cambridge Bible for Schools and Colleges; Cambridge: Cambridge University Press, 1892), 175; Leslie C. Allen, *Ezekiel 20–48* (WBC 29; Dallas, Tex.: Word Books, 1990), 53, 56–57, 59; Greenberg, *Ezekiel 21–37,* 499. Cf. Ezekiel 15:6; 17:19.

9. The characterizations of Jerusalem as "the city of blood(guilt)" follow on a series of denunciations of the injustice and violence committed in the city. See Ezek 7:23; 9:9; 22 (esp. vv. 2–4, 6, 9, 12–14, 27). The blood referred to in v. 6a is the blood of the victims of injustice.

10. The suggested renderings follow Greenberg's interpretation (*Ezekiel 21–37,* 499). See also Targum of Ezekiel; NIV. Other translations render the term as "rust" or "corrosion." See LXX; RSV, NRSV; Walther Eichrodt, *Ezekiel: A Commentary* (trans. Cosslett Quin; OTL; London: SCM Press, 1970), 338; Allen, *Ezekiel 20–48,* 53; Block, *Ezekiel, Chapters 1–24,* 777 n. 67, for further examples.

11. Alfred Bertholet, *Das Buch Hesekiel* (KHC12; Tübingen: J. C. B. Mohr [Paul Siebeck], 1897), 127; G. A. Cooke, *The Book of Ezekiel* (ICC; Edinburgh: T & T Clark, 1936), 267; Eichrodt, *Ezekiel,* 339; Wevers, *Ezekiel,* 189; Zimmerli, *Ezekiel 1,* 500; Greenberg, *Ezekiel 21–37,* 499.

12. Lit. "her blood." See Eichrodt, *Ezekiel,* 335 note g.

13. Eichrodt, *Ezekiel,* 339; Block, *Ezekiel, Chapters 1–24,* 779.

14. Zimmerli, *Ezekiel 1,* 500–501. Some commentators emend the text and read third-person, feminine singular ("she has placed") instead of first-person, common singular. See, e.g., Eichrodt, *Ezekiel,* 334, 335 note h. This is an unnecessary emendation and robs the text of its special twist, as Zimmerli notes.

15. See, e.g., Block, *Ezekiel, Chapters 1–24,* 778–79 (along with Lev 17:13–14); Eichrodt, *Ezekiel,* 338 (along with Gen 4:10); Allen, *Ezekiel 20–48,* 60 (along with Gen 4:10).

16. The book of Jubilees expresses concern about the blood of a slaughtered animal being seen and relates this concern to the commandment to cover it (see, e.g., Jub 7:30–31; 21:16–18).

17. Block (*Ezekiel, Chapters 1–24,* 779) conflates Deut 12:16, 24; 15:23 with Lev 17:13, citing the former verses as if they too require the covering of animal blood.

18. This text prescribes the construction of an altar consisting of several progressively smaller stages, with steps leading to the top of the altar. The text is ambiguous and obviously disturbed, and scholars have interpreted it in a number of different ways, leading to different reconstructions of the form of the altar. For our present purposes, it suffices to note that Ezekiel's altar has a "platform" (*'ăzārâ*) halfway up the altar, upon which the topmost stage, the altar hearth, sits. This results in a ledge running around the upper stage. As well, there are four horns on the altar hearth, one on each corner, and a rim running around the base. For reconstructions of the altar, with diagrams, see Alfred Bertholet, *Hesekiel* (HAT 13; Tübingen: J. C. B. Mohr [Paul Siebeck], 1936), 153–55; Wright, *Disposal,* 149–54; Allen, *Ezekiel 20–48,* 257–58. On the place of the description of the altar in the Temple Vision, see Tuell, *Law of the Temple,*

46–51. Tuell makes a convincing case for identifying the altar description as an older source document inserted in its present context by a redactor.

19. I have rendered *wĕ'el-'arba' pinot hā'ăzārâ wĕ'el-haggĕbûl sābîb* in Ezek 43:20 with "and *onto* the four corners of the platform, and *onto* the rim round about" since Ezekiel appears frequently to use *'el* as if it were *'al*, and visa versa. On this phenomenon, see Zimmerli, *Ezekiel 1*, 85–86 n. 17a.

20. Lit. "the second day." For the translation "the following day," see Milgrom, *Leviticus 1–16*, 282.

21. Rendtorff, *Studien*, 27, 31, 87, 98, 131 (esp. pp. 98, 131); Milgrom, *Leviticus 1–16*, 222–23, 416.

22. Noted, e.g., by Eichrodt, *Ezekiel*, 558; Allen, *Ezekiel 20–48*, 258.

23. Gese, *Verfassungsentwurf*, 47. Although Ezek 44:11 assigns the task of slaughtering to the Levites, that verse refers to burnt offerings and eaten sacrifices of the people (*lā'ām*). Since the *ḥaṭṭā't* here is a priestly offering, it is most appropriately slaughtered by priests.

24. LXX, however, has third-person, masculine plural verbs in v. 20, apparently indicating a group of priests as those who perform the blood manipulations. On the basis of the fact that third-person, masculine plural verbs appear in vv. 22ff., some scholars suggest that an earlier form of this pericope had a group of priests performing all of the rites. The identification of Ezekiel as the actor in v. 20 would, therefore, be the result of secondary editing. See Gese, *Verfassungsentwurf*, 47–49; Eichrodt, *Ezekiel*, 558. Gese, it should be noted, denies that the LXX rendering of v. 20 is a witness to the earlier form of the text. Rather, he asserts, LXX secondarily "corrects" the MT reading (*Verfassungsentwurf*, 49). My analysis here will be based on the Massoretic text, although I do not reject the possibility that the present form of the text is the result of editorial modifications.

25. Since Ezekiel's altar has two platforms (see Ezek 43:14), we may wonder which of the two is intended here. I assume that it is the upper platform, called "the greater platform" because it is two times the height of the lower platform.

26. See Lev 4:5–7, 16–18; Lev 16:14–19. See chapter 5 in this study for discussion of these texts.

27. On *leḥem* as "food" rather than "bread," see BDB, 537a; G. R. Driver, "Ezekiel: Linguistic and Textual Problems," *Biblica* 35 (1954): 309; Allen, *Ezekiel*, 239, 245 n. 7c; NRSV. Cf. Judg 13:16; Prov 28:27.

28. G. R. Driver, "Ezekiel," 299.

29. The foreigners whom Ezekiel bans from the sanctuary are likely cult servants, and this fact explains why he turns his attention to identifying those who could legitimately function as cult servants. On the identity of the foreigners, see Eichrodt, *Ezekiel*, 564; Wevers, *Ezekiel*, 318.

30. On the larger ideological context of such restrictions of access, see Olyan, *Rites and Rank*, 27–35.

31. On the lay offerer's loss of cultic duties, see Olyan, *Rites and Rank*, 138–39 n. 81.

32. On Ezekiel's unique and striking restriction of the priesthood to the line of Zadok, see Olyan, *Rites and Rank*, 30, 138 n. 78.

33. Olyan makes similar observations about the significance of reserving the offering of fat and blood to the Zadokite priests (*Rites and Rank*, 30).

34. The following commentaries provide useful introductions to 1–2 Chronicles: H. G. M. Williamson, *1 and 2 Chronicles* (NCB; Grand Rapids, Mich.: Eerdmans, 1982);

Sara Japhet, *I & II Chronicles: A Commentary* (OTL; Louisville, Ky.: Westminster/John Knox, 1993). The following commentaries are also cited in this section: Peter R. Ackroyd, *I & II Chronicles, Ezra, Nehemiah* (London: SCM Press, 1973); Simon J. De Vries, *1 and 2 Chronicles* (Forms of the Old Testament Literature 11; Grand Rapids, Mich.: Eerdmans, 1989); Raymond B. Dillard, *2 Chronicles* (WBC 15; Waco, Tex.: Word Books, 1987); William Johnstone, *2 Chronicles 10–36; Guilt and Atonement;* vol. 2 of *1 and 2 Chronicles* (JSOTSup 254; Sheffield: Sheffield Academic Press, 1997).

35. Ackroyd, *I & II Chronicles,* 203.

36. The listed animals are burnt offerings (see v. 24b). I have inserted the identification, following the suggestion of *BHS* n. *a* on 2 Chron 29:21, in order to avoid confusion about the identity of the sacrifices. The *BHS* note reflects the view of some scholars that *lĕ ʿōlâ* was omitted by a scribe. Note, however, Dillard's comment: "It may assist the reader to insert the phrase 'for burnt offerings' into the text of a translation (e.g., NEB) in order to anticipate at an earlier point the distinction made between the burnt offerings and the sin offering (vv. 22–23), but no versional evidence suggests the phrase was original, and the case for its accidental omission is poor" (*2 Chronicles,* 232 n. 21a); see also Japhet, *I and II Chronicles,* 925.

37. De Vries identifies the subjects as the Levites, citing 2 Chron 30:16, where the Levites are explicitly assigned the task of slaughtering (*1 and 2* Chronicles, 376). Dillard writes that the verb "appears to refer to the priests" (*2 Chronicles,* 236). Williamson asserts that the verb is used impersonally, or might have the king and the officials as its subjects (*1 and 2 Chronicles,* 356–57). Johnstone writes that "it is not quite clear in v. 22 whether as in Leviticus it is the laity who slaughter, not the priests (contrast Ezek. 44.11)" (*2 Chronicles 10–36,* 195).

38. Japhet, *I & II Chronicles,* 926; Williamson, *1 and 2 Chronicles,* 356.

39. As De Vries puts it, "the priests are definitely the ones who kill them" (*1 and 2 Chronicles,* 376).

40. Noted by Johnstone (*2 Chronicles 10–36,* 195).

41. Williamson maintains that the events of vv. 25–30 should be understood to occur simultaneously with the events of vv. 20–24. Moreover, v. 27 duplicates v. 22 (*1 and 2 Chronicles,* 356).

42. Johnstone suggests, however, that vv. 27–30 refers to the offering of the daily burnt offering and not to the previously mentioned burnt offerings (*2 Chronicles 10–36,* 197).

43. Johnstone interprets 2 Chron 30:15 to indicate that some laypersons did, in fact, slaughter their own animals (*2 Chronicles 10–36,* 249).

44. Ackroyd, *I & II Chronicles,* 185.

45. As Johnstone suggests, "Josiah's concern must be that, at this moment of solemn reinauguration, no mischance befall the people" (*2 Chronicles 10–36,* 249).

CHAPTER 7: Leviticus 17:11 and the Power of Blood

1. See, e.g., Kiuchi, *Purification Offering,* 109; Rodriguez, *Substitution,* 241; Rendtorff, *Leviticus,* 169; Schenker, "Zeichen," 210.

2. Füglister, "Sühne durch Blut," 147. See also Ibn Ezra, discussed later.

3. See also Gese, "Atonement," 107–8; Janowski, *Sühne,* 247.

4. Füglister, "Sühne durch Blut," 160. Note his use of the Polynesian term *mana,* borrowed from anthropological literature. See also Sabourin, "Nefesh," 43–45.

5. Ibn Ezra on Lev 1:1. Note his reference there to Exod 30:11ff., on which, see below in this chapter.

6. See Ibn Ezra on Lev 1:4 (blood of the burnt offering as a "ransom" [*kōper*]); on Lev 8:23 (blood applied to Aaron serves as a "ransom" for his life; with direct citation of Lev 17:11 and cross-reference to Exod 4:25); on Exod 12:7 (Long and Short Commentaries) (blood of the Passover sacrifice as a *kōper*); on Exod 4:25 (Long Commentary) (Zipporah touches her son's foreskin to Moses' feet, which has the same effect as the Passover blood applied to the doorposts and lintels; cross-reference to Exod 12:23).

7. Schmid, *Bundesopfer,* 30–31. See chapter 4 for discussion of Schmid's interpretation of the blood manipulation of the well-being sacrifice in the light of Exod 24:3–8.

8. Janowski devotes most of *Sühne als Heilsgeschehen* to the *ḥaṭṭā't* and its blood manipulations, which he explains on the basis of his understanding of Lev 17:11. He deals with other sacrificial offerings only in passing. Note, in particular, the conclusion to his treatment of Lev 17:11 (*Sühne,* 247).

9. Levine, "Prolegomenon," xxvii–xxviii; Levine, *Presence,* 67–73; Levine, *Leviticus,* 6–7, 115–16.

10. Milgrom, "Prolegomenon," *SCTT,* 99–103; Milgrom, *Leviticus 1–16,* 708–12, 1083. Brichto, "On Slaughter and Sacrifice," 26–28, 34. Note, however, that Milgrom also applies the verse to the burnt offering. See his comment on Lev 1:5 in *Leviticus 1–16,* 156.

11. Füglister, "Sühne"; Sabourin, "Nefesh."

12. Janowski, *Sühne,* 221–47. See also Gese, "Atonement," 104–8, 111–14.

13. Schenker, "Zeichen," 195–96 (esp. 196 n. 2).

14. Recall that this is also Ibn Ezra's understanding. See also Schwartz, "Prohibitions," 52–56.

15. Schwartz, "Prohibitions," 36–37; see also, Elliger, *Leviticus,* 219–21; Jacob Milgrom, *Leviticus 17–22* (AB 3A; New York: Doubleday, 2000), 1448.

16. Schwartz, "Prohibitions," 36–43.

17. Ibid., 42.

18. Ibid., 43.

19. Ibid., 43, and n. 1, where Schwartz identifies other interpreters who have identified this thematic link. See also Milgrom, *Leviticus 17–22,* 1448.

20. Milgrom, *Leviticus 1–16,* 417.

21. As Schwartz notes, "These two paragraphs [vv. 3–7 and 8–9] speak of acts which are permissible in themselves—slaughtering and sacrificing—but which lead to ["severing"] when certain restrictions are not observed" ("Prohibitions," 39).

22. Milgrom, "Prolegomenon," 101. See also Rashi (ad loc.); Ramban (ad loc.).

23. Milgrom, *Leviticus 1–16,* 417.

24. See Schwartz, "Prohibitions," 46, on the relationship between threat and prohibitive command.

25. The translation "which they are wont to slaughter in sacrifice" reflects Rashi's explanation (ad loc.) of the participle *zōbĕḥîm* as indicating habitual action. I render the verb *zbḥ* here as "slaughter in sacrifice" to highlight the fact that it refers to the act of slaughter and not to the whole sacrificial ritual, as is especially clear from its use at the end of v. 5b.

26. Ibn Ezra, ad loc.

27. The specification that the blood is dashed "round about" (*sābîb*), which we commonly find in P, is lacking here in MT. LXX, however, translates as if *sābîb* was

present in its Vorlage. This is not likely to reflect an original reading, but rather is an example of harmonization with the language of P. Note that the LXX rendering also eliminates the unusual formulation, "upon Yahweh's altar," in favor of a more typically P formulation, "before Yahweh."

28. There is only one other explicit reference to cultic blood manipulation in H. Num 18:17 prescribes that a priest is to toss (*zrq*) the blood of the firstborn of a sacrificable animal (ox, sheep, or goat) onto the altar and to turn the fat into smoke "as a food gift for a soothing odor for Yahweh," after which he may have the flesh for his own use (v. 18). For the H identification of the whole of Num 18, see Knohl, *Sanctuary*, 53–54. Note that, as in Lev 17:6, *sābîb* (round about) is lacking, the two priestly duties of manipulating the blood and burning the fat offering are prescribed in sequence, and the purpose of the fat-burning is indicated while the blood manipulation is not explained. The fact that *sābîb* is also absent from this H text supports my contention that the LXX reading in Lev 17:6 reflects a secondary addition to the text.

29. Knohl, *Sanctuary*, 99. See also Milgrom, *Leviticus 17–22*, 1344.

30. Ibid. Compare Num 35:34 with Lev 18:25–29.

31. Reading *lannās* instead of MT's *lānûs*; see *BHS*, note *a* to Num 35:32; see also RSV; NRSV; NIV.

32. See Adrian Schenker, "kōper et expiation," *Biblica* 63 (1982): 32–46. I am persuaded by Schenker's argument, that the *kōper* is an "appeasement price," by which an endangered party gains peace with the one who threatens him.

33. This is also the conclusion of Schwartz ("Prohibitions," 56 n. 1).

34. Jacob Milgrom, *Numbers* (JPS Torah Commentary; Philadelphia: Jewish Publication Society, 1990), 295.

35. This point has been noted in a general way by Kiuchi in his response to Milgrom's interpretation of Lev 17:11 (*Purification Offering*, 102–3). However, I believe I am alone in indicating the extent to which Num 35:30–34 functions as a resource for understanding the ideological background of the text. I believe that my treatment of Num 35:30–34 here significantly reinforces the case against Milgrom's interpretation by highlighting the fact that slaughter outside the shrine cannot be "expiated," while slaughter in the shrine is fully legitimate and requires no expiation. In short, there is no such thing as an expiable murder in H's ideology, and the slaughter of an animal in the shrine *cannot* be regarded as a murder, unless one is prepared to accept that it is unexpiable, which is, of course, patently absurd.

36. The verb *znh*, which I render here as "go like loose women," and the image it conveys, still awaits a full treatment, which makes sense of its use to indicate the sexual behavior of professional prostitutes as well as of unmarried girls and married women, and to indicate cultic behavior that is regarded as non-Yahwistic. Tentatively, see Phyllis Bird, "'To Play the Harlot': An Inquiry into an Old Testament Metaphor," in *Gender and Difference in Ancient Israel* (ed. Peggy L. Day; Minneapolis: Fortress Press, 1989), 75–94. My understanding of the verb is that it primarily indicates "unregulated sexual behavior" by women, and that the meaning "act as a prostitute" is a secondary one rooted in the primary sense, since prostitutes in ancient Israel were "independent business women," who acted independently of the sexual proprietorship of fathers, husbands, or other male power holders. The figurative usage (as in Lev 17:7) likens Israelites to women who fail to accept the sexual proprietorship of Yahweh (who is variously characterized as father or husband).

37. See Levine, *Leviticus,* 102, 114, 251–52; Hartley, *Leviticus,* 272.

38. Cf. Rodriguez, *Substitution,* 240. Rodriguez, however, goes too far into speculation with his suggestion that the blood was offered to the "satyrs." It is best, I believe, to abstain from speculation and simply affirm that the blood was spilled illegitimately because the sacrifice had an illegitimate object.

39. Gorman (*Ideology of Ritual,* 186) correctly affirms that the unit is "clearly directed at the appropriate place for sacrifice," and identifies the ban on offering sacrifices outside of the Tent of Meeting as a "ritual prescription regarding sacrificial space." He fails to note, however, that the unit also indicates *to whom* the offering is to be made.

40. There are, however, some notable differences between the formulation here and in the previous two units, on which, see Schwartz, "Prohibitions," 39–40.

41. This structural analysis follows Schwartz, "Prohibitions," 46.

42. Ibid., 45.

43. Ibid., 46–47.

44. Ibid.

45. Elliger, *Leviticus,* 219. See also GKC §32b; 135a.

46. Milgrom, "Prolegomenon," *SCTT,* 97.

47. *Pace* Schwartz, "Prohibitions," 50–51. Schwartz maintains that the use of *ntn* indicates that the human act of placing blood on the altar is actually the means by which Yahweh executes his own application of blood to the altar. Schwartz's interpretation falters, however, on the fact that there is not actually a standard idiom, "put blood," that would include all of the specific modes of applying blood. Rather, in biblical Hebrew, *ntn* indicates a specific manipulation, the daubing of blood. Schwartz's interpretation seems to have been influenced by mishnaic Hebrew terminology, in which the noun *mattānâ* does in fact mean "application," and indicates any blood manipulation. In P and H, however, *ntn* is not used in this general sense.

48. Despite my disagreement with Schwartz's explanation of *ntn* in the clause, I fully affirm his conclusions about the significance of Yahweh's claim: application of blood to the altar is something Yahweh does for Israel's benefit, rather than something Israel does for Yahweh ("Prohibitions," 51).

49. Contra, e.g., Elliger, *Leviticus,* 218; Füglister, "Sühne," 145; NIV. The use of the possessive suffix distinguishes the Israelites who are addressed in the verse from their "lives." In addition, the prior and succeeding uses of *nepeš* in the verse with the meaning "life," suggest that also here the noun should be understood to mean "life," and not simply "self." On this latter point, see Hartley, *Leviticus,* 262 n. 11e. For the rendering "for your lives," see also Hoffmann, *Leviticus,* 1:474; Wenham, *Leviticus,* 239; Brichto, "On Slaughter and Sacrifice," 23; Schwartz, "Prohibitions," 51; Milgrom, *Leviticus 1–16,* 707–8; NRSV; NJPS.

50. See AV; RSV; NRSV; Hartley, *Leviticus,* 261; Elliger, *Leviticus,* 218 ("Sühne damit zu schaffen"); Schenker, "Zeichen," 195–96, esp. 196 n. 2 ("sühnen").

51. Levine, *Presence,* 67–68; Milgrom, "Prolegomenon," *SCTT,* 97–98; Milgrom, *Leviticus 1–16,* 707–8; Schwartz, "Prohibitions," 55.

52. Exod 30:11–16 is identified by most interpreters, including Israel Knohl, as a P text. However, Knohl identifies Num 31:48–54 as an H text. He offers no specific analysis of the pericope, but demonstrates convincingly the distinctive language and concerns of its wider context (Numbers 31 as a whole), and indicates that these distinctive

elements point to the H tradition. Other scholars, before Knohl, have recognized that Num 31 is unlike indisputably P texts. Philip J. Budd (*Numbers* [WBC 5; Waco: Tex.: Word Books, 1984], 327) lists A. Dillmann, J. Wellhausen, A. Kuenen, H. Holzinger, and B. Baentsch as scholars who identify Num 31 as "a very late addition to the priestly document." See also George Buchanan Gray, *Numbers,* 419–20.

53. Num 31:50a refers to "Yahweh's offering" (*qorban yhwh*), made up of gifts given by each man from the booty. The gold was not simply donated by the commanders, as some commentators suggest; it was taken from the whole army. Note v. 53: "The men of the army had taken plunder, each one for himself." This verse explains the source of the donation. It came from the plunder each man had taken. Thus, it was a gift from the whole army. For this interpretation, see Eryl W. Davies, *Numbers* (NCB; Grand Rapids, Mich.: Eerdmans, 1995), 328.

54. The offering of the army in Num 31 was made "to effect removal for our lives before Yahweh" (Num 31:50b).

55. According to Num 31:54, the donated gold was taken by Moses and Elazar and conveyed into the Tent of Meeting "as a memorial for the children of Israel before Yahweh." The offering, therefore, benefited all Israel, not just the officers or the men of the army.

56. Note that I characterize the verb as being *employed* as a denominative, without taking a firm position on whether it actually *is* a denominative, that is, a verbal form created on the basis of a preexisting nominal form. Levine (*Presence,* 67) affirms that *kipper,* as used in Exod 30:11–16, is "a secondary denominative, from the noun *kôper,*" and adds that "the fact that *kippēr* in Ex 30:15–16 is a denominative is suggested by the occurrence of the word *kôper* in v. 12" (Ibid., 67 n. 36).

57. See the discussion of the use of *kōper* in Num 35:31–32 above in this chapter.

58. Schenker, "*kōper* et expiation."

59. Levine, *Presence,* 67.

60. See, e.g., Hyatt, *Exodus,* 293; Hertzberg, *I & II Samuel,* 411–12; Cassuto, *Exodus,* 393; Schenker, "kōper et expiation," 41. George A. F. Knight (*Theology as Narration: A Commentary on the Book of Exodus* [Grand Rapids: Mich.: Eerdmans, 1976], 180) refers to the danger of gathering information useful to the enemy, which amounts to disloyalty to Yahweh. W. H. Gispen (*Exodus,* 283) states that "it is perhaps better to think here of the Lord's jealousy in connection with the fact that this census could lead to pride," adding that "we should also think of the sins of those who are counted." E. A. Speiser ("Census and Ritual Expiation in Mari and Israel," *BASOR* 149 [February 1958]: 17–25), followed by P. Kyle McCarter (*II Samuel* [AB 9; Garden City, N.Y.: Doubleday, 1984], 513–14) and Durham (*Exodus,* 402), argues that the payment of the silver purifies the people. Although the analogy with practices at Mari is suggestive, there is nothing in the biblical texts to suggest that the silver effects purification. Substances that purify are applied to the person or thing they purify. The silver, however, is given as a donation and used to provide for the needs of the cult. Speiser, McCarter, and Durham seem to have been misled by assuming that *kipper* always means "purify," and that the meaning of *kōper* is based on the meaning of the verb. However, as I have indicated above, the reverse is the case. The meaning of the verb *kipper* here follows from the meaning of the noun.

61. As Sarna correctly notes (*Exodus,* 196), "a census places the lives of those counted in jeopardy." Compare 2 Sam 24: David counts Israel, and the Israelites suffer as a result.

62. According to Milgrom, the threat of a plague, and the payment of a *kōper* to ward it off, indicate "that a census is a capital offense in the sight of God" ("Prolegomenon," *SCTT*, 98).

63. For the view that the counting itself endangers the men of the army, see L. Elliott Binns, *The Book of Numbers* (WC; London: Methuen, 1927), 207. See also Eryl W. Davies, *Numbers,* 328: Davies suggests that the act of counting the men was a sin requiring atonement, but also proposes that the donation was given to thank Yahweh that no lives had been lost.

64. Noth, *Exodus,* 236.

65. Numbers records the carrying out of two censuses of the type described in Exod 30:11–16 (Num 1 and 26). In each case, Yahweh commands the making of the count (Num 1:1–3; 26:1–2). There is no reference in either pericope to the threat of plague or the payment of the half sheqel, as Noth notes (*Numbers,* 19). Thus, the two pericopes seem not to presuppose Exod 30:11–16. Knohl regards both as part of the P stratum of Numbers (*Sanctuary,* 100–101).

66. Cassuto, *Exodus,* 393; Sarna, *Exodus,* 195.

67. Knohl, *Sanctuary,* 29, 32, 105; Milgrom, *Leviticus 1–16,* 1062–63.

68. See Knohl, *Sanctuary,* 108, on H's construct juxtaposition of the name Yahweh with offerings and sancta.

69. Noth (*Exodus,* 236) identifies the obtrusive second-person plural address as a later addition to the pericope.

70. My argument builds on a thesis advanced by Schwartz ("Prohibitions," 55–56, 59–60).

71. Ibid., 59–60.

72. Milgrom, *Leviticus 1–16,* 156, 416–17, 704–13.

73. Schwartz, "Prohibitions," 47–48.

74. Ibid., 47 and n. 2. Schwartz embraces the position of the vast majority of modern scholars, who identify the *bet* here as instrumental. See, e.g., M. M. Kalisch, *Leviticus* (vol. 2; vol. 3.2 of *A Historical and Critical Commentary on the Old Testament, with a New Translation;* London: Longmans, Green, Reader, and Dyer, 1872), 349; Keil and Delitzsch, *Pentateuch,* 2:410; Hoffmann, *Leviticus,* 1:474; Bertholet, *Leviticus,* 60; Elliger, *Leviticus,* 218; Rendtorff, *Studien,* 231; Kiuchi, *Purification Offering,* 105–6; Füglister, "Sühne," 143, 145–46; Hartley, *Leviticus,* 261; Janowski, *Sühne,* 246; Milgrom, *Leviticus 1–16,* 417, 706; RSV; see Rodriguez, *Substitution,* 245 n. 3, for references to others who advocate this interpretation. See also Ibn Ezra (ad loc.). Ibn Ezra is the only medieval Jewish commentator to identify the *nepeš* in Lev 17:11b as the life of the animal and to interpret the *bet* preposition as instrumental. On *bet* of means or instrument (*instrumentii*), see GCK §119o; Williams, *Hebrew Syntax* §243 (p. 44); BDB, 89b–90a.

75. Levine, "Prolegomenon," xxvii–xxviii; Levine, *Presence,* 68. See also Brichto, "On Slaughter and Sacrifice," 27–28. Brichto distinguishes his interpretation of *bannepeš* from Levine's by employing the designation "*bet* of exchange." However, "*bet* of exchange" is simply a different way of designating what has traditionally been labeled *beth pretii.* Note that Williams refers to *bet* indicating "price or exchange" as a single category (*Hebrew Syntax* §246 [p. 45]). See also GKC §119p.

76. See also Saadiah, ad loc.; Rashi, ad loc.; Ḥizquni, ad loc.; NIV.

77. Janowski, *Sühne,* 245–46; Milgrom, *Leviticus 1–16,* 706.

78. Milgrom, *Leviticus 1–16*, 1082.

79. The same confusion is present in Levine's explanation that the idiom *lĕkappēr 'al-napšōtêkem* refers to "expiation by substitution" (*Presence*, 67).

80. For this distinction between ransom and substitution, see Schenker, "kōper et expiation," 45.

81. A point made by a number of the medieval Jewish commentators. See, e.g., Ibn Ezra's concise comment (on Lev 17:11): "The sense is life in place of life" (*wht 'm npš ṭḥt npš*).

82. Thus, Janowski's identification of Lev 17:11 as the "Summe der kultischen Sühnetheologie" (*Sühne*, 242) must be rejected.

83. Knohl, *Sanctuary*, 29, 32; Milgrom, *Leviticus 1–16*, 1062–63.

84. The referent of the third-person, masculine singular pronominal suffix with *'al* must be the incense altar.

85. See Lev 15:30 and Num 19:13, 20, H texts that warn of the severe consequences of remaining impure and thereby contaminating Yahweh's shrine.

86. This perspective clearly lies behind Milgrom's interpretation of Lev 17:11 in "Prolegomenon," originally published in 1971.

87. Stowers, "On the Comparison of Blood."

Conclusions

1. R. K. Merton, *Social Theory and Social Structure* (enlarged ed.; New York: Free Press, 1968), 73–138 (esp. pp. 114–20).

2. Stowers, "On the Comparison of Blood," 189.

3. Cf. Stowers' statement on this issue: "Lev 17:11 is an interpretation of sacrifice by a person or group of people inside the culture. There may have been many other such sentences by different persons that sound to us like definitions or theories of sacrifice. But none of these interpretations could be sufficient for the kind of understanding that scholars in the university ought to seek" ("On the Comparison of Blood," 189).

4. My observations on the status indexing functions of the Passover blood manipulations build on those offered by Olyan, *Rites and Rank*, 11.

5. As I noted in my discussion of Exod 12:6–7 in chapter 2, the tradent(s) responsible for the pericope seem(s) not to have assigned the slaughter and blood manipulation to particular individuals. Exodus 12:6 says that "the whole assembly of the congregation of Israel" is to slaughter the lambs, and in verse 7, the assembly of the congregation seems to continue as the subject of the verbs referring to the blood manipulation.

6. In P and H, the Levites are prohibited from acting as priests (see Num 16:9–10; 17:5 [ET, 16:40]). However, they are not present in most of P's and H's representations of sacrificial activity. Thus, we cannot speak of their relatively lower status in relation to the priests being explicitly indexed in those texts. Rather, the indexing of their status vis-à-vis the Aaronids is implicit in the fact that they are absent from the representations, and assigned no activities at the altar.

7. Similarly, in the nonpriestly covenant ritual represented in Exod 24:3–8, the tossing of blood onto an altar and then onto the people creates a bond between the people and the altar. If, as I suggested in chapter 2, the altar is understood to represent Yahweh, we may speak of the blood rite as creating an existential bond between Yahweh and his people.

8. As I noted in chapter 6, Ezekiel's specification that only the descendants of Zadok may offer fat and blood implicitly also excludes non-Zadokite Aaronids from functioning as priests. Indeed, Ezekiel seems to identify these non-Zadokites as "Levites."

9. Compare P's description of the inaugural sacrifices offered by Aaron and his sons (Lev 9), discussed earlier. There, Aaron's sons convey the blood to him and he applies it to the altar. Like the Levites in 2 Chron, the subordinate status of Aaron's sons is ritually inscribed by their place in the blood manipulation complex.

Bibliography

Ackroyd, Peter R. *I & II Chronicles, Ezra, Nehemiah.* London: SCM Press, 1973.

Allen, Leslie C. *Ezekiel 20–48.* Word Biblical Commentary 29. Dallas, Tex.: Word Books, 1990.

Anderson, Gary A. "Sacrifice and Sacrificial Offerings. Old Testament." Pages 870–86 in vol. 5 of *The Anchor Bible Dictionary,* edited by David Noel Freedman, Gary A. Herion, David F. Graf, John David Pleins, and Astrid B. Beck. 6 vols. New York: Doubleday, 1992.

———. *A Time to Mourn, a Time to Dance: The Expression of Grief and Joy in Israelite Religion.* University Park: Pennsylvania State University Press, 1991.

Barr, James. "Etymology and the Old Testament." Pages 1–28 in *Language and Meaning: Studies in Hebrew Language and Biblical Exegesis. Oudtestamentische Studiën* 19. Leiden: E. J. Brill, 1974.

———. "Sacrifice and Offering." Pages 868–76 in *Dictionary of the Bible,* edited by James Hastings. Rev. ed., edited by F. C. Grant and H. H. Rowley. New York: Scribners, 1963.

———. *The Semantics of Biblical Language.* London: Oxford University Press, 1961.

Bell, Catherine. *Ritual: Perspectives and Dimensions.* New York: Oxford University Press, 1997.

———. *Ritual Theory, Ritual Practice.* New York: Oxford University Press, 1992.

Bertholet, Alfred. *Das Buch Hesekiel.* Kurzer Hand-Commentar zum Alten Testament 12. Tübingen: J. C. B. Mohr (Paul Siebeck), 1897.

———. *Hesekiel.* Handbuch zum Alten Testament 13. Tübingen: J. C. B. Mohr (Paul Siebeck), 1936.

———. *Leviticus.* Kurzer Hand-Commentar zum Alten Testament 3. Tübingen: J. C. B. Mohr (Paul Siebeck), 1901.

Binns, L. Elliott. *The Book of Numbers.* Westminster Commentaries. London: Methuen, 1927.

Bird, Phyllis. "'To Play the Harlot': An Inquiry into an Old Testament Metaphor." Pages 75–94 in *Gender and Difference in Ancient Israel,* edited by Peggy L. Day. Minneapolis: Fortress Press, 1989.

Block, Daniel I. *The Book of Ezekiel, Chapters 1–24.* New International Commentary on the Old Testament. Grand Rapids, Mich.: William B. Eerdmans, 1997.

———. *The Book of Ezekiel, Chapters 25–48.* New International Commentary on the Old Testament. Grand Rapids, Mich.: Eerdmans, 1998.

Botterweck, G. J., and H. Ringgren, eds. *Theologisches Wörterbuch zum Alten Testament.* Stuttgart: W. Kohlhammer, 1970–. Translated by J. T. Willis, G. W. Bromiley, and D. E. Green as *Theological Dictionary of the Old Testament*. Grand Rapids, Mich.: Eerdmans, 1974–.

Brichto, Herbert Chanan. "On Slaughter and Sacrifice, Blood and Atonement." *Hebrew Union College Annual* 47 (1976): 19–55.

Brueggemann, Walter. *First and Second Samuel*. Interpretation. Louisville, Ky.: John Knox Press, 1990.

Buchler, Justus. *The Philosophical Writings of Peirce*. New York: Dover, 1955

Budd, Philip J. *Leviticus*. New Century Bible. Grand Rapids, Mich.: Eerdmans, 1996.

―――. *Numbers*. Word Biblical Commentary 5. Waco, Tex.: Word Books, 1984.

Budde, Karl. *Die Bücher Samuel*. Kurzer Hand-Commentar zum Alten Testament 8. Tübingen: J. C. B. Mohr (Paul Siebeck), 1902.

Buis, Pierre, and Jacques Le Clercq. *Le Deutéronome*. Sources Bibliques. Paris: Librairie Lecoffre, 1963.

Campbell, Anthony F., and Mark A. O'Brien. *Sources of the Pentateuch: Texts, Introductions, Annotations*. Minneapolis: Fortress Press, 1993.

Cassuto, U. *A Commentary on the Book of Exodus*. [In Hebrew.] 1942. Reprint, Jerusalem: Magnes Press, 1987.

―――. *A Commentary on the Book of Genesis*. Vol. 2. Translated by Israel Abrahams. Jerusalem: Magnes Press, 1964.

Childs, Brevard S. *The Book of Exodus*. Old Testament Library. Philadelphia: Westminster Press, 1974.

Clarke, E. G., W. E. Aufrecht, J. C. Hurd, and F. Spitzer, eds. *Targum Pseudo-Jonathan of the Pentateuch: Text and Concordance*. Hoboken, N.J.: Ktav, 1984.

Clements, Ronald E. *Exodus*. Cambridge Bible Commentary. Cambridge: Cambridge University Press, 1972.

Cogan, Mordechai, and Hayim Tadmor. *II Kings*. Anchor Bible 11. New York: Doubleday, 1988.

Cohen, Menachem, ed. *Miqra'ot Gedolot, I & II Samuel*. HaKeter Edition. Ramat-Gan, Israel: Bar Ilan University, 1993.

Cooke, G. A. *The Book of Ezekiel*. International Critical Commentary. Edinburgh: T & T Clark, 1936.

Craigie, Peter C. *The Book of Deuteronomy*. New International Commentary on the Old Testament. Grand Rapids, Mich.: Eerdmans, 1976.

Cross, Frank Moore. *Canaanite Myth and Hebrew Epic: Essays in the History of the Religion of Israel*. Cambridge, Mass.: Harvard University Press, 1973.

Davidson, A. B. *The Book of the Prophet Ezekiel*. Cambridge Bible for Schools and Colleges. Cambridge: Cambridge University Press, 1892.

Davies, Eryl W. *Numbers*. New Century Bible. Grand Rapids, Mich.: Eerdmans, 1995.

Davies, G. Henton. *Exodus: Introduction and Commentary*. Torch Bible Commentaries. London: SCM Press, 1967.

De Vries, Simon J. *1 and 2 Chronicles*. Forms of the Old Testament Literature 11. Grand Rapids, Mich.: Eerdmans, 1989.

Dhorme, Paul. *Les Livres de Samuel*. Études bibliques. Paris: Librairie Victor Lecoffre/ J. Gabalda, 1910.

Dillard, Raymond B. *2 Chronicles*. Word Biblical Commentary 15. Waco, Tex.: Word Books, 1987.

Dillmann, August. *Die Bücher Exodus und Leviticus*. 2d ed. Kurtzgefasstes exegetisches Handbuch zum Alten Testament 12. Leipzig: S. Hirzel, 1880.

Dion, Paul E. "Early Evidence for the Ritual Significance of the 'Base of the Altar.'" *Journal of Biblical Literature* 106 (1987): 487–92.

Douglas, Mary. *Natural Symbols: Explorations in Cosmology.* New York: Random House, 1970.

Driver, G. R. "Ezekiel: Linguistic and Textual Problems." *Biblica* 35 (1954): 299–312.

Driver, S. R. *The Book of Exodus* . Cambridge Bible for Schools and Colleges. Cambridge: Cambridge University Press, 1911. Reprint, 1918.

———. *The Book of Genesis.* 5th ed. Westminster Commentaries. London: Methuen, 1906.

———. *A Critical and Exegetical Commentary on Deuteronomy.* 3d ed. International Critical Commentary. Edinburg: T & T Clark, 1901.

———. *An Introduction to the Literature of the Old Testament.* Meridian Library 3. 1891. Reprint, New York: Meridian Books, 1956.

———. *Notes on the Hebrew Text and the Topography of the Books of Samuel.* 2d ed. Oxford: Clarendon Press, 1913.

Durham, John I. *Exodus.* Word Biblical Commentary 3. Waco, Tex.: Word Books, 1987.

Eichrodt, Walther. *Ezekiel: A Commentary.* Translated by Cosslett Quin. Old Testament Library. Philadelphia: SCM Press, 1970.

Elliger, Karl. *Leviticus.* Handbuch zum Alten Testament 4. Tübingen: J. C. B. Mohr (Paul Siebeck), 1966.

Fernandez, James W. "Symbolic Consensus in a Fang Reformative Cult." *American Anthropologist* 67 (1965): 902–29.

Finkelstein, Louis. *Sifra on Leviticus.* Vol. 2. New York: Jewish Theological Seminary of America, 1983.

Firth, Raymond. *Symbols: Public and Private.* Symbol, Myth, and Ritual Series, edited by Victor Turner. Ithaca, N.Y.: Cornell University Press, 1973.

Fish, Stanley. *Is There a Text in This Class? The Authority of Interpretive Communities.* Cambridge, Mass.: Harvard University Press, 1980.

Fox, Michael V., Victor Avigdor Hurowitz, Avi Hurvitz, Michael L. Klein, Baruch J. Schwartz, and Nili Shupak, eds. *Texts, Temples and Traditions: A Tribute to Menahem Haran.* Winona Lake, Ind.: Eisenbrauns, 1996.

Fretheim, Terence E. *Exodus.* Interpretation. Louisville, Ky.: John Knox Press, 1991.

Friedman, Richard Elliott. *The Exile and Biblical Narrative: The Formation of the Deuteronomistic and Priestly Works.* Harvard Semitic Monographs 22. Chico, Calif: Scholars Press, 1981.

———. "Torah (Pentateuch)." Pages 605–22 in vol. 6 of *The Anchor Bible Dictionary,* edited by David Noel Freedman, Gary A. Herion, David F. Graf, John David Pleins, and Astrid B. Beck. 6 vols. New York: Doubleday, 1992.

Füglister, Notker. "Sühne durch Blut: Zur Bedeutung von Leviticus 17,11." Pages 143–64 in *Studien zum Pentateuch: Walter Kornfeld zum 60. Geburtstag,* edited by Georg Braulik. Vienna: Herder, 1977.

Gerstenberger, Erhard S. *Leviticus: A Commentary.* Translated by Douglas W. Stott. Old Testament Library. Louisville, Ky.: Westminster John Knox Press, 1996.

Gese, Hartmut. "The Atonement." Pages 93–116 in *Essays on Biblical Theology,* translated by Keith Crim. Minneapolis: Augsburg Publishing House, 1981. 2d ed., 2000. Translation of "Die Sühne." Pages 85–106 in *Zur Biblischen Theologie: Alttestamentliche Vorträge.* Beiträge zur evangelischen Theologie 78. Munich: Chr. Kaiser Verlag, 1977.

———. *Der Verfassungsentwurf des Ezechiel (Kap. 40–48): Traditionsgeschichtlich Untersucht.* Beiträge zur historischen Theologie 25. Tübingen: J. C. B. Mohr (Paul Siebeck), 1957.

Ginsberg, Morris. *Sifra: With Translation and Commentary: Dibura Denedabah.* University of South Florida Studies in the History of Judaism 194. Atlanta: Scholars Press, 1999. Originally published, Jerusalem: Gainsford Family-Leshon Limudim, 1994.

Gispen, W. H. *Exodus.* Translated by Ed van der Maas. Bible Student's Commentary. Grand Rapids, Mich.: Eerdmans, 1982.

Gorman, Frank H. *The Ideology of Ritual: Space, Time and Status in the Priestly Theology.* Journal for the Study of the Old Testament: Supplement Series 91. Sheffield: JSOT Press, 1990.

———. Review of Gerald A. Klingbeil, *A Comparative Study of the Ritual of Ordination as Found in Leviticus 8 and Emar 369. Journal of Biblical Literature* 118 (1999): 534–36.

Gray, George Buchanan. *A Critical and Exegetical Commentary on Numbers.* International Critical Commentary. Edinburgh: T & T Clark, 1903.

———. *Sacrifice in the Old Testament: Its Theory and Practice.* 1925. Reprint, New York: Ktav, 1971.

Gray, John. *I & II Kings: A Commentary.* 2d ed. Old Testament Library. London: SCM Press, 1970.

Greenberg, Moshe. *Ezekiel 1–20.* Anchor Bible 22. New York: Doubleday, 1983.

———. *Ezekiel 21–37.* Anchor Bible 22A. New York: Doubleday, 1997.

Grintz, J. M. "'Do Not Eat on the Blood': Reconsiderations in Setting and Dating of the Priestly Code." *Annual of the Swedish Theological Institute* 8 (1970–71): 78–105.

Gunkel, Herman. *Genesis.* Translated by Mark E. Biddle. Macon, Georgia: Mercer University Press, 1997.

Hamilton, Victor P. *The Book of Genesis, Chapters 1–17.* New International Commentary on the Old Testament. Grand Rapids, Mich.: Eerdmans, 1990.

Haran, Menahem. "The Character of the Priestly Source: Utopian and Exclusive Features." Pages 131–38 in *Proceedings of the Eighth World Congress of Jewish Studies: Panel Sessions: Bible Studies and Hebrew Language.* Jerusalem: World Union of Jewish Studies, 1983.

———. *Temples and Temple Service in Ancient Israel.* Oxford: Clarendon Press, 1978. Reprint, Winona Lake, Ind.: Eisenbrauns, 1985.

Hartley, John E. *Leviticus.* Word Biblical Commentary 4. Dallas, Tex.: Word Books, 1992.

Hendel, Ronald S. "Sacrifice as a Cultural System: The Ritual Symbolism of Exodus 24,3–8." *Zeitschrift für die alttestamentliche Wissenschaft* 101 (1989): 366–90.

Herrmann, Johannes. *Ezechiel.* Leipzig: A. Deichertsche Verlagsbuchhandlung W. Scholl, 1924.

Hertzberg, Hans Wilhelm. *I & II Samuel.* Translated by J. S. Bowden. Old Testament Library. Philadelphia: Westminster Press, 1964.

Ḥizquni (Hazzequni; Hezekiah ben Manoah). Commentary on the Torah. Edited by H. D. Chavel and Zeev Gottlieb. In Katzenelenbogen, *tôrat ḥayyîm.*

Hobbs, T. R. *2 Kings.* Word Biblical Commentary 13. Waco, Tex.: Word Books, 1985.

Hoffman, Lawrence A. *Covenant of Blood: Circumcision and Gender in Rabbinic Judaism.* Chicago: University of Chicago Press, 1996.

Hoffmann, David. *Das Buch Deuteronomium.* Vol. 1. Berlin: M. Poppelauer, 1913.

———. *Das Buch Leviticus: Übersetzt und Erklärt.* Vol. 1. Berlin: M. Poppelauer, 1905.

Holzinger, H. *Exodus.* Kurzer Hand-Commentar zum Alten Testemant 2. Tübingen: J. C. B. Mohr (Paul Siebeck), 1900.

———. *Genesis.* Kurzer Hand-Commentar zum Alten Testament 1. Freiburg: J. C. B. Mohr (Paul Siebeck), 1898.

Honeyman, A. M. "Hebrew *sap* 'Basin, Goblet.'" *Journal of Theological Studies* 37 (1936): 56–59.

Houtman, Cornelis. *Exodus.* 3 vols. Translated by Johan Rebel and Sierd Woudstra. Historical Commentary on the Old Testament. Kampen: Kok Publishing House, 1993–96 (vols. 1–2); Leuven: Peeters, 2000 (vol. 3).

Hurvitz, Avi. "The Evidence of Language in Dating the Priestly Code." *Revue Biblique* 81 (1974): 24–56.

———. "The Language of the Priestly Source and Its Historical Setting—The Case for an Early Date." Pages 83–94 in *Proceedings of the Eighth World Congress of Jewish Studies: Panel Sessions: Bible Studies and Hebrew Language.* Jerusalem: World Union of Jewish Studies, 1983.

———. *A Linguistic Study of the Relationship between the Priestly Source and the Book of Ezekiel: A New Approach to an Old Problem.* Cahiers de la Revue Biblique 20. Paris: J. Gabalda, 1982.

Hyatt, J. Philip. *Exodus.* Rev. ed. New Century Bible. Grand Rapids, Mich.: Eerdmans, 1980.

Ibn Ezra, Abraham. Commentary on the Torah. Ed. Asher Weiser. In Katzenelenbogen, *tôrat ḥayyîm.*

———. *Leviticus.* Translated by Jay F. Shachter. Vol. 3 of *The Commentary of Abraham Ibn Ezra on the Pentateuch.* Hoboken, N.J.: Ktav, 1986.

Iser, Wolfgang. "The Reading Process: A Phenomenological Approach." Pages 50–69 in *Reader-Response Criticism: From Formalism to Post-Structuralism,* edited by Jane P. Tompkins. Baltimore: Johns Hopkins University Press, 1980.

Jacob, Benno. *The Second Book of the Bible: Exodus.* Translated by Walter Jacob. Hoboken, N.J.: Ktav, 1992.

Janowski, Bernd. *Sühne als Heilsgeschehen: Studien zur Sühnetheologie der Priesterschrift und zur Wurzel KPR im Alten Orient und im Alten Testament.* Wissenschaftliche Monographien zum Alten und Neuen Testament 55. Neukirchen-Vluyn: Neukirchener Verlag, 1982. 2d ed., 2000.

Japhet, Sara. *I & II Chronicles: A Commentary.* Old Testament Library. Louisville, Ky.: Westminster/John Knox Press, 1993.

Jastrow, Marcus. *A Dictionary of the Targumim, the Talmud Babli and Yerushalmi, and the Midrashic Literature.* 2d ed., 1903. Reprint, New York: Judaica Press, 1992.

Jay, Nancy. *Throughout Your Generations Forever: Sacrifice, Religion, and Paternity.* Chicago: University of Chicago Press, 1992.

Jenni, E., and C. Westermann, eds. *Theologisches Handwörterbuch zum Alten Testament.* 2 vols. Munich: C. Kaiser, 1971–76. Translated by M. E. Biddle as *Theological Lexicon of the Old Testament.* 3 vols. Peabody, Mass.: Hendrikson, 1997.

Johnstone, William. *2 Chronicles 10–36; Guilt and Atonement.* Vol. 2 of *1 and 2 Chronicles.* Journal for the Study of the Old Testament: Supplement Series 254. Sheffield: Sheffield Academic Press, 1997.

Jones, Gwilym H. *1 and 2 Kings.* Vol. 2. New Century Bible. Grand Rapids, Mich.: Eerdmans, 1984.

Kalisch, M. M. *Exodus.* Vol. 2 of *A Historical and Critical Commentary on the Old Testament, with a New Translation.* London: Longman, Brown, Green and Longmans, 1855.

———. *Leviticus.* 2 vols. Vols. 3.1 and 3.2 of *A Historical and Critical Commentary on the Old Testament, with a New Translation.* London: Longmans, Green, Reader, and Dyer, 1867–1872.

Katzenelenbogen, Mordechai L., ed. *tôrat ḥayyîm ḥămiššâ ḥûmšê tôrâ.* 6 vols. Jerusalem: Mossad Harav Kook, 1986–91.

Kaufmann, Yehezkel. *History of Israelite Religion from Early Times to the End of the Second Temple Era.* [In Hebrew.] 8 vols. [= Vols. 1.1–4.1]. Tel Aviv: Mosad Bialik, 1937. Translated by Moshe Greenberg as *The Religion of Israel: From Its Beginnings to the Babylonian Exile.* Abridged, vols. 1–7. Chicago: University of Chicago Press, 1960.

Keil, C. F., and F. Delitzsch. *Biblical Commentary on the Books of Samuel.* Translated by James Martin. Clark's Foreign Theological Library, Fourth Series, vol. 9. Edinburgh: T & T Clark, 1880.

———. *The Pentateuch.* Translated by James Martin as vol. 2 of *Biblical Commentary on the Old Testament.* Clark's Foreign Theological Library, Fourth Series, vol. 2. Edinburgh: T & T Clark, 1891.

Kertzer, David I. *Ritual, Politics, and Power.* New Haven: Yale University Press, 1988.

Kiuchi, N. *The Purification Offering in the Priestly Literature: Its Meaning and Function.* Journal for the Study of the Old Testament: Supplement Series 56. Sheffield: JSOT Press, 1987.

Klein, Ralph W. *1 Samuel.* Word Biblical Commentary 10. Waco, Tex.: Word Books, 1983.

Knierim, Rolf P. *Text and Concept in Leviticus 1:1–9.* Forschungen zum Alten Testament 2. Tübingen: J. C. B. Mohr (Paul Siebeck), 1992.

Knight, Douglas A. "The Pentateuch." Pages 263–96 in *The Hebrew Bible and Its Modern Interpreters,* edited by Douglas A. Knight and Gene M. Tucker. Philadelphia: Fortress Press, 1985.

Knight, Douglas A. "Deuteronomy and the Deuteronomists." Pages 61–79 in *Old Testament Interpretation: Past, Present, and Future,* edited by James Luther Mays, David L. Petersen, and Kent Harold Richards. Nashville: Abingdon Press, 1995.

———. Foreword to *Prolegomena to the History of Israel,* by Julius Wellhausen. Scholars Press Reprints and Translations Series. Atlanta: Scholars Press, 1994. Reprint of *Prolegomena to the History of Israel.* Translated by J. Sutherland Black and Allan Menzies, with preface by W. Roberston Smith. Edinburgh: Adam & Charles Black, 1885.

Knight, George A. F. *Theology as Narration: A Commentary on the Book of Exodus.* Grand Rapids: Mich.: Eerdmans, 1976.

Knohl, Israel. *The Sanctuary of Silence: The Priestly Torah and the Holiness School.* Minneapolis: Fortress Press, 1995.

Koch, Klaus. *Die Priesterschrift von Exodus 25 bis Leviticus 16: Eine überlieferungsgeschichtliche und literarkritische Untersuchung.* Forschungen zur Religion und Literatur des Alten und Neuen Testaments, New Series 53. Göttingen: Vandenhoeck & Ruprecht, 1959.

Kurtz, J. H., *Sacrificial Worship of the Old Testament*. Translated by James Martin. 1863. Reprint, Minneapolis: Klock and Klock, 1980.

Kutsch, E. *Verheissung und Gesetz: Untersuchung zum Sogenannten "Bund" im Alten Testament*. Beihefte zur Zeitschrift für die alttestamentliche Wissenschaft 131. Berlin: Walter de Gruyter, 1973.

Labuschagne, C. J. *Deuteronomium*. Vol. 2. De Prediking van het Oude Testament. Nijkerk: Uitgeverij G. F. Callenbach, 1990.

————. "'You Shall Not Boil a Kid in Its Mother's Milk': A New Proposal for the Origin of the Prohibition." Pages 6–17 in *The Scriptures and the Scrolls: Studies in Honour of A. S. vander Woude on the Occasion of his 65th Birthday,* edited by F. García Martínez, A. Hilhorst, and C. J. Labuschagne. Vetus Testamentum Supplements 49. Leiden: E. J. Brill, 1992.

Leach, Edmund R. *The Political Systems of Highland Burma: A Study of Kachin Social Structure*. 2d ed. London: Athlone Press, 1964.

————. "Ritual." Pages 520–26 in vol. 13 of *International Encyclopedia of the Social Sciences*. New York: Macmillan, 1968.

Levenson, Jon D. *Theology of the Program of Restoration of Ezekiel 40–48*. Harvard Semitic Monograph 10. Missoula, Mont.: Scholars Press, 1976.

Levey, Samson H. *The Targum of Ezekiel*. Vol. 13 of *The Aramaic Bible,* edited by Michael McNamara et al. Wilmington, Del.: Michael Glazier, 1987.

Levine, Baruch A. *In the Presence of the Lord: A Study of Cult and Some Cultic Terms in Ancient Israel*. Studies in Judaism in Late Antiquity 5. Leiden: E. J. Brill, 1974.

————. "Late Language in the Priestly Source: Some Literary and Historical Observations." Pages 69–82 in *Proceedings of the Eighth World Congress of Jewish Studies: Panel Sessions: Bible Studies and Hebrew Language*. Jerusalem: World Union of Jewish Studies, 1983.

————. *Leviticus*. JPS Torah Commentary. Philadelphia: Jewish Publication Society, 1989.

————. *Numbers 1–20*. Anchor Bible 4. New York: Doubleday, 1993.

————. "The Priestly Writers." Pages 683–87 in *The Interpreter's Dictionary of the Bible: Supplementary Volume,* edited by Keith Crim. Nashville: Abingdon Press, 1976.

————. Prolegomenon to *Sacrifice in the Old Testament: Its Theory and Practice,* by George Buchanan Gray. 1925. Reprint, New York: Ktav, 1971.

Levinson, Bernard M. *Deuteronomy and the Hermeneutics of Legal Innovation*. New York: Oxford University Press, 1997.

Licht, J. "*zebaḥ*." [In Hebrew.] Pages 901–2 in vol. 2 of *'enṣîqlopedyâ miqrā'ît,* edited by U. Cassuto et al. Jerusalem: Mosad Bialik, 1950–88.

Loewenstamm, S. E. "'anōkî 'ăhaṭṭennâ." [In Hebrew.] *Leshonenu* 29 (1965): 69–70. English translation in *Comparative Studies in Biblical and Ancient Oriental Literatures,* 225–27. Alter Orient und Altes Testament 204. Neukirchen-Vluyn: Neukirchener Verlag, 1980.

————. "yôm hakkippurîm." [In Hebrew.] Pages 595–600 in vol. 3 of *'enṣîqlopedyâ miqrā'ît,* edited by U. Cassuto et al. Jerusalem: Mosad Bialik, 1950–88.

Löhr, Max. *Das Ritual von Lev. 16 (Untersuchungen zum Hexateuchproblem III)*. Schriften der Königsberger Gelehrten Gesellschaft 2.1. Berlin: Deutsche Verlagsgesellschaft für Politik und Geschichte, 1925.

Long, Burke O. *2 Kings*. Forms of the Old Testament Literature 10. Grand Rapids, Mich.: Eerdmans, 1991.

Mayes, A. D. H. *Deuteronomy.* New Century Bible. Grand Rapids, Mich.: Eerdmans, 1979.

McCarter, P. Kyle. *I Samuel.* Anchor Bible 8. Garden City, N.Y.: Doubleday, 1980.

———. *II Samuel.* Anchor Bible 9. Garden City, N.Y.: Doubleday, 1984.

McCarthy, Dennis J. "Further Notes on the Symbolism of Blood and Sacrifice." *Journal of Biblical Literature* 92 (1973): 205–10.

———. "The Symbolism of Blood and Sacrifice." *Journal of Biblical Literature* 88 (1969): 166–76.

McConville, J. G. *Law and Theology in Deuteronomy.* Journal for the Study of the Old Testament: Supplement Series 33. Sheffield: JSOT Press, 1984.

McKenzie, Steven L. "Deuteronomistic History." Pages 160–68 in vol. 2 of *The Anchor Bible Dictionary,* edited by David Noel Freedman, Gary A. Herion, David F. Graf, John David Pleins, and Astrid B. Beck. 6 vols. New York: Doubleday, 1992.

McNeile, A. H. *The Book of Exodus.* Westminster Commentaries. London: Methuen, 1908.

Meigs, Anna S. *Food, Sex, and Pollution: A New Guinean Religion.* New Brunswick, N.J.: Rutgers University Press, 1984.

Merton, R. K. *Social Theory and Social Structure.* Enlarged ed. New York: Free Press, 1968.

Metzinger, A. "Die Substitutionstheorie und das alttestamentliche Opfer mit besonderer Berücksichtigung von Lev. 17,11." *Biblica* 21 (1940): 159–87, 247–72, 353–77.

Milgrom, Jacob. *Cult and Conscience: The* asham *and the Priestly Doctrine of Repentance.* Studies in Judaism in Late Antiquity 18. Leiden: E. J. Brill, 1976.

———. "The Cultic Šᵉgāgāh and Its Influence in Psalms and Job." *Jewish Quarterly Review* 58 (1967) 115–25. [Reprinted in *SCTT,* 122–32.]

———. "The Function of the *ḥaṭṭā't* Sacrifice." [In Hebrew.] *Tarbiz* 40 (1970–71): 1–8.

———. "The Graduated *ḥaṭṭā't* of Lev 5:1–13." *Journal of the American Oriental Society* 103 (1983): 249–54.

———. "Israel's Sanctuary: The Priestly 'Picture of Dorian Gray.'" *Revue Biblique* 83 (1976): 390–99. [Reprinted in *SCTT,* 75–84.]

———. *Leviticus 1–16.* Anchor Bible 3. New York: Doubleday, 1991.

———. *Leviticus 17–22.* Anchor Bible 3A. New York: Doubleday, 2000.

———. "The *Modus Operandi* of the *ḥaṭṭā't:* A Rejoinder." *Journal of Biblical Literature* 109 (1990): 111–13.

———. *Numbers.* JPS Torah Commentary. Philadelphia: Jewish Publication Society, 1990.

———. "The Paradox of the Red Cow (Num. xix)." *Vetus Testamentum* 31 (1981): 62–72. [Reprinted in *SCTT,* 85–95.]

———. "A Prolegomoenon to Leviticus 17:11." *Journal of Biblical Literature* 90 (1971): 149–56. [Reprinted in *SCTT,* 96–103.]

———. Review of Bernd Janowski, *Sühne als Heilsgeschehen. Journal of Biblical Literature* 104 (1985): 302–30.

———. "Sacrifices and Offerings, OT." Pages 763–71 in *Interpreter's Dictionary of the Bible: Supplementary Volume,* edited by K. Crim. Nashville: Abingdon Press, 1976.

———. "Sin-Offering or Purification-Offering?" *Vetus Testamentum* 21 (1971): 237–39. [Reprinted in *SCTT,* 67–69.]

———. *Studies in Cultic Theology and Terminology.* Studies in Judaism in Late Antiquity. Leiden: E. J. Brill, 1983.

———. "Two Kinds of *ḥaṭṭā't*." *Vetus Testamentum* 26 (1976): 333–37. [Reprinted in *SCTT*, 70–74.]

Morris, Leon. *The Apostolic Preaching of the Cross*. Grand Rapids, Mich.: Eerdmans, 1956.

———. "Blood." Page 143 in *New Bible Dictionary*. 3d ed. Leicester: Inter-Varsity Press, 1996.

Nelson, Richard D. *The Double Redaction of the Deuteronomistic History*. Journal for the Study of the Old Testament Supplement Series 18. Sheffield: JSOT Press, 1973.

———. *First and Second Kings*. Interpretation. Atlanta: John Knox Press, 1987.

Neusner, Jacob. *Sifra: An Analytical Translation*. 3 vols. Atlanta: Scholars Press, 1988.

Nicholson, E. W. "The Covenant Ritual in Exodus XXIV 3–8." *Vetus Testamentum* 32 (1982): 74–86.

———. *God and His People: Covenant Theology in the Old Testament*. Oxford: Clarendon Press, 1986.

Nielsen, Eduard. *Deuteronomium*. Handbuch sum Alten Testament 1.6. Tübingen: J. C. B. Mohr (Paul Siebeck), 1995.

Noordtzij, A. *Leviticus*. Bible Student's Commentary. Translated by Raymond Togtman. Grand Rapids, Mich.: Zondervan, 1982.

Noth, Martin. *Exodus: A Commentary*. Trans. J. S. Bowden. Old Testament Library. Philadelphia: Westminster Press, 1962. Originally *Das zweite Buch Mose, Exodus*. Das Alte Testament Deutsch 5. Göttingen: Vandenhoeck & Ruprecht, 1959.

———. *A History of Pentateuchal Traditions*. Translated by Bernard W. Anderson. Englewood Cliffs, N.J.: Prentice-Hall, 1972. Originally *Überlieferungsgeschichte des Pentateuch*. Stuttgart: W. Kohlhammer Verlag, 1948.

———. *Leviticus: A Commentary*. Trans. J. E. Anderson. Old Testament Library. London: SCM Press, 1965. Originally *Das dritte Buch Mose, Leviticus,* Das Alte Testament Deutsch 6. Göttingen: Vandenhoeck & Ruprecht, 1962.

———. *Numbers: A Commentary*. Trans. J. D. Martin. Old Testament Library. London: SCM Press, 1962. Originally *Das vierte Buch Mose, Numeri*. Das Alte Testament Deutsch 7. Göttingen: Vandenhoeck & Ruprecht, 1966.

———. *Überlieferungsgeschichtliche Studien: Die Sammelnden und Bearbeitenden Geschichtswerke im Alten Testament*. 3d ed. Tübingen: Max Niemeyer Verlag, 1967. English translation of pp. 1–110 in *The Deuteronomistic History,* translated by Jane Doull, John Barton, Michael D. Rutter, and D. R. Ap-Thomas. Journal for the Study of the Old Testament: Supplement Series 15. Sheffield: JSOT Press, 1981.

Olyan, Saul M. "Honor, Shame, and Covenant Relations in Ancient Israel and Its Environment." *Journal of Biblical Literature* 115 (1996): 201–18.

———. *Rites and Rank: Hierarchy in Biblical Representations of Cult*. Princeton, N.J.: Princeton University Press, 2000.

———. "What Do Shaving Rites Accomplish and What Do They Signal in Biblical Ritual Contexts?" *Journal of Biblical Literature* 117 (1998): 611–22.

Osumi, Yuichi. *Die Kompositionsgeschichte des Bundesbuches Exodus 20, 22b–23,33*. Orbis Biblicus et Orientalis 105. Göttingen: Vandenhoeck & Ruprecht, 1991.

Perlitt, L. *Bundestheologie im Alten Testament*. Neukirchen-Vluyn: Neukirchenere Verlag, 1969.

Péter-Contesse, René. *Lévitique 1–16*. Commentaire de l'Ancien Testament 3a. Geneva: Éditions Labor et Fides, 1993.

Phillips, Anthony. *Deuteronomy*. Cambridge Bible Commentary. Cambridge: Cambridge University Press, 1973.

Polzin, Robert. *Late Biblical Hebrew: Toward an Historical Typology of Biblical Hebrew Prose.* Harvard Semitic Monographs 12. Missoula, Montana: Scholars Press, 1976.

Porter, J. R. *Leviticus.* Cambridge Bible Commentary. Cambridge: Cambridge University Press, 1976.

Pritchard, James B., ed. *Ancient Near Eastern Texts Relating to the Old Testament.* 3d ed. Princeton, N.J.: Princeton University Press, 1969.

Rad, Gerhard von. *Deuteronomy: A Commentary.* Old Testament Library. Translated by Dorothea Barton. Philadelphia: Westminster Press, 1966.

———. *Genesis: A Commentary.* Translated by John H. Marks. Old Testament Library. Philadelphia: Westminster Press, 1961.

———. *Old Testament Theology.* 2 vols. Translated by D. M. G. Stalker. New York: Harper and Row, 1962–65.

———. *Die Priesterschrift im Hexateuch: Literarisch Untersucht und Theologisch Gewertet.* Beiträge zur Wissenschaft vom Alten Testament und Neuen Testament 4.13. Stuttgart: Verlag W. Kohlhammer, 1934.

Ramban (Nachmanides). Commentary on the Torah. Edited by H. D. Chavel. In Katzenelenbogen, *tôrat ḥayyîm.*

Rappaport, Roy A. *Ecology, Meaning and Religion.* Richmond, Calif.: North Atlantic Books, 1979.

———. *Ritual and Religion in the Making of Humanity.* Cambridge Studies in Social and Cultural Anthropology 110. Cambridge: Cambridge University Press, 1999.

Rashbam. Commentary on the Torah. Edited by David Rosen. In Katzenelenbogen, *tôrat ḥayyîm.*

Rashi. Commentary on the Torah. Edited by H. D. Chavel. In Katzenelenbogen, *tôrat ḥayyîm.*

Redpath, Henry A. *The Book of the Prophet Ezekiel.* Westminster Commentaries. London: Methuen, 1907.

Rendtorff, Rolf. "Another Prolegomenon to Leviticus 17:11." Pages 23–28 in Wright, Freedman, and Hurvitz, eds., *Pomegranates and Golden Bells.*

———. *Leviticus.* Biblischer Kommentar Altes Testament 3.1–3. Neukirchener-Vluyn: Neukirchener Verlag, 1985–92.

———. *Studien zur Geschichte des Opfers im Alten Israel.* Wissenschaftliche Monographien zum Alten und Neuen Testament 24. Neukirchen-Vluyn: Neukirchener Verlag, 1967.

Reviv, Hanoch. *The Elders in Ancient Israel: A Study of a Biblical Institution.* Translated by Lucy Pitmann. Jerusalem: Magnes Press, 1989.

Ridderbos, J. *Deuteronomy.* Translated by Ed M. van der Maas. Bible Student's Commentary. Grand Rapids, Mich.: Zondervan, 1984.

Robertson Smith, William. *Lectures on the Religion of the Semites: The Fundamental Institutions.* 3d ed. 1927. Library of Biblical Studies. Hoboken, N.J.: Ktav, 1969.

Robinson, J. *The Second Book of Kings.* Cambridge Bible Commentary. London: Cambridge University Press, 1976,

Rodriguez, Angel M. *Substitution in the Hebrew Cultus.* Andrews University Seminary Doctoral Dissertation Series 3. Berrien Springs, Mich.: Andrews University Press, 1979.

Rudolph, Wilhelm. *Chronikbücher.* Handbuch zum Alten Testament 21. Tübingen: J. C. B. Mohr (Paul Siebeck), 1955.

Saadiah Gaon. Commentary on the Torah. In Katzenelenbogen, *tôrat ḥayyîm*.

Sabourin, Léopold. "Nefesh, sang et expiation (*Lv* 17,11.14)." *Sciences ecclésiastiques* 18 (1966): 25–45.

Sarna, Nahum M. *Exodus*. JPS Torah Commentary. Philadelphia: Jewish Publication Society, 1991.

———. *Genesis*. JPS Torah Commentary. Philadelphia: Jewish Publication Society, 1989.

Scharbert, Josef. "Blood." Pages 75–79 in vol. 1 of *Encyclopedia of Biblical Theology*, edited by Joannes B. Bauer, translated by Joseph Blenkinsopp, David J. Bourke, N. D. Smith, and Walter P. van Stigt. 3 vols. London: Sheed and Ward, 1976.

Schenker, Adrian. "kōper et expiation." *Biblica* 63 (1982): 32–46.

———. "Das Zeichen des Blutes und die Gewißheit der Vergebung im Alten Testament: Die sühnende Funktion des Blutes auf dem Altar nach Lev 17.10–12." *Münchener theologische Zeitschrift* 34 (1983): 195–213.

Schmid, Rudolf. *Das Bundesopfer in Israel: Wesen, Ursprung und Bedeutung der alttestamentlishen Schelamim*. Studien zum Alten und Neuen Testament 9. Munich: Kösel-Verlag, 1964.

Schwartz, Baruch J. "The Bearing of Sin in the Priestly Literature." Pages 3–21 in Wright, Freedman, and Hurvitz, eds., *Pomegranates and Golden Bells*.

———. *The Holiness Legislation: Studies in the Priestly Code*. [In Hebrew.] Jerusalem: Magnes Press, 1999.

———. "The Prohibitions Concerning the 'Eating' of Blood in Leviticus 17." Pages 34–66 in *Priesthood and Cult in Ancient Israel*, edited by Gary A. Anderson and Saul M. Olyan. Journal for the Study of the Old Testament: Supplement Series 125. Sheffield: Sheffield Academic Press, 1991.

Sforno, Ovadiah. Commentary on the Torah. Edited by Abraham Darom and Zeev Gottlieb. In Katzenelenbogen, ed., *tōrat ḥayyim*.

Skinner, John. *A Critical and Exegetical Commentary on Genesis*. International Critical Commentary. New York: Charles Scribner's Sons, 1910.

Smith, Jonathan Z. "The Bare Facts of Ritual." Pages 53–65 in *Imagining Religion: From Babylon to Jonestown*. Chicago: University of Chicago Press, 1982.

Snaith, Norman H. *Leviticus and Numbers*. Century Bible. London: Thomas Nelson and Sons, 1967.

———. "Sacrifices in the Old Testament." *Vetus Testamentum* 7 (1957): 308–17.

———. "The Sprinkling of Blood." *Expository Times* 82 (1970–71): 23–24.

———. "The Verbs *zābaḥ* and *šāḥat*." *Vetus Testamentum* 25 (1975): 242–46.

Speiser, E. A. "Census and Ritual Expiation in Mari and Israel." *Bulletin of the American Schools of Oriental Research* 149 (February 1958): 17–25.

———. *Genesis*. Anchor Bible 1. Garden City, N.Y.: Doubleday, 1964.

Sperling, S. David. "Pants, Persians, and the Priestly Source." Pages 373–85 in *Ki Baruch Hu: Ancient Near Eastern, Biblical, and Judaic Studies in Honor of Baruch A. Levine*, edited by Robert Chazan, William W. Hallo, and Lawrence H. Schiffman. Winona Lake, Ind.: Eisenbrauns, 1999.

Staal, Frits. "The Meaninglessness of Ritual." *Numen* 26 (1979): 2–22.

Stevenson, William Barron. "Hebrew 'Olah and Zebach Sacrifices." Pages 488–97 in *Festschrift Alfred Bertholet zum 80. Geburtstag*, edited by Walter Baumgartner, Otto Eissfeldt, Karl Elliger, and Leonhard Rost. Tübingen: J. C. B. Mohr (Paul Siebeck), 1950.

Stoebe, Hans Joachim. *Das erste Buch Samuelis.* Kommentar zum Alten Testament. Gütersloh: Gütersloher Verlagshaus Gerd Mohn, 1973.

Stowers, Stanley K. "On the Comparison of Blood in Greek and Israelite Ritual." Pages 179–88 in *Hesed ve-Emet: Studies in Honor of Ernest S. Frerichs,* edited by Jodi Magness and Seymour Gitin. Brown Judaic Studies 320. Atlanta: Scholars Press, 1998.

Talmon, S. "Conflate Readings (OT)." Pages 170–73 in *Interpreter's Dictionary of the Bible: Supplementary Volume,* edited by K. Crim. Nasheville, 1976.

Thompson, R. J. *Penitence and Sacrifice in Early Israel Outside the Levitical Law: An Examination of the Fellowship Theory of Early Israelite Sacrifice.* Leiden: E. J. Brill, 1963.

Thureau-Dangin, F. *Rituels accadiens.* Paris: E. Leroux, 1921.

Tigay, Jeffrey H. *Deuteronomy.* JPS Torah Commentary. Philadelphia: Jewish Publication Society, 1996.

Tuell, Steven S. *The Law of the Temple in Ezekiel 40–48.* Harvard Semitic Monographs 49. Atlanta, Ga.: Scholars Press, 1992.

Turner, Victor. "Symbols in African Religion." Pages 55–63 in *Magic, Witchcraft, and Religion: An Anthropological Study of the Supernatural,* 2d ed., edited by Arthur C. Lehmann and James E. Myers. Mountain View, Calif.: Mayfield Publishing, 1989. Reprinted from *Science* 179 (1973): 1100–1105.

Vaux, Roland de. *Studies in Old Testament Sacrifice.* Cardiff: University of Wales Press, 1964.

Vawter, Bruce. *On Genesis: A New Reading.* Garden City, N.Y.: Doubleday, 1977.

Vervenne, M. "'The Blood Is the Life and the Life Is the Blood': Blood as Symbol of Life and Death in Biblical Tradition (Gen. 9,4)." Pages 451–67 in *Ritual and Sacrifice in the Ancient Near East,* edited by J. Quaegebeur. Orientalia Lovaniensia Analecta 55. Leuven: Uitgeverij Peeters en Departement Oriëntalistiek, 1993.

Vinson, Richard B. "Blood in the Old Testament." Page 119 in *Mercer Dictionary of the Bible.* Macon, Ga.: Mercer University Press, 1990.

Vriezen, Th. C. "The Term *hizza:* Lustration and Consecration." *Oudtestamentische Studiën* 7 (1950): 201–35.

Warning, Wilfried. *Literary Artistry in Leviticus.* Biblical Interpretation Series 35. Leiden: E. J. Brill, 1999.

Weinfeld, Moshe. *Deuteronomy 1–11: A New Translation with Introduction and Commentary.* Anchor Bible 5. New York: Doubleday, 1991.

———. *Deuteronomy and the Deuteronomic School.* Oxford: Clarendon Oxford University Press, 1972.

———. "Deuteronomy, Book of." Pages 168–83 in vol. 2 of *The Anchor Bible Dictionary,* edited by David Noel Freedman, Gary A. Herion, David F. Graf, John David Pleins, and Astrid B. Beck. 6 vols. New York: Doubleday, 1992.

———. "Social and Cultic Institutions in the Priestly Source against Their Ancient Near Eastern Background." Pages 95–129 in *Proceedings of the Eighth World Congress of Jewish Studies: Panel Sessions: Bible Studies and Hebrew Language.* Jerusalem: World Union of Jewish Studies, 1983.

Wenham, Gordon J. *The Book of Leviticus.* New International Commentary on the Old Testament. Grand Rapids, Mich.: Eerdmans, 1979.

———. *Genesis 1–15.* Word Biblical Commentary 1. Waco, Tex.: Word Books, 1987.

Werman, Cana. "The Rules of Consuming and Covering the Blood in Priestly and Rabbinic Law." *Revue de Qumran* 16 (1993–95): 621–36.

Westermann, Claus. *Genesis 1–11: A Commentary.* Translated by John J. Scullion. Minneapolis: Augsburg Publishing House, 1984.

Wevers, John W. *Ezekiel.* Century Bible. London: Thomas Nelson and Sons, 1969.

Williamson, H. G. M. *1 and 2 Chronicles.* New Century Bible. Grand Rapids, Mich.: Eerdmans, 1982.

Willis, Timothy M. "Elders in Pre-Exilic Israelite Society." Ph.D. diss., Harvard University, 1990.

Wilms, Franz-Elmar. *Das Jahwistische Bundesbuch in Exodus 34.* Studien zum Alten und Neuen Testament 32. Munich: Kösel-Verlag, 1973.

Wold, D. J. "The KARETH Penalty in P: Rationale and Cases." Pages 1–45 in vol. 1 of *SBL Seminar Papers, 1979.* Society of Biblical Literature Seminar Papers 16. Chico, Calif.: Scholars Press, 1979.

———. "The Meaning of the Biblical Penalty of KARETH." Ph.D. diss., University of California at Berkeley, 1978.

Wright, David P. *The Disposal of Impurity.* Society of Biblical Literature Dissertation Series 101. Atlanta: Scholars Press, 1987.

———. "The Gesture of Hand Placement in the Hebrew Bible and in Hittite Literature." *Journal of the American Oriental Society* 106 (1986): 433–46.

———. "Holiness (OT)." Pages 237–49 in vol. 3 of *The Anchor Bible Dictionary,* edited by David Noel Freedman, Gary A. Herion, David F. Graf, John David Pleins, and Astrid B. Beck. 6 vols. New York: Doubleday, 1992.

Wright, David P., David Noel Freedman, and Avi Hurvitz, eds. *Pomegranates and Golden Bells: Studies in Biblical, Jewish, and Near Eastern Ritual, Law, and Literature in Honor of Jacob Milgrom.* Winona Lake, Ind.: Eisenbrauns, 1995.

Würthwein, Ernst. *Die Bücher der Könige: 1. Kön. 17—2. Kön. 25.* Das Alte Testament Deutsch 11.2. Göttingen: Vandenhoeck & Ruprecht, 1984.

Zenger, E. *Die Sinaitheophanie: Untersuchungen zum Jahwistischen und Elohistischen Geschichtwerk.* Forshung zur Bibel. Würzburg: Echter-Verlag, 1971.

Zevit, Ziony. "The Earthen Altar Laws of Exodus 20:24–26 and Related Sacrificial Restrictions in their Cultural Context." Pages 53–62 in *Texts, Temples, and Traditions: A Tribute to Menahem Haran,* edited by Michael V. Fox et al. Winona Lake, Ind.: Eisenbrauns, 1996.

———. "Philology, Archaeology, and a Terminus a Quo for P's *ḥaṭṭā't* Legislation." Pages 29–38 in Wright, Freedman, and Hurvitz, eds., *Pomegranates and Golden Bells.*

Zimmerli, Walter. *A Commentary on the Book of the Prophet Ezekiel.* 2 vols. Translated by Ronald E. Clements (vol. 1) and James D. Martin (vol. 2). Hermeneia. Philadelphia: Fortress Press, 1979–83. Originally *Ezekiel.* 2 vols. Biblischer Kommentar Altes Testament 13.1–2. Neukirchen-Vluyn: Neukirchener Verlag, 1969.

Zohar, Noam. "Repentance and Purification: The Significance and Semantics of *ḥaṭṭā't* in the Pentateuch." *Journal of Biblical Literature* 107 (1988): 609–18.

Index of Biblical Citations

General Index

Aaron: performing blood manipulation, 67–68, 83, 95, 121, 122, 123, 125, 126, 130, 140, 176, 189, 219n52; as recipient of blood manipulation, 39, 96, 97, 101, 102, 103, 107, 131, 136, 147, 159, 189, 222n88, 228n6; status in relation to sons, 83, 95–96, 102, 103, 107, 122, 189, 224n111

Aaronids/Aaronid priesthood: and access to altar and other sancta, 52, 102, 103; and blood manipulation, 59, 139, 188, 189, 190; distinction from Levites, 217n39; distinction from non-Aaronids, 189; holiness of, 214n44

altar: built by Moses, 37–38; in Ezekiel, 145, 225n18; of King Ahaz, 52, 53; in Mishnah, 66–67; in Priestly texts, 66–67, 69

ambiguity, of symbols, 4, 6

atonement, 25, 46, 139, 159, 160, 170, 206n50. *See also* removal

Barr, James, 30

Bell, Catherine, 5, 6–7, 40, 42, 58, 100, 126, 141, 180

blood: as apotropaic, 44, 97, 183; in Christian teaching, 1, 46; of circumcision, 97, 159; and covenant, 37–43, 89–90, 182; exposed, 24, 143–44, 225n16; as "food" (*leḥem*), 150, 226n27; human, 19, 24, 164–65; of Jesus Christ, 1, 2; and leaven, 34, 36; as "sacred" or "holy," 18, 198n30; as "sign" (*'ōt*), 50–49. *See also* bloodguilt; blood manipulation; consumption of animal blood; consumption of human blood; ransom, blood as

bloodguilt, 143, 144, 161, 165, 225n9

blood manipulation: basic definition, 1; instrumental effects of, 5, 8, 42, 44, 70, 131, 182, 186. *See also* collection of blood; cover-ing of blood; daubing (*nātan*) blood; pour-ing (*šāpak* or *yāṣaq*) blood; presenting (*hiqrîb*) blood; sprinkling (*hizzâ*) blood; tossing (*zāraq*) blood

bloodshed, 24, 144, 164–65, 166. *See also* pour-ing (*šāpak* or *yāṣaq*) blood

Book of the Covenant, 34, 37, 40, 203n2

Brichto, Herbert Chanan, 159, 160, 167, 223n106, 232n75

Budde, Karl, 56

burnt offering: and blood manipulation, 11, 26, 50, 51, 61–84 passim, 86, 87, 88–89, 90, 91, 109, 119, 120 121–22, 154, 155, 159; in Deuterono-mistic History, 52–54; in Deuteronomy, 50; in Ezekiel, 145, 146, 148; in H texts, 167; in Priestly (P) texts, 61–84 passim, 111, 119, 120, 127, 138; in 2 Chronicles, 152, 153, 154, 227n36. *See also* tossing (*zāraq*) blood

Cassuto, U., 18, 34–35, 42, 172, 177

Clements, Ronald E., 41

collection of blood, 38, 47, 65, 69, 113, 123, 153

condensation of meaning, of symbols, 4, 6

consumption of animal blood, prohibitions of, 182; in Deuteronomy, 14–17, 49, 55–56; in H texts, 20, 21, 22, 23, 55–56, 168, 169, 198n19; in P texts, 55

consumption of human blood, 197n18

covenant, 37–42 passim, 89–90

covering of blood, 23–24, 28, 144, 145, 200n51

cult centralization, 14, 49, 197n13

dashing blood. *See* tossing (*zāraq*) blood

daubing (*nātan*) blood, 27, 169, 230n47; on altar, 1, 5, 27–28, 98, 101, 109, 115, 117, 118, 121, 125, 126, 129, 131, 136, 141, 146, 147, 149, 169,